# Belief and Meaning

TO MY MOTHER AND FATHER

# Belief and Meaning

## The Unity and Locality of Mental Content

AKEEL BILGRAMI

**BLACKWELL**
*Oxford UK & Cambridge USA*

First published 1992

Blackwell Publishers
Three Cambridge Centre
Cambridge, Massachusetts 02142
USA

108 Cowley Road
Oxford OX4 1JF
UK

*Library of Congress Cataloging in Publication Data*
Bilgrami, Akeel, 1950-
Belief and meaning: the unity and locality of mental content/ Akeel Bilgrami.
p.    cm.

91-22287
CIP

Includes bibliographical references and index.
ISBN 0-631-17776-0
1. Intentionality (Philosophy) 2. Meaning (Philosophy)
I. Title
B105.I56B55  1992
121'.6—dc20

A CIP catalogue record for this book is available from the British Library

Typeset in 10 on 12pt Times by Interpress Magazines Pvt Ltd, New Delhi, India
Printed in Great Britain by Billing & Sons Ltd, Worcester
This book is printed on acid-free paper

# Contents

# Preface

This book offers a philosophical account of intentionality which conceives of intentional content as being at once radically local or contextual and radically unified in the sense that it rejects the entire current way of thinking which bifurcates content into wide and narrow. The locality of content has the effect of denying the importance that has been given in the past several decades to the idea of a theory of meaning; and the unity of content is achieved by denying not only that meaning is normative or social in any interesting sense, but also by severing all of the standard associations of meaning or content with the official notion of truth-conditions. And though the account views content as externally rather than solipsistically constituted, it is nevertheless based on a repudiation of all the recent orthodox ways of thinking of its external constitution. An alternative version of externalism is at the heart of the account, and the claim is that the unity of content can only be achieved on the basis of this alternative.

For all this distance from contemporary philosophical thinking on the subject, however, the view that emerges owes greatly to what I have learnt from reading and talking to contemporary philosophers. Philosophy is a gregarious discipline, more so than any other, I think. Despite all the hours of solitary reflection, a philosophy book, to a large extent, emerges out of conversations both in and out of classrooms. I owe thanks to a mass of people who have heard me out on the themes of this book and responded – far too many to name here – but I have relied much more on some than others.

I came to America to study philosophy with Donald Davidson in Chicago. From the beginning, I would waste his time in hours of conversation, which have, to a considerable extent, shaped my interests and my thinking. The relationship has been only slightly interrupted since then by the distance between Berkeley and New York. Every summer since Chicago, we have spent a month or so in Berkeley or New York or some neutral territory in Europe, and kept up what has been, for me, a wonderful intellectual companionship. The disagreements with his views that emerge in different parts of the book exemplify, more vividly than most, his own philosophical principle that disagreements can only be registered against a large background of agreement.

I have discussed philosophy with Carol Rovane ever since we were both students in Chicago. It is hard to believe that anything in this book is not much the better for having had her acute critical scrutiny and her imaginative suggestions for change and improvement.

Stephen While, whom I knew in Oxford when he was a postgraduate and I an undergraduate, has also had to suffer hours of philosophical conversations for some years now. I have leaned on him repeatedly when I was defeated by some philosophical issue and unable to think it through to my satisfaction. I owe him more than an intellectual debt. In a period when I was laid up with a back injury, he looked after me and distracted me from pain with marvelous conversations about books, paintings, films – and intentionality.

Josh Guttmann, despite his defection to research in computer science, has been a longstanding source of criticism and encouragement. Many long conversations with Bill Tait as a graduate student in Chicago were an early influence, and I am sure that some of it shows in the discussion of Wittgenstein in chapter 3.

At Columbia, Isaac Levi has been both a serious philosophical influence and an unswerving critic. He has constantly alerted me to the implications of my own views, and even though I often find myself resisting the directions in which he thinks they lead, I am struck by how often he has seen something further along than I have, and, in his way, already made the point in a somewhat different setting in his own work. Everybody should have a colleague like him.

John McDowell, whose writing has occupied my interest for some years, has shown the sort of intellectual generosity one would not expect even from close friends, teachers and colleagues. His comments on the book, a third the length of the manuscript itself, reflected a remarkable capacity for genuinely sympathetic understanding as well as passionate criticism. Though I still find myself in deep disagreement with him on fundamental points of philosophy, this book has been thoroughly revised and immeasurably improved by his detailed criticism and advice.

Several other philosophers have written responses to material which has affected one or other part of the book and have helped to make it better. Tyler Burge, Noam Chomsky and Brian Loar, in particular, have been very helpful; and, for all the divergence between us in ideas and ideologies, it will also be evident to the reader that the book owes enormously to the instruction I have had from their books and articles.

I must also thank Marcia Cavell, Dan Dennett, Jerry Fodor, Jim Higginbotham, Jerry Katz, Barry Loewer, Sidney Morgenbesser, Calvin Normore, Chris Peacocke, Hilary Putnam, Georges Rey, Peter Railton, John Searle, Steve Schiffer and Palle Yourgrau for helpful comments and conversations at various stages of writing.

A number of graduate students have made valuable responses to the ideas in the book, in particular Muhammad Ali Khalidi, Claudine Verheggen, Steven Yalowitz, and most of all Asa Wikforss who laid a restraining hand on some misleading rhetorical excesses I was prone to while writing chapter 3. She also prepared the bibliography.

I have also profited from discussions with audiences after papers, presenting material from this book, given at colloquia at the University of California at

Berkeley, the University of California at Riverside, Boston University, the University of Chicago, the City University of New York's Graduate Centre, Columbia University, the University of Illinois, Jadavpur University, Massachusetts Institute of Technology, the University of Michigan, New York University, Northwestern University, Oxford University, Princeton University, the University of St Andrew, the State University of New York at Stonybrook, the University of Toronto and Vassar College.

Akeel Bilgrami
New York

# 1

# Belief, Meaning, and the External World

Bertrand Russell called mental states which possess intentionality "propositional attitudes" and thus gave a name to something that was familiar long before him: the fact that, of all the states of mind there are, intentional states are unique in possessing *content*. Content is what is specified by sentences or propositions in that-clauses when we attribute intentional states to agents. Thus, in the attribution, "Smith believes that Bigmouth has struck again," the sentence or proposition (Bigmouth has struck again) which follows the "that" specifies the content.[1]

Though, of course, all intentional states possess content, for the sake of convenience the discussion and examples given in this book will be restricted to beliefs. The 'belief' in the title of the book emphasizes nothing more than this adopted convenience. The book's subject is not specifically belief, but intentionality.

The "meaning" in the title of the book acknowledges the close and familiar connection between intentionality and meaning. The connection holds between the meaning of the sentence Smith utters when he utters "Bigmouth has struck again" and his belief that Bigmouth has struck again. The idea of this close relation is not intended to convey the obvious falsehood that the meanings of the sentences which an agent utters *always* express the contents of his beliefs. Utterances which are lies or metaphors, for instance, spoil the generality of that relation. Rather, the relation is conveyed by the fact that a sincere, non-self-deceived, utterance of (or assent to) a sentence by an agent is an utterance of something whose literal meaning gives the content of the belief that is expressed by that utterance. The fact that sentences are often not uttered this way does not spoil the connection between belief and meaning, though it obviously makes it necessary to produce an appropriately nuanced formulation of the connection for those utterances. The underlying effect of acknowledging the connection, of course, is to make the study of an agent's mind integral to the study of his meanings, and vice versa.[2]

The central core of my account of intentionality will be stated, very briefly and in broad outline, in this chapter; and then, in each subsequent chapter, detail will be added to the core doctrine, often by justifying various features of it or by seeing through its relation to, and significance for, other themes and positions in the philosophy of mind and language.

The book is framed by two principal theses about the nature of intentional content: the "unity of content" and the "locality of content." Central to these theses, is a very specific *externalist* picture of content.

A *general* characterization of the doctrine of externalism is that the contents of an agent's beliefs are not independent of the world external to the agent. It is a denial of the view that intentionality is fully characterizable independent of the external world, or to put it in terms of Descartes's First Meditation, it denies the view that an agent's intentional contents would be just what they are even if it turned out that there was no external world. Externalism, so characterized, is an important truth about intentionality.[3]

The externalism proposed in this book adds to this general idea a very crucial constraint and thus gives a very specific reading to this general doctrine. For two reasons it may with some justification be called a Kantian reading. First, it shows how in its representations, the mind may depend upon the world at the same time as it mediates the world upon which it depends; and it shows this without surrender to idealism with regard to the world or naturalism with regard to the mind. And, second, the externalism itself is argued for on perfectly general and negative grounds. That is, like Kant's strategy against idealism (though without any claims to transcendental arguments), externalism is established on the basis of perfectly general arguments (given in chapter 5) which show that internalism or the scenario of Descartes's First Meditation is unacceptable. Having argued for externalism on such general and negative grounds makes it possible for me to deny that *de re* senses or direct referential links between words and the world are necessary in order to be an externalist. It is possible for me to be an externalist and yet deny that reference in *any* standard sense has anything to do with content. That amounts to a recognizable parallel with Kant. My way of arguing for externalism avoids all the commitment of contemporary externalisms' to direct referential links or to *de re* senses without any surrender to internalism, just as Kant's "refutation of idealism" purports to avoid direct Lockean realism without surrender to Berkeley. More is said about this Kantian strategy for externalism in chapters 4 and 5.

The two framing theses of the book hang crucially on this specific version of externalism. Each thesis bears a slightly different relation to it. On the one hand, my specific externalism alone makes it possible to maintain the thesis of the unity of content. On the other hand, my specific externalism requires the locality of content, for without the locality of content my externalism would give rise to serious problems in the study of content. Thus my version of externalism is necessary to have unity, but locality is necessary to my version of externalism if it is not to be rendered wholly implausible.

The rest of this first chapter sketches in a summary way my externalist picture of content and the two framing theses which depend on it. Subsequent chapters elaborate upon, motivate, and defend what is summarized here and in doing so also elaborate in detail the many diverse implications which derive from these basic claims, implications for some of the most central and significant questions in philosophy: the social nature of thought and language, the normative element in thought and language, the role of content and meaning in the explanation of behavior, the distinction between theory-change and meaning-change, the relationship among truth and reference and intentionality, the status of theories of meaning, the nature of self-knowledge, the relationship between intentionaltiy and moral responsibility, holism about the mental, realism about the mental, the indeterminacy of meaning, skepticism about other minds and skepticism about the external world. The subjects of intentionality and meaning are not narrow topics in the philosophy of mind and language; they pervade almost every aspect of this and surrounding disciplines.[4]

## WHAT IS MEANT BY THE UNITY OF CONTENT?

The thesis of the "unity of content" claims that there is only one notion of content, which is externally determined and which explains actions. Much of the point of the thesis becomes vivid only when one enters into recent ways of thinking about the nature of content. The thesis of unity rejects both sides of the now orthodox distinction between "narrow" and "wide" content. It rejects the whole way of thinking that leads to that distinction.

The distinction is most often based on the claim that if content is externally determined in the way that is suggested by the well-known views on reference of Putnam, Kripke and, more recently, Burge's (i.e. if it is "wide" content), then it cannot be used in the commonsense explanation or rationalization of behavior, and another notion of internal (i.e. "narrow") content is needed for such explanation. Much more will be said about this distinction and its basis in chapter 2.

My thesis, by contrast, states simply that contents are externally determined but it is these *same* contents which go into the commonsense psychological explanation or rationalization of behavior. There is no need for a second internal (or, for that matter, a second external)[5] notion of content to explain behavior. It is thus a unified notion of content.

This thesis is not to be confused with another view superficially like it and assumed to be true by many philosophers who, like me, would like to reject the idea that there are two notions of content, external and internal. This is the view which says that wide content, i.e. content determined externally along the lines suggested by Putnam, Kripke and Burge, is sufficient to explain action. (Since "wide content" is a term coined by Putnam and is everywhere used to describe the views of these philosophers, it is used here in the restricted sense, not of *any* externalist content but of content which is externalist in the sense defined by their theories of reference.)[6]

I believe this view to be false and it is important to distinguish it from the unity thesis, which acknowledges the explanation-threatening potential of "wide" content and shuns it in an effort to unify the external element in content with the explanatory role of content. The difference between my view and this superficially similar but much less radical view is that my view rejects both sides of the distinction between wide and narrow content, whereas this view rejects only the idea of narrow content. So, it is part of my argument for the thesis of the unity of content that unity, in the sense I intend it, is only possible if one abandons the externalism derived from these standard theories of reference and content, and if one develops instead a quite different externalism. In order to defend the thesis I will be arguing that philosophers have been blind to the idea of unity because they have assumed that externalist content must be in accord with one or other of these orthodox forms of externalism. They have quite simply and uncritically conflated the more general doctrine of externalism as defined above with the specific version of it due to these orthodox theories of reference. They have not explored the possibility that there are other specific versions which do not depend on these theories. Though they often talk of wide content as just being defined very generally, i.e. by the general externalism stated above, their actual arguments and examples invoke specific orthodox views of reference that promote a specific version of externalism which threatens the unity of content. Thus, not externalism generally, but these *orthodox* externalisms have indeed spoiled content for explanatory uses, and have forced the disunity of content, because they have made it seem that only a second (usually internal) notion of content will have an explanatory use.

How exactly the orthodox externalisms spoil content for explanation, and how exactly my externalism does not, will only emerge in chapter 2. A full defense of the unity thesis will then be given in chapter 3. A full defense of the unity thesis against the orthodox externalisms requires one to look at all the different and often inter-related motivations and arguments of the philosophers who have proposed these orthodox externalisms and either show them to be poor motivations or show that what they are after can be captured by my unified view of content. My externalism is motivated quite differently from the motivations of these orthodox externalisms. My motivation, which is presented in detail in chapter 5, is that externalism is necessary because if the external world does not determine the thoughts of an agent as is suggested, for instance, in the scenario of Descartes's First Meditation, then it is an utter mystery how that agent's thoughts can be publicly available to another. Externalism makes the publicness of thought and meaning possible, but this need not be an externalism which posits wide contents, i.e. it need not be founded on the views of reference of terms due to Kripke, Putnam, Burge etc. Here now is a very smudged summary of my alternative externalist position.

## MY EXTERNALISM

The challenge to be met in order to attain or preserve unity against bifurcation is: how to appeal to the elements in the external environment as constituting the content of thoughts without giving up on those contents' explanatory potential in doing so? Virtually every known externalist position fails to meet this challenge in a satisfactory way: Kripke and Putnam's causal-essentialist view, Burge's social view, Fodor's causal-information-theoretic view.[7]

In my account, this challenge is met by imposing an absolutely crucial constraint on the way the externalist element determines content and, as will be argued later, there is no chance that the challenge can be met without constraining the external element in this way. The constraint can be stated thus:

(C): When fixing an externally determined concept of an agent, one must do so by looking to indexically formulated utterances of the agent which express indexical contents containing that concept and then *picking that external determinant for the concept which is in consonance with other contents that have been fixed for the agent.*

The emphasis in (C) is the constraint itself and that is the heart of my externalism, but there are several other things, which are not fully explicit in this brief statement and which also need elaboration and clarification in order to get straight on the overall externalism itself.

First, although the constraint and the whole question of externalism are formulated in the context of how we "fix" an agent's concepts and contents, this does not mean that I am interested only or even primarily in the epistemological question: how do we find out about another's concepts and contents. That would be to get things entirely the wrong way round. It is because I take concepts to be externally constituted that I allow myself to believe that the contents of an agent's mind are necessarily public. And it is because they are public items, items available to one another, that a scrutiny of what goes into the fixing of one's concepts and contents by another is illuminating. So, one should not be misled by my talk of concept-attribution and content-attribution to get things the wrong way round. Also, it should be obvious that when I talk of fixing concepts and attributing contents, I do not have in mind the everyday scenario where we interpret the sayings and doings of others by seeing them as contentful. I do not have in mind everyday understanding of each other but, rather, what underlies everyday understanding or what everyday understanding consists in. The question, what is it for agents to have the concepts and contents that we attribute to them in our everyday understanding of them, cannot be answered by looking to the way in which we attribute those concepts and contents to them in the everyday situations. Quine(1960), Davidson(1973), David Lewis (1973), and several others have recognized this obvious distinction when they distinguish between interpretation and what they call "radical interpretation." My talk of fixing and attributing follows them in this.[8]

Second, assuming the close connection between intentionality and meaning, the word "concept" will be used merely to talk of the counterpart to "term" in just the way that "content" is thought of as the counterpart to "sentence" . Just as the content of an agent's belief that arthritis is painful is cashed out in terms of the meaning of the sentence "arthritis is painful," so also the concept of arthritis which, in part, composes that content is cashed out in terms of the meaning of the term "arthritis" which, in part, composes that sentence.[9]

Third, the fixing of externally determined concepts takes place, as one might expect, by looking at the indexical contents (and the utterances expressing them) in which they occur. One should expect this because it is indexical contents and utterances ("It's cold," "Here comes Maggie," "That's a Bosendorfer," "This is a gazelle") which can be correlated most obviously with saliencies in the external world that are supposed to be determining the concepts they contain. It is with these that one can most easily identify the external determinants. Indexical contents and utterances are, therefore, the points of entry into another's mind, since they are the first clear clues to the external (and public) sources of another's meanings. One fixes concepts first by correlating them, or at any rate, correlating the terms in the utterances in which they are expressed, with items in the environment of the agent who thinks and expresses them. Thus these correlations consist in finding some sort of salient item regularly present in the environment when indexical utterances with a given term expressing some concept are uttered. The centrality of indexical utterances and thoughts, however, should not give the impression of any commitment to anything like direct reference. Indexicals are central because they are essential clues to an agent's perceptions and responses to things and events around him. This centrality is not lost if it is unaccompanied by doctrines of direct reference, as we shall see later.

Fourth, clearly one has to distinguish between those indexical utterances which are sincere and literal and those which are not, else we will not correlate them with the right item in the environment or perhaps we will not find any sort of item regularly present. Only the former must be correlated with external saliencies. If I was uttering a lie or a metaphor when I said "He's a beast" the correlated external salience would not help much in fixing the concept correctly. There is, however, no algorithm for sifting out the sincere and literal utterances from the lies, the metaphors, the stage-performances etc. Nor is there any reason to assume that a concept or term occurs more frequently in sincere and literal utterances than in this vast variety of other uses. But one may assume that the lies and metaphors and so on, even if more frequent, will bring no single item in the environment to the fore since they will be used with an indefinite variety of motives; so over time if there *is* a correlation at all with something in the environment then we can proceed on the assumption that we *had* got hold of the sincere utterances and, therefore, have the right external determinant. All this is, of course, a dynamic process of theory-building (of concept attribution or fixing) and, as with all theories, one may revise earlier attributions if they turn out to fail to provide a coherent theoretical picture due to having fastened on some non-literal or insincere indexical utterances in the early phases.

Fifth, obviously not all concepts will be externally determined. Not, for example, the concept of a unicorn nor the concept of the number five. But these concepts will in one way or another be related to others which will be determined externally. In the case of the concept of the unicorn, it will be related by *composition* to other concepts which are externally determined: the concept of a horse, the concept of a horn etc.; not so in the case of the concept of the number five, which will not be composed of externally determined concepts but rather related to externally determined concepts by more complicated relations. This general admission that not all concepts need themselves be externally determined makes clear that externalism is a weak and general doctrine which merely rules out the scenario of Descartes's First Meditation by saying that *some* at least (and very likely very many) of our concepts are the concepts they are because of the relations between us and the world around us.[10] It does not require that all our concepts are themselves exceptionlessly externally determined.

Finally, we come to the heart of the externalism, the constraint itself. What makes one an externalist at all is that in looking to fix concepts one looks to correlations with *external* things. But that is just externalism in the very general sense defined at the beginning of this chapter. My constraint on externalism gives rise to a more specific version of this externalism. It asserts that in selecting the item in the environment which is supposed to fix the concept that is being expressed, one has not only to pick what is salient and is correlated with that term but one has to be very careful how one *describes* this external determinant of the concept. One has to describe it in a way that fits in with the other *contents* one has attributed to the agent. Expressions such as "fits in with" or, as in the original formulation, "in consonance with" are vague, so a sharper intuitive sense to what I have in mind may be given by way of an example.

Finding the right gross external item to correlate with an agent's concept requires no more than (a) shared similarity standards, presumably wired into us all, so that what is grossly salient to him is not wholly at odds with what is salient to us, and (b) Mill's methods. These two things, however, will only get us the relevant gross and regular saliencies in the environment and no more. But it is the selection, not of the regular gross salience in the environment, but the right description of it, which the constraint is meant to address; and its claim is that the right description turns on looking to other beliefs attributed to the agent.

So, to give a very crude example, let us suppose that, by an application of Mill's methods and by shared similarity standards, we have noticed that there is pedal regularly present under the left foot of an agent when he utters indexical utterances with a certain term. Then the constraint says not to describe this external determinant of his concept expressed by that term as a 'clutch' if one has no confidence that he has other beliefs, however rudimentary, regarding the inner workings of an automobile. If, by this method in which external items determine concepts, one could not describe the determinant that way, one would not end up attributing the determined concept of a clutch to the agent and so no contents relating to clutches. For some agents we may find ourselves, for similar sorts of reasons, withholding from the external determinant even the description "pedal" (i.e. in such a case the regular gross salience will not even get the initial description "pedal") with similar consequences for concepts and contents.

Various features of this constraint need to be brought to notice. First, the word "cause" has not been used while talking of external things. Instead of talking of "external cause" I have used "external determinants." This is not because I want to specially deny that these are external causal determinants but only to avoid a wholly unnecessary discussion at this stage about whether in insisting on the right description of the external item I am emphasizing causal "explanations" rather than causal "relations" in my externalist account. No doubt I am doing precisely that and I do not see how it can be avoided. It seems to me that all the interesting action in this account (and I would say in every other interesting and important philosophical account of anything in which causality enters) lies at the level of causal explanation rather than causal relations. Causal relations no doubt exist but they are an idle metaphysical wheel. It is precisely in order not to elaborate on prejudices of this kind that using the word "cause" has been avoided.

Notice also that there is a strong element of anti-foundationalism built into this constraint. One may have thought otherwise, misled by my insistence that there is something basic about the indexical utterances which correlate with saliencies in the environment. One may have thought that this insistence on seeing the indexical utterances as a starting point makes for an externalist foundationalism.[11] The thought is not intended at all and the constraint makes that clear. Even for this basic level, this ground floor of indexically formulated utterances and beliefs by which one enters another's mind, the external determinants we pick out and correlate them with have to be described only as they cohere with the other beliefs. Hence the method at the ground floor is a convenient starting point in the building of a theoretical structure of another's beliefs and concepts, but it is built like Neurath's boat, and conclusions about the ground floor are just as mediated by belief, and just as revisable as we proceed with the theorizing if they will not lend themselves to a coherent theoretical picture. There are no Archimedean points in this externalism. Some causal links may be more direct than others, i.e. less mediated by surrounding beliefs than others: for instance, those that determine the concept of a pedal rather than those that determine the concept of a clutch. But there are no unmediated causal links. There is no getting away from this mediation and the appeal to external causality is not intended to stop or interrupt a holistic (by which I only mean anti-foundationalist)[12] pattern. Anti-foundationalist holism and externalism are both absolutely essential features of content and they are perfectly compatible. My eventual claim is that the latter allows for the public character of content and the former, as it constrains the later, allows for its explanatory potential. Together they allow for the unity of content.

This insistence on describing the external in terms of the beliefs of the agent may give rise to two impressions, one wrong, one right. First, it will give the impression that I am, after all, an internalist since the appeal to the agent's beliefs in fastening on an appropriate description of the external determinant is an appeal to an internalist filter upon the external. It is false, however, to think of the filter as internal since the belief contents of an agent which provide the filter will contain concepts which are themselves externally determined. There is nothing internal about the filter at all, if internal is defined in contrast to externally constituted content. But, that apart, the impression appears to arise from a tedious and misguided oscillation between a false pair of choices: a highly direct externalism and internalism (see chapters 4 and 5). Even *prima facie*, if a position is incompatible with the scenario entertained in Descartes's First Meditation, as mine certainly is (after all it denies that one could have the thoughts one has if there were no external world, something explicitly implied by that scenario), then it is "externalist" in a perfectly clear sense of that term. It is external in precisely the sense that was defined as externalism at the beginning of this chapter and commented on in note 3.

Second, it will give the impression that since the external items that fix concepts and give meaning to terms are *always* mediated by other beliefs, my notion of meaning and intentionality will never be naturalistically reducible. That impression is quite correct. I think the irreducibility of semantics and intentionality lies in the necessity of imposing my constraint at all levels. I see the unity of content, as I intend it, as only possible if one believes in the irreducibility of the mental. Unity and irreducibility require each other (more will be said about irreducibility in chapter 3.)[13]

Also, notice that the constraint only explicitly mentions that it is concepts and not contents which are externally determined. That is important since in my view content itself is only derivatively determined externally. That is content is external only in the sense that it is concepts of which it is composed that are externally determined. There is no requirement that any specific given content itself must be directly externally determined, not even singular contents, not even singular contents containing non-fictional concepts. This point should not be obscured by the fact that the externalist fixing of concepts by the method suggested above is only done by first looking at whole utterances (and the belief contents they express) and correlating them with the presence of external things. That is mere *procedural* priority, forced by the fact that the evidence for finding out what external things determine our concepts can only be found in the external correlations made with whole utterances in which terms expressing those concepts occur. There is no direct way of fastening on the external determinants of concepts. There is no observable evidence except via the utterances in which they are expressed. But this point is merely about the evidence, merely epistemological if you like. It does not show that the contents of utterances (or the beliefs they express) are directly constituted externally, even though they are often caused by external things. It merely shows that because they are often so caused, the correlating of them with external things provides *evidence* for external determination of concepts contained in those belief contents.[14] My reason for insisting on this point is this. I do not want to be in the position of having to say that an intuitively indexical or singular content cannot really be an indexical content if there is no external object, as when one is hallucinating. This is a thoroughly unintutive consequence and no externalism should be saddled with it. But there is no way of avoiding it unless one insists that it is not contents but concepts which are externally constituted. Once we are in possession of externally constituted concepts, we can allow that some of our indexical perceptual contents in which they occur may turn out to be hallucinatory. This theme is elaborated in my criticism of Evan's and McDowell's externalist Russellian view of singular thought in chapter 4.

## WHAT IS MEANT BY THE LOCALITY OF CONTENT?

My constraint on externalism requires that no concept be attributed along externalist lines, unless it is in consonance with the other contents of the agent to whom it is being attributed. This leads to a rather alarmingly fine-grained notion of concepts. After all, the beliefs of an agent that are relevant to (and that she associates with) her term "clutch" might be very numerous and very diverse. This is alarming because no two people are ever likely to have the same concepts since they will almost certainly associate different beliefs with their respective terms. But in my picture of things this does not matter for the following reason.

My use of the term "concept" to describe what is attributed in this way needs a serious qualification. These attributions of concepts are attributions of things that do not go directly into the attribution of specific contents to explain behavior. All that they do at this stage is to provide a pool of resources which one uses in a selective way in order to attribute specific contents in the explanation of behavior.

Suppose you know a fair amount of chemistry and I know none, i.e. you have various chemical beliefs and I do not. The concept "water" attributed to you in accord with the constraint requires that it be different from the concept attributed to me. Your beliefs which constrain the description of the external substance with which your "water" utterances are correlated will be different from mine since you have beliefs about its chemical composition which I do not. The case is exactly like the one about the concept of clutch and pedal for two agents who respectively do and do not have beliefs about the workings of automobiles. At this general – or, as I will call it, the "meaning-theoretic" or "aggregative" – level of concept attribution it is unlikely that any two people will have the same concept of anything since it is unlikely that they have the same beliefs associated with the term which expresses that concept. This is the level on which theories of meaning do their work: they specify the concepts or the term-meanings of an agent along the lines of this constrained externalist method. At the meaning-theoretic level, the concepts are very fine-grained and they are hardly ever shared by people.

But this does not matter since it is not *these* "concepts," so thought of, which go into the contents that explain action. Action-explanation always takes place at a much more local level than the meaning-theoretic level. Here, the entire aggregate of beliefs that an agent associates with "water" are not all relevant. One distils out of the aggregate of resources provided by the meaning-theory only those beliefs that are relevant to the action-explanation at the local level. Thus, if you and I are both drinking some substance from the kitchen tap because we want to quench our thirst with the cheapest available drink, we may *in this locality* both be attributed the same content: "...that water will quench thirst." In this locality of explanation, your chemical beliefs are simply not among the beliefs selected from the specifications of the meaning-theory (for your idiolect). The specification of your local water-concept in the attribution of content which explains your behavior does not contain your chemical beliefs. Those beliefs are not needed in this locality so the specification of the local water-concept ignores them. Hence, although our idiolects are never likely to be the same for any single concept, in many localities we may nevertheless share many contents. There will obviously be other localities in which we will not share contents because in those localities we *will* find it necessary to use your chemical beliefs from the overall pool in order to explain your action. This thesis is the "locality of content."

The locality of content is forced by the sort of anti-foundationalist holism which is essential to the thesis of the unity of content. Without locality there would be, as we shall see in chapter 4, a serious problem with how my holistic anti-foundationalism threatens realism about content.

One of the chief points underlying the locality of content is that it shows that the idea of a theory of meaning, which has been so important to the past several decades of philosophizing about mind and language, is not really as important as it has been taken to be. The deliverances of a holistic meaning-theory do not, in my picture, have anything directly to do with contents as we attribute them in explanations of behaviour. Meaning-theories merely provide a pool of resources and no more. Content as it enters into the explanation of behavior, content as it is attributed in response to the specific questions such as what does so and so believe about …?, is always local because the questions asked and the explanations sought are always in particular contexts.

One may, thus, see theories of meaning for terms such as "clutch" and "water" in particular agents' language as idealized constructions, i.e. as ideally complete specifications of their "concepts," which hypothesize on the basis of ideally complete evidence or, as Quine would say, "all possible evidence,"[15] all the beliefs that an agent associates with each such term in his language. Of course, we cannot make such idealized spesifications explicitly because we usually cannot list all the beliefs an agent associates with these terms of his language. (More will be said about this problem in the discussion of the point and nature of theories of meaning in chapter 4.) But the crucial point for now is that, these "concepts" are *not* the concepts that then go into the attribution of a content in an explanation of action. This meaning-theoretic notion of "concepts" has no psychological reality in the sense that it does not ever pull its weight in explanations. It is a trumped up theoretical posit which provides a pool of resources from which local concepts are selected to compose the contents which do explain behavior in particular localities. Hence the entire idea of meaning-theory and the concepts or meanings it specifies is exhausted by its role in the following scheme. Contents attributed in particular localities are comprised of concepts, which are themselves cashed out in terms of a selection of beliefs, and the idea of a selection of beliefs innocuously requires the idea of some place from which the selection is made. The idea of a meaning-theory is merely a gesture acknowledging that a selection has to be a selection from somewhere.[16] It has no further role than one of marking that place. I will say more about the locality of content in chapter 4.

Since the "unity thesis" is based on the rejection of a whole way of thinking which leads to certain basic distinctions about intentional content, and since the "locality thesis" dissolves the very idea of content composed of context-invariant concepts, this account of intentionality is genuinely radical. For if, as in the eyes of most contemporary philosophers of mind, wide content and narrow content are the only sorts of content there can be, and if, in their eyes, the whole interest in content is an interest in something much less contextual, then this book will be seen to be claiming that there is no such thing as content. And I can see the finger pointing, hear the voice saying: yours is nothing but a total skepticism about content. Perhaps, but I would prefer to put things differently. I think I have offered a way out of the dogmas of a certain way of thinking which leave us on the one hand with a false distinction and, on the other, with an artificially tidy picture of the mind, a way of thinking which gets wrong both the external and the internal nature of the human mind, and which pretends that there are context-independent intentional phenomena that need to be studied. The alternative account given here redefines our conception of internal and external in a way that sees them as part of a unified picture of the mind at the same time as it acknowledges that any picture of the mind needs to accurately portray the messy local realities about our intentional states and their explanatory functions.

## OUTLINE OF THE FOLLOWING CHAPTERS

Here, in brief outline, is the plan of the rest of the book. Chapter 2 discusses fully how unity of content is redeemed by my externalism but destroyed by the orthodox externalisms I have mentioned. In other words, it shows how my externalism alone allows the external nature of thought to be reconciled with the explanatory power of thought. It also shows how only my externalism allows for the possibility of self-knowledge of intentional states. (This discussion of self-knowledge is supplemented in the Appendix to the book, where it is argued that self-knowledge has important links with moral responsibility and that its justification has very little to do with epistemology as standardly conceived.)

Chapter 3 further justifies my externalism and the unified view of content proposed by looking to various motivations for being an orthodox externalist and either showing them to be poor motivations or, when good, showing that they can be satisfied by my externalism. By the end of the chapter, it is claimed that there is absolutely no reason to believe that wide content has any worthy role to play in the study of the mind, and therefore that the orthodox externalisms are misguided and wholly unnecessary. In the course of the discussion the question of normativity, which is widely taken to be essential to language and intentionality, is examined, and the relevance of normativity, is shown to be much more restricted than it is generally taken to be. In arguing this, I show how much of the recent discussions of "rule-following," which stresses a wholly unnecessary element of normativity, betrays an *ersatz* Platonism in the philosophy of language and mind. It is also argued in this chapter that though there is an obvious sense in which language and thought are social, that sense is not of much *philosophical* interest or significance. And, finally, it is argued that it is not necessary to embrace the views of reference which define the orthodox externalist accounts of content in order to allow a distinction between theory-change and meaning-change, proposing an alternative way of grounding the distinction.

One way of describing the dialectic of chapters 2 and 3 is to see the former as repudiating the suggestion that my notion of content is not necessary (repudiating the suggestion that the orthodox externalist picture is quite adequate) and the latter as repudiating the suggestion that it is not sufficient (repudiating the suggestion that it leaves out things which only wide content can capture). This two-part dialectic defending my account of content helps to bring out a number of details of the account which I have not mentioned in this first chapter.

Chapter 4 discusses the relationship among intentionality, truth-conditions and truth-theories of meaning and content. It argues that though truth-theories may still be used to theorize about meaning and content, my externalism forces a different picture of the relationship than is found in the seminal writings of Davidson. In the course of this my externalism and my conception of truth-theories of meaning are also contrasted with those of Gareth Evans and John McDowell, and, in spelling out the contrast, bring out the specifically Kantian way in which I hope to argue for my externalism in chapter 5. The externalism that my argument tries to establish has no place for reference, not even a description-mediated or belief-mediated theory of reference. Chapter 4 also elaborates on some implications of the locality of content and shows how locality allows one to be a holist about content and meaning without compromising a realism about them. The discussion of locality in this chapter also goes some way toward deflating the pretensions of the theory of meaning in the study of mind and language.

The idea of the unity of content is defined upon an externalist view of content. Chapter 5 justifies this general commitment to externalism made, without argument, throughout the first four chapters of the book. This is done by presenting a detailed case against internalism which is based on two different sorts of epistemological considerations: the publicness of meaning and mind, and skepticism about the external world. It is then shown how externalism can capture all that is worth capturing in the "first-person point of view," and a criterion for realism about content itself is given, showing how externalism can remain part of a non-naturalistic doctrine and still be resolutely anti-instrumentalist.

# 2

# The Unity of Intentional Content

## THE THREAT TO THE UNITY OF CONTENT

There are two longstanding, widely held, and plausible assumptions about intentional content. First, ever since Aristotle invented the practical syllogism, it has been assumed that intentional states such as beliefs and desires get their point and rationale from the role they play in the commonsense psychological explanation of human behavior.[1] This is not one of their features which can be repealed.

Second, there is the general assumption of the externalist constitution of content (see chapter 1). It is widely believed, for one reason or another, for good reasons and bad, that content as it is specifiable in that-clauses is, partly at least, constituted by the external environment of agents who possess intentional or contentful states. Though this assumption was made explicit only in recent years, it is plausible to think that in the very general form in which it is stated here and at the very beginning of chapter 1,[2] it too has been implicitly believed by many philosophers ever since Aristotle.

As one must expect in philosophy, neither of these assumptions is wholly uncontroversial. Philosophers have opposed the first assumption on the grounds that an undue stress on the explanatory role of content will make us instrumentalists about content. Philosophers have opposed the second assumption on a variety of grounds which will not be listed here. Both these assumptions will be defended in chapter 5; until then they will be taken to be uncontroversial.

The aim of this chapter is not to defend these assumptions but to defend a thesis which rests on them. This is the thesis of the "unity of content." To repeat, the thesis is simply this: what makes it possible for intentional states to have a role in the commonsense psychological explanation of behavior (the first assumption) is the very fact of their possessing content which is externally constituted (the second assumption). This thesis has been implicitly assumed to be true for at least as long as the two assumptions upon which it is defined. But in the past 15 years or so most philosophers who accept the two assumptions have turned to denying the unity defined upon them.

What is it to deny the unity of content? It is to say that we need two notions of content, each satisfying one of the two assumptions: one notion which is used in the explanation of behavior, and the other which is externally constituted. This denial of unity can be called the "bifurcation" of content.

Why should philosophers have turned against unity? Obviously, because they have felt a sense of tension between the two assumptions. This tension is usually brought out by way of examples. The general point of these examples is to show that if, as the second assumption says, content harbors elements that are external to agents, then intentional states will be impaired for the explanatory tasks demanded by the first assumption. The basic idea seems to be that since the object of explanations is to illuminate the behavior of individual agents, anything that is cited in these explanations must be constituted within these agents. The examples are supposed to establish this idea by making vivid the explanatory failures of those explanations which cite externally constituted contents. So, it is argued, one must posit a second notion of content, fumigated of these outlying elements which contaminate the externalist notion of content. This second notion will now carry out the explanatory tasks. In a word, then, the denial of unity is the denial that explanatory tasks can be carried out by externally constituted content, and various examples are urged upon us to prove this.

My own claim will be that the examples only intuitively point to bifurcation if one assumes, in the spelling out of the examples, a commitment to one or other of the orthodox externalisms.[3] But first the examples. They can be usefully divided into two sorts, each making trouble for unity for the same general reason, but from opposite directions.

The first sort of example is familiar from Kripke's (1979) well-known puzzle about belief.[4] In the present context, it is perhaps easier to understand the bifurcatory point, for which the example is being exploited, if we work, not with Kripke's own example, but with a variant of it suggested in a lucid and stimulating paper by Brian Loar (1985a). In this variant, someone called Pierre learns from his nanny, while growing up monolingually in Paris, something which he expresses by saying "*Londres est jolie.*" When, later, Pierre settles in a pretty section of London, after picking up the native language, he is disposed to say "London is pretty." However, he does not realize that the city he learnt about in Paris is the city of which he is now a resident.

Now, assuming the close connection between meaning and belief mentioned at the very beginning of chapter 1, we will want to say that if Pierre is disposed to (sincerely etc.) utter or assent to "London is pretty" (when prompted), then he believes that London is pretty. Kripke himself is explicit about this assumption and formulates it in something he calls "the principle of disquotation." The question is, what is it that Pierre is assenting to? And, in particular, does he believe the same thing (have the same content) when he assents to "*Londres est jolie?*"

Those who cite such examples to raise difficulties for the explanatory powers of externally determined content would answer this question in the affirmative. What is their reason for doing so?

Apart from the assumption of the close connection between belief and meaning (i.e. "the principle of disquotation" ), this affirmative issues from two further assumptions they make. First, externalism for them is tied to a certain notion of reference. And, second, they assume that translation preserves reference (and, therefore, truth, of the sentences which are assented to).[4] Since, on that view of reference, *"Londres"* refers to London, and since "London" translates *"Londres"* , the two belief contents must be the same.

It is these three assumptions that are also crucial to Kripke's use of his own original and somewhat different example to raise his "puzzle about belief." [5] It may be useful now, before showing how the variant example raises the difficulty about explanation, to compare it to the point of Kripke's original example when he raises his puzzle about belief.

In Kripke's example, Pierre's upbringing in Paris is the same as in the variant example, but things are different when he goes to London: he settles in an ugly section of the city and is disposed to utter or assent to "London is not pretty." The example gives rise to a puzzle because, given the assumptions about reference and translation (and the earlier one captured in the principle of disquotation), one would, by a short step, conclude by attributing inconsistent beliefs to Pierre. And since we may take for granted on the basis of the rest of his behavior that Pierre is a logically acute man, there is a *prima facie* puzzle generated by the fact that he must be attributed an inconsistent belief.[6] Charity requires that we do not rest with the charge of inconsistency but somehow explain it away. The puzzle is supposed to lie in the fact that explaining it away means giving up on the above, seemingly obvious, assumptions about the nature of content and its attribution.

The problem raised by the variant example is not that inconsistent beliefs are attributed to Pierre. In the variant example Pierre has the same belief attributed to him (earlier) in Paris and (later) in London. But that difference is due to the contingencies of the example. There is, however, a more general description of the difficulty involved in these examples, a description common to both examples, which is independent of the contingent circumstance of where Pierre settles in London. The source of this common difficulty lies in an element that is essential to both examples, which is that Pierre does not know of the identity that holds between London and *Londres*. This common element in the examples gives rise to the perfectly general difficulty which has nothing to do specifically with Pierre being attributed inconsistent beliefs. The more general difficulty rather is this. Beliefs attributed, under the assumptions mentioned, simply cannot account for the inferences that an agent such as Pierre might make or fail to make. So, since the inferences they are unable to capture might be practical as well as theoretical, and since explanation of behavior turns on capturing the practical inferences of agents, these examples bring out the fact that content attributed under these assumptions will not always be efficacious in explanations.

What is meant by saying that inferences are not captured, in these examples, by contents attributed under the foregoing assumptions? Taking an example from Brian Loar, let us say that among the things his nanny told him about *Londres* was that Oscar Wilde lived there. Recall that included in the governing assumptions are the assumptions that concepts are tied to reference and that translation preserves truth and reference. On the basis of these assumptions we may attribute to Pierre, while he is in Paris, the belief that London is the city in which Oscar Wilde lived. We may also plausibly attribute to him when he is in London, the belief that he is now in London. One would, therefore, expect that he can infer from these two beliefs, the beliefs that he is now in the city in which Oscar Wilde lived. But since, in the example, Pierre does not know that London and *Londres* are identical, he fails to infer this. Thus content, so attributed, does not always have the resources to capture an agent's failure to make theoretical inferences. Everything about content and its attribution leads us to think that he will make an inference which he does not and cannot make. It is obvious that things are just as badly off when it comes to practical inferences. So suppose that when he was in Paris, Pierre had assented to *"Je voudrais visiter la maison d'Oscar Wilde quand j'arriverai a Londres."* We can, given the assumptions about disquotation, reference, and translation, make the attribution "Pierre desires that he visit Oscar Wilde's house when he arrives in London." He then goes to London and, plausibly, comes to believe that he is in London. (Let us also assume that he has not, in the lapsed period, lost his interest in Oscar Wilde.) One would now expect that he would have plans to do something about visiting Oscar Wilde's home. But again, he simply does not. The desire and belief attributions, made on these assumptions, simply fail to capture the fact that he has not made the practical inference and they therefore fail to explain his (in) action.

What has gone wrong with these content attributions? Why are they inefficacious in explanation? The answer is straightforward. They are inefficacious because they are insensitive to Pierre's different (earlier and later) *conceptions* of London. Pierre conceives of London differently when he is in Paris and when he is in London. It is because he has different conceptions earlier and later that it is possible for him to fail to know or realize the identity of London and *Londres*. And, conversely, the fact that he does not know of the identity should tip us off to the fact that he has different conceptions. What goes into Pierre's inferences and therefore into the explanations of his actions are Pierre's conceptions of London and so it is not surprising that these contents will fail to capture his inferences and explain his actions.

How, then, may we arrange things so that we have content which *is* efficacious in explanations? The answer which is usually given (and given by Loar himself, 1985a) is that the problematic content attributions are made under an externalist view of content and in the external world there is only one city, so it is not surprising that externally determined contents will not capture Pierre's two different conceptions of the city which go into his inferences and into the explanations of his actions. What we need to do, it is said, is to posit a second notion of content which is not externalist but which looks to Pierre's inner conceptions, and actions will be explained by this second notion of content. This second notion will impose a taxonomy on intentional states that will be more fine-grained than the one provided when content is thought of externalistically. In this example Pierre will, by the new taxonomy, no longer have one belief but *two* beliefs about the city of London, as different from each other, as Loar points out, as the beliefs "London is pretty" and "Rio is pretty." No problem remains any longer of accounting for why he fails to make the inferences. (He certainly would not believe that he was in London now if he believes that he was in Rio! He certainly would not make plans to visit Oscar Wilde's home if he believed that he was in Rio!) The failure to make the inferences is accounted for precisely because the second notion of content which captures Pierre's conceptions is individuated in terms of the role of intentional states in inferences, both theoretical and practical.

That is the response of the reigning orthodoxy on the subject of content. The first notion of content which is externally constituted in accordance with these assumptions and which gives rise to the problem is called "wide" content, and the second internal notion of content which is determined by inferential or conceptual role and which is used in explanations is called "narrow" content.[7] It should be obvious how this appeal to Pierre's conceptions of London in a second notion of content will also furnish the resources to prevent any attribution of inconsistent beliefs to him in Kripke's original puzzle. (After all, "Pierre believes that London is pretty and that Rio is not pretty" do not strain our charitable impulses!)

The variation on the Kripke example is particularly useful because it displays why the lesson to be learnt from the Kripke example is not just that a puzzle needs to be solved in the sense that an unjust attribution of inconsistency needs to be removed. The unjust attribution of inconsistency in the Kripke example is just a symptom of a perfectly general malaise: One has failed to capture the inferential patterns which give rise to an agent's behavior. And this is diagnosed as flowing from a general source: an agent's conceptions are being ignored in the attribution of externalist content. This means that externalist content will not be that in virtue of which behavior is being explained, thus undermining the thesis of the unity of content which insists precisely that it also be that.

The second sort of example is equally familiar from the thought-experiment about twin-earth (Putnam 1975). It too is invoked to emphasize the explanatory irrelevance of externalist content. The familiarity of the example allows me to be brief. An agent on earth and his twin on twin-earth are internally identical but their environments are different in a very specific way: what is called "water" on twin-earth has a different chemical composition, XYZ rather than $H_2O$.

In this sort of example the problem arises in a form which is opposite to the case of Pierre. That is, considerations of agents' conceptions and inferential role force a taxonomy in the opposite direction. Where with Pierre, external elements were supposed to impose too coarse-grained a taxonomy (one London-belief instead of two conceptions-of-London-beliefs), in the twin-earth cases they are supposed to impose an unnecessarily fine-grained one; unnecessarily fine-grained, that is, for psychological explanation.

An agent and his twin on twin-earth, both innocent of chemistry, might use a word like "water" in expressing beliefs and desires which explain some action of theirs, say, the action of drinking a tumbler filled with some substance, because each desires that his thirst be quenched and believes that drinking it will quench his thirst. The argument, as it standardly proceeds, points out that the chemical composition of the substance in their external environment being talked and thought about is quite different and so, therefore, given externalism, is the content of their thought and their talk. But, in a quite other sense of thought and talk (the "narrow", internalist sense, the sense relevant to psychological explanation), the thought and the talk are not interestingly different. One would not think of the explanations of their respective actions as being different in any interesting sense. Their actions both get a common description and are both explained by the same things: they both drink a tumbler full of a substance (which they both call "water") because they are both thirsty and they both believe that drinking it will quench their thirst. The fact that, unknown to them, the chemical composition of what they are respectively drinking is different makes no difference to the psychological springs of their action, so described.[8] Our interest as explainers or rationalizers of their actions is simply not in a chemical fact that neither of them is aware of. As far as the interests of such explainers is concerned, that chemical fact does not have the effect of showing that their respective actions must be differently described. And so it does not have the effect of showing that they must have different water-beliefs and water-desires. No doubt their actions *can* get different descriptions but those descriptions are not of interest to us while our interest is in psychological explanation.

But, the story goes on, if we looked to the external element (the substance with its chemical composition) as constitutive of content, we would turn up two different beliefs for the twins since the substances have different chemical compositions in their respective external environments; while looking to psychologically relevant facts (involving the twins' conceptions of the substance or the inferential roles of the beliefs), we would turn up just one since neither twin knows any chemistry.

So, the taxonomy dictated by externalism in the twin-earth example has us attributing two beliefs where explanation requires one, whereas externalism in the Pierre example dictated that there be one belief where explanation requires two. The point in both cases is that a second notion of content, which shuns externalism and which tunes into the twins' and to Pierre's conceptions, will have to be introduced to capture their respective coarseness and fineness of grain. Psychological explanation requires this appropriateness of grain and the appeal just to externalist elements is bound to fail in providing it.[9]

It seems that if we did not already have a notion of the content of propositional attitudes which captures an agent's conception of things and the inferential roles of the propositional attitudes, we would have to invent one. For it is surely in virtue of our conceptions of things that we, in our behavior, act upon things; so, if we admitted that externalist content did not capture these conceptions, that would be tantamount to rejecting the unity thesis which insists that what explains behavior is externalist content.

The pull towards a more and less fine-grained taxonomy in these respective sorts of examples is thoroughly convincing, and more will be said to justify this conviction a little later. However, it is my claim that it is not necessary to bifurcate content to capture agents' conceptions and the appropriate grain; it is my claim that an externally constituted notion of content is quite flexible enough to give us these taxonomies without surrendering the externalism. So I shall be arguing that there is a way of reconciling the external constitution of content with the role of intentional states in psychological explanation. But in order to do that it will be necessary to say more about which assumptions in these examples have given rise to such a strong impression of the need for bifurcation.

My discussion has so far spoken rather vaguely of "externalism" and how, according to the bifurcationists, "externalism" seems to get the wrong grain by leaving out agents' conceptions. While discussing the Pierre example, I referred without much detail or precision to "a certain view of reference" of singular terms and concepts such as "London." While on the second sort of example, I spoke equally vaguely of how "given externalism and given that the chemical structure of the external substance is different on earth and twin-earth, twin agents must have different concepts of water." These remarks only gestured at the standard and orthodox externalisms which pervade the use of these examples. The time has come to say something more detailed about them because they are at the centre of my diagnosis of the disunity of content which these examples generate. It is these externalisms which are responsible for the failure to capture agents' conceptions. It will be my claim, therefore, that it is not any externalism but the commitment to one or other of the orthodox externalisms that threatens unity.

The next section sketches the orthodox externalisms and the following section discusses how the assumption of their truth in the examples is the source of the threat to unity.

### THE ORTHODOX EXTERNALISMS

There are at least three substantially different orthodox externalist positions, with a measure of overlap of doctrine and motivation. They can be discussed under two headings: social externalism and non-social externalism, with two positions falling under the latter heading.

The most interesting and influential proponent of social externalisms is Tyler Burge, and the view is most explicitly proposed and defended in Burge (1979).[10] Unfortunately, social externalism is not all that apparent in the two examples cited above and Burge presents it with a lengthy example of his own which bears close similarities to the structure of the twin-earth example. Since it too is, by now, very familiar, I will be brief in the exposition.

There is a man, Bert, who thinks that arthritis is a disease that can strike the thigh as well as the joints; in this, of course, he is mistaken since, as his doctor will tell him, arthritis is a disease of the joints only. Burge insists that despite this, Bert's concept of arthritis is the same concept as the doctor's. So, when Bert thinks or utters various things about arthritis such as "Arthritis is a disease" or "I have arthritis in my ankles" and even "I have arthritis in my thigh," he is thinking and talking about the same thing as the doctor when *he* says some of these things, i.e. they are all arthritis-thoughts and utterances. Why? Because that is how the society and its experts use the term and their usage *constitutes* the concepts and, therefore, the contents of individuals in the society, even of such medically ignorant individuals as Bert.

This constitutive social thesis is fortified by the following thought-experiment. Imagine, counter to fact, another social environment in which the same word "arthritis," that is to say, the same shapes when inscribed or the same phonetic vocable, is applied to a larger class of rheumatoid ailments, one that can strike the thigh as well as the joints. Imagine also that there is a counterfactual Bert who is, internally, in no way different from the actual Bert. Only his environment is different in the sense just mentioned. All that is internal to him is the same. He is, as they say, molecule for molecule identical, his inner functional states are identical, and he utters the same sounds and writes the same shapes. In this counterfactual social setting, Burge explains, we must not say that Bert's belief which he expresses by saying, for instance, "I have arthritis in my thigh" is the belief that he has arthritis in his thigh. Whatever else it is a belief about, it is not about arthritis which is a disease only of the joints. Only the actual Bert will be talking about and have beliefs about arthritis, even when he wrongly thinks it is lodged in his thigh. In the counterfactual situation, the man's belief is about another disease which, to keep things distinct, deserves another name. Why is his belief about another disease? Because counterfactual Bert's community, in particular its experts, have a quite distinct linguistic usage for the term and it is their linguistic practices that constitute his concepts and contents.

In order to have clearly in mind what exactly Burge's social externalism is, it is good to be clear about what one means here by words like "constitute" and "constitutive." It is quite a strong and interesting thesis and ought not to be confused with the much less controversial and less interesting claims about the general relevance and influence of various social linguistic factors on the individual. To put the constitutive thesis of social externalism in a word: the linguistic practices of a community can often[11] affect the individual mind in the sense that we attribute to an individual the same concepts as his fellows, even where he has quite divergent beliefs.[12] That is quite a strong thesis. In chapter 3 there will be occasion to mention some of the weaker and less-interesting, more contingent and non-constitutive theses about the social nature of language. Let me just cite one weaker thesis now, partly because I expect to exploit its difference from Burge's view a little later in this chapter.

This is the thesis, stressed perhaps first by Putnam, called "the division of linguistic labor," and it is often confused with Burge's stronger thesis.[13] It points to a fact, a fairly widespread fact, about the linguistic practice of individuals. Take a well-known example, due also to Putnam. An individual agent often relies on experts in his society to pick out a certain kind of thing from others (an elm tree from a beech tree or from other trees in general) without in any serious way getting fully educated into the criteria for such individuation. This does mean that we will only accurately discover what he means and believes by observing his dependence on at least some others in his community; and so, in a sense, his concept of an elm is not entirely independent of his social environment. However, the reason this is not equivalent to Burge's thesis is that, to put it crudely, his reliance on others is *part* of his concept of an elm tree. He does *not* have the same concept of an elm tree as the experts themselves have. He may, when asked to pick out an elm, pick out the same thing as they do but the beliefs via which he does so will be different from those by which the experts pick them out. Essential to his picking out those things is that those are the things that the expert has told him are elms. Unlike Burge's thesis, we can stress the individual's own beliefs rather than the expert's as determining what concepts are to be attributed to him, and we can therefore distinguish between the concepts of an elm tree that the relying agent has and the relied-upon experts have. And, in turn, we will have to distinguish their relevant contents. It will be a crucial part of the relying agent's concept of an elm tree that he believes that elm trees are what the experts around him call "elms." The experts' concepts will presumably be determined by more purely botanical or dendrological beliefs. If the thesis of the linguistic division of labor, then does not imply that individual agents have the experts' concepts when they rely on them,[14] then it cannot amount to Burge's stronger thesis. I will reserve words like "constitutive" for the stronger view. Social externalism is defined by this constitutive thesis.

Social externalism can be described as the thesis that an individual's concepts (such as that of arthritis) are often determined by the experts in his or her society. Another natural way to describe it is to say that his concepts are based on a socially mediated account of *reference*. What a term (such as "arthritis" ) in an individual's speech refers to or what her concept applies to is determined by things as the experts take those things to be. Holding to the close connection between concepts and terms, the sequence which introduces social externalism is something like: (1) her concept is given by the reference of the relevant term, (2) reference is determined by something(s) in the world external to her but, (3) only as the experts takes the thing(s) to be. It is (3) which brings in the specifically *social* externalism.

Now, if we drop the specifically social externalism introduced by (3), we are left with the idea of reference, not socially determined or mediated, but just simply reference. A word that naturally comes to mind and that has often been used to describe the doctrine is "direct" reference.[15] This is the general idea underlying what we have called non-social externalism.

There is, as is well known, a mountain of writing on the idea of "direct" reference ever since the early papers of Kripke (1972) and Putnam (1975) first formulated the idea. The writing elaborates several different aspects of the idea. One aspect that does not especially concern us here is its implications for the theory of possibility and necessity. But there is an aspect that is of relevance to our interest in concepts and content, and it emerges if one asks how exactly we must understand (2) in the sequence above. How does the thing(s) external to the agent determine her concept, or more immediately, the reference of her term? One must say something about that or else "direct reference" will remain quite mysterious.

The proposal in Kripke's own writing, and developed in detail by others (see especially Devitt 1981), is, for terms such as proper names, roughly as follows. A thing, a person, a place, is first named at some point, say, in a baptismal ceremony or in some less ceremonial (possibly even inadvertent) way. This sets up the beginning of a causal story which, if ever it were told, would describe an elaborate chain of events, all causally linking this initial episode with any subsequent use of that term, even centuries later and in distant places. If, in different languages (sociolects), the term is translated into a different inscription or vocable, those translational events will form part of the causal chain which will connect any use of the term (by a speaker whose idiolect contributes to that sociolect) with the initiating event.

Thus, to take Pierre in our first example, we may say that his use of *"Londres,"* while he was in Paris, is connected causally by some elaborate chain of events, including some relevant translational events, to some initial event in which a city got named, whether ceremoniously or even inadvertently. His later use of "London" is similarly connected to that initial event, though of course without any translational events forming part of the connecting chain. Both terms in his use can therefore, and must, be said to refer to the city, London. They do so in virtue of the relationship they bear to the city via the initial event to which they are distantly connected by all these other events. The idea of direct reference is grounded in this elaborate causal story. The fact that the connection of Pierre's uses of the term with the city London is so distant does not spoil the idea of reference being direct. The directness of the reference can only be spoilt by a *conceptual* mediation of the object named, not by distance of causal mediation.[16] It would be quite wrong to think that there is any conceptual mediation in the proposed story.

One may be tempted to think that there is conceptual mediation because, let us say, in some initial ceremony some official said, "I now name this city, which flanks both sides of the Thames at the head of tidewater and which housed the fort of Londinium that was sacked by the followers of Queen Boadicea in AD 61, 'London'." One might think these brief descriptions of the city's geography and history must count as a conceptual mediation. The thought, according to the theory, would be quite wrong. Such descriptions may count as descriptions which *fix the reference* of the term "London" as that particular city but they may not count as conceptually mediating subsequent referrings to that city by the use of "London."[17] (or to put it in Fregean term, they may not count as the "sense" of "London.") All referrings, after the descriptions in the initial event have fixed the referent, are direct. The descriptions drop out.

That is one version of non-social externalism. This externalism is by no means restricted to proper names or singular concepts but extends to many common nouns, most famously, natural kind terms or concepts. The story that fills out (2) in the sequence is somewhat different for common nouns but it produces a similar overall account of concepts. The rough idea is this. Many of our general terms, for example, "water," which we have already considered, or "gold" or "lemon," refer directly to things with a certain nature. Our use of these terms first turns on there being some paradigm or example that set the standard for reference. Then, anything with the same nature will count as a thing or substance falling under that concept. Both with proper names and natural kind terms, things which are, as it were, present (the person baptized, the paradigm examples) provide the basis for reference. They do so by bearing the right relation to our subsequent use of these terms. Just as in the case of proper names it was the proper causal connections which were crucial, in the case of natural kind terms it is the sameness of the nature. It is a completely objective matter what these natures are, and our evolving scientific investigations tell us what they are. In the case of water, it is sharing a certain chemical composition with the paradigm; in the case of lemon, the same DNA. Things may look and be like these paradigms in all sorts of superficial respects but these terms and concepts would not apply to them if they did not share their "natures." Once again these things are not conceptually mediated, our words refer directly to things which share this essence with the paradigms.

While somewhat rudely conflating this externalism's treatment of common nouns with its treatment of proper names, this form of non-social externalism can be called "causal-essentialist" externalism.

A second, more recently influential, version of non-social externalism may be found in a book by Jerry Fodor (1987, ch. 4). It is an externalist account of content built on a refinement of information-based semantics as it is found in the work of Fred Dretske (1981) and Dennis Stampe (1977). After criticizing Kripke-style causal accounts for concentrating on the causal history of terms, Fodor stresses that the causal links one must look to are those between tokens of mental representations and properties in the external environment.[18]

His question is: what does the fact that a certain mental representation means horse, say, consist in? An information-based semantics aims to provide a naturalistic answer to this sort of question by looking to the information carried by the internal symbols; and the idea of information-carrying is naturalized by appeal to relations of causal covariance between symbols (the information-carriers) and things symbolized (the things that the information carried is about). As Fodor says, "In a word, $A$s carry information about $B$s if the generalization '$B$s cause $A$s' is true and counterfactual-supporting." There are plenty of refinements that Fodor introduces to this basic externalism; most of them enter to account for the possibility of misrepresentations or false beliefs and he finds himself having to make the most convoluted maneuvers to do so. But once the refinements are in place the basic idea remains: "horse" means what it does because of the causal connections that hold between horses and tokens of "horse." By contrast with "causal-essentialist" , this externalism can be called "causal-informational" externalism.

## WHY THE ORTHODOX EXTERNALISMS THREATEN UNITY AND MINE DOES NOT

The diagnosis of disunity is that content's unity is disrupted when content leaves out agents' conceptions of things. One reason why content would leave out agents' conceptions of things is (to put it a little crudely) that the story by which content was determined stressed the external things themselves to the exclusion of the agent's conceptions of those things.

Each of the orthodox externalisms does precisely that. The one which does it most explicitly is the non-social, causal-essentialist externalism. The whole point of its emphasis on *direct* reference to external things is to leave out the mediation that might be brought by agent's conceptions. That is the point of the insistence that the only place where descriptions or beliefs have any relevance to reference and, therefore, to concepts is in the initial fixing of reference. They have no relevance in the actual exercise of the concepts and they play no part, not even an implicit part, in the individuation or the specification of the concept.

Let us bring this out with the first sort of example exploited to threaten unity. As far as this version of non-social externalism goes, the descriptions or beliefs that might have been invoked in any initial ceremony in the inception of the term "London" are, as we saw, irrelevant once the reference to the city is fixed. This means that Pierre's term "London" refers to that city because it stands in a certain historical, causal relation to that city. But so does his term "*Londres.*" The historical, causal story always gets us to the same city. No doubt the causal chains are not identical but this does not affect the reference nor the concept since the causal story is not being allowed to be reflected in any mediating descriptive or intentional element in Pierre. Pointing to the differences in the causal chains themselves does not solve the difficulties of capturing Pierre's inferences and explaining his behaviour. For that, those differences would have to make a difference in Pierre's concepts; but that could only be done if they were reflected as different conceptions of his. That is precisely what the Kripkean view is determined to leave out. And that is why, on its view, the reference of "London" and "*Londres*" are the same and Pierre expresses the same concept by those terms. Since the diagonisis of disunity laid the blame on externalism's inability to provide two concepts of London rather than one, it is clear now how this version of non-social externalism fits the diagnosis.

We need not restrict ourselves to proper names to prove this point. Let us take "water." Though it is perfectly possible to run examples such as those in a Kripke-style puzzle (or its variant) on general terms as well, let us instead consider "water" in relation to the second sort of example we discussed in the diagnosis of unity. The diagnosis showed that unity is disrupted when twin-agents' actions, which were intuitively to be explained by the same intentional contents, were instead being explained by different intentional contents due to an externalism insensitive to the agents' shared conceptions of the things that they were acting upon. The non-social externalism we are considering is explicitly insensitive in precisely this way. According to it the term "water" refers to that substance which shares the objective nature of the paradigm samples. We know from the example that twin-agent live in environments in which the paradigm samples have different objective natures. So their concepts will, according to this account, be different. This means that according to it, the intentional contents which contain these concepts will be different even if, as we saw, their chemical ignorance points intuitively to their having shared conceptions of the substance and to shared explanations of their behavior. The diagnosis once again fits this externalism perfectly.

Fodor's causal-informational version of non-social externalism is different from the other version only in having shed some of its features of appealing to the causal links with an original baptism or reference-fixing event. It shares with it a determined effort to keep out of the determination of content exactly those features that the diagnosis of disunity makes clear are needed if unity is not to be undermined. Causal, historical links are given up for causal covariance between tokens of (mental) symbols and items in the world, such as horses. But it still explicitly keeps out anything which might introduce agents' conceptions and inferential roles. Fodor has a reason for this exclusion, which will be discussed in chapter 4 along with holism and the locality of content. For now, we need only note that his is a strict denotational semantics.[19] Though Fodor's causal story, which grounds step (2) of the sequence above, is different from Putnam and Kripke's way of grounding it, what it grounds is denotation or direct reference. In the story of grounding, it is items in the external world without mediation which must co-vary with our symbol-tokens.

Social externalism gives an initial impression of standing apart from these other two externalisms which depend on direct reference because it demands a mental mediation of the reference of many terms, a mediation usually by the beliefs and linguistic practices of an agent's community. However, this difference does not prevent the diagnosis of disunity from applying it it. The diagnosis says that any view of content that fails to capture an agent's conceptions of things will fail to explain the agent's behavior and will fail, therefore, to avoid the bifurcation of content. What the mediation in social externalism allows is of no help in capturing an individual agent's conceptions. There are bound to be agents who lack the knowledge of experts and whose linguistic practices will be out of tune with the community, agents such as Bert in Burge's example. For these agents, social externalist content will ignore the individual conceptions and another notion of content will have to be posited to capture them. Just as with the non-social externalism, where twin-agents get different explanations when intuitively they should get the same, so with social externalism, Bert and counterfactual Bert will get different explanations when intuitively they should get the same. They will get different explanations because their concepts will be different. Their concepts will be different for slightly different reasons from the reasons why the non-social externalisms attributed different concepts to twin-agents. But the central point is that they *will* be different, whereas our intuitions about explanation require that they be the same. If, for instance, both Bert and counterfactual Bert put a balm on their respective thighs because they want to relieve what they take to be their painful arthritis, our intuitions tell us that no matter what their community and its experts think, they have the same psychological conceptions, and therefore as far as psychology is concerned these amount to being the same explanations. The case is no different from the case of chemically ignorant twin-agents drinking water from thirst. If our diagnosis of disunity is right, then social externalism's failure to allow the coarseness of grain in their contents means it too must be diagnosed as threatening unity.

Social externalism may have some serious advantages over the non-social ones and social externalists have pointed these out. Brian Loar, for example, says this against non-social externalism:

> A non-social causal theory requires non-socially-mediated causal-reference relations. I doubt that we have conceptions of such relations.... Consider the simple fact that there is no such thing as *the* natural kind to which paradigms of a predicate like "dog" belong: they are dogs, members of the family Canidae, mammals. A person's term "dog" does not acquire a natural kind as its reference merely by pointing to paradigms. (Loar 1985b, pp. 128-9)

Even though I reject the social externalism that Loar accepts in the paper, I am sympathetic to this criticism of non-social orthodox externalism, and those who accept the latter ought to address it.[20] The point can be elaborated as part of a general criticism of essentialist assumptions in the study of content, but I will not do it here since my focus is not on that at the moment. Suffice it here to say that what the social considerations add to this externalism is a way of removing some of the mystery that attaches to the idea of *the* natural kind which is the referent of a predicate like "dog" or any other such predicate. The objective natures that Putnam and Kripke appeal to are, after all, specifiable properties and they are specified in the investigations of experts; so why not make that explicit by bringing in the social mediations of reference? Adding the social intermediary also makes it possible for the externalism to affect many more kinds of terms and concepts, rather than restrict itself to proper names and names for natural kinds. This is exactly what Burge has done in various papers when he extends his view of concepts from "arthritis" to "contract," "sofa," etc. Contracts many not have an essence but still experts tell us what they are when we are in a difficulty.

More will be said about this dispute between the social and the non-social views; the point for now is that it is an in-house quarrel between two versions of externalisms. It is a house and a quarrel that I do not particularly wish to enter since I wish to reject both these versions of externalism as undermining the unity of content.

Now that the diagnosis of disunity has explicitly been made and now that it has been shown how it fits the orthodox externalisms, it should be clear and obvious why it does not fit the externalism sketched in chapter 1. The threat, as we saw, comes from the fact that an externalism may appeal to the external world in the determination of content in a way that leaves out the agent's conceptions of things. But if one appeals to external items in the way proposed by my constraint (C), there is no reason to expect that agent's conceptions will be left out in the individuation of content. Let me state the constraint again.

C): When fixing an externally determined concept of an agent, one must do so by looking to indexically formulated utterances of the agent which express indexical contents containing that concept and then *picking that external determinant for the concept which is in consonance with other contents that have been fixed for the agent.*

The constraint's demand that the external item correlated with an agent's concepts be described in a way that is in consonance with the other contents attributed to the agent should have precisely the effect of including his or her conceptions of the external items. The constraint is there to make sure that we get the right descriptions of the external items which determine an agent's concepts, and that is just to say that those descriptions will be dictated not from God's point of view, not from the point of view of the expert or other members in the agent's community, not even from the point of view of a radical interpreter, not from any other point of view than the point of view of the agent himself. The concepts that are determined and the contents they compose can now hardly suffer from the bifurcation-inducing effect of omitting the agent's conceptions.

For example, if one allows the external elements to enter content under this constraint, the Pierre and the twin-earth examples do not have any bifurcatory consequences. In Pierre's case, the city in question, which is correlated with Pierre's earlier use of the term "*Londres*" and later use of the term "London" will be under different beliefs (or descriptions) of his. The recording of the correlations will make that explicit. One crucially important difference will be that the correlation in the later phase will not be between the use of the term and the city which his nanny told him of. So these different correlations between Pierre's utterances and the city will constitute two different concepts (the earlier and the later). Thus we will have the fineness of grain necessary for psychological explanation in examples of this kind.

In saying this one should not lose sight of some of the caveats in chapter 1. Of course, there is a slight oddity in talking of the correlations being between a city and earlier and later uses of a term, and of saying also that a description of the city drops out in the later phase. If the correlation is with the city, it is with the city, someone might say. This objection is fair enough and it echoes the worry mentioned in chapter 1 about causality and causal explanation: if it is causal (co) relations between utterances of a term and a city which are doing the determining work, what have descriptions of the city got to do with it? All the same, my point should be clear, if one understands that it would be to misdescribe my position if all one said was that my talk of correlations made under a certain constraint *merely* gives a twist to the orthodox causal accounts by bringing in their external causes under different descriptions. The departure from them is more radical. As already hinted at in chapter 1, in the analogy with Neurath's boat and in the point about anti-foundationalist holism, the selection of the descriptions cannot come prior to coming to grips with the agent's psychology. What that really amounts to is that in my externalism one looks at the agent's relations with the world around him with the task of imposing characterizations in which the concepts that we find composing the agent's contents can also be used to describe the world around him with which he relates. No doubt causation holds, but the role it plays is not at all the role it has in the orthodox externalisms, because when one looks at the relations with the world around him one is looking at cognitive and practical interactions. I will not keep repeating this caveat very time I talk of correlations or causal relations between agents and their environments.

The problem for unity in the twin-earth examples came from the opposite direction to the one from the Pierre example. We needed a more coarse-grained taxonomy in order to get the twins' psychologically efficacious contents. Where the orthodox externalisms gave us different contents, what psychology demanded was for the twins to share the relevant concepts and contents (about a substance, a disease, whatever.) The constraint I place on external causality allows me these shared contents. If we take the case where the substancs on the two planets are chemically distinct but neither of the twin-agents have any knowledge (beliefs) about chemistry, then the constraint, which requires that the substances in their environments (which are correlated with their indexical "water" utterances and thoughts) be described in consonance with their other beliefs, can see to it that they are described by the same descriptions. Thus the concepts these external substances determine can be the same for both agents. We can have the necessary coarseness of grain. I conclude that my externalism poses no threat to the unity of content.

There is, therefore, no need to posit a second notion of internalist content in order to produce a psychologically satisfying notion of content. Philosophers have jumped to positing it because they have simply been blind to the possibility of there being an externalism which is not one the the orthodox externalisms.

Whence this blindness? They have defined externalism in *general* terms as the non-independence of content from the external world.[21] They have then fashioned a specific externalist doctrine based on one or other of the views of reference discussed above. And they have assumed without question that their specific doctrine is the only way to cash out the general idea of externalism. And when some of them discovered that the specific doctrine seems to spoil the explanatory function of content, they have, therefore, jumped to the conclusion that only narrow or internalist content will carry out that function. My opposition to their entire way of thinking has been based on the following argument.

It first accepts the explanatory inefficacy of content as defined by their specific externalist commitments, i.e. it accepts the explanatory inefficacy of "wide" content. It then points out that the general doctrine of externalism need not be cashed out by their specific externalist commitments and can instead be redeemed in my externalism. In other words, wide content is not the only externalist content there is. And, finally, it shows how my externalism is not susceptible to charges of inefficacy in psychological explanation. It therefore establishes that there is no need for a second notion of "narrow" or internalist content. It thus rejects both wide and narrow content. It offers, instead, a unified notion of content, externalist and explanatory.

Having given, with my commitment to the unity of content, my opposition to the orthodox externalisms which disrupt unity, it is very important to warn against a certain misunderstanding. In opposing them I have denied that the general doctrine of externalism needs to be specifically thought of in terms of the orthodox externalisms, in terms of certain orthodox theories of reference. This may give the impression that, in offering an alternative specific way of thinking of externalism, I have offered an alternative view of reference. That impression would be wrong. One can see, though, how the impression would be formed. Are not the beliefs appealed to by my constraint (C) in the externalist determination of concepts just an appeal to a description - or belief-theoretic account of reference? Am I not, in insisting on the relevance of these descriptions and beliefs, just providing for a description-theoretic alternative to the orthodox causal theoretic account of reference? I think it would be highly misleading to say so. The idea of a description-theoretic account of reference as competing with a causal-theory of reference suggests that there is something called "refer-ence" and these are alternative theories of it. I do not believe that that notion of reference has anything to do with meaning and content. I am, therefore, inclined to deny that I am providing a version of a description-theory of reference. Even though in my criticism of direct reference in the study of concepts, I will occasionally contrast it with "reference being mediated by descriptions or beliefs" , that should not be taken to mean that in my own view there is some independently definable thing called "reference," which individuates concepts and which I think of as mediated, and the view I oppose thinks of as unmediated. Reference in that sense has no role in my account of concepts and contents. What I have in mind, when attacking the idea of direct reference in the study of concepts and content for leaving out conceptual or descriptional mediation, is not that one should replace direct reference with a mediated conception of reference. Rather, I am only stressing that concepts are determined by external things under my constraint (C). The idea that meaning and concepts are agents' conceptions of things is what my constraint gains for me. But the idea of "*conceptions* of *things*" should not be heard as an echo of "*descriptional* view of *reference*." The idea of agents' "conceptions of things" which individuate meanings is not the idea of things which can be severed from the conceptions or of things which different agents can have different conceptions of. Of course, there *are* things which are independent of conceptions and which different people have different conceptions of. But they do not play any role in the individuation of concepts and meanings. That is what is implied by my denial that reference does not individuate content even when reference is mediated by conceptions.

Does this mean that I am really an internalist? Not in the slightest. What makes me an externalist is that external things are necessarily involved in the determination of meaning and content. But, for me, being an externalist just does not bring with it the idea that reference, even mediated reference, has anything to do with the meaning of terms or with content. If it did, the external things which play a role in the determination of content would be decouplable from the conceptions or mediating descriptions. Though external things are involved in their determination, the meanings of terms are specified not by specifying their mediated reference but simply by specifying an agent's beliefs. This in no way threatens externalism since one could not arrive at those meanings except by looking at the correlations between indexical utterances and external things.[22]

I hope it is clear now how I manage to have it both ways. On the one hand, my constraint on the externalist determination of concepts rules out all standard (direct and descriptional) referential accounts of concepts. It does so by insisting that what are determined are concepts not referentially individuated but individuated in terms of an agent's beliefs. On the other hand, this involves no surrender to internalism because of my equal insistence that the constraint is a constraint on a determination of concepts which proceeds by correlating indexical utterances in which they occur with *external* things.

Chapter 4 will say more on this point about how one can see meaning and concepts as given only and entirely in terms of beliefs (and not as given, at best, by beliefs mediating reference) without compromising externalism. The point is emphasized now to warn as early as possible against misunderstanding of my view because of the widespread tendency to think that all externalism must involve some standard view of reference, either direct or descriptional. That is a tendency that my rejection of both wide and narrow content is intended to repudiate.

The rejection of that distinction might appear to be incoherent, since it seems that there can be no other option on content than that there is either narrow or wide content, or both narrow and wide content, as the bifurcationist wants. How can one reject all these three options? One can reject them because the distinction is made on the basis of two different criteria which are run together. Let me explain.

On the one hand, there is a distinction between taking an externalist view of content in the general sense mentioned at the very beginning of chapter 1, and denying such an externalist view and insisting that nothing external enters into the individuation of content. The former is wide content and the latter is narrow content. Let us call this the first criterion.

On the other hand, there is the distinction that the concepts which compose contents are individuated by the notion of reference in the official sense (orthodox externalisms being the most prominent accounts of such reference), and a denial of the view that reference in this sense has any thing to do with concepts and contents. The former is wide content and the latter is narrow. Let us call this the second criterion.

These two criteria are not always kept apart. The orthodox externalists, especially, do not keep them apart, and it is easy to understand why. They believe in wide content by both criteria. And so, they do not worry about the fact that wide content can be one of two distinguishable things. Many orthodox externalists – the bifurcationists – believe in narrow content too. And, in doing so, they, in a parallel way, again run together the different criteria. They assume – without explicitly making the distinction – that to believe in narrow content is to believe in something which both rejects a referential account of content and rejects something much more general, viz. that there is a notion of content which has *some* external element or other in its characterization.

Now, my view of unified content emerges from a careful separation of the two criteria. The reason why I reject the distinction between wide and narrow precisely flows from the observation that the distinction is based on two conflated but separable criteria, and that once one separates them, there is no single distinction there. By the first criterion, my notion of content as spelt out in chapter 1, is wide content. But it should be equally clear from chapter 1, and the discussion in this chapter, that, by the second criterion, my notion of content is narrow content. This is because I believe in an externalist notion of content which *rejects* the referential accounts of content. And this leaves my position open for dual misinterpretation and criticism. Those who are committed to a referential view of concepts and wide content will think I am committed to narrow content, when it suits them to think so, ignoring the fact that I am denying internalism. Those who are committed to an internalist conception of narrow content will think that I am committed to wide content, when it suits them, ignoring the fact that I am denying all referential views of concepts and contents. I do not know what a "double whammy" exactly is, but this sounds to me like one. For this reason, I do not associate my position with either wide or narrow content, but a rejection of the distinction altogether. It would be to positively encourage misunderstanding to call it either.

Now that the distinctions and terminology are all out in the open, it is necessary to confess (as I did in chapter 1, note 6) to a slightly misleading use of terminology so far. For the sake of convenience the term "wide" content has been used to talk of content characterized by an externalism based on the orthodox accounts of reference. That is, I have used the term "wide" in the sense defined by the second of the two criteria mentioned above. I have done this because I have been focusing so far on attacking orthodox externalists, and I have needed a convenient label for their view of content. But the reader should by now be sufficiently aware of my own externalist commitments to know that just because I have opposed "wide" content, so defined, I have not surrendered all externalism. For this reason, I have, despite this convenient terminological lapse, tried to keep the reader unconfused about my notion of content, by refusing to call it "narrow" content and choosing instead to use the term "unified" content to describe my position. The reader is urged, therefore, to keep the two criteria separate in the discussion that follows, especially since I will continue to describe the orthodox externalist view of content as "wide" content, throughout my critical discussion of their view. I contrast "wide" content defined by the second criterion with a notion of content that is non-referential but nevertheless externalist. This is what I mean by "unified" content. And in spelling out the role of constraint (C), I have said something about the specific nature of the non-referential externalism which characterizes my view of unified content.

I have criticized "wide" content, as defined by the second criterion, for not always being efficacious in the explanation of content. But I have denied that this means that "wide" content, defined by the first criterion, is necessarily subject to the same criticism. I have forged a view of externalist content (i.e. wide content, by the first criterion) which is always efficacious in explanation, and which, therefore, avoids the criticism. I have not called this notion of content I have forged "wide" content because I have already used that term to describe the referentially characterized notion of content of the second criterion. And so it would be to encourage misunderstanding to call my notion "wide" content. I would not want my notion of content to be confused with content thought of as referentially characterized any more than I want it confused with internalist content. That is why I am insisting on calling my view "unified" content rather than either "wide" or "narrow" content.


## SOME OBJECTIONS TO THE CHARGE OF DISUNITY

Though many orthodox externalists – the bifurcationists – would accept the charge that their position disrupts the unity of content, there are also many others who have denied the charge. They have denied that their notion of content needs supplementation with another notion of "narrow" content in order to explain behavior.[23] Burge, for instance, has all along resisted the call for a bifurcation of content. I will restrict my discussion to Burge and the claim that his orthodox externalism does not force bifurcation.

So far two sorts of examples have been invoked to raise trouble for the unity of content. There is first the example of Pierre, which showed that orthodox externalism imposed too coarse-grained a taxonomy on content and therefore forced a second notion of content for psychological explanation. And there is the twin-earth example and the closely similiar example of Bert and his arthritis, which showed that orthodox externalism imposed too fine-grained a taxonomy and therefore also forced bifurcation.

Someone may complain that the Pierre example serves well my purpose of charging orthodox externalism with disunity but there simply is not a similar use I can make of the twin-earth or Bert example. The parallel between the two sorts of examples, this complainer will say, simply does not hold because there is no threat to agents' conceptions in the second sort of example. The worry about appropriateness of grain in content attribution is a genuine worry for Pierre but not for the other sort of case. Pierre, he will admit, does need a finer grain of content but there is need to insist that the twins or that Bert and counterfactual Bert get a coarser grain. Why not? Because the Pierre case, as Kripke's puzzle makes clear, leads to blatantly inconsistent attributions, whereas there is no reason to think that anything as unpalatable happens in either the twins' case or in Bert and counterfactual Bert's case. There is thus no similarly compelling reason to fuss about the appropriate grain in these latter cases as there is in Pierre's case. In short, the complaint is that unless there is the possibility of something as serious as blatantly inconsistent attributions (or as failing to account for inferences of the agent) there is just not enough motive to deny that the twins' concepts or the two Berts' concepts are different.

The complainer is apparently simply unpersuaded by my appeal to the intuition about shared explanations of the twins drinking a certain substance to quench their thirst, or similar shared explanations of Bert and counterfactual Bert applying balm to their thighs to ease their pain. He is simply unpersuaded that as far as our interest in the twins' or in the Berts' *psychological or mental life* goes their actions should, intuitively, get the same descriptions and the same explanations. He simply denies that he has any such intuitions about psychological or mental life. So he insists that unless there is an inconsistency attributed and therefore unless there is a threat of Kripke-style puzzles about belief, one should leave things as they are and not worry about appropriateness of grain and agents' conceptions. The case of Pierre raises the threat of such puzzles but the other cases do not. He concludes that I should not, therefore, have extended my point about agents' conceptions to the other cases. Don't scratch where it doesn't itch, he might say.[24]

As the intuition about shared explanations that I appeal to in the twin-earth examples seems fairly decisive to me, I am not actually persuaded by this complaint; but it would be unwise to rest my case on an intuition that others claim not to share. The complainer can be seen as having thrown down a certain challenge. Insisting that only examples which lead to something as serious as blatantly inconsistent attributions will raise the question and problems I am raising, he has asked how I can use what the orthodox externalists say about the twins or about the Berts to raise them.

I accept the challenge. I will for the sake of argument, accept that the litmus test lies in falling prey to the charge of inconsistent attributions. And I will show that the orthodox externalisms fail the test and that they lend themselves to inconsistent attributions in all the examples we have considered (not just Pierre, but the twins and the Berts as well).

Once I have shown that, I will have made a more elaborate charge of disunity against the externalist and we will be ready to take three objections against the charge. And as we successively reply to each of the objections the charge will get more and more elaborate, thereby bringing out the widely different philosophical issues at stake in the thesis of the unity of content: the analytic-synthetic distinction, the linguistic division of labor, disquotational accounts of truth and reference, the nature of self-knowledge, to name some of the more central of them.

It is not, at least at first sight, hard to show that, if one believes in orthodox externalism, blatantly inconsistent attributions must sometimes be made to the twins and to the Berts. Since inconsistencies hold between the beliefs of a single agent, we will need to look at the agents in question singly rather than compare them as we did in my appeal to the intuition about shared explanations. For the sake of brevity, I will concentrate only on Bert and Burge's social externalism. The extrapolation to the other externalisms will be obvious.

Recall how we came to conclude that social externalism fails to capture agents' conceptions and the inferential and explanatory role of their contents. We imagined that we came across Bert who knows there is special balm for arthritis and thinks that he should apply it to ease the condition in his thigh. And we pointed out that counterfactual Bert reasoned in exactly the same way, even though his society had a different use for "arthritis" from Bert's society. Let us drop counterfactual Bert and stick to the task of attributing an inconsistency to the single agent Bert.

If we took the view that contents are socially constituted in Burge's sense, as sketched above, notice that we ought not, on the face of it, to be in a position to capture the practical reasoning by which Bert came to think that he should apply the balm to his thigh. After all, the concept being attributed to him, on Burge's externalist view, is the same as the one the medical expert has and that is the notion of a disease which only afflicts joints. Why, in that case, does he want to apply it to his thigh? (Let us assume that we know that he does not think that the thigh is a joint.)

The response will be that there is no problem in accounting for the inference; it goes through because there is a step in it which makes clear that he wants to apply the balm to the place where he things (falsely) that he has arthritis. But now notice that in an explicit statement of the inference which ends with the conclusion that he should apply the balm to his *thigh*, there must be a step which asserts that he believes that the place where he has arthritis is his thigh. However, this does look now as if the man is being attributed a thought that involves something inconsistent. He is supposed to be predicating his concept of arthritis which is supposed to be the same as the expert's (i.e. the concept of a disease only of the joints) to his thigh, which we have already said he knows is not a joint.

The examples can be multiplied to make this point. Think of the chemically ignorant agent saying or thinking, as he brashly might, "Water is not $H_2O$;" or his twin on twin-earth thinking "Water is not XYZ." None of these cases is, in its essentials, different from Kripke's Pierre.[25] And if there was no problem with the claim about the Pierre example threatening unity, there is no problem with the claim about Bert and twin-earth example doing so. Even if we accept the (to my mind, unreasonable) claim that the *only* test for unity being genuinely threatened comes from the fact that externalism strains the principle of charity by attributing blatantly inconsistent thoughts, we now have shown that the orthodox externalists do strain it in this way in both sorts of examples. They will, therefore, have to appeal to a second notion of content which will not lead to these inconsistencies being attributed.

Notice that if it is right that these attributions are inconsistent, the following argument against Burge's having to bifurcate is pre-empted: social externalism makes clear that Bert's belief that he has arthritis in his thigh is a false belief but false beliefs can be employed in the explanation of actions, so what is the problem, why do we need another notion of content to explain actions, why is unity threatened? This false belief of Bert's perfectly well explains various actions of his such as putting a balm for arthritis on his thigh. To deny that these beliefs explain his actions is to take the implausible view that only true beliefs can explain actions. I have no quarrel with the claims of this argument. But if I am right that the social externalist is stuck with having to say that Bert's belief that he has arthritis in his thigh is not just false but inconsistent, this argument is irrelevant to Bert's case. Like Pierre, Bert believes something inconsistent.

My insistence on finding inconsistency here is intended to challenge the orthodox externalists with a dilemma. Either they must admit that their position can always (that is, not merely in the Pierre example but in the others as well) lead to inconsistent attributions or they must relinquish unity and bifurcate content. Since, in this chapter, I am only attacking the orthodox externalists who deny that unity is being threatened by their externalism, this dilemma constitutes a sufficient case against them, if they also accept (as they surely must) that blatantly inconsistent attributions intolerably strain the most elementary principle of charity. They strain it just as badly in Bert's case as they did in Kripke's puzzle about the Pierre case. Burge and several others, sympathetic to one or other orthodox externalism, have wanted to preserve unity and avoid the bifurcation of content. So we have now given them a task: the only way for them to avoid bifurcation (the second horn of the dilemma) is to somehow avoid being impaled by the first horn of the dilemma.

Hence any effort on the orthodox externalists' part to deny the charge of disunity has the task of dealing with this dilemma and showing how they will avoid the first horn, avoid the possibility of there being these blatantly inconsistent attributions.

We are now ready to look at objections that someone might make on their behalf against the charge, objections which will try to carry out this very task. All these objections will try to show that orthodox externalism is not forced to attribute inconsistencies in the way I have insisted above. There are three lines of objection available to Burge and the orthodox externalists, which need careful elaboration and consideration, and which reveal interesting and significant features of the nature of intentional content. These will be spelt out once again with Burge's example of Bert and arthritis, though once again the point can be extended easily to other examples.

## First Objection

It is an important step, in making the point about how Burge's externalism can lead to inconsistent attributions, that one has interpreted his point about the expert's concept being attributed to Bert, as taking the form of attributing to him the concept of a disease which strikes the joints only. If the step did not establish this we could not charge him with attributing to Bert the inconsistent thought that it is a disease of the joint only which has afflicted his thigh. Now someone may resist this interpretation of Burge's point, and in a recent paper Burge himself has introduced certain distinctions which someone may invoke in this resistance. Here is the passage with the distinctions:

> I distinguish between a lexical item and the explication of its meaning that articulates what the individual would give, under some reflection, as his understanding of the word. I also distinguish between the concept associated with the word and the concept(s) associated with the entry. Call the former 'the concept' and the latter 'the conceptual explication'. Finally, I distinguish between a type of meaning associated with the word, 'translational meaning', and the meaning associated with its entry, 'explicational meaning'. For our purposes, the explicational meaning is the semantical analogy of the conceptual explication. The translational meaning of a word can be articulated through exact translation and sometimes through such trivial thoughts as *my word 'tiger' applies to tigers*, but need not be exhaustively expressible in other terms in an idiolect. (Burge 1989, pp. 12-13)

He goes on to criticize the view (he calls it the "traditional" view) which claims that:

> a word's explicational meaning and its traditional meaning are, for purposes of

characterizing the individual's idiolect, always interchangeable; and that the individual's conceptual explication always completely exhausts his or her concept.
This view is incorrect. It is incorrect because of the role that the referent [presum-
ably socially mediated referent] plays in individuating the concept and translational
meaning, and because of the role that non-explicational abilities play in the
individual's application of the word and concept. Accounting for a person's lexical
entry or conceptual explication is relevant to determining the nature of a person's
meaning or concept. But the two enterprises are not the same. (Burge 1984, p. 13)

Now all this is relevant because someone may think that in the crucial step
above, my insistence that Burge's social view amounts to taking the agent's
concept of arthritis as involving an attribution of the concept of a disease of the
joints only, is a running together of the agent's concept with the conceptual
explication, his "translational meaning" with his "explicational meaning" – just
what he warns us against in the "traditional view." An inconsistency is only
attributed if the agent can, on reflection, exhaustively articulate (recall the
definition of "explication" at the beginning of the first quotation) the concept of
arthritis, in particular articulate that it is a disease of the joints only. Clearly, the
medically ignorant Bert cannot, not even after the most assiduous reflection.[26]
And clearly also since we are in advance convinced by considerations of charity
that the agent is not being blatantly inconsistent, we may, armed now with these
distinctions, attribute to him only the explicatory portion of the concept of
arthritis and thereby ensure that no inconsistency is being attributed. For this is
a case of his explicational meaning of his term not exhausting the translational
meaning.[27]

The trouble with this objection, however, is that it has surreptitiously, that is
to say with other words and labels, conceded that his externalism and his position
on what is attributed to Bert, forces a second notion of content. Contents, as we
said, are composed of concepts. And now we are being told that there are two
notions of concepts: (a) concepts proper, given by socially mediated reference,
and (b) concepts in the sense of conceptual explications that the agent can, on
reflection, articulate. It is only when the second of these is attributed that an
attribution or inconsistency is avoided. And it is only contents composed by these
that are relevant for psychological explanation. They alone can enter into the
sorts of inferential relations that explain agents' behaviors. Contents composed
of the former, whatever it is they are good for, will fail to capture an agent's
psychologically efficacious states without opening up the possibility of attributing a mess of internal inconsistencies every time the agent is seriously misin-
formed about the (socially mediated) reference. The explication of "arthritis" in
Bert's case will consist, say, of his belief that it is a disease, that it is a painful
disease, that it occurs more often in older people, etc., but nowhere in the
explication will there be the belief that it is a disease of the joints only. And it is

this explicational concept that goes into our attribution of the psychologically explanatory state, his belief that he has arthritis in his thigh, which explains why he wants to, and perhaps does, apply the balm to his thigh. This explication, of course, does not get us to the reference of "arthritis" (in any official sense of reference) and it does not coincide with the explication of the experts. It is concepts proper which are tied to that sort of thing. If one attributes contents composed of *concepts proper* to Bert, as Burge's social externalism demands that we do, and if we want to avoid an intentional psychology for him that often attributes inconsistencies and therefore runs afoul of the most elementary principle of charity, we had better also attribute to him the other kind of content which is composed of *explicational concepts*.

Hence an appeal to these distinctions to save the thesis against the difficulty I raised can only be made by accepting my initial claim that Burge's view of content destroys its unity and forces a bifurcation. It avoids the first horn of the dilemma only to be impaled on the second.

## Second Objection

I repeat that the problem about attributions of inconsistent beliefs arose for Burge's view because we allowed ourselves to rewrite "arthritis" in the representation of the agent's belief with, among other things, "a disease of the joints only." Only thus the inconsistency in his thinking, "I have arthritis in my thigh" (assuming still that he knows that the thigh is not a joint). Our justification for allowing ourselves the rewrite was just Burge's claim that the expert's notion or the socially determined notion must be attributed to the agent – that *is* the expert's notion.

It is this substitution or rewrite that the distinctions invoked by the first objection were trying to finesse. Here is another reason why the inconsistency-inducing rewrites might be resisted. It might be said that the rewrite is only permissible if one believes in something like the analytic-synthetic distinction. Only if one thought that concepts or terms, such as "arthritis," have definite meanings which include "a disease of the joints only," is it permitted. But why, it will be protested, should we hitch this old cart-horse of a distinction to a shiny new buggy like Burge's social externalism? Indeed, Burge has explicitly denied that he embraces the distinction in another recent paper (Burge 1986b). It is unfair to him, then, to interpret his idea of the social element's constitutive relevance to concepts and contents as the idea that we take any definite belief or set of beliefs of the experts as defining "arthritis" and plug them into the representations of individual agent's beliefs whenever we might have said "arthritis." But without plugging it in we cannot have the first horn, we cannot have our inconsistent belief attributed.

This objection is fair enough only if the social externalist tell us of an alternative way of saying what the agent's concept is to the one which is specified by the substitution of some set of beliefs of the community and its experts. What, according to social externalism, are we attributing to the agent when we say that he believes that he has arthritis in his thigh, if it is not, among other things, the belief that he has a disease, which afflicts the joints only, in his thigh? The expert and most other people do, after all, think that is what arthritis is, i.e. that is what it refers to; so what is left of the social externalism if the substitution is not allowed? How can we retain the relevance of the society and its experts to this agent's concepts and contents and fail to specify things this way?

The only alternative specification of his concept of arthritis, *which retains the relevance of the social environment* is one which appeals to a very much more general belief of the agent himself: "arthritis is whatever the others in my society, in particular the experts, call 'arthritis.'" This metalinguistic specification is a convenient way of bringing in the social element without saying anything specific by way of a definition of "arthritis," and it thus avoids saying anything that smacks of a commitment to the analytic-synthetic distinction. And because it does not say anything very specific it does not involve the agent in any inconsistency.

But notice that this way of retaining the social element may get rid of the problem of inconsistent attributions but it does so only by retaining the wrong thing. The social element it retains does not amount to social externalism. The social now enters in a way that is perfectly compatible with the "*individualism* about the mental" that Burge was attacking in his paper with roughly that title (Burge 1979). This point has been made clear in the discussion of the linguistic division of labor. In fact, this sort of specification makes Burge's view indistinguishable, for the most part, from the thesis of the linguistic division of labor, a much weaker view. The social now enters through a belief of the agent's, even if the belief is metalinguistically specified.[28] It thus meets the constraint I have imposed since the external (social) element enters only via how the agent himself conceives of it. The agent in this case conceives of it very generally as something that the expert knows much more about than he does. And because it meets the constraint, this externalism avoids the strictly social anti-individualist externalism defined in terms of Burge's constitutive thesis.[29] The constitutive thesis had it that Bert is attributed the expert's concept. But this metalinguistic specification does not attribute the expert's concept to him at all. It would be absurd to suggest that the expert's concept is: "the disease which experts call 'arthritis.'"

Burge can therefore only endorse this second line of objection by abandoning the strong constitutive thesis that the objection was supposed to defend. He could endorse it only by giving up his social externalism for a basically individualist externalist position since the social would only come in filtered by an individualist constraint upon which I have insisted, viz. that the external items (even if, as in this case, socially mediated) always be described keeping in mind the other beliefs of the agent in question. In this case the beliefs in play would be the metalinguistically specified beliefs which would capture the fact of his reliance on others in his society, a fact adumbrated in the often plausible (but not in itself anti-individualist) thesis of the division of linguistic labor.

## Third Objection

It may still seem that Burge has not been allowed the most sympathetic exposition of his own position so that he can avoid the problem of having to attribute an inconsistency and, thus, avoid the first horn. Someone may deny that the only way for a social externalist to avoid a commitment to the analytic-synthetic distinction is to rewrite "arthritis" along the metalinguistic lines suggested in the second objection. Someone might say that there is no reason to plug in for "arthritis," in the specification of the agent's content, either the individualist metalinguistic rewrite ("whatever the experts call 'arthritis'") or the anti individualist inconsistency-inducing rewrite ("a disease of the joints only"). There is no need for *any* rewrite. Rather what is needed, it might be said, is simply the concept of *arthritis*. There is nothing else to say. So to the question: what does he think he has in his thigh, the answer simply is: arthritis. He is able to think this because he thinks, falsely, that one can have arthritis in one's thigh. That the concept is the concept of *arthritis* (which is a disease one can only have in the joints) allows us to say no more, Burge might say, that something harmless such as "He thinks, *of* a disease which one can (in fact) only have in one's joints, that he has it in his thigh." No need to rewrite things either as the inconsistency-inducing belief that he thinks that he has a disease in his thigh which is among other things a disease of the joints only, or to rewrite it as the non-Burgean, non-social externalist, individualist, specification of the second objection, viz. the belief that he has whatever is called "arthritis" by his community and its experts, in his thigh.

This third objection leaves things with a mystery. One is being left with what is sometimes called a purely "disquotational" specification of the concept. If we were to persisit, well what is it that you are attributing when you say that he has arthritis in his thigh, what does "arthritis" *in the de dicto specification of the content* tell us? – the answer will simply be that "'arthritis' refers to arthritis." [30] To the question, what's *that*?, what does the right-hand occurrence of the term convey, the protest will be that I am insisting on definitions, an insistence from the dark ages when the analytic-synthetic distinction was still in currency. Notice, though, that I am asking for what "arthritis" in the specification tells us, I am not asking for *further* information about something which has already been conveyed by the disquotational specification. The protest, then, has got to be that even this minimal and initial demand smacks of a commitment to definitions and therefore to the analytic-synthetic distinction.

This protest against my rewrite is not the same as another more clearly mistaken protest. It is not the protest which says that I am missing the obvious point that *de dicto* attributions do not allow of substitutions. Such a protest would itself be missing the obvious point that it cannot be that *de dicto* attributions allow of *no* substitutions. The prohibition of substitutions in *de dicto* attributions turns on the attribute *not knowing* of the coextensiveness of the expressions involved. Such substitutions would threaten self-knowledge of one's own thoughts, if thoughts are individuated in terms of truth-conditions and reference. I will return to this point below after discussing the relevance of this question of self-knowledge.

The more serious protest under consideration charges my insistence on rewrites with the more specific charge of being committed to the idea of analyticity. I have no particular wish to defend the analytic-synthetic distinction and below will say something to make clear that my view does not require any commitment to it. But it does seem quite wrong to think that if one persists with the question, what is it that the reference-giving assertion above is really saying, one must be doing so because of a desire for definitions. All that the persistence reflects is a dissatisfaction with a disquotational specification of the term "arthritis" when one is asking for the concept being specified in the content attribution. Disquotation cannot be a merely syntactic device, for if it were, it could never specify the concept of arthritis in content attributions. Indeed, it could never specify any meaning of anything at all. Disquotation, if it is to be in the service of an account of meaning, is not a wholly trivial idea. It must be anchored in something which is not made explicit in the disquotational clause itself. The right-hand side occurrence of "arthritis," after all, is a *use* of the term. It expresses something.

And so if disquotation is not a mere syntactic device, one does, if not explicitly at least implicitly, get an answer to the question one is persisting with, the question what is it that one is saying when one says that Bert thinks that he has *arthritis* in his thigh. And then one wants to know, if the right-hand side of the reference-giving statement expresses something, why – *for the social externalist* – it does not express the inconsistency-inducing "a disease of the joints only" since that is what the community and its experts think arthritis is. What remains of social externalism if that is not what the right-hand side occurrence expresses?

One answer to this criticism might be that the appeal to the idea that "arthritis" refers to arthritis in specifying Bert's concept is not an appeal to disquotation as a syntactic device at all. Rather the disquoted term conveys that the term "arthritis" links up with something in the world by a causal relation which is unmediated by any description. It is linked up with an *object,* and *not,* as I am insisting, an *object under some beliefs or descriptions.*

Now, first of all, this answer, though it may support the other orthodox externalists, cannot entirely provide solace to the *social* externalist, who allows the beliefs of the expert to play some mediating role. But even putting that aside, it is hard to understand how terms like reference (and truth) can possibly have a theoretical role to play in the study of concepts (and contents) if the right-hand sides of the statements attributing reference (and truth-conditions) reduce us to utter ineffability about what the concept is. This way of avoiding the triviality of disquotation as a syntactic device makes things trivial not by making something syntactic out of something semantic, but rather by making semantics ineffable and mysterious. The highly metaphysical nature of the link-up has the same trivializing effect. Both convey no information at all as to what the concept being attributed is.

Here is a way of bringing this out more vividly. Nobody can deny that there is, at least, a *prima facie* difference between the sentence "Vermeer's *View of the Delft* is beautiful" and "Vermeer's *View of the Delft* is painted on a canvas," between "Nehru was a good man" and "Nehru was born in Allahabad." Nobody can deny that predicates like "is beautiful" and "is good" are, *prima facie,* different from predicates like "is painted on canvas" and "is born in Allahabad." We might say that the difference consists in the fact that, at least *prima facie,* there is a difference in the way we think of how they stand in relation to concepts like truth and reference. The application of concepts like reference and truth is, at least *prima facie* to be thought of as problematic when we are dealing with evaluative predicates and sentences. No doubt many will eventually want to say that evaluative predicates like "is good" and "is beautiful" are susceptible to a naturalistic treatment and so there is not a serious difference between them and the other predicates. But that is something we might *eventually* say, so it does not spoil the observation that there is a *prima facie* difference. That is, it takes a lot of philosophical work to put oneself in an eventual position of being able to say that there is no serious difference. But if one took reference and truth in a disquotational way in either of the two senses we are considering (the syntactic or the highly metaphysical causal link-up with objects), we will not be able even to acknowledge that there is a *prima facie* difference between these two sorts of sentences and predicates. We will not be in a position to acknowledge that there is even a *prima facie* problem in thinking of truth-conditions and reference as applying to the evaluative sentences and evaluative predicates respectively. If disquotation is a purely syntactic device then it is indifferent to the *prime facie* distinction we are marking between these two sorts of sentences and predicates. Equally, if descriptions and beliefs are wholly irrelevant to the link-up with objects which these disquotational assertions are supposed to convey, then there are no resources to state the problem that evaluative predicates might *prima facie* raise for the application of notions like truth and reference. For all we have said and can say, these predicates link-up with objects (goodness, beauty) just like any other predicate, so there cannot even be a *prima facie* problem of this kind. But we started by saying that there *is*, undeniably, a *prima facie* problem; so there is nothing else to conclude but that this way of thinking of the specification of Bert's concept, "'arthritis' refers to arthritis," is just as unsatisfactory as the syntactic treatment of the disquotation involved in it. It papers over a genuine *prima facie* problem and distinction. It does not even allow us to raise the problem or make the distinction.

It has been said that concepts are "primitive" things about which one can say no more than what this pure notion of disquotation allows. The disquotation does not convey any further explication because if it did it would deny the primitiveness of concepts. "Primitive" merely labels what I find mysterious. In any case, Burge himself ought not really to count concepts as being "primitive" in this way since he himself does, after all, offer an account of them and their place in content; an account along social externalist lines. The account tells us something about them. Therefore, he cannot object to my using what he tells us about them in the way I do, by saying that I am refusing to see that concepts are primitive. What, then, would be the point of his account of them and their place. in content?

Some may object that surely *some* concepts have to be primitive. Not all concepts can be such that they get a rewritable explication, because explications themselves invoke other concepts and it would make things circular or infinitely regressive unless some concepts did not get explications. This view comes from an altogether uncompulsory foundationalist picture of a bedrock of concepts on which others are founded. It is an important consequence of, and indeed partial motive for, my constraint (C) that such a foundationalism is unnecessary. No doubt, we hold some concepts steady in the background in order to explicate what others mean. But that does not mean that the ones we held steady are primitive in the sense of not themselves susceptible to explication, holding *other* concepts steady. Illumination about concepts comes from this dialectic between background and explication, and not from some foundationalist bedrock.

This third objection, which tries to deal with the first horn of the dilemma by invoking disquotational specification of concepts and thereby avoids any kind of rewrite of the concept of arthritis, will not work either. It avoids the first horn at the cost of making it wholly mysterious what concept, and therefore what content, is being attributed to Bert.

Someone may be tempted to say that my complaint about how there is a mystery at the heart of the orthodox externalist's appeal to disquotation is unfair because such a mystery arises for my own view as well. They may say that I just assume that there is no mystery about how beliefs or descriptions get us the meaning of "arthritis." Why should we find agents' conceptions less mysterious than direct unmediated reference? In short, as I have often heard it said, if direct "reference" is mysterious why is "sense" any less mysterious? It is just as mysterious to say that words get meaning via sense as it is to say that they get it via reference.

I would deny this on the ground that what I find mysterious (about the claim that there are in principle no beliefs or descriptions which can be substituted) is perfectly easy to state, and state precisely. And I would claim that it is a notion of mysteriousness simply missing in the idea that there are beliefs or descriptions which give meaning and which are substitutable for the terms in appropriate contexts.

Following Wittgenstein, I find mystery in these matters if something is altogether and by its very nature inexpressible. Whereof one cannot speak, thereof one is mystery-mongering. By inexpressibility here I do not mean merely that something cannot be explicitly listed because it would take longer than we have, but something which is by its very nature not the sort of thing which is expressible, something for which descriptions are the wrong sort of things to demand. Such inexpressibility is implied by the appeal to disquotation and primitiveness in the third objection. It is said that Wittgenestein himself took a rather glamorous view of the inexpressible at the end of the *Tractatus*. That may or may not be so. I do not take such a view. In not allowing that there is anything to be said in answer to the question: what does the right-hand side of the occurrence of "arthritis" in a reference-giving statement convey?, the orthodox externalist is being mysterious, by this criterion of what is mysterious. But by the same criterion my insistence on beliefs or descriptions being brought in to answer these questions precisely eschews this mysteriousness.

Of course, for any term in any of the descriptions given to answer the questions above, more such questions can be raised. And the point is that more such answers appealing to further descriptions will be given. There is no reason to admit to inexpressibility and reduce oneself to silence. Therefore there is no mystery, at least as defined above. It is true that I have traded mystery for other things such as a seemingly infinitely regressive appeal to descriptions. But I have already addressed that difficulty as inherent in anti-foundationalism, a difficulty which can be overcome in routine pragmatist ways by tentatively holding some descriptions unquestioned in the background while answering questions about others in the foreground. This is all, of course, much messier than the view that concepts are primitive and that they must be purely disquotationally charac-terized. But life is a mess, and theoretical and philosophical reflection on these matters would do well to acknowledge the mess and keep faith with it, rather than produce an artificially tidy theory with a mystery at its very core.

In a word, then, I have stated clearly what I mean by mysterious and I have found the view I am opposing (the view that permits no rewrite) guilty of it in precisely the way that my own view (which demands a rewrite) is not. If someone is going to turn on me and say that I too am being mysterious in insisting on descriptions and beliefs they must have in mind another sense of what is mysterious. And as I do not know what that is, I cannot answer the charge.

It remains for me to say a little about why my insistence that there must be some form of implicit rewrite in order to specify a concept, does not, at least on my view of intentional content, bring with it any commitment to an analytic-synthetic distinction. This is a very important part of my overall view of intentionality. It is one more thing that separates my notion of concepts, which in superficial respects is like a description-theoretic view. It is not at all the traditional descriptional view of concepts nor even subsequent refinements of the traditional view which account for concepts by bringing in clusters of descriptions with weighted majorities among these descriptions to explicate the concept. Let me explain.

My insistence on the rewrite flows merely from the fact that the alternative leaves unexplained what the concept in question is. Now it is *only* if one holds a view like Burge's social externalism or Putnam's view of natural kinds, that the insistence on the rewrite looks as if it will lead to definitions, and therefore to what looks like a commitment to the analytic-synthetic distinction. This is because on Burge's view or on the scientific-essentialist view there is some privileged belief or beliefs of the expert or some paradigm instance of a natural kind which fixes the reference and meaning of agents' concepts and terms. Thus I am claiming that the insistence on the rewrite (an insistence forced by the mystery attaching to any view that denies it) *by itself* does not commit one to the analytic-synthetic distinction. It is only if one combines the insistence with certain accounts of concepts or the meaning of terms that one is committed to analyticity.[31]

If instead one combines the insistence on rewrites with an account like the one sketched in chapter 1, there is no such commitment. Recall that a concept, at the level at which concepts are attributed by a theory of meaning, is nothing but a carrier of all the beliefs an agent associates with the term which expresses the concept. There are no weights placed on some beliefs over others which might give the impression of definitional status or of the notion of criteria (versus symptom) or anything like that. There is, or course, another level over and above the meaning-theoretic level: the local level. But the whole point of distinguishing between the aggregative, meaning-theoretic level and the local level was to allow that there can be lots of different localities at the local level. This means that there is no single rewrite because there is no single locality. There is no definition. Different localities dictate different selections or distillation from these aggregates, but there is no fixed concept, no canonical selection or distillation, at the local level. Different localities will distil out different beliefs and thus sanction different rewrites. Though there might be overlap and coincidence in what is distilled in different localities, there is no saying in advance what these are. Thus there are no weights imposed on any of beliefs within the aggregate of beliefs at the meaning-theoretic level such that some beliefs are more important than others and must be distilled out in all localities. So the rewrites I insist on will have no fixed criteria, if one adopts my picture of concepts and contents. They cannot, therefore, count as a commitment to the analytic-synthetic distinction.

By contrast, once one forces the need for rewrites, as I have with the charge of mystery, the orthodox accounts I oppose are bound to provide the more rigid definitional rewrites which give rise to analyticity. Given their accounts, the rewrites *will* be canonical, e.g. the expert's beliefs. No wonder they worry about and resist having to allow rewrites.

So, my response to those who charge my demand for a rewrite with a commitment to the analytic-synthetic distinction is simply this. There is nothing in the demand itself which makes that commitment. The demand merely flows from the inability to specify what a concept is if one did not meet the demand. Only if one were already given to certain specific views on meaning and concepts, would the commitment be made with the rewrites. My view of meaning and concepts makes no such commitment, but the externalisms I am opposing, given the need to rewrite, do.

Three objections to the specific charge of disunity, made against the orthodox externalism, have been considered. That charge consisted in the posing of a dilemma. Either one ends up often, and uncharitably, attributing blatant inconsistencies or one bifurcates. To avoid the charge of disunity the orthodox externalist has to somehow avoid attributing inconsistencies in the examples we discussed. The three objections made on behalf of the orthodox externalist wrestled with this first horn of the dilemma but have not succeed in resisting it. The first surreptitiously embraced bifurcation and thus avoided it by being impaled on the second horn, i.e. by succumbing to the charge of disunity. The second relinquished orthodox externalism and embraced my externalism. The third objection avoided the first horn by leaving it a complete mystery what concept and content is being attributed to the agent in question. If I am right, then, there is no way for the orthdox externalist to avoid the first horn and it would appear that he has no way out but to resort to bifurcation.

There is one possibility left. It is a way out that cannot possibly have any attraction for the orthodox externalist or anyone else for it avoids the first horn of the dilemma by saying that agents do not have the most ordinary kind of self-knowledge of their own intentional states. This way out could be proposed as a fourth objection which seeks to avoid the dilemma, but given the special importance and independent interest of the subject of self-knowledge, a special section will be devoted to it.

## SELF-KNOWLEDGE

Let me first raise a general problem that self-knowledge is supposed to pose for externalism and then bring in the relevance of the problem of self-knowledge to the dilemma we have been posing for the orthodox externalist in particular. I will be arguing that there is no threat to self-knowledge which issues from externalism, unless one is an orthodox externalist.

Externalism has notoriously been at least a *prima facie* threat to the very possibility of self-knowledge of intentional states in cases where it seems self-knowledge should uncontroversially and intuitively exist.[32] If things outside the agent's ken determine the contents of an agent's intentional states then, *prima facie*, that raises a question about how the agent can always have knowledge, or at any rate full knowledge, of those contents. That is, to the extent that there might be features of the external things that the agent does not know, then to that extent he would not fully know the concepts and contents that those external things determine.

Some philosophers, including Putnam, have happily embraced this implication and have claimed that a proper understanding of the fact that content and meaning are external should make one suspicious of (what they take to be) the internalist-bred intuition that we always have knowledge of our intentional states (Putnam 1975, pp. 164–5). These philosophers have, of course, gone on to deny that content is a unified thing and pointed out that there is one notion of content which is externalist about which they embrace this conclusion regarding absence of self-knowledge, and another which is internalist and about which this particular problem, *ex hypothesi*, does not arise.[33] Other externalists, however, may not (and, in the case of Tyler Burge, laudably, do not) wish to embrace such a conclusion about self-knowledge, nor may they want to introduce a second notion of content; but the fact that there is this *prima facie* difficulty suggests that they have some work to do to give themselves the right to say that the agent knows what whose contents are. Burge recognizes this and takes on the task of giving himself the right (Burge 1988).[34]

His proposal is straightforward. An agent's belief that p, says Burge, has certain ncessary conditions, and he adds that since when one knows that one is thinking that p, one is also thinking that p, it follows that those necessary conditions for believing that p carry over to the self-knowledge, carry over to the iterated state, too. If the necessary conditions are external to the agent, that makes no difference. This point seems to be impecable.

Someone might worry that it assumes the very thing that there is supposed to be a *prima facie* difficulty about. It assumes self-knowledge and says that if one has self-knowledge of one's thought that p, then what goes into the individuation of p carries over to the iterated thought that expresses the self-knowledge. But with what right does one say, given one's commitment to externalism, that one knows one's thought? This question seems to be missing Burge's point which is to turn the tables around on the question, to make the questioner do some more work himself to raise a problem about self-knowledge. Burge says that one does not have to know the necessary conditions that go into the thought that p being the thought it is in order to have that thought. And so if one is unaware of the various external factors that go into its being that thought, it neither follows that one does not have that thought nor, given their common necessary conditions, that one does not have the iterated thought that expresses self-knowledge of the thought.

By the strategy of his proposal, it looks as if Burge is going to insist that one can never argue directly from externalism to a *prima facie* threat to self-knowledge. So far as I can see the strategy, as it stands, looks reasonable and anybody who argues simply that Burge's (or Putnam's, Kripke's etc.) externalism leads directly to absence of self-knowledge has not said enough to resisit the strategy. For instance, for all that Davidson says in his paper criticizing Burge's externalism for threatening self-knowledge,[35] Burge's response sketched above seems to answer him quite satisfactorily. It is not enough just to say that there is a *prima facie* problem that externalism poses for self-knowledge because Burge's proposal simply shows us a way of denying that there is a *prima facie* problem.

Burge, then, is right and more work needs to be done by those posing the problem for the orthodox externalist. The way in which Burge's externalist position on content threatens self-knowledge must be spelt out and set up properly. So let us try a less direct and more round-about strategy for setting up the difficulty for Burge and the other orthodox externalists. Though my round-about strategy will apply to all the externalisms under criticism, attention will be restricted to Burge's social externalism since it is his proposal that we are considering. Once again the extrapolations of all points made here to the other orthodox externalisms will be obvious.

In order to float the round-about strategy against Burge all one has to do is to reintroduce my dilemma. The last section led up to the conclusion that Burge and the other orthodox externalists are faced with one of two choices: either they must conclude with a view of content that has the possibility of attributing inconsistencies to agents or they must bifurcate content. The first choice is wholly implausible and unacceptable to Burge and everyone else, and the second choice is, as we said, unacceptable to Burge and anybody else who denies that orthodox externalism threatens unity. So someone must say something on behalf of Burge to get him out of the dilemma. Someone might say this.

Granted that Burge does not want to bifurcate content. Granted also that the failure of the three objections above show that we are faced with the possibility of having to attribute implausibly inconsistent attributions. But perhaps the three objections have been taking the wrong line on this dilemma. They should not be denying that inconsistent attributions are forced by their externalisms. They should be arguing instead that even if inconsistent attributions are forced, that need not amount to an implausible position on the nature of intentional content.

What makes blatantly inconsistent attributions, such as the ones we are considering in these puzzle cases, seem implausible is that they lead to a violation of the most elementary and undeniably plausible principle of charity. It is not disputed that such violations would render the position on content, which leads to these violations, implausible. But it is disputable that the principle is being violated just or simply by the attribution of blatant inconsistency. Blatantly inconsistent attributions only violate the principle under a certain condition, the condition of self-knowledge. If the condition is missing, then there is no violation. That is, only if an agent can be said to be knowingly contradicting himself is there a violation of the principle of charity. But if we say that the agent does not know that he is being inconsistent, whatever else is wrong with him, he is not being shown up to be a logical idiot. If he does not (fully) know what he believes, then his belief could be inconsistent without straining charity. If Pierre does not know that he believes that London is pretty and London is not pretty, if Bert does not know that he believes that he has arthritis in his thigh, then there is no strain on charity. Charity is only strained if the person comes out a logical idiot, but an admission to the failure of self-knowledge absolves him of that. So in a round-about way the orthodox externalist has arrived at a denial of self-knowledge: the denial is the only way for him to avoid the dilemma we have posed for him.

Notice that this way out of the dilemma is not the same as the following suggestion: an agent is *uttering* a contradiction when he says "I have arthritis in my thigh" or "Water is not $H_2O$," but that does not imply that he *believes* anything inconsistent, since the meanings of his utterances are one thing and the content of his beliefs another; i.e. one can admit that one has no (full) knowledge of the meaning of what one has uttered without admitting anything problematic about self-knowledge of one's beliefs. This may be something people are tempted to suggest, and no doubt have suggested (see Salmon 1986). But it amounts to a denial of one of the basic premises of this book, a premise expressed in its title and mentioned at the outset of chapter 1: the inseparability of meaning and content, or what Kripke calls "the principle of disquotation." The premise will not be defended here since I assume it to be widely held and, more to the point, it is held by Burge himself. Remember Burge is interested in an externalism (as he would call it, anti-individualism) about the *mental*, as his own title of his classic paper makes clear, and remember that his argument for it turns on the *linguistic* practices of the community. For him what the *term* "arthritis" means is vital in determining the *concept* of arthritis. The suggestion we are discussing by contrast wishes to treat the meaning of "arthritis" (the term) which is contained in his utterance as being one thing and the concept of arthritis that goes into the content of the agent's belief as another, thereby avoiding an inconsistency in the *belief* while admitting it in the meaning of the *utterance* (containing that term). Burge, therefore, cannot possibly accept this suggestion. In any case, quite apart from Burge there is a sense in which the suggestion is futile because it implicitly concedes the power of the second horn of the dilemma. It implicitly concedes bifurcation. It is true that it does so only implicitly and in different words. It severs meaning from content rather than bifurcating content. But it is always possible for Burge and other orthodox externalists who share my premise to say that what the suggestion is calling separable meaning is just what the bifurcationist are calling separable (wide) content. The suggestion is separating the same thing off from belief that the bifurcationists are separating off from narrow content. The substance of the distinctions is the same; what the suggestion must call "meaning" and "content," others will call "wide content" and "narrow content." The suggestion is a desperate terminological begging-off. It can only pretend that it has not been impaled on the second horn of the dilemma by changing the terminology.

Let us leave this futile suggestion and return instead to the original interpretation of the idea that charity is preserved if we abandon the assumption of the inconsistent agent's self-knowledge of his *beliefs*. This interpretation, as we saw, denies that Bert is being treated uncharitably. It denies it simply because the uncharitableness of inconsistent attributions depends on a condition of self-knowledge about the beliefs that are supposed to be inconsistent, and Bert can be said to fail to meet this condition. He simply does not (fully) know the contents of his own beliefs in this case.

All this has been said about inconsistency and self-knowledge in order to make clear that my strategy for raising the problem of self-knowledge for Burge and the other orthodox externalists is not to simply and directly pose the *prima facie* problem we posed at the beginning of this section. As we saw, Burge's counter-strategy shows that this simple and direct ploy is too simple and direct. My more round-about strategy raises the problem of self-knowledge by first showing that Burge's externalism is stuck with a dilemma and then arguing that the only way out of the dilemma (given the failure of the three earlier objections) is to admit to lack of self-knowledge on the part of the agent in question.

We can therefore conclude: my round-about way of posing the problem for Burge makes his proposal about how externalism can accommodate self-knowledge unsatisfyingly general. His proposal does not at all address the question of self-knowledge as it arises out of a specific dilemma we have posed for his specific externalism. It addresses a much more general question about self-knowledge. We have replaced this general question (how can one reconcile self-knowledge with externalism?) with another question for him (how can one reconcile self-knowledge with externalism when externalism – in the sense you mean it – can only be made plausible, can only avoid a crippling dilemma, if you abandon self-knowledge?). And once one poses this question, it looks as if he must admit to a problem about self-knowledge or else, for one reason or the other specified in the two horns of the dilemma, be convicted of holding an implausible position about content. Or, at any rate, he must admit that his own proposal for solving the problem and reconciling self-knowledge with externalism is now quite inadequate.

Indeed, since we know that Burge does not want to deny that we by and large have knowledge of our own thoughts – nobody should, and indeed, as far as I know nobody does – we can now pose the whole matter to Burge in the form of a *trilemma*. Burge must allow that on his view of content agents are in many cases going to be uncharitably accused of logical idiocy (something no view of content should allow) or he must bifurcate content to deal with those cases (which he, sensibly, does not wish to) *or* he must admit that in those cases agents lack self-knowledge of their own contents (which nobody should admit, even if they admit it for other more Freudian sorts of cases).

This move from confronting the orthodox externalist with a dilemma to confronting him with a trilemma is forced by the relevance of self-knowledge to the question of content. Self-knowledge is essential to understanding all the examples we are considering including the examples in Kripke's puzzle. (As stated earlier, if we allowed that Pierre did not have self-knowledge the inconsistencies we were forced to attribute to him on an unbifurcated orthodox view of content would not amount to being implausibly uncharitable.) Once we comprehend the relevance of self-knowledge to this entire question, we can see that *de dicto* attributions of content to an agent like Bert do permit of substitution of terms in the specification of contents so long as there is self-knowledge. It is only where we would withold self-knowledge that we would not allow substitutions. So if Burge avoids the third horn and insists that his social externalism determines contents which agents have self-knowledge of, then he must allow the substitution of "is a disease of the joints only" for "arthritis" in "Bert believes that he has arthritis in his thigh." That is what social externalism says his concept of arthritis is. And the trilemma consists precisely in the fact that such a substitution forced by a desire to avoid the third horn, in turn, either forces uncharitable attributions or it forces bifurcation.

He could, of course, say that social externalism allows that Bert has only partial knowledge of his own concept of arthritis and, in allowing that, it allows that he partly knows and partly does not know his thought when he believes that he has arthritis in his thigh. The part of the concept that Bert does not know is the part that is determined by the expert's knowledge. But to say this is to be impaled on the second horn, i.e. it is to admit that social externalism forces a bifurcation, it is to admit that when we attribute to him the belief that he has arthritis in his thigh we are really attributing two contents to him, only one of which is known to him and which explains his behavior. The other is the one not known to him because it carries that part of the content which is socially determined. There just is no way to avoid the trilemma.

The remaining question about self-knowledge is: why is my externalism any better off than the orthodox externalisms on the subject? Why does my externalism not entail a similar threat to self-knowledge? The rest of this section will be devoted to giving a brief answer to this and to drawing out some implications of the answer.

So long as one raised the issue of self-knowledge and externalism as the *prima facie* problem posed at the beginning of the section, it is not at all obvious how any advantage can be claimed for my externalism on the issue. But once one appreciates the round-about way of raising the problem, the answer to this question is really straightforward and obvious.

Threatening self-knowledge is the only way which will allow the orthodox externalisms to refrain from attributing certain internal inconsistencies to agents, without bifurcating content. But my externalism, unlike these others, has no problems with inconsistent attributions in the first place. Neither dilemma nor therefore trilemma ever exits for my view. My constraint on externalism sees to it that external items which determine concepts do not determine concepts that are at such odds with his other beliefs that he will fall into the situation of uttering or thinking inconsistent thoughts just on the basis of the concepts attributed to him. Agents, on my view, may think thoughts that we specify as "Water is not $H_2O$" or "I have arthritis in my thigh" but the concept of water or arthritis in these cases will not be determined by the experts' beliefs or by scientific essence etc. The sorts of inconsistency, which follow upon these other externalist views of concepts, therefore, are simply not entailed if one applies my constraint. If the agent lacks certain chemical or medical beliefs he will not be attributed the same concept as the members of his society and its experts. Thus if he goes on to say things like "I have arthritis in my thigh" etc., this will not be inconsistent. My constraint has the effect of bringing in the external determining item under descriptions, or more properly under beliefs, of the agent. Let me show the relevance of this in both the case of social and non-social external elements.

We have already seen in countering the second objection to the trilemma that my constraint suggests that the social external items should enter content routed through the agent's own beliefs (and specified by the metalinguistic specifications), beliefs such as "water is whatever my social fellows, in particular the experts, call 'water.'" We have seen that this removes the threat of inconsistent attributions and the eventual threat to self-knowledge. The social enters into the concept without losing respect for the fact that the relevant individual agent himself knows very little about the chemical composition of various substances.

Where the external items are not taken to be social, the beliefs my constraint insists on will not be metalinguistically specified, they will just be ordinary beliefs of the kind "water is the substance that comes out of the tap" etc. The point is that for chemically ignorant agents the concept of water will not be determined by an external substance under any chemical descriptions or beliefs. So if such an agent were to brashly think that water is not $H_2O$, he would not be thinking something inconsistent.[36] If he is not thinking something inconsistent, then the first horn in the round-about strategy which leads eventually, in the third horn, to a threat to self-knowledge, is unavailable. Thus neither social nor non-social external elements raise any threat to self-knowledge if one adopts my constrained externalism. It is only if one adopts one of the orthodox externalisms that there is a threat.

This way of avoiding the threat to self-knowledge within externalism is, of course, very different from Burge's way, sketched at the beginning of this section. It is different because it addresses a problem that arises for the misguided externalisms (including Burge's own) in a way that his solution does not. He gets away with the impression that he has avoided the threat because, as we saw, he raises the threat in a way that does not bring out why his own specific externalist position really gives rise to the threat.[37] Once one sees via the round-about strategy why his externalism gives rise to the threat in a very specific way, only then does one see clearly why my constraint on externalism alone will provide for the compatibility of externalism with self-knowledge. His more general solution avoids the hard problem for his own externalist position, a problem hidden from view because he raises a much less hard (much more general) problem for externalism by the more direct route and provides his solution to it.


## MORE OBJECTIONS TO THE CHARGE OF DISUNITY

In this section some features of my unified view of content will be elaborated by discussing a few more objections, the point of which will still be to reject the charge of disunity and to show that there is no need for my unified notion of content. These objections are not addressed in particular to the dilemma I posed for the orthodox externalists but are of a more general kind.


### *Objection A*

*Agents' conceptions or "senses" are just as much subject to some of the puzzles that afflict reference, so there is no special or unique problem issuing from orthodox externalism's appeal to reference.*


Though, unlike Loar and others, I have insisted that agents' conceptions be externalistically constituted and insisted also that there is no other notion of content than that, I have nevertheless followed Loar and many others in demanding that one can only give a resolution to Kripke's and variant puzzles by introducing the idea of agents' conceptions.

Against this resolution of the puzzles by the introdction of agents' conceptions, one often hears the following complaint. It is just as possible that an agent not know that one way in which he conceives of something (a city, a heavenly body) is the same as another way that he conceives of it. This parallels the possibility of him not knowing that the thing a concept or term of his refers to is not the same as what some other concept refers to. If so, there is no advance in positing agents' conceptions. In short, parallel puzzles can be generated for content even if we individuate concepts in terms of agents' conceptions rather than reference.

In claiming that one can fail to know of the identity of one's conceptions or contents, this complaint presupposes that there is a philosophical way of making self-knowledge come apart from content, something we have been resisting in the last section. We have been assuming that agents (except in the cases explainable psychologically as self-deception and other Freudian kinds of case) by and large know what their contents are. But this is precisely the assumption that this complaint is questioning.

But the complaint is able to question this assumption only because it makes a highly questionable philosophical assumption of its own. It assumes that senses or agents' conceptions are *objects* of an agent's thinking and that an agent can therefore fail to know of the identity of some of them. This is to allow for failure of self-knowledge of contents, not due to factors like self-deception but rather because of an assumption that one's contents are the objects or targets of thought, about which we can fail to know identities in the way that we may fail to know the identity of Hesperus and Phosphorus, London and *Londres*. Contents are *objects* of thoughts. Hence, and only hence, the possibility of these parallel puzzles. In rejecting this complaint, therefore, we can deny its assumption that there are objects of thought.

As Davidson has argued (1987, and in more detail in 1991), this assumption is wholly unmotivated and unnecessary for anything we want from content. There is absolutely nothing gained in our understanding of the nature of content to see contents as objects of thought. Philosophers have thought that there must be objects of thoughts for various reasons. Some, in earlier times, thought that they are necessary to account for the fact that we can make mistakes about the world. Only if we have intermediary epistemological objects of thought between us and the world could we make mistakes about what is in the world. Such Cartesian epistemological intermediaries are wholly unnecessary, as Davidson and others have argued. Others more recently have posited such objects (this time sentential objects) because it seemed to follow from the fact that thoughts have specifiable contents at all. Davidson is equally persuasive that this is not necessary. No doubt we need sentences of ours to keep track of and report an agent's thoughts but it simply does not follow from this that an agent's thoughts have sentential objects.

But, quite apart from the fact that the thesis that there are objects of thoughts is totally unnecessary for anything, the fact is that it seems also to be positively implausible because of the very fact that the objection we are considering exploits. It seems to allow for the possibility of lack of self-knowlege in a way that we should want to rule out. Self-knowledge of many contents may indeed be missing in agents. But that is because of specific psychological reasons, the most interesting of which were studied by Freud. But we should not want to threaten self-knowledge on abstract philosophical grounds, such as that there are objects of thoughts which we may fail to grasp, or identities between such objects which we may fail to grasp. Objects of thought are, therefore, not merely unnecessary, they are a positive menace because they overturn a very strong intuition we have, the intuition that we have self-knowledge of our contents except when there are good psychological obstacles to having it.

In a different but not wholly dissimilar objection, it has been said – and Kripke (1979) himself says it – that agents' conceptions or senses do not help resolve the puzzles because in the specifications of the conceptions we have to use terms, which themselves may be subject to the puzzle phenomena. Thus if it is part of Pierre's conception of London that London is in England, "England" in the specification of his conception may be subject to the problem of Pierre not knowing that it is identical with Angleterre. And so on for all specifications of all conceptions. To this there can be no response but to say that these too must be dealt with in the same way as we dealt with the initial puzzle, i.e. by bringing in Pierre's different conceptions of that country. It cannot be an argument against the introduction of conceptions that conceptions will have to be introduced whenever it is necessary. Of course, this means that there is a certain messiness to the idea of concepts and contents, but once again if the explanatory function of contents requires that things be messy, it is wrong to turn a blind eye to this fact and impose a distorting neatness upon the idea.

## Objection B

*We need "causal roles" to deal with the puzzle but we don't need "conceptual roles" or conceptions of things, so we don't need another notion of content to deal with the puzzles.*

In a recent unpublished manuscript Jerry Fodor has acknowledged that his causal-informational externalism (as well as the orthodox positions we have been discussing) gives rise to problems such as Kripke's puzzle and its variant, as well as Fregean puzzles about identity. I have been saying that such an acknowledgement is *eo ipso* an acknowledgement that these externalist views of content fail to capture an agent's conceptions of things. It is that failure which accounts for why these puzzles arise. And I have also said that it is not surprising, therefore, that many orthodox externalists have had to posit a second notion of content to capture conceptions of things.

Fodor denies this. He denies that one needs anything like *content* to get around the puzzles, *a fortiori*, one does not need a second notion of content.[38] Is he then rejecting the claim that the idea of an agent's conception of things is tantamount to a notion of content? Or is he rather rejecting that the resolution of these puzzles (which he has acknowledged as arising) requires positing agent's conceptions? It is the latter that he seems to be rejecting.

How could he, given all that we have been saying so far? His view seems to be this. The puzzles do arise for orthodox externalist content but that does not mean that we need to posit anything like agent's conceptions to explain the puzzles away. They can be explained away by something less than or other than an agent's conceptions. All that is needed to explain the puzzles away is a difference in causal dispositions or causal roles, not an agent's conceptions of things. Fodor does not specially want to deny that bringing in agent's conceptions will also solve the puzzles. He merely wants to say that it is not necessary to bring them in to solve them. So he concludes: If causal roles alone are enough to solve the puzzles, if it is not necessary to introduce agents' conceptions to solve them, then there is no need to introduce a second notion of content. Only something like *conceptions of the world* warrant our saying that *content* is involved. Pure causal dispositions do not warrant saying that. And if he is denying that a second notion of content is necessary to deal with the Pierre example, he is, in effect, denying my claim that the example can be used to pose a threat to the unity of content.

Let me go over this again with reference to Pierre.[39] Recall that to capture Pierre's psychology (that is, to account for his failure to make the theoretical and practical inferences having to do with Oscar Wilde and London etc.) we had said that one must find a way of attributing two London-beliefs to him. Even when "believes that London is pretty" and "*croit que Londres est jolie*" were attributed to him, we had to find a way of saying that these were different beliefs so long as we were interested in his psychology. Externalism, in one or other of the orthodox versions, since it fails to find a way of saying that, whatever else it succeeds in doing, fails to capture his psychology. Fodor acknowledges all this. He grants that Pierre must be attributed two beliefs. What he denies is that he has to be attributed two belief *contents*. He distinguishes between beliefs and belief contents, saying that though sameness and difference in content is a necessary condition for sameness and difference in beliefs, it is not a sufficient condition. Sameness and difference in another (necessary) condition is required before we get the sufficient conditions. And that is sameness and difference in causal or functional role. He says: "Two belief tokens are tokens of the same type iff they are identical in their content and relevantly similar in their causal dispositions," adding in parenthesis "I take it that talk about the functional roles of attitude types is cashed by talking about the causal dispositions of their tokens" (p. 4). The idea is that causal role ought not to be conflated with anything like agents' conceptions, i.e. with *conceptual* role[40] Thus it does not amount to content.

The distinction between pure causal role and conceptual role is easy enough to accept in general. Intentional states have contents which are related inferentially to one another and to actions as well as perceptions (intentionally characterized). But they also stand in causal relations with one another and with motor output as well as perceptual stimuli or input (non-intentionally and non-relationally characterized). That is, intentional states form part of a system that is at once both causal and mechanistic as well as conceptual and contentful.

But it is highly questionable whether the way in which the distinction between causal and conceptual role is being invoked by Fodor, in this particular context, can be justified. Causal roles are being invoked by him to account (just by themselves) for the failure of some of Pierre's beliefs about London to interact with his other beliefs about London. And this means that the causal role of beliefs in mental processing is sensitive to how its objects (London, water) are specified.[41] It is hard to see how such a notion of causal role, which presupposes sensitivity to something like modes of presentation in order to account for Pierre's failures of reasoning, can be individuated without bringing in his conceptions of the world, without bringing in what the world is like for him. In short, such a powerful notion of causal role *is* content whether we like it or not, whether we *call* it that or not.[42]

### Objection C

*Why not yoke together conceptual and inferential role with orthodox externalism?*

It might seem that there is no need to worry about creating a new-fangled externalism in order to capture the inferential role and conceptions of agents in a unified notion of content: why not simply attain unity by taking inferential role and conceptions to reach out and range over the very external things that constitute concepts and contents for the orthodox externalist? Thus water on earth and water on twin-earth would affect twin-agents in ways that would give rise to different conceptual and inferential roles for them, but they would still be inferential and conceptual roles. Why not just bring together the externalism of the orthodoxy and the explanatory aspects of content by brute force in what has been called "long-armed" conceptual roles? Such a view of content has been proposed by Gilbert Harman (1982).

As Ned Block (1987) demonstrates, this view is an acceptance, by the back door, of a bifurcated notion of content. Block points out that this would require that the conceptual and inferential role of my word "Moses", say, will have to "extend through my sensory inputs back thousands of years into the past." He

adds "The point also holds for kind-terms e.g., 'manna' rather than 'Moses'."
Block then points out that, on scrutiny, it is not clear in what sense the appeal to
the outlying things have any part to play in the inferential relations which hold
between the thought of the agent. If they do not, it looks as though, if they have
anything to do with content, it can only be wide content. This leaves it possible
to say that there is a common internal part which is what people have all along
called narrow content. The latter alone on scrutiny, he adds, plays an inferential
role. Since I wholly agree with Block's analysis of this view, there is nothing to
add or subtract from it, except to say, that if there needs to be proof that he is
right, all one has to do is to pose a challenge to Harman: how is she going to deal
with Kripke's puzzle or with the dilemma we have raised for the orthodox
externalisms (whose externalism he has, in part adopted) without falling prey to
Block's objection that there really are two notions of content hidden in his view?

We can, of course, reject Block's own account of content in that paper because
it bifurcates content and because it thinks that conceptual roles are to be
internalistically characterized. Hence in a sense, and up to a point, Harman and
I share a view here: we both agree that the conceptual roles which are used to
explain actions need not be internalistically characterized. What we disagree
about is the requisite externalism. What Block and I share is the idea that
conceptual roles cannot be made by brute fiat to embrace orthodox externalism
because that provides us with no way of dealing with the issues which give rise
to bifurcation. There is no way to deal with those issues by simply *saying* that
one should unite the explanatory aspects of content with the old externalisms.
To achieve genuine unity of content one has to forge a new externalism.

### Objection D

*Agents' conceptions can be captured by externalism without appeal to constraint
(C).*

This is an objection that Fodor does not himself make but someone may make
on behalf of his externalist account against the charge of disunity. Recall that the
charge was made against him because his account stressed the naturalistic notion
of information based on causal covariances between properties in the world and
tokens of mental representations. There was no room in this causal, naturalistic
underpinning of the external determination of concepts and contents for the
mediating beliefs of the agent. These were deliberately shunned by him because
they would introduce a holistic, anti-foundationalist element which he opposes.
His account, as we saw, is nothing if it is not denotational and foundationalist.
But our diagonisis of disunity showed that without bringing in the beliefs of the
agent (something my own externalist account with its constraint allows and

insists on) there is no hope of an account capturing the agents' conceptions which alone will explain actions. Without them we would not get the right descriptions of the external causes with which the mental tokens are supposed to covary. It would not, therefore, capture the right fineness or coarseness of grain in the contents, as the examples we discussed demanded.

It might, however, seem that a careful enough scrutiny of these causal covariances may deliver up the right grain, in which case we would not need my constraint and the agent's beliefs, in order to get the right descriptions of the external items that the mental tokens covary with. It might seem that all we need is a fine (or coarse) enough discrimination of the *properties in the environment* of the agent which are causally covarying with the token mental representations–the property of being merely a pedal but not a clutch in the case of some ignorant agents but not in the case of knowledgeable others.

But it is hard to see how this discrimination can be achieved unless one does impose my constraint. Simply staring at the external world repeatedly whenever the mental tokens are "tokened" is not going to help unless we do appeal to the agent's other beliefs. The world does not discriminately wear its properties on its sleeve in a way that allows my constraint to be by-passed. How do we investigate the difference between these properties that are causally covarying with the tokenings except by first looking to the other beliefs the agent in question has been or not been attributed, beliefs about the inner workings of an automobile? Of course, it is possible to say that all those other beliefs are also to be thought of as consisting of concepts determined in terms of the causal covariance story. That is true, but the fact remains that the fixing of any one concept rather than another (pedal rather than clutch, say) requires looking to the other beliefs and not just looking at the causal covariances, and that just is to concede the anti-foundationalist holism of my constraint that Fodor despises. It is no serious defence of Fodor to say that the properties out there are providing for the right grain and the right description, if an agent's concepts and beliefs are really always needed to establish the different properties in question. One can always take our concepts and the beliefs and inferences that make them the concepts they are and project it all on the world, calling these external properties. But it should be clear that this notion of property is an idle metaphysical wheel. The real work in getting the right grain has been done by the beliefs and inferences, as my constraint suggests.

In these last three sections I have rejected various objections philosophers have given against my claim that orthodox externalism (unlike my externalism) destroys the unity of content because its notion of wide content cannot be used to explain behavior. If I am right, there is a fundamental question which looms for contemporary philosophy of mind and language: why, if it does not explain action, should we believe in "wide" content at all? Why should anybody have ever been an orthodox externalist? In the next chapter I take this question up by arguing against the claim that there are things that we want content to do which only "wide" content (but not unified content) can do.

In short, this chapter demonstrated that my notion of content is necessary by showing that wide content is not sufficient for certain tasks we expect from contents. The next chapter will show that the wide content of the orthodox externalists is not necessary for anything we demand of content and, therefore, that my unified notion is sufficient for all that we demand from content.

# 3

# Society and Norm

Since we have now seen that the orthodox externalist idea of wide content puts the unity of content in jeopardy, there needs to be very powerful reasons to retain a notion of wide content at all in the study of intentionality. This chapter will therefore look at various arguments philosophers have or might have for thinking that something deep and important is being left out of the unified notion of content that has been sketched in the first two chapters. Are there any worthy motivations for positing content that only wide content – but not unified content – can fulfill?

The widespread commitment among philosophers today to orthodox externalism and its notion of wide content is often a result of an appeal to *intuitions* that we are supposed to have in thought-experiments (thought-experiments such as the ones about the twin-earths or about Bert's actual and counterfactual social surroundings). This procedure has often made these philosophers impervious to the need to further argue for and motivate the commitment. But intuitions often have their source in hidden presuppositions in the background. Some of the lines of motivation for wide content which will be discussed in this chapter can be seen as the *hidden* philosophical sources which help jog the intuitions in favour of wide content in these thought-experiments. Hence a good deal, though by no means all, of what follows will take the form of reconstruction on the basis of remarks not always consciously and systematically constructed and presented in the literature to motivate the commitment to wide content. This is inevitable with any commitment which is so widely taken for granted in philosophy.

There are roughly two large and inter-related motivating lines of argument which will be considered, one in each of the next two sections. The first argues that something essentially social is left out of my externalism and the notion of content it delivers; the second that an essential normativity of mind and language is missing from my account. Though these can be discussed as self-standing arguments for wide content, there are points when one is not complete without the other, as we shall see. So, to a large extent, their separation is artificial. Their separation is nevertheless justified within my dialectic because these two lines of argument do not both support all of the versions of orthodox externalism. The first line of argument lends its support exclusively to the social version of orthodox externalism, whereas the second could, in principle, be used to support all versions.

## THE RELEVANCE OF SOCIETY TO MEANING AND BELIEF

It is widely thought that language, and therefore thought itself, is a social phenomenon. To some extent, and in more than one sense, this is obviously true. This section will explore the senses and the extent to which it is true. I believe that it is much less true than is commonly supposed, and the senses in which it is true ought to be of much less significance or interest to philosophers than post-Hegelian philosophers have taken them to be. The senses and the extent to which the social is relevant to meaning is of no more and no other interest to philosophy than it is to commonsense sociology.

Hence, though my rejection of social externalism in the study of content and meaning will be seen, *prima facie*, as a rejection of some essentially social aspect of content and meaning,[1] I will argue that my account has captured what needs to be captured about this aspect and the rest is not needed. The sense in which it is not needed is precisely the sense in which philosophers like Burge and more recently even Kripke (1982, on behalf of the mature Wittgenstein) have demanded it.[2] Their views on this subject offer a more or less precise statement of an ideological tradition regarding the social nature of the mental which began, with somewhat less precision, most explicitly with Hegel and which is widely taken for granted in current thinking about language and mind in both Anglo-American and European philosophy.[3] Much of this section will be spent examining the arguments that could be made on behalf of this philosophical demand of the relevance of the social. Though my target will be the wider tradition, I will direct most of my explicit remarks against Burge, Kripke and Wittgenstein.[4]

Let me briefly sketch the "individualistic" position implied by my unified notion of content, which stands in opposition to this tradition.

### *What is my Individualism?*

There are some confusing uses of the term "individualism" , which should be warned against. Since "internalism" is a term that provides a natural contrast to "externalism" , it would seem natural that "individualism" is best characterized as a contrast to "*social* externalism." Burge himself, however, has tended to define individualism in contrast with *all* externalism: as a view of content which denies that content is determined by anything which is not *internal* to *individual* agents.[5] So I must warn against a confusion. In chapter 1, I have embraced externalism. Yet I am opposing Burge and social externalism. So I am making a claim for what my be called "*individualistic externalism*." I, therefore, cannot follow Burge's broader characterization of individualism here. The individualism I will be defending is only a part of the "individualism" Burge is attacking.

Now, though the crucial point about my own view is that it is an *individualistic* externalism, it is very important to remember also that the externalist part of my individualistic externalism is not one of the non-social orthodox externalisms but rather the externalism sketched in chapter 1. So though the phrase "individualistic externalism" distinguishes me from Burge, it does not by itself distinguish my externalism from the non-social orthodox externalisms we discussed in chapter 2.[6] There is no evidence in Kripke's work on reference prior to his book on Wittgenstein that suggests his view has anything much to do with social externalism. There is more of a suggestion of it in Putnam who tended to bring in the social in his use of the thesis of the linguistic division of labor. But I have argued that thesis can be seen in individualistic terms, so Putnam's externalism in the end must also be read as largely causal-essentialist rather than social. And Fodor's information-theoretic denotational account does not particularly stress the social at all. All these positions *can* be thought of as individualistic externalisms.

Of course, the phrase "individualistic unified externalism" would distinguish me from these non-social orthodox externalists since, if I am right, despite their indifference to the social in Burge's sense, they all nevertheless also force a bifurcation of content. From now on, however, I will not constantly use this long-winded phrase to describe the position I am defending. Since I have made it abundantly clear that mine is an externalist position, and since my concern in this section is only to defend it against Burge's social externalism and not the other orthodox externalisms, I will drop both "externalism" and "unified." I will talk simply of my "individualism" and hope that these warnings will have helped the reader to keep in mind the difference between my view and the other positions that have and might be called "individualism" and "externalism."

One way of bringing out the form of my commitment to individualism is by seeing how the distinction between my externalism and social externalism is founded on another distinction. Among my own motivations for being an externalist (see chapter 1 and chapter 5), is the claim that externalism alone provides a satisfactory basis for the public nature of meaning and content. So I am thoroughly committed to publicness. It follows, then, that I am obliged to distinguish between the *public* nature of content and the *social* nature of content since I want the former but not the latter.[7] Hence my individualistic externalism is individualistic because it denies the latter, it is externalist because externalism makes possible the former.

Individualism, for me, contrasts with a social externalist view of language and mind. To begin with, we need some basic terms. One needs to distinguish the different objects or phenomena to be philosophically studied from the different philosophical positions about those phenomena or objects of study. Let us use the terms "idiolect" and "sociolect" to mark the different objects of study, And "individualism" and "social externalism" to mark the different philosophical positions in the study of them.

The notion of the idiolect is the notion of language or meaning which we study when we study the individual. It is the idiolect which is most immediately connected with intentionality as our brief discussion of the close relation between meaning and content in chapter 1 made clear. It is individuals who have thoughts and it is their language which expresses them. An individual's intentional contents are, thus, just as much the object of study as his language is, when we study idiolects. Now, when studying idiolects philosophically, we may arrive at either an individualistic conception of them or a social externalist conception of them. Social externalism, as we found it in Burge (and, as we shall find it in Kripke's Wittgenstein), is a social externalist conception of idiolects. When I rejected social externalism, I was promoting an individualistic conception of idiolects. (Those who find the very idea of a non-individualistic conception of idiolects disturbing should be patient enough to read on until their worry is addressed below.)

Idiolects as an object of study may be contrasted with a quite different object of study, the language of the community in which individuals live and speak. These communities and their languages may be more and less local. English, as it might be, or Oxford English, Urdu or Hyderabadi Urdu, French or Parisian French. These objects of study we can call sociolects. And about these, too, one's study may arrive at different philosophical positions. One may come to think of them individualistically or not. That is, one could think of them as nothing but an overlap of individualistically conceived idiolects or one could think of them as something over and above that, some form of linguistic idealization. Let us look closer at the dispute between individualistic and social externalist positions on idiolects first, and sociolects second.

In the discussion of Burge in chapter 2 we, like Burge himself, concentrated on the idiolect as the basis object of philosophical study but, unlike him, insisted on an individualistic position about it rather than a social externalist position. What is this individualistic position on idiolects? It is most conveniently characterized by attending to his own way of setting things up in his example about Bert and arthritis. The first thing to notice in the example, as he sets it up, is that it requires there to be some (initial) misalignment between what Bert means and what the community means by "arthritis." The word "initial" was added deliberately since it is clear that the social externalist will not want to rest with this description of things. He will eventually deny that Bert means anything by "arthritis" other than what the community and its experts mean by it. But whatever description we rest with, even Burge must allow that something describable initially as Bert's "meaning" is discoverable in order to make the observation that Bert is in some sense different from his community. Otherwise we cannot even set up his example, which requires that Bert is misaligned with his community in some way; that is to say, Burge's own example could not be given, unless we could notice that there was some fact about how he uses words and thinks about a disease which was different from theirs.

If that is so, then the individualistic suggestion is: why not just stop there and say that what is initially revealed in Bert's sayings and doings, and described prior to the socially constitutive redescriptions (of the sayings and doings, and the contents they reveal)is of *primary* significance in the philosophical study of the propositional attitudes and in the study of the notion of meaning that is relevant to the attitudes? Thus, from this point of view, the eventual social externalist redescriptions, by which Bert ends up having the same concept as the community and its experts, is of no interest in the study of Bert's idiolect. While the subject is intentionality (the "mental" in the title of Burge's paper under discussion), one can begin with and rest with these initial individualistic descriptions.

Before looking at Bert's fellows and making the social externalist redescriptions, Bert will be attributed the concept of a disease which afflicts both joints and ligaments for that is what his sayings and doings must be described as revealing at this stage. If that is what we rest with, then that just is his concept. Not surprisingly this concept will find a place in the contents which will explain his behavior (at least until he is corrected by the doctor), and they will do so without the problems of being either inconsistent or unavailable to Bert himself, and without, therefore, making necessary the coining of another notion of content which explains his behavior without these problems. In short, attributing these sorts of concepts will not involve us in the trilemma of chapter 2.

Notice that though this alternative individualist position on idiolects is introduced by looking to Burge's example of Bert and his misalignment from the community, the point does not in any way turn on the fact of such misalignment. Misalignment requires that we first attribute something to an agent and then notice a misalignment with the community. The situation is no different if we do not notice any misalignment. The point is that we can think of what we *initially* attribute as meaning and belief.

I am not here trying to argue for this individualistic alternative to social externalism nor to show that the redescriptions that the latter demands are unjustified. I have done whatever I could towards these ends in chapter 2 by showing the undesirable trilemma-inducing consequence of taking the social externalist view. Here I am merely trying to define a coherent individualist contrast to social externalism. And my strategy for doing so has been to appeal to the observation of individuals that even a social externalist must begin with (no position can avoid observing individuals to begin with since everyone must begin with the observation of linguistic and other behavior) and then claim that what one attributes at this beginning stage is all that one needs in the study of intentionality. At this beginning stage one notices that Bert uses a certain noise in the presence of afflictions in joints *and* ligaments, and the misalignment is noticed when one notices that others in his community use it more restrictedly. The individualist rests with the conclusion that his meaning or concept of arthritis is different from the community. Even if one did *not* notice any misalignment between individual and community (as say, in the case of counterfactual Bert) one would, on the basis of observation of individual behavior, rest with these initial attributions. In neither the cases of misalignment nor of alignment is there any constitutive relevance of the community and its experts to the attribution of meaning and concepts to individuals.[8]

The social externalist will often want to go on and redescribe the individual's meanings as something else. He will see these initial discoveries as merely initial hypotheses which are confirmed but also (as with Bert) often overturned, as more and more individuals are observed. He may grant that when we say that Bert is misaligned with his social fellows, we are in an *initial* way also saying that for him "arthritis " is not used to talk of a disease of the joints only. But he will overturn this initial concession as mere procedural conjecture or early hypothesis-formation in a method of inquiry which, when it eventually delivers a full theory, will have no place for this initial description of Bert's concept. Once the full theory is available there will be place only for the non-contentful noise ("arthritis") on Bert's lips and the social concept that it is assigned: there is no individualistically conceived concept associated with that noise. The temptation to say that there is, he will say, is to be seen at best as a temptation formed by a temporary phase in the procedure by which the full theory is arrived at.

That is certainly a position one may take (if one is prepared to live with chapter 2's trilemma.) But my point for now is that the individualist has an equal right to deny that it be seen as a merely temporary phase, and insist instead that one rests with attributing an idiosyncratic concept to Bert's idiolect. That, in a word, is the dispute between the two positions on idiolects.

What, then, of the dispute between the individualist position and the social externalist position on sociolects? No more needs to be said in characterizing the former than already has: an individualist conception of the sociolect could see the language of a community as merely an overlap of such individualistically conceived idiolects.

If one thought of idiolects anti-individualistically as the social externalist does, then there is no sense to thinking of the sociolects as overlapping idiolects. This might seem obvious if one is clear about the distinctions I am making. But I am stating the obvious because it is sometimes hidden from view. In a recent paper, supporting Burge's anti-individualistic conception of the idiolect, James Higginbotham (1989, p. 155) falls into this odd combination of positions I am warning against. He argues that sociolects are derivative of idiolects in the sense that they can be constructed from overlapping idiolects, at the same time as he argues for an anti-individualist conception of idiolects. There does not appear to be a sensible point behind this combination of views. The anti-individualism about idiolects should make the task of constructing sociolects out of overlapping idiolects unnecessary in a way that an individualism about idiolects does not.

A question, then, arises about what story to tell for how sociolects are to be constructed, if one takes a social externalist view of idiolects. The story cannot avoid the appeal to the behavior and languages of individuals in order to do so. Only a position which implausibly reifies the social would deny that. But what facts about individuals may a social externalist look to in the construction of sociolects, if they are not the facts that an "overlapping" story looks to? What other facts are there? What is it to look at individual behavior without looking to idiolects and the overlap between them?

It could be a story in which the theorist constructing the theory of the sociolect would look at individual behavior with special attention to how people correct one another's speech, and how individual informants refer the theorist to experts they rely on, who in turn would do the same for things which they thought they had only a partial knowledge of, and so on, until the theory for the sociolect was secured. Such a story, then, would not be a story of the derivation from overlap of idiolects, but a construction upon the interdependencies among individuals.

There is a subtle point worth being careful about here. I am not suggesting that telling this last ("interdependencies") story about the construction of sociolects forces an anti-individualist conception of the idiolect. In fact, it does not do that. Its appeal to individuals relying on one another, as I have already established in my discussion of the division of linguistic labor, can be accommodated within individualism. Its appeal to correcting one another is also describable in individualist terms if one describes the correction as ones in which the corrected agents come to have new and different concepts from the hitherto idiosyncratic ones. So, my suggestion is really the other way round. All the story does is to suggest how sociolects may be thought of as constructed out of an observation of individuals even when one adopts an anti-individualistic conception of idiolects. It does not imply that one *must* adopt such a conception.

Note, on the other hand, that it does not force any concession to an individualistic conception of idiolects either. Just because the story appeals to individual informants and their behavior does not imply that one cannot return and give an anti-individualist account of their idiolects. To give such an account all one has to do is to take the sociolects, so constructed, as having a fundamentally constitutive role in the way we think of the concepts and meanings of the individuals; even ignorant individuals like Bert. In short, the anti-individualist first constructs sociolects on the basis of observation of individual behavior along the lines of the "interdependencies" story just mentioned; and then uses these sociolects to constitute the idiolects of those individuals in the way favored by Burge.[9]

But now someone may wonder whether there is any point left to the very idea of an idiolect, if an idiolect is socially constituted in this way. Someone may ask questions like: if an idiolect is socially constituted, what is idiolectical about it? Why call it an "idiolect?" Is not the point of an idiolect that it be thought of individualistically? Why not just say that there is a sociolect – constructed along the lines just mentioned – and individuals in a community speak it? This list of questions has a point but it also misses a point or two.

First of all, it is not the case that social externalists about idiolects, like Burge, want to allow for *no* idiosyncratic concepts. He often explicitly denies that he wants to do this.[10] And if individuals have some idiosyncratic concepts, then it would be wrong to say that, when the terms expressing those concepts are on their lips, they are speaking the sociolect.

It is true that if there were absolutely no idiosyncratic concepts, then there would be some excess and redundant terminology in the way I have presented things. But that – and this the second point these questions miss – is harmless. It is not as if the term idiolect (introduced innocuously, as I have introduced it) does any question-begging harm in favor of individualism. The distinction between idiolects and sociolects was only introduced to talk of certain objects of study and my idea was merely to have a neutral description or word for things about which the individualist and anti-individualist could quarrel. At no stage of the discussion have I begged any questions in favor of individualism by using the term "idiolect;" the anti-individualist should have no reason to be disturbed by my use of "idiolect" since I have gone out of my way to sketch a coherent position on his behalf, despite my use of the term. Similarly, the individualist should have no quarrel with my use of the term "sociolect" (once again innocuously defined as merely an object of study) since even he should at least allow the dispute with his opponent to be stateable; and one way of stating it is to say that his view of a sociolect is that they are overlapping individualistically conceived idiolects, while his opponent constructs them by the interdependencies story suggested above.

Noam Chomsky has sometimes written in favor of a more radical individualist position than mine. He writes as if the very idea of a sociolect as an object of study is incoherent (Chomsky 1986). If he were right, it would give rise to a much more radical critique of Burge's view than anything I have hinted at so far. Burge takes sociolects, that is, social or communal linguistic practices and conventions as constituting many items in agents' idiolects. So far I have allowed this as a coherent way of doing things. I have only said what its destructive implications are for the unity assumption and I am about to argue against the motivations for doing things in this way. If Chomsky is right, however, this is not even a coherent and allowable way of doing things since there are no sociolects to play this anti-individualistic constitutive role.

Chomsky's reason for rejecting the very idea of sociolect is that it is an idea which is impossible to pin down, even roughly, there being far too little in common between any two persons' speech, let alone a community of persons. Even granting this diversity in individual speech, and granting that most theoretical linguists since Chomsky's pioneering work do not any longer study sociolects, I wonder whether there is not a lot evidence for the fact that, in the interpretation of speech and in the attribution of thoughts in many common contexts, there is a certain amount of abstraction from the diversity in individuals' speech.

Such abstraction is reflected in our talk of whether a learner has mastered a term or concept. This talk would lose its point if there was not some notion of a language over and above the idiolect. No doubt, such talk might still have point within idiolects individualistically conceived, e.g. it would have point retrospectively as when we say of some one after he has gained linguistic maturity that at an earlier stage he had not mastered his term $x$. But the talk of mastery is not restricted to such retrospective observations within idiolects. We do, after all, say of someone who may never go on to learn anything further, that he has not mastered the use of this or that term.

It is true that it is hard to expect agreement over when exactly such mastery is acquired. It is also very hard to delineate the community which speaks the sociolect that sets the standard by which we judge the mastery of a term. Sociolects can be more or less local, and it is surely true that what will count as a community for one term in a natural language will not count as the community for another; that what will count as a community might be far-flung and not necessarily in the near vicinity; and certainly that no single community exists which sets the standard for all terms of a given natural language. In all this Chomsky is undoubtedly right and he, more than any one else, is responsible for our resistance to approaches to the study of language which uncritically assume more social convention than there is. Nevertheless, abstractions from diversity might be said to exist, which set some vaguely demarcated standards and which ground our talk of the "mastery" of particular terms. And one has to look at persons other than the individual whose mastery is in question to discover these standards.

However, conceding this implication of our talk of mastery forces no anti-individualist concessions regarding the idiolect. It is perfectly compatible with individualism about the idiolect, so long as one is careful to describe the point about mastery as follows: we may say that an individual has not mastered one or other term in his sociolect and when he masters it he would have given up his idiosyncratic concept for a new concept. The point against Chomsky is that even to be able to say that, even on this individualist picture of the idiolect, we would still have to appeal to the abstractions from diversity in order to talk of mastery in this way at all. That is, we would still have to appeal to sociolects.

Another fact which reflects our appeal to such abstractions from diversity is this: were Bert my neighbor in my Upper West Side academic community in New York City, and were he to utter the words "arthritis is painful" or "I am suffering from arthritis this morning," and I had no clue about his ignorance, I would assume that he was speaking the sociolect of our medically (relatively) well-informed community. Burge wishes to say that not only are we correct in assuming it, the assumption itself is the philosophically correct position. For Burge, facts which underlie the assumption carry far more philosophical significance than individualists allow. An individualist, on the other hand, would only wish to say that we are correct in assuming it but may often have to give the assumption up. But what makes possible the assumption (that both parties to this dispute allow) is the underlying notion of a sociolect, however vaguely delineated. However, if Chomsky is right it makes no sense even to assume it. For him there is no coherent idea of the sociolect which supports even the assumption. This does not even allow the social externalist to have a stateable position. For Chomsky, the social externalist's mistake is not merely that he sees philosophical significance in facts that individualists see as lacking that significance. For Chomsky, the social externalist (and I) are mistaken in thinking that there are facts here which are coherently describable. I am inclined to think that this exaggerates things a bit because the assumption requires a very minimal and imprecise notion of a linguistic community. And, in any case, individualism is not in any way threatened by granting this minimal notion of sociolect.[11]

I have tried to give a sense of what basic claims the philosophical doctrine of individualism makes about two objects of study: idiolects and sociolects. From now on I will concentrate on its claims about idiolects because it is these claims that are most immediately relevant to the study of intentionality and, in particular, these claims follow from my commitment to the unified view of intentionality as it emerged in chapter 2. Individualism about idiolects is the only plausible way to retain unity of content unless, as two of the horns of the trilemma posed against social externalism in the last chapter made clear, one was prepared to be so implausible as to give up on basic commitments to charity and self-knowledge.[12] In the following pages, I will consider arguments to the effect that there are social features essential to idiolects and essential to intentionality, which individualism fails to capture and which only social externalism about idiolects can capture.

### *Does Individualism Fail to Capture Social Features Essential to Belief and Meaning?*

I will consider and reject two arguments in favor of an affirmative answer to this question.

*First*: It will and has been protested that my individualist alternative to social externalism about idiolects, as sketched above, proposes a *revisionist* conception of that-clause content; that it is a philosopher's invention which distorts our ordinary, everyday practice of the attribution and the reporting of people's beliefs, which is non-individualistic.[13] Let us call this *the argument from common usage* against individualism. According to this argument, individualism fails to capture the most ordinary facts about our everyday reporting of people's beliefs, which is thoroughly social externalist.

Burge extensively discusses how individualistic reinterpretations of the socially constituted attributions he proposes are a departure from common usage and so are not warranted. The claim underlying this argument is simply that in common usage we more often than not do attribute contents as if the ignorant have the concepts of the learned. We would, in everyday reporting of belief, say "Bert believes that he has arthritis in his thigh." I do not deny this claim on the general grounds that one should not deny facts. Of course, if Bert is too wildly idiosyncratic, if, for instance, he thinks arthritis is a bunch of bullets, we will not be inclined to report the thought he expresses when he says, "I have arthritis in my thigh" as "Bert believes that he has arthritis in his thigh." But for the Bert in the example which we have so far been considering (who at least believes that it is a disease, a painful disease...) our common practice of reporting is likely to support Burge's conclusion that that is how we would report his belief.

It is quite open, however, whether this fact about everyday reports has anything to do with the issue before us. The issue before us is a philosophical one. Discussion of this issue began in chapter 2 with a question about which picture of content (individualist or social externalist) is to be preferred. The question was decided in favor of the former on the grounds that the latter would disrupt the unity of content. A question was then posed at the beginning of this chapter about whether there are compelling reasons in a philosophical treatment of the propositional attitudes to give up on the unity of content and accept the latter picture despite this theoretically undesirable consequence of multiplying notions of content. The appeal to ordinary practice of reporting seems hardly to acknowledge that the question here is a thoroughly philosophical one. The notion of content which is the subject of this philosophical question is a notion which has a theoretical status because the very issue underlying the philosophical question is a theoretical one: what notion of content to posit such that it will serve in the explanation of content as well as stand in essential relations with the external world? Why should we take facts about ordinary, everyday reports to be relevant to this theoretical notion? If Burge's example tells us anything, it is that ordinary, everyday practice is neglectful of the fairly serious differences between Bert and his fellows. The common practice of reporting does not fine-tune its tracking of the states of mind of the person on whom it reports and whose behavior it has to explain. Surely one needs, therefore, to be given reasons as to why in a philosophical and theoretical treatment of the propositional attitudes, one must be slavish to the details of common practice. Is there some philosophical urge or goal that remains ungratified by deviating from it?

This last question's point will be better appreciated with the help of a contrast. In chapter 2 and earlier in this section the public nature of meaning was mentioned. For the moment let me assume the intolerability to most philosophers of the view that meaning and thought are essentially private and inner things. The view is despised by many, whether rightly or wrongly, because it generates a skepticism about other minds. Thus the widespread assumption among philosophers that content and meaning must be governed by the constraint that they are publicly discoverable things. This suggests that there is a philosophical goal, a certain widely held epistemological urge, which motivates the imposing of the *publicness constraint* on meaning and belief. The question is whether there is anything so philosophically urgent and compelling about imposing the further *social constraint*. The argument from common usage cites the urge to keep faith with the common practice of everyday reports of belief as something that would justify imposing the social externalist constraint. And my claim is that whether the epistemological considerations just cited in favor of the publicness constraint are persuasive or not, they are recognizably philosophical considerations in a way that the considerations from common usage are not. The contrast with what underlies the publicness constraint is unconvincing because it is not of the same philosophical relevance. Ordinary chat, unlike epistemology, is not in itself of relevance or interest in the philosophical study of anything.

Someone may think it is relevant to turn one of my own restrictions against me here. It might be objected that in failing to respect common practice, I am rescinding on my commitment (made at the very outset in chapter 2)[14] that my interest in intentional states was primarily restricted to their place in common-sense psychology and not their refinement and eventual reduction to a quite different place: in a highly scientific theory of human behavior. This objection is guilty of a fairly widespread but unnoticed confusion. The question posed in the last paragraph in no way compromises my concern to restrict the discussion of intentional states to within the bounds of common-sense psychological considerations. The term "commonsense" in the restriction was intended to sound a contrast with efforts at scientific psychological explanations which have no eventual place for the intentional idiom in their specifications of the explanans or the explananda. Thus "common-sense" is not to be confused with the haphazard and inattentive attribution of that-clause content which might occur in the "common" practice of everyday reporting of an agent's intentional states. Insistence on care and attention in attribution of these states need not, therefore, require giving up intentional attributions; it merely implies that worrying about revising everyday practice is a form of fastidiousness quite unnecessary in a philosophical account of intentionality. It would be uncritical to be misled by the superficially common use of "common" in "commonsense psychology" and "common practice," to think that departure from the latter involves abandoning the former. That

would only be so if there was a well-motivated prior desideratum for a philosophical account of content (within the bounds of its role in commonsense
psychology) to keep faith with the common practice of content-attribution. It
would not and should not be so because of the confusing use of the equivocal
description "common."

The conflation is perhaps encouraged by an expression like "folk-psycho-
logy," which is so much in currency today. Is the expression meant to sound the
contrast between, on the one hand, the theoretical pursuits of a living tradition
of philosophy of mind and action issuing from Aristotle's work on the practical
syllogism and, on the other, the theoretical pursuits of more scientifically
ambitious contemporary philosophers of psychology?[15] Or is the stress by "folk"
meant to sound a contrast between, on the one hand, the ordinary linguistic
practice of belief attribution by ordinary folk (in the sense of non-philosophers
who are not caught up in any of the themes of the philosophy of mind and action)
and, on the other, any philosophical or theoretical treatment of intentionality
whatsoever?

The term is certainly introduced in the literature as a way of making the former
contrast, a contrast with neuroscience in particular, but sometimes even with the
further recesses of cognitive science, where computations seem to be working
on items hardly recognizable as intentional.[16] But despite this mode of introduction it often slides to describe something much more specific than this contrast
dictates; it slides to describe, that is, the psychology (such as it is) contained in
the reports of ordinary, non-philosophical chat. But in that case we should be
careful if we adopt the terminology of a "folk" psychology not to make this slide.
I suggest that there is no special and pressing reason for philospohers to be
interested in such untheoretical chat, especially if it conflicts, as I claim it does,
with the specifically philosophical goal of clarifying and codifying the contents
of states (and their inter-relations) which commonsensically explain or rationalize individual behavior. It is not as if this suggestion is a new-fangled turn in
our subject, departing radically from the practice of the tradition. It is no
departure at all. The psychology contained in the idea of a practical syllogism
and its (non-scientific) refinements are through and through theoretical and there
is no evidence whatsoever, as far as I know, that Aristotle, for instance, or Kant
or Davidson (just to include names from the wider tradition) ever had in mind to
keep faith with the details of everyday practice of reports.

The fact that one is interested in something theoretical and philosophical
forces one to attribute different contents to agents than the ones we do in ordinary
chat. It is undeniable, of course, that even to do so, one has to use everyday
vocabulary which will often give the impression to the everyday listener that the
contents being attributed are the ones that Burge has in mind rather than
individualist ones. But this too is irrelevant to the philosophical issues. Just
because our words will automatically convey something to an unphilosophical

listener does not mean that philosophers have to draw the wrong conclusions about what notion of content is relevant to theoretical issues like the common-sense explanation of action. One may, of course, raise a question about whether, in that case, the content I have in mind are ever specificable. The answer to this is not that they are not specifiable at all but that in order to specify them explicitly one may have to bring in various additional descriptions to capture an agent's conceptions ("a disease of the joints and ligaments," "the only English city his nanny told him about," "the city he is now living in" etc.). In chapter 4, I will discuss how we may not always be able to make such explicit descriptional specifications of the concepts involved in the specifications of content and how we may therefore have to view the terms we use in content attribution as summaries of these descriptions which capture an agent's conceptions, how in many cases we may have to provide neologistic terms in order to summarize agents' conceptions.[17] For now it is enough to say that it cannot be a serious argument against the need for a non-orthodox externalist notion of concept individuation, that its contents are much more difficult to specify than the contents of the orthodox notions which we use in everyday reports of a person's contents. One cannot rest with a wrong view of concept and content individuation just because it is easier to specify contents on that view. And, in any case, if we did rest with it, the other harder-to-specify contents will crop up somewhere else because we have to explain behavior and, we have already seen, that orthodox externalist content will not do that.

All this was said by way of general criticism of the fetishization of common usage and everyday reports in the study of content. There is actually something stronger and more specific to be said, something more internally unsatisfactory in the appeal to the everyday in support of the social externalist view of content. And that is, even in many everyday contexts, and with everyday and non-theoretical goals in mind, it can be perverse and misleading to attribute to agents the content that Burge's position demands. It does not need much imagination to think of various quotidian contexts in which we will not want to say that Bert believes that he has arthritis in his thigh unless we hastily add that he is medically incompetent in the use of that term. (For instance, in the context of, and with the perfectly non-theoretical goal of, communicating his medical history to an insurance agent.) And so for any number of terms in which such misalignments may occur between agents and their communities. Without the qualification, in these contexts, such reports could seriously misinform and deceive those to whom the reports are being made. Burge himself admits to this when he says, "But frequently, common practice seems to allow us to cancel the misleading suggestions by making explicit the subject's deviance" (1979, p. 91). He seems content to rest with that point and does not see it as undermining the significance of the everyday. Yet if these qualifications must so often accompany everyday style reporting of a person's beliefs, the great importance being attached to the everyday diminishes considerably. There is nothing of any moment that turns on it. It does not seem to matter which way one tracks an agent's states of mind: in individualist terms or the socially constituted terms with the qualifications attached.[18]

To insist even so that its importance is not undermined and that everyday practice is still of decisive philosophical moment is, in my view, as idle as anything we have become used to complaining about in the philosophical style of mid-century Oxford. That style, was, if anything, a departure from the tradition of philosophizing on these themes. Russell, if we recall, famously lost his patience with Strawson for objecting that everyday practice did not reflect Russell's views on reference; and the general situation here is not very different from that in the dispute between them.[19] Even if there is no analogue here to a whole program of the regimentation of language in Russell, the general point is that (quite apart from that program) just as Russell had theoretical goals in the study of reference (goals which have exercised philosophers ever since, who have no interest in his program of regimentation), philosophers long interested in the nature of commonsense psychology have certain theoretical aims in their study of intentional states and their contents. The appeal to everyday practice is equally irrelevant and equally exasperating to both enterprises. So, to the protest that the individualist picture offers a notion of content that is "revisionist" and "a philosopher's invention," I reply with exasperation that it is indeed that and indeed that I am a philosopher. And as a philosopher, though I am moved by certain epistemological anxieties and goals to view content as public, I am altogether unmoved by the anxieties about keeping fastidious faith with everyday reports to view it as, in this further sense, social.

*Second*: To be fair, neither Burge nor most of those who embrace social externalism trivialize their position by resting their entire case on our slovenly, everyday announcements of other people's beliefs. They gather other sorts of phenomena to build up the case, facts such as the pervasive tendency to correct our own usage and to bend to the standards of the community. Let us call this *the argument from deference* for social externalism.[20]

Bert's case can again be used to bring out the argument. Let us say that Bert is told by his doctor that he is mistaken in his belief that he has arthritis in his thigh and that arthritis can only occur in the joints. It is very likely that Bert will now defer to the doctor and adjust his usage accordingly. This sort of example turns up all the time in all of our lives. There is no denying the fact that we have very well established (as well as quite specific) ways of admitting error in our linguistic usage. And it is a fact that needs an explanation. The argument from deference proposes that we explain it by adopting Burge's social externalism about concepts and contents. The claim is that the fact that Bert (and all of us) so readily changes his ways to conform to the standards of his community and its experts is to be explained by saying that he all along had the expert's concept.

He was just misapplying it. He has now come to have a fuller understanding of it.

I have admitted to the *fact* of deference. (Some, like Chomsky, think even this should not be conceded.[21] I wish to avoid taking such a controversial stance so as to focus the controversy where I think Burge's anti-individualism enters. The concession to the fact of deference in my view concedes nothing to the anti-individualism.) But here again, as with facts of common usage, we ought to pause at the philosophical significance that Burge and others tend to see in such facts. The question once more is why should these facts force us to impose the social externalist constraint on the attribution of content. If the facts have an explanation that does not imply that we must impose that constraint; would it not be better to stick with just the constraints that one cannot do without (such as the publicness constraint).[22] And surely there are such alternative explanations for the fact of deference.

In order to see the persuasiveness of the alternative explanations I am about to suggest, it should perhaps first be pointed out that, in any case, linguistic deference is by no means universal, irrespective of contexts. This is not to take Chomsky's more radical stance since I am happy to admit that these may be seen as mere exceptions; point it out rather because something deflationary about deference can be learned from these exceptions. In many contexts, agents resist deference and do so quite sensibly. Take the case of an agent who has been misusing a term in his community's tongue for some time and who suddenly realizes, after looking at a dictionary (or a medical manual), that he has been wrong all along. It is possible to imagine situations in which he next meets someone and will find it much more sensible to continue using the term as he always has rather than defer to the community's usage. In these situations he may think it will cause more strain and confusion among his audience, which is used to hearing his idiosyncratic usage, if he were to suddenly start speaking differently. In these contexts, he has a pragmatic reason not to defer. Decisions about deference are, thus, dictated by specific situations and these are too unsystematic to warrant any single conclusion about what an agent will or must do when he realizes he has been misapplying a term.

This point about pragmatic reasons to explain non-deference opens up the possibility of showing that deference itself can be explained pragmatically, and in other similar ways, and need not be explained along social externalist lines. There is a common underlying explanation of both deference and the exceptions to deference which makes no appeal to Burge-like considerations. More obvious commonsense sociological explanations, i.e. more pragmatic and historical explanations of deference, can be introduced instead of Burge's explanations, such as: if we wish to be understood and understood without strain, we will by and large (except in the admittedly exceptional contexts mentioned in the last paragraph) use words as others do;[23] if we have been brought up in the same social environment and our words and beliefs have been formed in it, our

meanings will tend to converge and especially so if we want to bring others up
in it.

These alternative explanations belong to commonsense sociology and have
no relevance to philosophy in the way that Burge insists on. With these alternative explanations in place, there is no compulsion to say that Bert all along had
the doctor's concept of arthritis. The alternative explanations support individualism for we can now just as easily say that Bert had a certain concept before he
was corrected by the doctor and, afterwards, came to have a different concept
(now perhaps the same as the doctor's, if he is fully informed).[24] The alternative
explanations allow us to say that because they make clear that he changes his
concept on the grounds that that is how his doctor and others around him speak
and understand each other and he wants to be understood easily by them. (Of
course, he does not have to want this consciously and explicitly, it is an
underlying tacit desire explaining both deference and the occasional non-deference.) This alternative explanations makes it unnecessary to say that Bert had
their concept of arthritis all along and his mistake was that he thought that *that*
disease had afflicted his thigh. The doctor's correction brings about a change of
his concepts not a realization of a misapplication of his concept.

It might be protested that that is not how we report the change that deference
brings about. We would not say that Bert's mistake lay in having a concept that
was different from the society's and the change brought about by his deferring
consisted in changing his concept to theirs (so as to be understood more easily).
Rather we would say that his mistake was to think that arthritis was in his thigh,
i.e. the mistake of a false belief not of a true belief containing a misaligned
concept. Indeed, it might be said that that is how Bert himself will report the
change.

There are two very different responses that need to be made to this protest,
depending on the spirit in which this protest is made. If it is made in the spirit of
stressing once again the importance of ordinary reporting I will simply repeat
my earlier response with renewed exasperation. But something more subtle and
philosophically significant can be made to inform the spirit in which it is made.
The talk of mistakes of a certain kind introduces the philosophical themes of
normativity and theory-change in the study of content. These themes are highly
relevant to the protest just made against my alternative explanations and the
consequences I am drawing from these explanations for how to understand the
fact of deference. I shall discuss them in the next section rather than immediately
here because they appeal to considerations which seem to favor all of the
orthodox externalisms I wish to oppose and not just social externalism. The
deference issue has been taken up on its own here because it is temporarily
separable in my dialectic since it alone bears specific relevance to the social
externalism now being considered.

In other words, though the argument from deference against individualism in the end may only be fully made by bringing in considerations about normativity etc., those considerations unlike the deference considerations also purport to have a much wider force than an anti-individualist force and deserve to be discussed separately. Though they affect the argument from deference, their significance is not restricted to the argument, which was introduced as a way of questioning whether my unified notion of content captures what is essentially social about language and thought. The considerations from normativity purport to show that my unified notion of content fails to capture much else besides the social, and hence they have a wider relevance than the restricted subject of this section.

So this discussion of the argument from deference must be concluded somewhat tentatively by saying: on the basis of my alternative explanations for deference given in this section, the argument from deference cannot by itself (that is, without these additional themes and considerations) compel us to shun individualism and adopt social externalism. After those additional considerations have been dealt with in the next section, we will be able to state this conclusion less tentatively.

### Society and Radical Interpretation

In a famous opening sentence of *Word and Object*, Quine (1960) makes a clear commitment to the idea that language is a "social art." But very quickly after that in the book, one finds that it would in a deep sense be question-begging if we believed that one's neighbors or even one's own family members spoke the same language as one. That is something we would really be allowed to say – even if we assume it all along – only if we turned up the same "analytical hypotheses" for them as someone might for us; turned up, that is, the same concepts associated with the same terms or sounds. It is true that there will be *some* society involved prior to this: the one for whom the hypotheses are being turned up and the one who is turning them up.[25] But the denial that, as philosophers, we may even assume, prior to the delivery of the hypotheses, that any *other* than the speaker speaks a given language (of course, keeping in mind the qualifications made in chapter 2 about the contingent fact of the linguistic division of labor), strongly suggests that what is essential to the philosophical understanding of language need not involve, in the sense required by Burge, what these others do or say.[26]

The suggestion is not that one cannot adopt the radical translation stance and still be a social externalist.[27] No, it is perfectly possible to adopt the radical interpretative stance and appeal to the linguistic practices of an agent's fellows to fix analytical hypotheses for her. It is also possible not to do so; the idea of radical translation opens one's eyes to the possibility of a coherent individualist position. And, in a sense, it would be to miss out on the beauty of the idea of radical translation if one adopted its stance and also embraced social externalism.

The point is that the very idea of *radical* interpretation shows that the interpreter does not have to have the same language as the interpretee to come to understand her; and so it shows that understanding in general does not absolutely require that one share a language. What is true of the radical interpreter and radical interpretee could, in principle, be true of any two people, of all pairs of people. If so, one can take this point about radical interpretation and extend it comprehensively, concluding that one's concepts and meanings are never *constituted* by the linguistic practices of one's social fellows, even if, in fact, any given speaker, for pragmatic and historical reasons, has the same linguistic practices as many others.

It is true that the idea of radical translation or interpretation has been taken to require that if interpretation is going to take place interpreter and interpretee must share a lot of beliefs and concepts.[28] The "principle of charity" taken to be so essential to the idea makes that absolutely clear. But that requirement is not at all the same as the social externalist requirement which has it that *linguistic practices* must be shared, if understanding is to take place, i.e. social externalism requires that one must by and large use the same words for the same things.[29]

It might be objected that thinking of the *social* aspects of language in terms of overlapping idiolects, as the individualist does, leaves out from that aspect its basic feature, viz. that we participate in a common practice and that we do not merely happen to do the same thing (as the overlapping idiolects idea suggests). However, that suggestion is not intended by that idea. The point is not to deny the element of participation but rather to insist that in order to get to the central core of meaning and content, that element is not essential. It is not essential – and this is what radical translation emphasizes and brings out – because one can manage with understanding what is communicated, without such participation. The element of participation can then be explained by giving the sort of socio-logical (pragmatic and historical) explanations cited above. We participate in the same practice because we have been brought up in the same social settings and bring others up in it, because we want to be easily understood, etc.

So, whatever Quine must have meant in that opening sentence when he described language as social, it could not and need not be what Burge intends. And whatever he meant, that is all that the publicness requirement demands and all that is necessary for the tasks at hand. If my overall argument so far has been persuasive, no unavoidable or otherwise unexplainable phenomenon has been cited which forces us to lay down social constraints stronger than that require-ment. Considerations of the everyday or common practice of that-clause attribu-tion, of linguistic deference and admission of error, of our reliance on others, of our participation in the linguistic practices of others, of the social formation of patterns of thought and speech, of the matchless convenience of speaking the way others do, are all considerations which in one way or another are lacking the significance or the particular sort of philosophical significance that Burge and his supporters have thought them to have. If I am right, these considerations have no other status than that of commonsense sociological observations about how and why we speak the way we do. They cannot be used to erect a philosophical doctrine about the socially constitutive nature of intentional content as we find it in social externalism.

## THE RELEVANCE OF NORMS AND RULES TO BELIEF AND MEANING

### *The Apparent Relevance of Norms*

The sense in which the question of normativity is relevant to the dispute between the unified view of content and the orthodox externalist may be put very simply and crudely to begin with. If one takes the unified view of content, it turns out that one could say that Bert has a different concept than the expert. On the other hand, if one took any of the orthodox externalisms, his concept is determined by the expert's beliefs or it is determined by a certain scientific essence etc.[30] So when Bert (sincerely and literally) says "I have arthritis in my thigh," it is only the orthodox externalist who is in a position to say that in making that utterance, Bert has made a mistake regarding the use of "arthritis," to say that Bert has misapplied his concept. The notion of a mistake is a normative notion, and the possibility of mistakes of this sort introduces a matter of rightness and wrongness regarding the use of terms or the application of concepts the terms express. Rightness or wrongness of this sort is essential to the idea of meaning and concepts, and therefore to the idea of content. My view does not allow one to say of Bert and others like him that they have made or can make these sorts of mistakes. As we saw toward the end of the discussion of the argument from deference in the last section, when it came to describing Bert's deference to his doctor, I did not describe it as learning from the doctor that he was all along mistaken about arthritis and had been wrongly applying his term for it, but rather as the doctor having helped him acquire a new concept so that he was now wielding a new term. Therefore my view has no place for an essential normativity that attaches to meaning and content. Only a notion of content like the orthodox externalist's will capture this normativity.

This notion of normativity introduces a certain matter of rightness and wrongness in the meaningful use of words or in the application of concepts. The point can be, and has been, made in terms of rules. That is, one can think of the use of terms and the application of concepts as being governed by rules, which are the standards by which particular uses and applications can be judged to be correct or mistaken. Thus if we answer "125" when asked "what is the sum of 68 and 57?," we might be said to have correctly applied the rule for the term "+"

or the rule associated with the concept of addition. So also I am following the rule for "arthritis" if I apply the term "arthritis" correctly. To have a concept is to follow a rule of this sort.

In recent years much of the discussion of normativity, and its relation to meaning and content, has concentrated on the nature and possibility of following linguistic rules. The discussion goes back to certain well-known sections in Wittgenstein's *Philosophical Investigations* (1953, sections 179-242) and has more recently been made the centre of philosophical attention by Kripke's (1982) brief and stimulating commentary on those sections. Kripke and Kripke's Wittgenstein stress this very normativity attaching to meaning, which seems to me also to motivate orthodox externalist views of meaning and content. It will be useful, therefore, to take up a discussion of the basic thrust of Kripke's Wittgenstein's argument, so as to elaborate on the crude and simple initial statement of the relevance of normativity to the dispute about wide content. In much of this section I will argue that this sense of normativity, which fuels Kripke's discussion and which also underlies the commitment to "wide" content, is not a deep or essential part of the notion of meaning and content. Though many have seen the obvious connections between Kripke's discussion of rules and the subject of intentionality, they have not often connected it specifically with the present dispute about wide content in particular. But anybody who has grasped the relevance of norms to the dispute as expounded in the first paragraph of this section will see immediately that the issue is just the same as Kripke's Wittgenstein's stress on normativity in the discussion of rules and meaning.

(Incidentally, those who have written on Kripke's book find it obligatory to say something at the outset about the relation between views expressed in the book and those whose views are being expressed. On the one hand there, are many who say that the views that Kripke attributes to him are not really Wittgenstein's. On the other hand, Kripke is coy about whether he himself holds the views that he attributes to Wittgenstein. I will from this moment on cease to be careful about either of these things. I will simply talk of the views expressed in Kripke's book as being, indifferently, Kripke's and Wittgenstein's views. The views are influential and interesting enough that they merit serious discussion and it does not matter whether either *really* believes them; and, in any case, in philosophical discussions in the past few years I have found that there are plenty of philosophers who do hold these views or views which very strongly imply them.)

Kripke introduces the idea of normativity via what he calls a "skeptical" problem about rules and the following of rules. Kripke and Wittgenstein raise the problem with arithmetical examples but are very clear that it holds generally for all terms and concepts. For the sake of continuity with the discussion of chapter 2, I will not work with an arithmetical example but instead with a variation on the example of Bert.

Imagine a man, call him KWert, who for several years has used the word arthritis (as we all do) to talk of a disease of the joints only. Then on and from January 1, 1989, he is heard to say things like "I have arthritis in my thigh." We are inclined to say that he is making a mistake. He is not applying the rule for the concept of arthritis correctly. But we are asked with what authority we say this? Why do we not say that he is quite correctly applying the rule and indeed was all along applying the rule for the concept of *quarthritis*. The rule for the concept quarthritis, unlike the one for the concept of arthritis, does not say: "Apply the term 'arthritis' to rheumatoid ailments with properties... and which afflict the joints only." Rather it says something more bizarre and complicated: "Until January 1, 1989 apply the term 'arthritis' to rheumatoid ailments with properties... and which afflict the joints only, after that apply it to rheumatoid ailments with properties... and which afflict the ligaments as well as the joints." The skeptical problem is just this: there is no fact about KWert that will decide for us that he has the concept of arthritis rather than of quarthritis. And this is a perfectly general problem. It is quite possible that any given concept of ours is afflicted with this sort of future possibility of what, to our commonsense, might appear as lunatic deviant application. In that case we are not sure what any of our concepts is at any time.

Various candidates for facts about KWert which might be thought to decide the matter about which of the two rules is being followed (which concept he really has) are canvassed and rejected by Kripke and Wittgenstein. In particular, facts about his neurophysiology, images of one kind or another, an inner conviction that he meant to be following one rule rather than another, and a variety of other sorts of mental occurrence which Bert may have undergone when he applied the term. All those facts are as much in need of interpretation as the behavior they are supposed to deliver a verdict on; and there is the problem that if such purely inner things gave our words meaning, we may render meanings private.[31] This is just Wittgenstein's version of anti-internalism.[32] ("An inner process stands in need of an outward criterion.")

There is a temptation to say that even if there is nothing introspectible and phenomenological which will provide the fact of the matter when it comes to meanings and concepts, the special authority that agents have of their own contents and meanings – something that Wittgenstein never denied – should surely decide the issue and remove the skeptical problem. Of course, it is a difficult question what account we must give of this special first-person authority of meaning and content, once one follows Wittgenstein in rejecting an internalist account of meaning and content, and, therefore, in rejecting an introspectionist model for our self-knowledge of them. (This question is taken up in the Appendix.) But on the assumption that there is such an account and that first-person authority is undeniable, why not say that such authoritative self-knowledge is the basis of a solution to Kripke's skepticism about there being no fact of the matter about meanings and rules? Kripke does not discuss this possibility in any detail but one would expect that he would reject it as well; and he would be right to do so. The authoritative nature of self-knowledge does not help a jot in providing an answer to Kripke's question about a fact of the matter as to what KWert means. This is because the *publicness* of meaning (something absolutely basic among Wittgenstein's commitments) makes it clear that no matter how specially authoritative KWert's self-knowledge of his own meanings is, no matter how different it is from the way *we* know his meanings, KWert does not know anything about his own meanings that any of us cannot know about his meanings. So, if there is no way for us to tell which rule he is following, there is no way for *him* to tell which rule he is following. There just is no fact of the matter. If this were not so, the specially authoritative nature of self-knowledge would amount to rejection of publicness of meaning and thought. But the special nature of self-knowledge cannot amount to that. It cannot amount to an agent knowing something about his mind that others cannot know, it can only amount to him knowing it in a way different from the way others know it. If that is right, the commitment to first-person authority is of no help with the skeptical problem.

There is yet another sort of fact that might be thought to decide the matter about which rule KWert is following. It is not internalistic and so one might think it would be acceptable to Wittgenstein. These are the dispositional facts about KWert, how he is disposed to use the term "arthritis." But, Kripke says, that will not help either. Dispositions are *descriptive* of the person to whom they are attributed, and they are read off his behavior. If so, we are never in a position to say that his behavior on January 1, 1989 counts as a mistake. To appeal merely to dispositions is to appeal to something that does not allow us to say anyone is mistaken in this way. Equally, therefore, it does not allow us to say of KWert's behavior and usage before that time (or anybody's at any time), that it is *correct*. But to be able to judge correctness and mistakenness, Kripke says is essential to our notion of rules, meanings and concepts. These are essentially normative notions. No amount of refinement of the idea of disposition will help unless it begs the question against the skeptic. People do what they do and they say what they say and they do so in relatively uniform and regular ways; and their dispositions are attributed to them on the basis of that. But these are just facts about regularities in their behavior and projections based on them. They cannot settle an issue which is in its essence an issue that goes beyond facts into matters of correctness and mistakenness. That is, into considerations of normativity.[33]

Nothing about KWert, then, decides the issue. Not his internal states, not his authority over his own mind, not his dispositions. And this is not just a difficulty about *finding out* which concept he has. There is nothing to find out, no fact of the matter. Thus it is a skepticism about all talk of concepts (and meanings) and since contents are composed of concepts, of content also.

Kripke admits that there is no solution to this skeptical problem, if the solution is to take the form of those rejected above. All those efforts fail and so if there is a solution, it must proceed from a recognition of something principled in those failures. Acknowledging the failure of these efforts is to concede something important to what the skeptic is saying. For this reason Kripke calls his own solution a "skeptical solution."[34] To put it roughly it is this. The skepticism consisted in saying that nothing about an agent determines which concept he has. The solution does not combat this claim. It concedes it. It proposes instead not to look merely at the agent for the solution, but to look at the community in which he lives and speaks. If the agent applies the concepts to things in a way that squares with the way the community applies it, then he is correct. If not, not. If his answers to addition problems, his judgments of the location of disease, square with the community's answers and judgments, then there will be no reason to count them as mistaken. If they do not square, then there will. The skeptical solution appeals to the community to bring in the normativity and thereby to bring in the fact of the matter which will decide which rule is being followed by KWert. If he is a member of our community he is following the rule for arthritis and he is mistaken on and after January 1, 1989.

It should be obvious where the role of normativity enters in Kripke's dialectic. Normativity is presupposed right from the start by Kripke as essential to the meaning of terms; and it is introduced into the dialectic of his skeptical problem at the point where one thought one could get away with an answer to his skeptic, an answer which appealed to the regularities in individual agent's behaviors and the dispositions attributed to agents on their basis. This "dispositional" view of the meanings of terms falls afoul of the demand for normativity. It does not allow us to say of KWert's answers after January 1989 (or any uses of terms, generally) that they are mistaken. We could just as easily see him as following the more bizarre and complicated rule mentioned earlier, and see him, therefore as making no mistake at all. But if we look to the members of his community and find that his answers after that date do not any longer square with the answers they give, we *do* have the resources to say that he is mistaken. Looking to the community, thus, captures the normativity.

It is not now hard to see the links between Bert and KWert; and between Kripke's Wittgenstein and Burge. When the individualist would have us say of Bert that he has his own idiosyncratic concept, it was because Bert's concept was attributed to him on the basis of his own behavior, his more or less *regularly* applying a certain term to a condition that afflicted ligaments as well as joints. On the basis of that, one said that he was disposed to apply the term to such a condition. That was all there was to his concept. So when he said that "he had arthritis in his thigh," one was not in a position to say that he was making a mistake. One could only be in a position to say that he was making a mistake if we followed Burge and looked to the way Bert's community used the term "arthritis" and attributed that concept to him. The similarities with Kripke are obvious. The difference is that Burge does not raise the example of Bert as one that might, if treated wrongly, threaten us with the spectre of skepticism, but rather of individualism. But just as with Kripke, where the consideration of normativity was introduced to say something other than what the dispositionalist says and thereby stave off a skepticism-generating reinterpretation of KWert's behavior as the application of a bizarre concept, so for Burge, it was important that Bert be taken to be making a mistaken judgment for that disallows us the individualism-generating reinterpretation of him as exercising an idiosyncratic concept. And in both cases only bringing in the community can afford us these things. The common factor in both Burge and Kripke is the stress on normativity as a motivation for their appeal to the community. That one of them is attacking a certain form of individualism and the other is attacking individualism as a way of responding to a skeptical problem is a minor difference of presentation compared to this shared conception being presented.

It is this shared conception of the normativity of meaning, a conception which only something as strong as a social externalist or Kripkean appeal to the community can capture, that I will be attacking in what follows. I am only attacking that demand for normativity in matters of meaning and content which *cannot* be met by my individualistic, unified, externalist, regularity-based view of concepts and content. I am only attacking that demand which can *only* be met by something as strong as the orthodox social externalist view of them.[35] The demand for normativity that can be met by something like my unified individualistic view is, as we shall see below, a quite different demand, much lower in profile and hardly interesting.

### The Irrelevance of Norms

Unified content, as sketched earlier has no place for Burge's and Kripke's view of the relevance of norms to content and meaning. Now, if my exposition of the view of their relevance is correct, the alleged relevance of norms enters by contrast to a dispositionalist view of content and meaning. Does it mean, then, that in rejecting the relevance, the unified picture is, at bottom, a dispositionalist picture? Obviously it shares something with the dispositionalist picture but, as will emerge below, there is more than one element in the unified view which is foreign to many people's view of what the dispositionalist picture is and so it is asking for confusion to call it that.

Recall that the method of concept attribution in my unified view suggested in chapter 1 requires one to look, under a certain constraint, at the circumstances in the external world in which agents utter or assent to sentences containing a specific term. Applying the method to the case at hand, it would say something very roughly like this: if the agent has regularly tended to use the term, say "arthritis," in one sort of circumstance, say the circumstance of people being afflicted by a disease of the joints and which has the other properties of being painful... attribute that particular (disposition?) concept to him. These are the regularities of usage which give rise to the correlations between his indexical utterances and some set of external circumstances. Remember that there was also a constraint which asked one to describe the external circumstances keeping in mind the *other* beliefs attributed to him. This is a holistic and anti-foundational constraint which was discussed in chapters 1 and 2. Its relevance here is that the insistence on the appeal to other beliefs highly qualifies the sense in which these regularities of the agent's usage may be thought of as issuing from "dispositions" in any strict naturalistic sense of dispositions. One crucial thing that the constraint does is to allow us to account for his occasional use of the term in other ("wrong?") external circumstances by appealing to some other belief or beliefs of his which will explain why he used them under these circumstances. But it does so at the cost of making dispositions irreducibly intentional: their characterization involves an essential tie to the other *intentional* states of the agent. For naturalists, these will be dispositions only by courtesy. For obvious reasons, externalists who do not impose this constraint (presumably because of the constraint's frank repudiation of a naturalistic reduction of concepts and content) will have a much harder time dealing with these occasional uses (as, for instance in Fodor 1987). A little later I will say more about what, if any, of a dispositionalist picture is shared by an individualism committed to a unified picture like mine which rejects the relevance of normativity demanded by Kripke.

Despite the irreducibility and the non-naturalism I have committed myself to, it is not hard to envisage what Kripke's general line of objection to my view of concepts or meaning will be. It will be that if all it does is appeal to the regular behavior of the agent (under a certain holistic constraint) then it does not give us the right to say that (Bert's behavior or) KWert's new behavior violates anything, no right to say what we intuitively might want to say: that an agent, who suddenly applies the term after a certain date to a condition in his thigh, is making a mistake. It, thus, leaves out the essential normativity of meaning. One might think that the way of accounting for deviation mentioned in the last paragraph could also be used to say to Bert and KWert that they have made mistakes? But that is wrong. Bert's and KWert's behavior are not deviations in anything like the same sense as we found in those accounted for in the last paragraph. Recall that Bert's behavior and KWert's new behavior are not the sorts of behavior that can be accounted for as exceptions to their past regular behavior and therefore explained away in the manner mentioned in the past paragraph by the resources provided by the holistic constraint. Bert does not even deviate from past regularity, so there is nothing to explain away. And yet Burge would have it that he is making a mistake. As for KWert, though he does deviate from his past behavior, the idea presumably is that he generates a new and different regularity and so there is no reason to call it an *exception* to the past regularity and explain it as a *mistake* by an appeal to the resources provided by the holistic constraint. On the other hand, Kripke's appeal to the community does provide the resources to treat KWert's post-1989 usage as mistaken.

The objection goes on: at best the individualist (for all her insistence on non-reduction and non-naturalism) can only say that Bert has his own idiosyncratic concept and that KWert used to do one sort of thing and now he does another sort of thing. She can only say that KWert's regularities, his tendencies or habits of speech (his "dispositions?") have changed. And, in that case, one can always find a rule which accommodates both patterns of behavior and allows us to see them as a *single* pattern (such as the rule for "quarthritis"). That means that he has not made any mistake at all. In fact, on this view, one cannot make this sort of mistake. Nothing can count as such a mistake because it is not a departure from a *norm*, at most a departure from a previous regularity, and therefore subsumable under a more accommodating conception of the regularity involved in the first place. And if one cannot give sense to his making the mistake, one cannot give sense to his using it correctly prior to the departure.[36] It is only by appeal to the practices of the community that one can provide a norm against which one can count an individual agent like Bert or KWert as making a mistake or as using a concept correctly. That alone gives us the right to talk of correctness or error, the right that is, to normativity.

The objector is perfectly right to point out that the required normativity is also missing in my non-reductionist, non-naturalist dispositionalist picture as it is in the naturalist dispositionalist picture. It would seem then that the objector's conclusion that the appeal to the community's practice is necessary in order to have the right to the desired normativity, would seem impeccable – at least so long as one does not see it as given by some set of internal mental states (neurophysiological states, inner feelings of conviction etc.) or alternatively some set of Platonistic abstractions or metaphors (forms or meanings or, paraphrasing a metaphor of Wittgenstein, "rails which are set up independently of our linguistic behaviour and which our linguistic behaviour tracks"). We have already seen that Wittgenstein rejects the internal candidates for being the fact of the matter at least as vehemently as he rejects the dispositionalist picture, and since Wittgenstein is the inspiration behind the objection we are discussing, one can ignore them. But ever since the middle period of his writing, Platonism is as much the target of Wittgenstein's attack as the internalist picture and the dispositional picture, so one can assume that the objector would not want the right to norms to come from the Platonistic sources either. What then can the source of the desired normativity be but the social element?

However, a question that does not seem to have occurred to the Wittgensteinian is this. Does the Platonist's mistake lie merely in thinking that the norm is afforded in the wrong sort of thing, an abstract entity or the "rails" metaphor; or is it rather that Platonism's mistake lies deeper – in the fact that it hankers for such normativity at all, hankers for such final judgments of rightness and wrongness in the use of words. It is possible to argue that the erecting of metaphysical abstractions or the metaphor of independent rails which our linguistic behavior tracks, is a relatively superficial shortcoming of the Platonist picture; and to argue that a deeper analysis would show that the real trouble with Platonism lies in the desire to see our concepts and meanings as governed by normativity in the sense of being demanded by Kripke and the orthodox externalist notion of concepts. It lies in the desire to find our use of terms right and wrong in the sense being demanded by them. Kripke and others never stop to ask what the compulsion is to conceive of the use of words in this way. They uncritically presuppose that it must be so conceived and then argue that unless one saw meanings as governed by abstractions or exaggerated metaphors on the one hand and inner or private mental states on the other, one would have to appeal to the social considerations of the sort we more recently find in Burge as well. Without this presupposition, however, the regularity-based view of concepts and contents being objected to is not obviously inadequate.

This may sound as if I am agreeing with Kripke that there is no non-skeptical solution to his problem and am offering an alternative skeptical solution to Kripke's own skeptical solution. But I think the more accurate description is that I am taking a way out that does not quite acknowledge that there was a very large problem in the first place and that I am giving a diagnosis as to why it has been thought to be a problem needing a solution of one kind or another. That is, I am not offering either a skeptical or a non-skeptical solution, I am rejecting the problem as being based on a misguided philosophical dogma, a residual Platonism.

(Such a description, in fact, fits a certain conception we have of Wittgenstein's attitude to philosophical problems; and for that reason one might be tempted to attribute this view to him rather than the view Kripke attributes to him. But this would imply that one can treat the regular patterns of linguistic behavior of an individual agent as the social practice of a society of one;[37] and I simply cannot say whether Wittgenstein would equally well allow this as an interpretation of his remarks about the relevance of "custom" and "practice," or whether he intended them to be interpreted as Kripke interprets them.[38])

The diagnosis I am giving for the anxiety which leads to posing a skeptical problem is this: in rejecting the abstractions of meanings on the one hand and the internalistic mentalism of inner facts of the matter on the other, one has not yet succeeded in rejecting what in Platonism underlies the search for these things being rejected. Without rejecting this deeper urge, one will no doubt find another such thing to gratify the Platonist urge and indeed one has found it in society and its experts, or, as in Putnam (rather than Wittgenstein or Burge), in the scientifically discoverable essences of the natural world around us. This deeper urge underlying Platonism is precisely the drive to see concepts and the meanings of terms as governed by such normativity. It is only because of this view of concepts, after all, that we are not able to be indifferent to the question: which concept does KWert really have, arthritis or the more accommodating notion of quarthritis? It is only because of it that we see the question as raising a problem, a "skeptical" problem about meaning and concepts. It is only if you have this residual and deeper Platonist picture of meanings and concepts that you will think that KWert raises a skeptical threat about them. For it will matter to you that he have one or the other concept. If it did not matter, you could not find him ever making the sort of mistake that the drive for normativity demands. And it is only because this matters to you that you will find some *ersatz* version of the Platonist picture, cleansed of its unpalatable metaphysics and metaphors. You will bring Plato's domain of forms down to earth and call it "Society."

Notice that my criticism of Kripke is *not* the, by now, familiar criticism of him which takes him to have failed to fully understand the full force of his own demand for normativity.[39] Philosophers have, like me, opposed Kripke's social view of meaning and concepts but on altogether different grounds from mine. They have argued that the way Kripke brings in the social is just an extension of the normativity-denying position of the dispositionalist because all Kripke does is bring in the dispositions of other members of the society to account for an individual's meanings. So they say if something was missing in the individualist dispositionalist account in the first place, then it will be missing in the social extension as well. This criticism, as a criticism of Kripke, may or may not be fair. The point is that it is only a criticism if one accepts the normativity demand as one finds it in Kripke. The criticism consists in accepting his demand and then saying that Kripke has himself failed to live up to that demand. But I do not accept the demand in the first place, so mine is a much more radical criticism of Kripke. The more radical position entailed by my constrained externalism is quite different from theirs. In my view, shedding the "Platonism" altogether,[40] one would instead have to give notions like meaning and concepts a much lower profile, whereby it does not matter very much that one is not able to say that KWert is making a mistake on January 1, 1989 or that Burge's protagonist has all along made a mistake when he applies the term to a condition in his thigh.

If KWert regularly persists with his new usage and makes accommodating changes with the use of other terms conceptually related to his term "arthritis," then on my individualist (but externalist) view we will say that he has a new concept after January 1989. But Kripke's skeptic may persist and say the question asked is not whether he has a new concept but whether he all along had the concept of arthritis or all along had the weird concept of quarthritis. To this question, the answer should be that it makes no difference to anything at all, which answer we give. His behavior is equally well explained no matter what we say. There is no problem, skeptical or otherwise. Taking one line, one could explain all his relevant behavior before and after 1989 by attributing contents containing the concept of quarthritis. Or, taking another line, one could explain his behavior prior to 1989 with contents containing the concept of arthritis and after that date with contents containing the concept of tharthritis. (The concept of tharthritis, you will recall from the earlier discussion of Bert, is the concept of a disease which afflicts both the joints and the ligaments. It differs from the concept of quarthritis.) Of course, the behavior itself would get somewhat different descriptions depending on which line we took. The point is that these would just amount to different ways of describing the same behavior (explanandum) and the same intentional states (explanans). There is no urgency any longer to the question which concept does KWert really have. No more urgency than there is to asking whether something is three feet or a yard long. The question certainly does not raise the threat of skepticism about meaning and content, once we shed the *ersatz* Platonism which finds my view of concepts unsatisfactory.

The analogy with yards and feet and others analogies like it are commonly invoked in discussions of indeterminacy and underdetermination of meaning, and my invoking it here may, therefore, give a slightly wrong impression. It is not that I am saying that the so-called skeptical paradox is like Quine's problem of the indeterminacy or underdetermination of semantic theory which may be, as it sometimes is, answered by invoking these analogies. There is at least one clear difference in that underdetermination is usually understood as something arising when all possible evidence is in, whereas the whole point of the skeptical paradox is that it arises precisely in situations of limited evidence in which rules have to be given that cover all future uses of the term. My point was only that it did not matter whether KWert should be described in one or the other ways we mentioned above, once he started "going on" in a bizarre and surprising way. If some (non-semantic, non-psychological) part of nature surprised us in a similarly bizarre way we would no doubt try to re-think our system of laws to account for the surprising turn. But holism required that we do so with KWert too by finding systematic ways in which his new usage regarding what he takes to be a certain disease is connected with his uses of other terms in utterances related inferentially with his beliefs about that disease. The point is that if there are systematic changes in all the other related terms, we have a harmless choice between saying he has a new set of rules or meanings for all these terms or we can say that he was all along following the bizarre rules for these terms, such as the rule for "quarthritis." It is true that this does not tell us what to say to the question which rule he or anyone of us is following *now*, given that we *might* go on in bizarre and surprising ways in the future. But once we shed what I am calling the *ersatz* Platonist hankering, that problem becomes just a general problem of how to project on the basis of (limited) evidence. We project in this way in every other empirical discipline, so why should there be a special problem about projection in the attribution of meaning on the basis of behavioral evidence?[41] It is indeed possible that any one of us right now is not really speaking according to the rule for arthritis but rather a bizarre rule akin to the rule for "quarthritis," but that is no different from saying that any projection in any discipline may be overturned. We need not be paralyzed in the theory of meaning from projecting (holistically, of course) on the basis of regularities of usage just because of the possibility of surprising behavior in the future, no more so than the possibility of a failed projection in any other discipline should (or does) paralyze empirical work from formulating a system of generalizations. Only a prior commitment to the normativity of an *ersatz* Platonist view of meaning would make one think the situation is different in the study of meaning.

### Normativity and Naturalism about Meaning are not the only Two Alternatives: Some Confusions about Irreducibility

This discussion of regularities and the deflation of the problem via a comparison with other empirical disciplines may give the impression that I am, after all, a dispositionalist. I have already said something to indicate that that would be a highly misleading impression, given the sort of highly naturalistic associations that come with the term "dispositional." A lot more should be said about this because it is an important point with important consequences, and it is a point which is often missed.

My discussion of regularities and tendencies is not intended to reduce the idea of meaning to something non-intentional. The regularities I have in mind cannot do the work they are supposed to do for me unless they are regularities in intentionally described behavior. I am only resisting the idea that the intentionally described behavior gets its right to being so described on the basis of the very powerful notion of rightness and wrongness which is necessarily supposed to attach to it. Thus it would be misleading to call my view dispositionalist, if that is supposed to mean that an individual's habits of speech or causal dispositions to speech must be fully characterized in non-intentional or, as is sometimes said, "naturalistic" terms.[42] I have no faith in that possibility and my opposition to it is already evident in the anti-foundationalist externalist holism expressed in my discussion of constraint (C) in chapter 1. There is no hope that one will be able to characterize an agent's dispositions to use a word under certain circumstances and account for the exceptions to that use (the use of it in different circumstances) without bringing in intentional or non-naturalistic characterizations, i.e. without bringing in the other intentional states of the agent.[43] I have sometimes used the word "fly" in the presence of black spots. This is easy to account for if one allows one to bring in my other beliefs about what flies look like, what the item in front of me then looked like, etc. My constraint has all along insisted on the appeal to such intentional states anyway. Error in the sense of deviation from regular use may be a problem for those who want to naturalistically reduce meaning and intentionality, but it is not a special problem for me.

Hence my position is distinct both from the naturalistic and reduction-minded dispositionalist as well as from the normativity-demanding position of Kripke and Burge. Those are not the only two options. It is easy to make an elementary confusion and miss this point.[44] It is easy to think that my opposition to the demand for normativity automatically makes me a reductionist.

One can start by insisting on the normativity demand in the sense which leads Kripke (rightly or wrongly) to posit his social view of concepts.[45] (I am emphasizing the normativity demand here, not the social view it leads him to embrace.) And one can say, as Kripke does, that a dispositional account will never capture this normativity. One can then worry that the purely naturalistic dispositional reductionist view of concepts is hopeless on the above grounds that it cannot deal with the manifest fact of exceptions to the regularities. And one can conclude on the basis of the latter criticism of the dispositional view that the normativity demand (which the view also fails to meet) is justified.

The obvious point that this reasoning misses is that granting the failure of this sort of reduction for this sort of reason does not in itself lend support to anything like the demand for the sort of normativity that is driving Kripke and others. The dispositional view is being rejected on two different grounds, but rejecting it on one ground is not a cue that the other ground is compulsory. One could perfectly easily deny the necessity of making the normativity demand on meaning and yet insist on the holistic irreducibility of meaning and content (inherent in may constraint (C)) which repudiates the naturalistic dispositionalist. Thus, defending the non-reductionist view of meaning and intentionality does not by any means constitute a defence of the idea of a notion of meaning based on the demand for the sort of normativity which is driving Kripke.

All that the concession to irreducibility of the intentional gives one is a certain kind of externalist *and* anti-foundationalist holistic conception of the idea of intentionality and meaning.[46] It is the externalist holism which accounts for the exceptions in the regularities, a problem that the pure naturalistic and dispositional view cannot deal with. It is only this externalist holism which spoils the reduction. But there is nothing in the idea of this externalist holism, by itself, which amounts to a capitulation to the normativity demand. Thus it would be a complacency based on a confusion to think that Kripke's demand for normativity has been met if one has established irreducibility of meaning and intentionality. The confusion I am trying to diagnose is, therefore, a result of not keeping apart *two* notions of reduction which are in play.

Here are the two notions. First, it is said that Kripke imposes his demand for normativity in matters of meaning and wishes to ground those norms, or to find the source of those norms, in the dispositions of the community. And it is said that to try to find a source of the norms governing meaning is to seek a reduction of them. We are told that we must resist the very idea of grounding norms in the fear that that will, to put it as John McDowell does, "dig down to a level at which we can no longer have application for normative notions" (McDowell 1986b, p. 63). This is an idea of irreducibility which insists on the *groundlessness* (a certain *sui generis* quality) of the norms which are supposed to be governing the use of terms and the application of concepts, i.e. the groundlessness of what gives us the right to say that Bert has made a mistake when he says "I have arthritis in my thigh" or gives us the right to say that someone has the concept of arthritis rather than quarthritis. John McDowell has been the most eloquent recent proponent of this notion of irreducibility.[47]

The second sort of irreducibility is the one we mentioned above, the idea of the impossibility of characterizing a person's possession of concepts in a way that leaves out the externalist-cum-holistic and non-naturalist dimension in the characterization.

But notice that the idea of the groundlessness of norms is quite different from an externalism's holism-invoking opposition to a naturalistic externalist reduction of meaning. It is easy to run these two irreducibilities together because in Kripke's dialectic so much of the force of the demand for normativity comes from his dissatisfaction with the "dispositionalist" picture. It is true that the naturalistic dispositionalist picture has no place for the sorts of norms that Kripke demands. But it equally has no place for something quite else, it has no place for my version of individualist, regularity-based, intentional, non-naturalistic characterization of the possession of concepts. Affirming the second kind of irreducibility – say, by introducing my constraint on externalism – does not amount to embracing anything about the sort of normativity Kripke and others demand.

Hence, Kripke is not just hostile to the ambitious non-intentional characterization of concept-possession, he is ultimately hostile to an idea of even an intentional and holistic characterization if it denies the importance of normativity as he demands it, if it is individualistic and regularity-based in the sense that I am insisting on. He is not going to accept that irreducibility in the sense given by externalist holism and anti-naturalism is by itself enough to get him the normativity he is demanding.[48] But once we ourselves are clear on this, we may accept one half of his view and reject the other. We may accept that the dispositionalist view is wrong because it leaves out the anti-foundationalist holism, but not accept the rest. It is precisely my claim that it is quite possible to deny that anything like the norms being demanded are necessary for possession of concepts, while insisting on the external, holistic anti-naturalist characterization of those concepts.

It is not that I think, with McDowell, that the normativity being demanded by Kripke is irreducible in the sense of groundless. It is not even that I think, with Kripke, that it is grounded. My efforts to separate out the two notions of irreducibility were not intended either with a view to accepting them both or with a view to accepting one of them and rejecting the other. No, I accept one notion of irreducibility but I neither accept nor reject the other. If I accepted *or* rejected McDowell's notion of irreducibility, I would be accepting that there is something there that is or is not reducible. But I am rejecting the very idea that there are these sorts of norms governing the meanings of terms, rejecting it as a residual Platonist yearning, and that makes me unanxious about the fact that Bert does not, on my view, count as making a mistake. For me, it does not matter if we instead say that he is quite correctly using *his* term "arthritis." The rejection makes me indifferent to the problem that exercises Kripke, the problem that there is no fact of the matter as to whether KWert's concept is arthritis and then (after 1989) tharthritis or whether it is quarthritis all along. For me, it is quite true that there is no fact of the matter about whether any of us right now is following the ordinary rule for our terms or whether for each of our terms we are following the sort of bizarre rules that define the concept of quarthritis. It does not matter to anything we are interested in which rule we say we are following. I can insist that there is no reduction of the intentional to purely causal and non-holistically and non-externalistically characterized dispositions and yet display this indifference and lack of anxiety.

Part of the reason why philosophers fail to keep the two different notions of irreducibility apart is that they have rather blunt and underdescribed ways of thinking of the irreducibility of meaning. It is both tempting and common to describe the idea of irreducibility of meaning bluntly by saying that the fact of the matter about KWert, which would solve Kripke's problem but to which Kripke is blind, is just the fact that KWert *means arthritis by "arthritis."* This is sometimes said in criticisms of Kripke's worries about there being a skeptical problem about meaning. The criticism is that Kripke fails to find this fact of the matter only because he assumes a reductionist attitude toward what could count as a fact of the matter and therefore only looks to such things as inner introspectible, phenomenological states on the one hand or to dispositions on the other. But, the criticism goes on, why not bluntly say that the fact of the matter just is *meaning itself* and not something that falls short of meaning in one or other of the above ways.[49] The fact of the matter just is that KWert means arthritis by "arthritis."

The temptation to say this is perfectly fair but one cannot stop with such a blunt description because unless one says something more about what the expression "meaning itself" means, we are left with something totally unhelpful. "Meaning itself" seems to be nothing but the idea that someone means *arthritis by "arthritis"* and that is altogether unilluminating. It is as unhelpful as the idea of pure disquotation. As argued in chapter 2, one wants to know what it is that the unquoted occurrence of the term conveys, and one cannot make reference so highly metaphysical or disquotation so purely syntactic, that there is no saying anything about what it conveys. Meaning does not have to become mysterious and ineffable just because it is irreducible.

No doubt the response will continue to be that this is to miss the point because if one said anything more, if one appealed to anything more than "meaning itself," one would say something which would reduce meaning to something else, something non-intentional, something naturalistic or phenomenological. The criticism of Kripke, then, is that it is precisely because he misses this point that he worries about a skeptical problem regarding meaning: he thinks you *must* say something more, so turns to these reductionist things, finds them unsatisfactory, and so worries about a skeptical problem regarding meaning. His mistake is supposed to lie in thinking that something more must be said. Nothing more can be said without surrendering to reductionism. Or so this response claims.

But the claim is quite false. One could say something more – thereby going beyond the blunt description of non-reductionism found in the idea of "meaning itself" – without falling into naturalistic or phenomenological idioms. One could point out the place of "arthritis" in a set of other concepts (and therefore beliefs) holistically linked with it and pinned down externalistically as suggested in chapter 1. This would amount to non-reductionism because it would all be in a decidedly intentional idiom since it would make an appeal to other beliefs of the agent. Seeing the place of the concept in this way would take the unhelpfulness out of the assertion that someone means arthritis by "arthritis." Or, to put it differently, it would give us a way of seeing that assertion as a summary or abbreviated way of stating its place in a holistic scheme of concepts and contents. And so for all other such unhelpful seeming assertions.[50]

This move would make the idea of non-reductionist meaning unmysterious and informative but it would do so without making any commitments to a notion of normativity which Kripke demands of meaning. Once we gave this informative characterization to the irreducibilist idea of "meaning itself," this informative substance to the irreducibilist idea that someone *means arthritis by "arthritis,"* we would immediately notice that it is no other than the idea of the externalist anti-foundational notion of irreducibility. It is one of the two irreducibilities mentioned above. But once it is given this informative substance, there is no longer any temptation to run it together with the other irreducibility. That is something we only fell into doing while we did not have an informative and fine-grained way of describing the irreducibility, while we talked of irreducibility in a monolithic and blunt way. The proof of the separability of these two reductions lies in the fact that the non-reductionism given in the informative claim of the last paragraph is perfectly compatible with my total indifference to, with my total denial of the importance of, the question: is KWert following the rule for "arthritis" or "quarthritis. It is thus a non-reductionist notion of meaning which does not provide a fact of the matter to decide that question but rather allows for an indifference to that question. It is also a notion of meaning which is compatible with my not being anxious to say that Bert is making a mistake.

On the other hand, anybody who takes Kripke's notion of normativity seriously cannot be indifferent and unanxious about those things. This notion of normativity gives rise to the prospect or possibility of there being another sense of non-reduction about meaning, the idea that this sense of normativity is ungrounded and *sui generis*. This non-reduction is something over and above the notion of non-reduction which, with its appeal to externalist holism, repudiates a naturalistic reduction. It is intended precisely to provide a fact of the matter to Kripke's question about which rule KWert is following.

So my claim is that it is easy to miss this difference between the two reductions because one has rather unhelpful ways of describing non-reductionist meaning (descriptions such as "he means arthritis by 'arthritis'." ) These descriptions serve two quite different ends.

First, they are intended to be the basis of the misguided protest that if one tries to say anything more about meaning than these unhelpful descriptions, one will give up on the irreducibility (in one sense) of the intentional idiom and turn to purely dispositional or introspectible phenomenological states. As soon as we give substance to the blunt initial descriptions of non-reductionist meaning in the way just mentioned, we can see that we have not turned to such states at all.

And second, they are meant to describe an irreducible notion of meaning (in the other sense) which will also provide a fact of the matter to a question which is a serious question only if one accepts that meaning is essentially normative in a rather powerful sense. This irreducibility insists on the groundlessness of that normativity, and if one embraces it, one rejects not only the naturalistic and phenomenological as being reductionist but one also rejects the externalist, anti-foundationalist and fully intentional, but nevertheless anti-(*ersatz*) Platonist, picture I am endorsing.

And my further claim is that if we unpack these two different non-reductionisms being served by the appeal to this blunt description of non-reductionism, we may then accept my holistic version of non-reduction, and not so much reject the groundlessness or irreducibility of norms but reject that there is anything of that kind to reduce or not reduce. That is, reject the very relevance of such normativity. It is the holistic non-reduction one embraces when one removes the uninformativeness of the blunt formulations of non-reduction along the lines I suggested above. And once one does this, once one displays the informative element and sees what it is exactly that stands in non-reductionist contrast with the strictly dispositional or phenomenological, it will be perfectly clear that this non-reductionist view of meaning is of no more help than the reductionist dispositional and phenomenological views when it comes to providing a fact of the matter to Kripke's skeptical problem: a problem which is only urgent if one is committed to a highly normative conception of meaning.

### What Sorts of Norms are Relevant to Intentionality?

A difference has been stressed between my appeal to regularities in the study of a person's concepts and the strict dispositionalist view which stresses regularities in a quite different sense, a sense in which the regularities are not caught up in an externalist and holistic theory of interpretation of an individual's behavior, as they are for me. Another difference has also been stressed: the difference between my view and Kripke's and Burge's view – my rejection of their normativity demand.

It is important to be clear about what exactly is denied when rejecting the notion of normativity here. There are two points to be made in order to be clear about this. First, I am only denying normativity in a certain domain and, second, even in that domain, I am only denying norms with a high profile. I will elaborate on each of these points in turn.

My rejection of Kripke's Wittgenstein's and Burge's insistence on normativity in the study of the meaning of terms is exactly that: a rejection of normativity in the study of *the meanings of terms*, in matters of the *lexicon*. It should not be taken to imply a similar rejection of normativity in other matters that affect the study of intentionality. Recall that my eventual aim is limited to arguing against the orthodox externalism, and my excursion into the question of normativity was necessitated by the fact that that question has been a motivating force in taking the orthodox externalist view of content. The orthodox externalist view of content, as we saw, appeals to a notion of concepts which, in turn, owes its motivation to the normativity that is supposed to govern the meanings of terms such as "arthritis," "water," "London," etc. These are the sorts of terms to which orthodox externalism addresses itself.[51] Rejecting this motivating normativity governing the meanings of such terms, I reject the orthodox externalist notion of content. But given this limited aim, I need make no anti-normative commitments about other related matters. It is important to be clear about this because it may be that those who have insisted on this normativity about the lexicon may themselves have been led to it by an illegitimate and unnecessary extension of a perfectly legitimate insistence on normativity regarding other matters that affect the intentional.

The point can be put very crudely at first and then qualified. It can be put by saying that I am only rejecting the idea that norms have a very high profile, when it comes to certain matters of *language*.[52] But there may be very good reason to think that the notion of norm has a much higher profile when we are talking, not about the meanings of words, but about the codifications of, say, deductive rationality (or of decision-theoretic rationality, possibly even of inductive rationality). For here we do not leave things to the regularities in the speech behavior of individuals but indeed assess individual behavioral performances themselves in terms of norms which are in place autonomously of such regularities. And, it is fair to conclude, in general, that if something which appears to be a norm is attributed merely on the basis of regularities in an individual's behavior, then it is not a norm in any interesting sense. If it is not derived from or attributed on the basis of such regularities, if it is autonomous from such regularities, then it has more of a right to be called a norm.

By this it is not suggested that when it comes to logical concepts and principles, we should endorse what I have been opposing in Kripke's Wittgenstein's proposal about meanings generally, viz. that the norms involved are determined by the practices of the community. The right thing to say is that they are autonomous in some further sense. This cannot be the place for me to explore the normative status of logic. The idea of the sort of autonomy we might allow for the norms of logic has already been explored in different ways by different philosophers. To take one prominent example, Davidson (1973b) has suggested that we could not make sense of an agent, could not attribute intentional states to him, if we did not see those states as satisfying those norms to a very great extent. This idea certainly puts those norms at an autonomous distance from the regularities in the behavior of individuals since it is a constraint on the very (holistic) assignability of propositional contents to agents based on the observation of their behavioral regularities. In order even to make sense of the regularities we have to impose these norms. We have no choice in the matter. So the norms cannot possibly be based on an observation of those regularities. They form an *a priori* constraint on the very possibility of interpretation. But when it comes to the lexicon, it is perfectly possible to attribute concepts and meanings on the basis of observation of regularities in the behavior of agents.

There is no *compulsion*, therefore, to impose the norms dictated by social practice on an individual agent's concepts and meanings. We do have a choice in the matter. We do have the choice as to whether Bert has the concept of arthritis or tharthritis. We do have a choice as to whether KWert has the concept of arthritis first and then later tharthritis or whether he has had the concept of quarthritis all along. It is possible to account for their behavior no matter which of these alter- natives we attribute to them. It is possible, therefore, to think of our attribution of such concepts as something done (holistically, of course) on the basis of observed regularities. Normativity, thus, simply does not have the same grip in this domain.[53]

That was a crude statement of the point. It needs to be made less crude because there is an obvious objection to it: I have made a distinction between lexical matters or matters having to do with concepts on the one hand and matters of *logical inferential* relations between sentences on the other, but I have failed to mention that there might be *conceptual inferential* relations which are relevant to the lexicon. That is, there might be inferential relations between items of the lexicon. And these too, it might be said, force a normativity which is autonomous from regularities in behavior and which is akin, therefore, to the normativity I am granting to logical matters. The objection is that one cannot distinguish too strictly between the formal norms of logical inference and the material norms of the inferential relations that hold between concepts and meanings; and one cannot do this because it is absurd to suggest that for all the sentences of someone's speech, one knows that this, that and the other sentence are logically related to one another but one does not know what any of them mean. Detection of logical inference in an agent is not altogether independent of detection of material inference.

Nobody can deny this point, but the comparison is inexact to a fault. It is still possible to argue, for instance, that the role that the requirement of (say) logical consistency plays as an *a priori* constraint on interpretation is very different from the role of the requirement which says that in order to have one concept one must have some other beliefs and concepts. The idea of material inference is just the idea that one cannot have a concept (say, the concept of table) without having some other concepts (say, the concept of a middle-sized object). But that merely says I cannot attribute *my* concept of table to someone who fails to have certain other beliefs or concepts. It does not require that any particular concept that *he* has must be the concept dictated by a norm set by my linguistic practice or by social linguistic practice more generally. The former requirement of logical inconsistency, therefore, still seems properly describable as an imposition of norm whereas the latter requirement does not. The latter merely says something rather general, viz. that an agent's concepts are interdependent on other concepts and beliefs; but the former has relatively clear and stable codifications as to what amounts to consistency and what does not. It, therefore, makes much more sense to think of the former as involving norms.

There will be a further protest to be addressed. Someone will say that I have failed to stress the autonomy (from regularities in behavior) that attaches to the idea of material inference. I have merely said that there is an interdependence of any given concept on other concepts. They will say that Davidson himself, whom I have invoked to make the point of the autonomy of logical norms, commits himself to a similar autonomy for lexical norms when he makes his famous (infamous) claim that an interpreter and interpretee, in radical interpretation, must by and large share concepts and beliefs if there is to be interpretation at all. That is, in interpretation, material disagreements or failure of overlap in concepts make sense against a background of agreement and conceptual overlap. So the radical interpreter is (by and large) willy-nilly imposing the material inferential relations between his concepts on to those whom he is interpreting. If this too is being done, not on the basis of the observation of regularities in the interpretee's intentional behavior, but is part of the very idea of making sense of those regularities, then by my own criterion (autonomy from regularities of behavior), one has just as much right to say that normativity governs the domain of concepts and the lexicon as the domain of logic. The idea is that it is not just that there be material inferential relations, nor merely that there be interdependence among an interpretee's concepts, but rather that there be *overlap* between the concepts of the interpretee and interpreter. So the protest is: why not say that the interpreter imposes not just logical norms but also his own concepts and beliefs. Does this not amount to conceding that there are norms of the lexicon? Does it not amount to conceding that both logical and lexical norms are autonomous of regularities in the interpretee's behavior and both are imposed on the regularities of an agent's behavior in order to assign contents at all?

Two initial points may be made in response. First of all, it should be pointed out that the idea of there being conceptual overlap between interpreter and interpretee is not the idea of social externalism at all, it is not the idea of norm that Burge and Kripke have invoked. It is an idea that is essential to certain conceptions of radical interpretation (Davidson's) and radical interpretation is perfectly compatible with individualism. Indeed, it would be to miss out on one of the special points of the very idea of radical interpretation if one practiced it along social externalist lines.[54] Conceding the point of by and large conceptual overlap in radical interpretation gives no comfort to Kripke and Burge's appeal to normativity, nor to the orthodox externalist view of content that their appeal to normativity might be exploited to motivate.[55] Conceding the point does not at all force me to withdraw my claim that there is no serious problem about meaning raised by Kripke's skeptical problem. Nor, if I were radically interpreting Bert, would it force me to say that Bert is making a mistake (when he utters "I have arthritis in my thigh") in the sense of mistake that the orthodox externalists can and want to say that he is making. All I need say, in having made the concession, is that despite by and large conceptual overlap, there is no overlap in this part of our idiolects, the part having to do with "arthritis." There is no further urge to call Bert mistaken as there would be if I, in radical interpretation, had found him guilty of a logical inconsistency. So I would argue that even if it were true that the rationality which one cannot help finding in a radical interpretee is a rationality which involves imposing not only the norms of one's logic but also involves finding a good deal of conceptual overlap between the interpretee's concepts and one's own, it still is unnecessary and wrong to think that there are norms which govern concepts and their linguistic expression in the sense of norms that one must concede in the case of logic.

Second, it is, in any case, a highly controversial claim for many that interpretation requires interpretee and interpreter to by and large share concepts and beliefs. Many have insisted on much more minimal *a priori* constraints on interpretation. But, even apart from these two points, even if we grant that there must be considerable conceptual overlap, and even if we put aside the difference between Kripke and Burge's idea of norms and Davidson's idea of conceptual overlap, it may still be possible to retain our qualms about seeing the lexicon as governed by norms. It may still be possible to say that Bert is not even violating a non-social norm, not even violating a norm generated by my (the radical interpreter's) idiolectical linguistic practice. I do not have a strict argument here, no strict criterion of the difference between the genuine norms of deductive rationality and the so-called (in my view spurious) norms of the lexicon, but I will briefly try to convey a rough sense of the difference.

One way of conveying it is to look at the different character of the exceptions to or violations of the "norms" in the two cases. When someone (an interpretee) falls short of deductive rationality, it is perfectly clear in advance what the norms will have to be which are violated. When there is a failure of conceptual overlap, that is, when there is disagreement in material inference, there are no such norms, clearly stateable in advance, which are violated. For if there are norms involved at all in the domain of material inference, then which one is violated in the case of a failure of overlap will differ with each particular failure. By my lights, some interpretee may violate the norm for "snow" by thinking that snow was warm, another by thinking that it was green, yet another by thinking that it grew underground, and so on and on. Things are not like that with failures of deductive rationality.

With regard to violations of deductive rationality, we can say something thing like:

*There is a norm, such that for any violation of deductive rationality, it is a violation of that norm.*

But, if I am right, with regard to the failure of conceptual overlap one has to say something quite different, something more like:

*For any failure of conceptual overlap (or material inference), there is a norm, such that the failure is a violation of that norm.*

This shift in the quantifier makes vivid what the difference is. It is only apparently the case that there are norms governing concepts, because – as the example of "snow" above makes clear – the material inferential relations that fail to hold, in the cases of failure of conceptual overlap, are so highly contextual, so highly situated in each given case that there is no sense in which it is useful or necessary to call them norms and to say that it is norms that are being violated. On the contrary, logical norms are highly context-free and one can say quite exhaustively and in advance what the principles are that are being violated in the case of logical failure.[56]

Here, two points must be made by way of qualification. First, I am assuming, as I have in chapter 2, that there is no clear analytic-synthetic distinction. If there were analytic truths, and in some uninteresting cases there may be,[57] then there would be clear norms governing concepts (norms of the lexicon) and the violations of material inferences would not be subject to the same situatedness as they are when there is no commitment to analyticity. Second, indeterminacy about some of the logical norms slightly spoils the distinction I am making between them and the so-called norms of the lexicon, but it would be utter hyperbole to think that they spoil it to the extent that the distinction loses its point. Both these qualifications may show that there is a spectrum rather than a sharp distinction. But the rough sense of the distinction between the genuineness and the spuriousness of norms in these different domains can be conveyed by looking at the two ends of the spectrum. If one just considers the principle of non-contradiction at one end and the so-called rule for "snow" at the other, it should be absolutely obvious what the distinction amounts to.

So, nothing about lexical norms follow even if we grant the Davidsonian point that if there is massive failure of conceptual overlap in interpretation one has violated an *a priori* constraint of rationality on interpretation. The *a priori* demands for logical consistency are wholly unlike this sort of *a priori* constraint. The latter does not warrant the claim that the meaning of our terms are governed by norms in a way that the former shows that thoughts are governed by a norm of logic. It is much more reasonable to say instead that particular cases of failure of conceptual overlap are not a violation of norms but just a matter of there being different meanings and concepts. That is exactly what has been said about Bert against Burge and the orthodox externalist. Considerations of normativity, therefore, fail to show my view of content to be wrong.

If I am right, then even this concession to the necessity of by and large conceptual overlap in interpretation does not amount to saying that the necessity issues from an imposition of norms in the way that the necessity for finding by and large logical consistency does. One could still continue to think of the concepts an agent has and the meanings of his terms as being given by a theory based on the regularities in his intentional behavior regarding the use of terms, while granting as a general constraint – but with no isolable and no very specific substance – that such a theory is bound to come up with by and large conceptual overlap. In particular, concession to the idea of a necessary overlap in beliefs and concepts does not fetch any concession to the idea that agents like Bert should be counted as making a mistake, an idea central to the orthodox externalist notion of content.

A number of philosophers appear to have unconsciously run together (or at any rate assumed an easy extension of) the undeniable normativity that attaches to the principles of logic and what they take unjustifiably to be the normativity ("rules") governing the meanings of words. I have tried also to diagnose why they should unconsciously fall into this assumption by looking to the similar status both sorts or norms might be thought to have as prerequisites for successful interpretation.[58] And I have criticized them for it. The work that the former kind of norm does as an *a priori* constraint on attribution of intentionality is wholly different from whatever work it is that the alleged norms of the latter kind are supposed to do. If I am right, the latter certainly do not get imposed as norms on those who are attributed intentionality in the clear sense that the former do. So it is not clear what rationale there could be for the idea that there are norms governing the use of words in the way that philosophers such as Kripke, Burge and McDowell claim.

The fact that the former are imposed as norms does make intentionality the sort of thing that is normatively constituted, and it does put into doubt that we can study intentional states and the behavior they explain on the model of the natural sciences.[59] Hence my earlier talk of there being no important difference between the study of semantics and the study of physical nature must be seen as restricted to the point about how the meanings of terms need not involve norms and need only involve regularities of intentional behavior. It was not meant to deny normativity altogether in the study of mind and it was not, in turn, meant to deny a significant difference between the study of mind and the study of physical nature. The point I will insist on is that since the normativity I have granted spoils the idea of a strict science of the mind, it is perfectly possible to oppose the norms regarding the lexicon, as I have, and yet rightfully make a claim *not* to have fallen into some scientistic conception of the mental. The acknowledgment that the former sense of normativity is a genuine sense and constitutive of intentionality is by itself sufficient for not having fallen into it. Normativity regarding the meanings of terms is not necessary to avoid the scientism. Scientism about the mind simply does not follow from a rejection of the normativity that Kripke and Burge are demanding.

Philosophers such as McDowell have criticized Kripke's "skeptical solution," despite his insistence on the latter sense of norms, because they think his appeal to communal dispositions in the solution has failed to live up to his own demand for such norms. They therefore claim that he too, in the solution, has succumbed to a scientistic conception of the mind. This does not follow. It may be true that Kripke is guilty of not living up to his own attack on dispositional answers to the skeptical problem because he goes on to invoke communal dispositions; but even if it were true, that does not mean that he ever had in mind to invoke dispositions in a naturalistic and reductionist sense, nor that he would deny that the *former* sense of (genuinely autonomous) norms govern the behavior of individuals. Again the point is that even if he has really failed to live up to the demand for normativity in the lexicon, it does not mean that he has succumbed to scientism about the mind. It is only a failure to keep apart the relevant sense of norms from the irrelevant latter idea of lexical norms that would tempt one to say that it does mean that.

Does all this mean that I am committed to saying that there is absolutely no sense of norm attaching to matters of the *lexicon* on my picture of intentionality?

That, of course, depends on what one means or intends by the term "norm." So long as one is clear that it is not the sense of norm that is driving Kripke, Burge and McDowell and others, I am happy to admit that there are norms with a much lower profile at play in the unified, individualist picture of intentionality. To repeat, what I am denying is only the conception of norms which drives either the anxieties about being able to say that Bert is making a mistake or which finds a skeptical problem in KWert. For that is the conception of norms that motivate the desire to posit "wide" content.

What sense of norm, then, is acceptable for the lexicon? This question can be answered in two stages.

*First*: I have already mentioned a sense of norm which is embodied in the notion of individual lexical competence based on (as opposed to autonomous from) the regularities of (intentionally described) individual linguistic behavior. These regularities will have exceptions, which are often pronounced to be "mistakes," as when someone calls an element in a class of things by a name he usually reserves for a quite different class of things, as in my example of "fly." The holistic constraint on regularities allows us to count these things as errors. If this means that it allows for norms, then so be it (though see the second point below for how odd it is to call what it allows "norms"). The explanations for such errors, however, will be very different from the explanation Burge gives for Bert's error. They may point out that the agent has been distracted or that he has been forgetful of how he has used the term in the past. Or, as in the case of the fly, it might be that he has misperceived the object. In Burge's example, his explanation of Bert's error was that Bert does not fully grasp what his own concept of arthritis is. My account has no place for errors based on such a description of Bert's concepts. Indeed, it denies that the facts about Bert's mind can be described that way at all.

But even allowing this sense of norms and this sense of mistakes might seem inconsistent to some. They may raise the following internal objection to my view. Take an example of the sort of mistake I am allowing. Suppose that an agent who has regularly used "arthritis" to talk of joints, says "I have arthritis in my thigh." The explanation may be that he is distracted and confused or forgetful of something that the regularities of his past behavior show him to know perfectly well, i.e. that arthritis is a disease of the joints only. The internal objection is that having denied Burge the right to say that Bert was mistaken, I should deny myself the right to call this a mistake on the agent's part. Just as I said that if Bert never knew that arthritis was a disease of the joints only, then he is not making any mistake because he does not have that concept of arthritis, so also I should be prepared to say that if he has been momentarily distracted and forgotten that arthritis is a disease of the joints only, then he has not made a mistake because he does not have the concept of arthritis *at that moment*. I should be prepared to say that at that moment he has a new meaning. Of course, we can only say this if he has made corresponding adjustments in all related meanings as the holistic constraint would demand. But, the objection would say, let us assume that he has made those changes. I cannot protest that if we observed and interrogated him he would reveal that he has not made those other changes and would therefore realize that he had made a mistake after all. This protest fails to see that the objection really is insisting on momentary meanings and these further interrogations and observations only reveal that he has gone back to his old meanings. The point of the objection is that at the point that the agent was distracted he really had a new meaning even if he reverts to the older ones again later. At that point we must assume that there are those other corresponding changes which meet the holistic constraint. At that moment there is an assumption of a whole new flood of momentary meanings. The holistic constraint is met and therefore cannot by itself rule out this objection. After all we have rejected calling up a background of *other* peoples' linguistic practices to judge an individual's error, so why not disallow the individual's own past regularities and future behaviors to judge his error on a particular occasion?

There is a serious question as to whether the holistic constraint can be met in the way the objection claims. It is possible that the very idea of holistic constraints requires the stabilities in behavior that the objection is denying as being necessary to meaning and belief. But even if that were not so, it is still possible to answer the objection by making a different, though not unrelated, point. The answer is simply that it is not compulsory to call it an error if one does not wish to. That is part of what it is to take my relaxed attitude to norms in these matters. But despite this, there is still a crucial distinction between the appeal to individual stabilities and the appeal to the community. Whether we call it an error or not, we cannot deny that were it not for the regularities in the individual's behaviors we would not be able to interpret him at all, we would not be able to attribute any meanings or concepts or contents to him. Without them we would have to abandon the distinction between semantics and pragmatics as well as the distinction between semantic competence and performance. These distinctions are based on a fact, the fact that individuals are more or less stable and regular in the way they use terms.[60] However, though this is a contingent fact about us, that does not mean that it is not a fact which is absolutely necessary for the intelligibility of those of whom the fact holds. If it did not hold, we would not be able to interpret their speech nor count them as linguistic agents.

Without regularities and stabilities in the speech of an individual agent, we would have to interpret his speech, performance by performance. This would leave us no basis or reason even to see each performance as composed of words, the thought as composed of concepts and so on. Any assignment of thoughts to an agent, any theory of interpretation of his speech must fulfill certain well-known theoretical desiderata. Such a theory or assignment must be finite and it must account for the fact that we understand sentences we have never encountered before. I will not elaborate on these desiderata because that would take us too far afield and because ever since Chomsky first announced them they are, in any case, very well known. Suffice it to say that in order to fulfill these desiderata we cannot solve for each sentence's meaning, utterance by utterance. We have to have a theory of sentence-meaning, of literal meaning, and to do this we have to have a theory of the parts of sentences, a theory of the meanings of words or of concepts.[61] Such a theory cannot therefore countenance that *all* deviance from past regularities can themselves be accounted for by the theory as new meanings rather than genuine deviances or "mistakes." That would force one to look at each utterance case by case and, therefore, to fail to meet the desiderata. hence, since these are desiderata for a theory of interpretation or meanings, the very idea of the interpretability of agents' meanings requires that we find in these agents, regularities in the use of their terms.

The situation is quite distinct for the linguistic practices of his community and its experts from what it is for the stabilities of individual behavior. These practices are not an essential requirement for the interpretation of an individual and are not a necessary precondition for the assignment of content to him. We can interpret someone who does not speak as others in her community do and we can, in principle, interpret a community of one. The contrasting point just made is that the theoretical desiderata mentioned above make clear that by and large regularity and stability in individual verbal behavior are essential to the very idea of attributing meaning and concepts. And not even Burge and Kripke can deny these theoretical desiderata. There is nothing analogous to which would make clear that the *social* practices are essential.

The moral to be drawn here is that one cannot fully extend the critique I have been making in which I have stressed the idea of the individual over the social, to a further critique in which one stresses the idea of the individual at a given moment over the *abiding individual*. This is quite simply because the idea of an abiding individual, defined as it is by the *stabilities* of individual speech and behavior, is not something we can do without in the attribution of speech and propositional attitudes to an individual. But none of this is a surrender to the demand of normativity we are discussing. The thesis that there are such general theoretical reasons to think that there must be by and large stabilities and regularities in an individual's linguistic behavior in order for her to be interpretable at all, cannot possibly be equivalent to the thesis about norms governing her use of particular terms that Kripke, Wittgenstein and McDowell are insisting on. I say a little more about this below.

*Second:* The sense of norms that can be accepted emerges from the fact that individuals *intend* to speak like others in the community speak and they intend to speak as they have in the past rather than waywardly.[62] This means that individuals do intend to speak in a way that is natural to describe as, and that they themselves describe as, *correctly*. Bert or the agent we just considered above would no doubt himself say that he was using words incorrectly when, respectively, he was informed by the doctor or when he got over his momentary distraction and memory loss. But, if my critique of the normativity demand is just, in both cases this can now be understood as pointing to norms in a much more low-profile sense of norms than Kripke and Burge's sense. And this is a sense of norms that emerges from the pragmatic explanations I gave for the fact of widespread deference among individual agents to the ways of speech of their communities.

Recall that Burge argues that the only satisfactory way to account for the ubiquitous phenomenon of deference is to take the social practice as constitutive of the individual's concepts. And I alternatively suggested (in the last section) that it was perfectly adequate to account for deference by giving such pragmatic reasons as: the individual defers to others around him because he wants to be understood by them without strain. These explanations have the following relevance to the question of normativity. To the extent that such explanations are true, one can conclude that individual agents tacitly operate linguistically with the following norm: "speak as others in the community do," a norm so obvious that we never make it explicit until we leave our own communities and go to others ("When in Rome..."). Now this is a norm that an individualist view can invoke to judge all the cases that Burge and Kripke count as errors to genuinely be errors. Bert, for instance, has violated *this* norm by not using the word arthritis as his fellows do.

However, once one sees the norm as motivated by pragmatic reasons, there is no reason to think that Bert has the same concept as his fellows. It is not that Bert possesses the same concept as his fellows and has made the mistake of misapplying a concept he possesses, rather he has made the mistake of not speaking as his fellows do, not having the same meaning and concept as his fellows when that is what he intended to do and have. It is a mistake because it violates a norm that tacitly instructed him against this. Thus we not only have a normative element in the individualist picture of content, we have a norm that is in fact perfectly sensitive to the social linguistic practices that surround an individual. But the pragmatic explanations underlying this norm make clear that it is a norm in a sense that is quite different from the one that Burge says is violated by Bert. It is an extrinsic norm which necessarily has a hypothetical formulation. It says "Speak like others do, *if it pays to do so*," or more specifically it might say "I ought to use words as others do, *if I want to be easily understood*." [63] Moving from Bert who deviates from social linguistic practices to the agent who departs from his own regularities, he too has a conditional norm which he violates. The norm says, "I ought to use words as I have used them in the past, if I want to be easily understood." [64] And to speak as I have in the past (or as others do), in turn, of course, means that I ought to use the word "fly" or "arthritis" to talk of this sort of thing rather than that or any other sort of thing.

These norms are necessarily hypothetical. If this is right, the idea that we *ought* to use the word *x* and not *y* to convey… because that is what *x means*, is strictly reducible to the idea that we ought to use *x* to convey that because we have done so in the past (or because others do so) and therefore using them will allow us to convey it without causing strain. The connection between "ought" and "mean" here is none other than this low-profile connection. The normativity involved, if it is strictly reducible in this way to something extrinsic like this, is certainly not groundless or *sui generis*. It is firmly grounded in our desire to communicate without strain.

In a sense, then, I am not denying that as philosophers interested in meaning our interest is not only in what KWert and Bert regualrly say but what it is they should or ought to say. But I insist that to say that is to say something that is very different from what the *ersatz* Platonist has said.

The "oughts" I am admitting are hypothetical and extrinsic in the sense that if one has a certain end and a certain view of the means to achieve the end then one ought to pursue those means. There is nothing special about the normativity which attaches to the meanings of words. Meanings are normative in the sense that a lot of other things might be: such as that I ought to play with a straight bat if I do not want to get caught in the slips, or that I ought to listen to songs by Hugo Wolf or the Cure if I want to get depressed. Similarly, there are certain things I ought to do if I want to be easily understood: I ought to speak as I have in the past or I ought to speak like others do. And, of course, in turn, if I want to speak as I have in the past or like others do, I ought to use words in some ways and not others. The point of these hypothetical, extrinsic norms is that neither intentionally conforming to others usage nor even intentionally sticking to the past ways of one's own usage, is a sign that meaning has an essential or primary aspect of correct and incorrect usage. The entire notion of correctness is entirely secondary to the desire and intention to communicate without causing strain, which underlies the notion of meaning.

My talk of hypothetical imperatives and of ends and means to describe my position on norms is a little misleading since "If you want to speak *English*, do not apply 'arthritis' to diseases of the ligaments" is hypothetical in form also and it too may be seen in terms of ends and means. But *qua* imperative it appeals to something intrinsic to language, it appeals to rules of language. It says that one ought to say *x* rather than *y* in certain circumstances because that is what *x* means. Meaning is the resting point in the unpacking of this ought. But it is not the resting point for me. My hypothetical imperatives appeal to something extrinsic, something it pays to do, such as not causing strain in understanding. So it is hypothetical *extrinsic* norms that I am stressing.

For me, in the end, all hypothetical imperatives of the kind "If you want to use the term *x* in a regular way you ought to use it under circumstances *c*" are imperatives which are necessarily grounded in another imperative: "And you ought to use term *x* in a regular way, if you want to be easily understood." This pragmatic element introduced by such expressions as "easily understood" or "understood without strain" is a very important part of my way of thinking of the norms. If I had left this element out and instead said "You ought to use *x* in a regular way, if you want to be understood," that would still be to appeal to an intrinsic consideration because it would be too much like resting with unpacking of the ought in the notion of meaning. Why do I insist on the extrinsic, pragmatic qualifications to the idea of understanding in these imperatives? Because it is a plain fact that for any given term, I *can* be understood even when I do not use it in a regular way. It is just that I will probably cause strain and not be understood easily. I may make a listener sit up, but its use can, with effort, be understood.

If it was not clear from earlier in this section, it should be clear by now that my attack on norms is not restricted to the norms of social externalism. The last paragraph extends the attack to individualism too, if the demand for individual regularities is viewed in the wrong way. Social externalism as one finds it is motivated by a demand for intrinsic norms of meaning but even an individualist who demands only individual regularity can slip into *ersatz* Platonism and demand an intrinsic view of norms. I have opposed that demand as well because the target of my attack in this section is not social externalism in particular but an *ersatz* Platonism about norms.

Someone might protest at my insistence on bringing in the pragmatic element into the norms on the following ground. They might say that an individual must behave in regular ways not just in order to be understood without strain, but to be generally understood at all. If there was not by and large regularity and stability in our linguistic usage we would not generally be understood at all and would not be counted as linguistic agents. I do not deny this last point and have, in fact, made the point myself in the discussion above of the Chomskyan desiderata imposed on the notion of meaning and understanding. However, the point does not support the protest at all. A claim about how for us to be *generally intelligible* there must be *by and large regularity* in our usage does not in any way contradict the point just made that in any given case, one may use a term which is not in accord with any regularity and yet be understood. The crucial point is that norms attach to *particular terms and they assess usage for correctness and incorrectness on particular occasions*. They allow us to say such things as "You ought to use the word 'water' as you have in the past" or "Bert used 'arthritis' incorrectly when he said 'I have arthritis in my thigh.'" And I am denying that there need be anything as specific needed to be generally understood. I can use a term once and never use it again and be understood on that occasion. I have said "The gavagai is too loud" and found that a friend of mine (who had never heard the sound "gavagai" before) turned the volume of the radio down; there is the famous story about a Cambridge philosopher who is supposed to have smiled politely as she was leaving a party and said "Fuck you very much" to the hosts, who we can imagine said "Come again." Examples can and have been multiplied.[65] I have never before used the term "gavagai" in such circumstances and probably never will. For all I know the Cambridge philosopher never uttered the word "fuck" at all in any circumstance before or since that occasion. So: no need for regularity with any given term in order to be understood. Of course, the utterances of these terms would not have been understood without a background of regular usage of a lot of other terms, but that is a general requirement which does not yield any particular norm for any particular term, no specific intrinsic lexical imperative such as "Use 'gavagai' under conditions... if you want to be understood!" Not even "Use the word 'loud' under conditions... if you want to be understood." The concession to by and large regularity needed for the intrinsic goal of general intelligibility does not translate at all into a claim about how one ought to follow this or that norm in order to be understood. And the latter is all I am denying is necessary for understanding and meaning. The latter is all that deserves to be called "a norm." I deny what Burge, Kripke and McDowell are demanding when they say that we should be able to call this or that idiosyncratic usage mistaken (whether idiosyncratic given social practice as in Bert or KWert or idiosyncratic given one's own by and large regular usages of other terms, as in the examples just given). Nothing but philosophical conflation and confusion is gained by insisting that the sort of thing they demand (norms for the meaning of words) in the examples and paradoxes they devise is the same as the demand that there be by and large regularity in our linguistic usage in order for us to be understood and counted as linguistic agents. Conceding by and large regularity for the intrinsic but general goal of intelligibility, therefore, does not in any way compromise my denial of intrinsic norms.

The only lexical norms I admit, the only imperatives directing usage of particular terms (and assessing individual usage for correctness) which I allow, are in the end supported by extrinsic and pragmatic considerations. The *ersatz* Platonist picture in Burge's and Kripke's views demands a more intrinsic sense of lexical norm. It demands that Bert and all the others we have been discussing be counted as mistaken but not just because they strain or mislead others (and because they have a tacit norm directing them not to strain or mislead them). Burge and Kripke do not cite these sorts of things as the reason for finding them mistaken. From their point of view these reasons for counting them mistaken would be far too instrumental. Their reasons for appealing to the social as constitutive, for rejecting an extrinsic regularity-based account of concepts like mine, makes clear that their protagonists are counted by them as mistaken because they have violated something more constitutive and intrinsic to the idea of meaning. Therefore, the idea of extrinsic hypothetical norms will not count as norms at all for the *ersatz* Platonist. They will not have a high enough profile. From his point of view one either has intrinsic norms or one has given up on normativity. If so I have given up on normativity.

114        *Society and Norm*

### Norms and Robinson Crusoe

The discussion of the first Section of this chapter closed by saying that I would not have fully argued against social externalism unless I took care of some of the motivations for it that it shares with the other orthodox externalisms. The second section turned to one such motivation: the motivation from normativity. If I am right in the argument of this section, that motivation is a bad one and I have, to that extent, redeemed my pledge and given a fuller argument against social externalism. To the same extent, then, my individualistic externalism stands vindicated.

Individualistic externalism, as previously stated, makes a distinction between the public nature of meaning and content and their social nature as proposed by the social externalism of Burge and Kripke. It does not necessarily deny social features of meaning, such as the individuals's reliance on other speakers or his deference to them. It does not deny them because it is unwise for anybody to deny facts. But it insists that these facts ought not to be exploited to erect the constitutive thesis of social externalism. It gives the facts of reliance and deference a quite different significance which is compatible with individualistic externalism. Now a question arises: if individualism is true and if reliance and deference are merely contingent facts with no constitutive significance, is it not possible that there be a solitary speaker with no society, who has meanings and contents? Or, to put it as it has often been put in the discussion of these themes: can Robinson Crusoe be said to have meanings and thoughts? Not, of course, the Robinson Crusoe of Defoe's novel who was a fictionalized version of the grown man Alexander Selkirk brought up in English society, but a Crusoe who has never had any society.

It would seem that there is no reason why my individualistic externalism should withhold meaning and thought from such a person if he produced a level of complexity of behavioral reactions to the world around him, and if we could with sufficient observation and interchange (the sort of interchange familiar from radical interpretation and presupposed in my constraint (C)) come up with a holistic theory of this behavior. It is surprising, therefore, to learn that Kripke (1982, p. 110) is also prepared to allow belief and meaning to such a Crusoe.[66]

How could he allow it, given that he thinks that the meanings of a person's words are constituted by the social practices of his fellows? Has he not insisted on something stronger in his skeptical solution to his own skeptical paradox? Is he, then, weakening the claim made there and allowing now for a position which is basically individualistic, a position in which the social nature of language is no longer distinguishable from the public nature of language as spelt out in the last section? Is he conceding that the strong sense of norms which for him is only given by the appeal to the social, is now no longer an essential part of meaning?

It is very hard to say, since he does not say anything very specific about what exactly he has in mind in allowing such a Crusoe meaning. But he certainly presents it as if it is of a piece with the social constitutive point he makes in the skeptical solution and there is no indication that he thinks that point is being weakened. Yet it is hard to see how it is not weakened. This will be briefly explored in order to round out this discussion of normativity and its relevance to meaning and belief.

Kripke says that Crusoe can be attributed thoughts and meanings if we can "take him into our community and apply our criteria of rule following to him" (1982 p. 110). Much of the problem is that it is not wholly clear what the phrase "take him into our community" is supposed to convey. Kripke says hardly anything about it in the short paragraph in which the phrase occurs. Does it mean that Crusoe follows the rules we follow if he utters the sounds we do in roughly the same circumstances we would utter them in? If so, that may be all right,[67] though it does seem a fantastic coincidence that he should utter the same sounds if he has not had any interactions with us, i.e. since the pragmatic and historical explanations I mentioned while discussing deference will not be in play, there is no sensible explanation for him uttering the same sounds.

The phrase "take him into our community," however, is presumably intended to cover cases where he makes quite different sounds. Here, if I were to take him into my community, that means I must be able to provide translations of his sounds into mine on the basis of observations of the patterns of circumstance under which he makes his sounds, and which allow me to correlate them with my sounds. This would be just good old radical interpretation. But it is not clear, as pointed out in the last section in the discussion of Quine, that this requires or forces accepting anything like the general view about the social constitution of meaning, which we get from Burge or Kripke's skeptical solution.

It allows, for instance, that I can take Crusoe's sound or word, let us say "gavagai," to be a word for a certain disease with certain characteristics and which afflicts the joints and ligaments. (Let us imagine that he uses "gavagai" in the same circumstances that Bert uses "arthritis," i.e. he uses it to talk of afflictions in his knee and his thigh.) And it allows this whether I come from a community in which there is a word "arthritis" which takes a disease with just those characteristics to be one that occurs in the joints only or whether I come from a community in which the word is taken to stand for a disease that is supposed to afflict joints and ligaments. If the latter I will translate "gavagai" into my "arthritis." If the former I will not and will translate it into a longer expression, say, "a disease which has characteristics... and which afflicts joints and ligaments." (If I wanted to avoid the longer phrase, I might coin a new word in my own language and think of myself as having acquired a new complex concept. There is nothing in the idea of radical interpretation that disallows any of this.) Whether I belong to the former or the latter community, in neither case will Crusoe be counted as mistaken about anything, whereas Bert on the social externalist view was said to be mistaken when the community standard for correct use was generated by the former sort of community. Thus a radical interpreter from either community can interpret Crusoe by "taking him into his community," without conceding anything to social externalism, without any surrender of individualistic externalism.

So if the phrase "taking him into our community" amounts to something like what radical interpretation permits us to set out to achieve, and if I am right that radical interpretation is compatible with individualism, then Kripke's skeptical solution's appeal to what he there calls an agent's "wider community" can be made to drop out of the picture. It can be made to collapse with my individualist externalist picture sketched in the last section. If Kripke, then, still wishes to retain the skeptical solution's claim, he cannot take the line on how to translate Crusoe suggested in the last paragraph. He must either abandon his idea that Crusoe may be allowed to have meanings and thoughts or he must take some other line on how to translate Crusoe.

But what other line could he take? There are two alternative lines he could take. Remember that his reading of Wittgenstein emphaiszed the normativity that was supposed to be essential to meaning, the possibility of finding usage correct or mistaken. So the alternative lines must see to it that the phrase "take into one's community" is made to relate to the idea of judging for correctness or mistakenness by the norms or standards of one's community. The two alternative lines are these.

First, assuming the interesting case where I belong to the former sort of community,[68] Kripke could say that I must not, as suggested above, translate "gavagai" into the longer expression, but instead I must translate it into "arthritis" and see Crusoe as making a mistake, when he says things that I would translate as "I have arthritis in my thigh."

This reading of the phrase "take him into our community" would indeed fit in with his (and Burge's social externalist) position on the non-Crusoe case. There is, however, an oddity in judging someone to be mistaken when he says this sort of thing, if he is not even a member of my community. And even apart from the question of judging him to be mistaken, one cannot even bring in deference and reliance in the use of his words (i.e. one cannot brings in the motivations for social externalism considered in the last section). That too would present an oddity. His deference and reliance would have to be on us the translators but that is absurd since we are not members of his community.

Second, Kripke could accept the implausibilities of the first line just pointed out and say instead that if I, the translator, belong to the former sort of community, then, at least as far as "gavagai" goes, I simply cannot "take Crusoe into my community." He could say that when the phrase "taking into one's community" is properly understood along social externalist lines, it would not allow the fragment of Crusoe's speech being considered as something covered by the phrase. A social externalist conception of norms would have it that the norms of my community would judge Crusoe's assertion that a disease which has characteristics... has afflicted his thigh, to be a mistake, were he a member of it. But, by definition, he is not a member of it. He is not relying on members of the community and their expertise, he does not defer to them nor is there any reason to think that he will defer if told everything. So that must mean that his assertion, since it cannot be judged a mistake, must be treated as something which leads me to say that he cannot be taken into my community. If we do not adopt the first line, then this is the only way to retain the Kripkean reading of Wittgenstein and its insistence on the social.

But this second line leads to a strangely relativistic result because presumably somebody from a relevantly different community from mine (where the term is used to cover a wider class of ailments) *could* "take him into his community." This means that by one community's lights Crusoe's term means something and by another's it means nothing at all. I assume from the other detailed assertions and commitments in his book that Kripke would find this relativistic result highly undesirable.

To sum up the discussion so far: my individualism allows that Crusoe has thoughts and meanings. Surprisingly, Kripke allows it too, despite the social externalism of his skeptical solution. I have argued that this is a surrender of the anti-individualist line he takes in the skeptical solution to his own skeptical problem. The crucial phrase in Kripke's allowing Crusoe to have thoughts is that he has them if he can be "taken into our community." Suppose Crusoe uses "gavagai" in the same circumstances that Bert uses "arthritis" and suppose I come from a community in which "arthritis" is used to talk of a disease of the joints only. What interpretation would my individualistic picture give to phrase like "take him into our community?" On my picture there is no difficulty in my "taking Crusoe into my community" since I will simply translate "gavagai" into the longer expression, mentioned earlier. In my picture, recall, an agent like Bert was allowed to have his own idiosyncratic concept of arthritis, a certain sort of disease of the joints and ligaments. For me the analogue of saying this of Crusoe is the position which allows his "gavagai" to be translated into my longer expression "a disease which has the features... and which afflicts joints and ligaments."

But the anti-individualist picture cannot say this of Crusoe. If he did, there is no way Crusoe could ever make a mistake of the kind that Kripke has said is essential to meaning. Kripke, therefore, better find something else to say of Crusoe. He could say one of two alternative things about how I should translate Crusoe. He could say that I should translate his "gavagai" into my "arthritis" and count some of his uses of the term as being mistakes. Or he could say that for that fragment of his speech I cannot "take him into my community." These are the only ways to make Kripke's remarks about Crusoe consistent with his socially oriented skeptical solution to the rule-following paradox. And I have said why both lines of response are most implausible. We can therefore conclude that the idea of normativity that fuels his social externalism cannot give any plausible reading to his phrase compatible with his position on Crusoe. One can only conclude that he has in mind to take the position I am taking on Crusoe, where one translates his "gavagai" into the longer expression. If so, his position on Crusoe is a surrender to a position which is compatible with individualistic externalism. It is a position to which only the public is central and not the social.[69] Thus, though Kripke in the skeptical solution presents the public character of meaning as something made possible only by an appeal to social or communal practices, the only plausible way of reading his own position on Crusoe is proof that that is not compulsory. His own position on Crusoe is proof that the separation of the public and the social as made in the last section is a coherent and viable way of thinking of meaning and intentionality.

What his position on Crusoe allows is that an agent may be attributed intentional states and meaning in a way that yields no concessions to the anxiety that Bert must be judged as making a mistake rather than having his own idiosyncratic meaning. It allows a view that has no place for the anxiety that KWert's behavior raises a skeptical paradox. It only requires that an agent must be attributed meaning by someone else's lights and that (given my commitment to publicness) is not something my individualism need deny. It does not require that any attributor judge the agent to be right or wrong in the use of a term because the agent may not even belong to the community of an attributor.

Notice also that the logic (or the "grammar" , as Wittgenstein would say) of allowing all this is that the someone else's lights need not be a whole community, but himself a Crusoe-like figure. For, once Crusoe is admitted in as an attributee, then there is no need to deny that the attributor himself is a solitary linguistic agent, since whatever justifies allowing us to say that the former is a linguistic agent can justify allowing us to say that the latter is one.

### Norms and Two

Now, of course, it is possible that someone will say that what Burge and Kripke really had in mind all along – even in the non-Crusoe cases of Bert and KWert – was not to embrace the social in the sense that I have been representing them; that all along they had in mind a sense of social which said merely this: in order to have meaning and belief at all, in order even to attribute meaning and belief to an agent holistically on the basis of the *individual* stabilities and regularities I have been restricting myself to, one would need to see the agent by the lights of other people, at the minimum, one other person. That is what Kripke meant by the phrase "taking an agent into one's community" and that is all he had in mind even in the non-Crusoe cases. That is all he had in mind in his appeal to the community in his skeptical solution to his skeptical problem. So the claim would be that there is no inconsistency between the stand Kripke takes on Crusoe and his stand in the skeptical solution to his skeptical problem. What Kripke and Burge had in mind all along in their appeal to the "community" was just that there be at least two people, the attributor and the attributee of beliefs and meanings. This is a much weaker relevance of the social factor to belief and meaning than I have all along represented them as claiming. It only requires two people, and so each of them could be like Robinson Crusoe, since they need not even belong to the same community.

This simply cannot, however, be what Kripke and Burge really had in mind, since this weakened, two-person view of the social does not have any place for a sense of norm that forces us to say that Bert is making a mistake (or forces us to see KWert as raising a genuine skeptical anxiety). As we have already seen in the Crusoe case, this view of the social can perfectly well take an agent like Bert to have his own concept of arthritis since it would be absurd for the attributor to judge Bert to be mistaken on this view. Bert, on this view, need not even be a member of the attributor's community or of any community, so one cannot judge him to be mistaken simply because the attributor's own word for a disease with certain characteristics is applied only to affliction of the joints. Much of the difficulty and point of the skeptical problem turned on a sense of normativity that was being demanded for meaning. If, on this weaker view, Bert's usage does not count as a mistake, then that sense of normativity has dropped out. This weaker view is just plain inconsistent with the social externalist view that found Bert to be mistaken when he was misaligned with his community. On the weaker view, it should have been possible to treat Bert as if he were a Crusoe and attribute his own individualistic meaning that was different from his community's. Thus the weaker view cannot be what Burge and Kripke had in mind all along.

What sense of norms, then, does this weaker view of the relevance of the social commit itself to? Does it involve anything over and above the low-profile sense of norms I conceded earlier? It does commit itself to a subtle underlying sense of norm over and above the extrinsic and hypothetical norms mentioned earlier. But I will argue again that this further sense of norm is nothing like the more intrinsic and categorical norms we find in Kripke and Burge.

The further sense of norms can be brought out by looking to Donald Davidson's conception of the social nature of meaning. It is a conception which is very akin to this two-person view of the relevance of the social; and Davidson actually offers an argument for his conception rather than talking cryptically of needing to "take an agent into one's community." My concern is not to assess the validity of the argument but only to see what further sense of norms it commits itself to over and above the hypothetical and extrinsic norms I have committed my individualism to.

Davidson's argument is for the conclusion that a necessary social condition for an agent's having thought and meaning is that there be at least a second agent with whom he is in communication (see esp. Davidson 1982. pp. 326-7). Davidson requires that an agent can be said to have thought only if there is a second person who interprets him. Why does he require that there actually be a second agent?

The answer cannot be just that the very idea of publicness of thought and meaning demand a second person. The idea of publicness demands only that an agent's thought be discoverable by another. It merely says that if there was another, he would discover it. It does not require that there be another for thought to be possible in the one, as Davidson requires. So Davidson demands more than just what the idea of the publicness of meaning demands. He demands at least a community of two.

In saying why he demands this, we would have answered our question about norms, the question what sense of norms is involved in the weakened, two-person view of the relevance of the social? This is because Davidson's argument for the necessity of the second person turns on how the second person alone eventually gives us the right to talk of a distinction between subjective and objective judgments, the possibility of right and wrong. For him the second person – the lights of another – gives rise to the very idea of the most primitive underlying norms which eventually make possible the idea of truth and falsehood.

The argument is this. If there was only one person who produced various reactions to things in the external world, there would be no right to call these anything other than physical or bodily reactions. We have no right to describe them in anything but non-intentional terms. Now I might protest: "But what if there was one person who was reacting in *regular and stable ways* to things around him and, of course, reacting in highly complex and inter-related ways. Why withhold intentional descriptions in describing him? How does bringing in another person with similar reactions help, if one person's reactions are not enough?" To this protest Davidson would give the following answer: "Your protest has itself described a scenario that is only possible if there was a second person. For, there cannot be any sense given to the idea of regular and stable reactions of an individual to which I am appealing, unless there is a second person. Regularity of reaction means that there are reactions which are similar to one another. But similarity is not an idea that can be cashed out or explained except as a similarity that is *noticed*, except as something that is *seen* to be similar. Nature does not announce its similarities, similarities have to be noticed in order to *be* similarities. And so one needs a noticer, a second person."

If Davidson is right, the very appeal to stabilities and regularities in the behavior of agents, which is central even to an individualist view of meaning as we saw a little earlier, presupposes that there be a second individual, at least. The very idea of similarity, which is implicit in the ideas of regularity and stability of behavior, is an idea that is dependent on there being a perceiver of similarity. It is an idea which brings with it a certain minimal sense of norms. "This reaction is similar to this reaction" is a *judgment* and it is always made by someone's lights. It introduces into the picture a distinction between the subjective and objective, a distinction that only comes in via the lights of another, a perceiver or noticer of the similarity being judged. Without a second person, a noticer of the similarity in the reactions of an agent, the question of regularities in the agent's linguistic behavior could not get any purchase. The agent himself could not serve as the noticer of the similarity between two reactions of his, presumably because, as Wittgenstein himself pointed out, memory is not a good enough basis for a judgment of similarity. The agent by himself could not in the full and proper sense judge a similarity since he does not have such a basis. There is no way to dispute with his memory and what seems the same will be the same. But a judgment, in the full and proper sense, requires that what *seems*, may not *be*. That, only a second person will bring.[70] This entry of the second person in the very possibility of similarity judgments is essential, therefore, to the idea of regularities which provide part of the basis of attributions of meaning and concepts to an individual. Judgments of similarity, essential to counting something as a regularity in an individual, involve us in norms, and a second person is, in turn, essential to having those norms.

Notice, however, that this notion of norm, adumbrated in this weaker (two-person) conception of the relevance of the social to intentionality, is a sense of norm that has not much to do with anything as specific as the question about how to individuate contents and concepts. But Burge and Kripke are interested in precisely that, the individuation of contents and concepts which, for reasons of normativity, they think must be done along social externalist lines. As we just said, this notion of norm merely provides for the seems same/is same distinction which underlies the idea even of regularity in an *individual* agent's behavior. Therefore on this conception of the relevance of the social, concepts and contents *can* be constituted and individuated on the basis of regularities in individual behavioral responses to the external world, i.e. they can be constituted along individualist lines. Individualism does not and need not deny that there must be a second person, so long as that does not amount to social externalism or a notion of norm that motivates social externalism. The question to which this two-person conception of the relevance of the social is addressed is a much more general and underlying question about the prerequisites for even observing regularities in an individual. If Davidson is right, the normative notion of similarity that underlies the notion of "regularity in usage" requires this two-person sense of the social. Since my account of meaning depends on regularities in the usage of individuals and since this sense of norm lies behind the idea of such regularity, even my individualist view of meaning must allow for these norms. But equally, since this sense of norms fuels an individualist regularity-based notion of meaning, it falls short of the sense of norms one finds in Kripke and Burge. It is not a sense of norms which can be gratified only if we find ourselves able to say that Bert is mistaken or that KWert is the source of a skepticism about meaning. One could easily admit to the sense of norms that attaches to this basic idea of similarity at the same time as on took a relaxed attitude towards Bert and KWert, i.e. it is a sense of norms that one could accept at the same time as one said that Bert had his own concept of arthritis which he applied correctly to his thigh and at the same time as one said that the problem raised by KWert was not a serious problem for any interest we have in the concept of intentionality or meaning.

So it would be thoroughly disingenuous to say that it is something like Davidson's idea of the social and of the normative that Kripke and Burge had in mind all along.[71]


## EXTERNALISM AND THEORY-CHANGE

My skepticism about normativity, however, is not yet fully justified. The question which remains to be addressed is whether in finding a certain normativity about meaning unnecessary, and in insisting instead that we can just as easily say that the protagonists in these examples have idiosyncratic concepts, I have given up entirely on the idea that there is something we would describe as theory-change over and above meaning-change. If I have, and if there is a strong intuition that there is a distinction between these two kinds of change, that would seem a reason to resist my line against normativity. The intuition that there are genuine cases of theory-change which ought not to be collapsed into cases of meaning-change, is an intuition that supports Burge and Kripke's insistence on normativity. For it supports their view of what sort of mistake their protagonists are making.

The question of theory-change and its connection with the question of normativity was already evident at the end of the first section of this chapter. There we had left my case against the argument from deference unfinished, saying that the question of norms and theory-change must be dealt with before the case is fully made. Recall that there the argument from deference for social externalism could be supported by saying that the right way to describe Bert's deference towards his doctor is to say (what he himself might very well say) that he was wrong about arthritis and was corrected by the doctor. My externalism, on the contrary, allows one to describe him not as having been wrong about anything, but as having one concept before the doctor informed him of the community's usage and then as having acquired another concept. I have at some length dismissed a certain objection to this which invokes considerations from normativity but that dismissal would not be complete, nor would the first section's case against the argument from deference, unless we can also dismiss the appeal to the intuition about theory-change which supports normativity. I will not have fully repudiated this line of motivation for wide content until I deal with the intuition.

In invoking the distinction between meaning-change and theory-change, the intuition invokes a distinction central to much philosophy. The distinction, in one form or another, is not only deeply entrenched in our philosophical thinking about the history of our theories about the world, but also in our everyday thinking about the nature of disagreement between people. On the one hand, we often want to say that our changing theories are about the same phenomena. On the other hand, we sometimes want to say that a later theory has changed the subject of the earlier one and is no longer "about the same thing." The same duality applies not to changes over time but disagreements between agents at a given time.

How can this distinction motivate the orthodox externalist idea of wide content? The motivating argument seems to be that unless we think of the content of our beliefs (taking theories to be systems of beliefs) as wide contents, we will lack the conceptual wherewithal to make the distinction, we will allow one half of the distinction to collapse into the other. Only wide content allows us to anchor the subject matter of a theory, which is then retained over changes of theories, or over disagreements. Without the notion of *reference* as characterized in chapter 2's discussion of Kripke, Putnam, Dretske, Fodor and Burge,[72] the subject of changes of mind will be unanchored and free-floating and there will be no saying ever that it is a change of belief or theory rather than a change of meaning.[73] (The same point and all the following points, of course, apply to disagreement as well as change but for the sake of convenience I will take that for granted and talk mostly of change rather than disagreement.) Theory-change will thus collapse into meaning-change. An anchor, then, is always needed, which pins down what it is that the changing theories are about unless we want to allow that when theories change so does their subject such that all theoretical change involves thorough-going change of subject or meaning, i.e. unless we want to allow that it is not really theory-change but meaning-change. If we do not wish to allow that, then the argument seems to suggest that we must accept an account of reference along one or other of the above lines, for that alone will provide such an anchor. Thus wide contents.

If this argument is correct, then a unified picture of content like mine, which has no place for wide contents, cannot make a theory-change/meaning-change distinction. The specific worry for my account would be that since my constraint (C) allows me to capture a far greater fineness of grain provided by the beliefs that go into individual conceptions, there is the danger that changes in belief will always amount to changes in meaning itself, for there will be no anchors to prevent this complete slide of one into the other. So, in order to allow for the distinction, my account must at least be supplemented by a notion of wide content which has these anchors.[74] My notion of content by itself is incapable of capturing our intuitions about theory-change versus meaning-change. Is this correct? I would deny it, so long as we have a plausible idea of what it is exactly that we wish to retain when we insist on having a theory-change/meaning-change distinction.[75]

We can, first of all, deny that there is any way of distinguishing between meaning-change and theory-change if that means that we have a way of telling, for any case of change presented to us, whether it is a case of change in theory or in meaning. However, for any given case of which we are convinced by our intuitions after a scrutiny of the details that it is a case of one rather than the other, what makes it one rather than the other can be characterized in terms that do not invoke any of the orthodox externalist accounts of concepts or contents.

Let us take an example about which we are so convinced. It is an example raised by Jerry Fodor (1987, p. 88). As we know, a contemporary astronomer has vastly different theories about the nature of stars from that which an ancient Greek astronomer would have held. Yet we feel convinced that the theories of these two astronomers are nevertheless about the same things, stars. We are not prepared to give up on this conviction and say that the theories are so divergent that what they are theories of is no longer the same. In short, we are loathe to say that it is a case of meaning-change, rather than theory-change.

Fodor and other theorists committed to a notion of wide content claim that the source of this conviction is an orthodox externalist causal[76] account of the concept of star, a causal account which anchors the concept as it is found in both the earlier and later theories.[77] Since I oppose their causal accounts because they lead to wide content, I must provide an alternative source of such a conviction. And the source is obvious, given my account of content and its constraint (C). It is the common beliefs shared by the temporally distant astronomers which fix the common subject matter of their theories and which underlie our conviction that it is a case of theory-change, rather than meaning-change.

It is true that we have already granted that the theories are highly divergent and this implies that there will not or may nor be many very important or interesting beliefs that are shared by them. But there is no reason to demand that what fixes the common subject matter of the two theories is itself theoretically interesting or important. After all, all it is doing is fixing the common subject for interesting and important theoretical developments, interesting and important theoretical disagreements and changes. It need not itself be interesting. Nor need these shared beliefs be numerous. It may be that all that we can find in common are a few beliefs like the belief that stars are the salient luminous pinpoints that we see when we look up at the sky at night. Switching to other sorts of examples we may even want to say of some contemporaneous disagreements that there is only one shared belief which fixes the common subject of what the disagreement is about and that belief can, in some cases, only be characterized metalinguistically. Thus I may disagree with someone whether elms have large trunks or not, and what decides that we have a common subject here may be merely the shared belief that an elm is the sort of tree that our friend the dendrologist pointed out to us and called "elm", when we were out for a walk the other day. The point is that though the shared beliefs may be few and uninteresting, without them there is nothing to fuel the conviction that there is a common subject, a case of theory-change. Or, to put it more correctly the other way round, if there were *no* shared beliefs, however few and uninteresting, in a case of change of this sort, I simply have no intuition at all that it must be counted as a case of theory-change rather than meaning-change.

What, then, does the difference between my view and the orthodox causal theorist's view on this question of theory-change versus meaning-change consist in? Not, as it should be clear by now, in that I am denying that external causality is involved at all in the fixing of concepts. But rather, in that for me the real anchors are provided by the shared beliefs which the theorists associate with the terms involved (say, stars are the salient luminous pinpoints...), beliefs that constrain our descriptions of the external causes in our causal account of their respective concepts. It is thus the beliefs that are emphasized and not just the external causality. But, for the view I oppose, beliefs are precisely what jeopardize the possibility of anchors since the two astronomers have such divergent beliefs. Thus the view's search for purely causal anchors.

Since for me the very idea of invoking external causality to fix concepts raises the question of how to describe the external causes (a question that the wide content view tends to pass over in silence) and since those descriptions must turn on agents' beliefs, beliefs can never be completely out of the picture. Of course, this does not yet fully establish my way of providing the anchors, which is to look for *shared beliefs* between the astronomers. What establishes that is my insistence that the beliefs that determine the right descriptions of the external causes in *each* case must be the beliefs of the *respective* astronomers involved. This is precisely what would seem to jeopardize a common subject matter for their disagreement since their beliefs are so different. But my point has been simply that if we have the intuition that this is a case of theory-change, then even though the beliefs are very different and very interestingly different, they cannot be entirely different. In a word the difference between us is that for my opponents the question – theory-change or meaning-change – turns on the question: is there a common causal link of the astronomers' usage of the relevant terms with *stars*? (I emphasize "stars" to bring out the idea that we are supposed somehow to be getting to the things themselves unmediated by belief and description.) For me, it turns on whether there are shared beliefs held by the two astronomers.

There is, of course, the question about how we know or decide which beliefs are shared. The point of this question is to express a skepticism about the proposal that shared beliefs account for our intuitions about theory-change, and to suggest that direct causal connections are necessary after all. But the proposal has an answer to the question. We decide what the shared beliefs are from a position of shared beliefs that we the deciders have with both the parties in the dispute, with both astronomers. These decisions like all decisions that go into intentional attributions (or anything else based on evidence) generally are initial hypotheses which we may revise if we run into trouble. There is no other method or way of deciding these things. Beliefs like everything else are attributed from a background of our own beliefs. There is no reason to think that in the study of meaning and intentionality there ought to be or could be any other method.

There are a few things worth bringing to notice about the proposal that invariance in belief will account for a given intuition that we have a case of theory-change rather than meaning-change.

The way I have put my point may mislead a reader about the role of causality in my view, in ways that I have warned of before. It is worth putting in a caveat again. Though, unlike the orthodox externalist, I emphasize beliefs it is not as if the causal relations do not have any role to play for me. This is because for me the question, why do just those shared beliefs count, cannot be answered outside the context of the constraints on interpretation, and we could not talk of those constraints without talking of the causal relations between the subjects of interpretation and the star, or whatever. So I do not want to give the impression that I am allowing causal relations no significance at all. For me it is not a choice between allowing just one or the other (causal links or beliefs) significance. That is a dichotomy set up by the orthodox externalists I am opposing. What I am really opposing, then, is the attempt to make causation do some work in the philosophy of mind and language outside the context of interpretation. Of course, talk of interpretation here is vague and one needs a more specific formulation. My constraint (C) offers that specific formulation.

Also, notice that my view allows for explicit appeal to indexical elements in specifying these shared beliefs: "stars are the salient pinpoints we see when we look up at the sky at night," "Elms are what the dendrologist pointed out to us the other day and called 'elms,'" and so on.[78] This may give the impression that my view only seemingly provides an alternative source for the conviction. It may give the impression that in the end it is the direct reference provided by the indexical element that provides the anchor even for me, the beliefs themselves being superfluous. But that impression would be quite wrong. Indexical elements, as said in chapter 1, necessarily come in because they initially are the clues that connect the individual's mind to the external world; but even if we grant that these indexical elements are ineliminable, no indexical element refers unmediated by descriptions altogether. The descriptions or beliefs are *integral* and essential to the way we think of the external causes that the indexical elements clue us into. Because my starting point is not the sort of causal theory of reference in Kripke and Putnam, mine is not an indexical-*cum*-description account such as the one Putnam (1975) proposes, even though there may be an indexical element involved in the beliefs or descriptions. Thus for me there is no temptation to say that just the indexical element provides the anchors. It is the common beliefs (admittedly involving indexical elements) which do so. If this means that when I say that my anchors allow us to say that the astronomers are disagreeing about the same *things*, I am only talking of "things" by courtesy, since the "things" are always *inseparably* under the descriptions or beliefs the astronomers share, I have no quarrel with that. After all, I have all along insisted that when it comes to their role in individuating concepts and contents things enter only as agents conceive them, and moreover the things cannot ever be decoupled from the conceptions. If this also means that I should not be allowed to talk of *anchors* as anything more than a metaphor since "anchors" strictly suggests much more the orthodox causal-theoretic nailing down to *things*, I am happy to grant that too. After all, "anchors" here is a metaphor anyway.

Finally, I also admit that if one took my view, talk of theories being "about the same thing" will not be transitive as they would for the orthodox externalist view I reject. When the anchors are given by the pure external cause or the unmediated indexical element (pretending that one understands what that means, which I do not), then, if a Greek astronomer has a theory about the same thing as a medieval astronomer, and if the medieval astronomer has a theory about the same thing as the contemporary astronomer, it follows that the Greek astronomer has a theory about the same thing as the contemporary astronomer. But when the common subject is provided by shared beliefs, as it does for me, that does not necessarily follow. It only follows if there are indeed shared beliefs between the Greek astronomer and the medieval astronomer which are also shared by the contemporary astronomer. If there are not, no purely causal element will retain the subject over the two sets of changes. This is how it should be. There is nothing counter-intuitive about this. It follows obviously from the suggestion, itself intuitive, that any intuition that two theories are about the same thing can have nothing more underlying it than that there is some shared belief(s) or description(s) involved.

I said that I would show that my view has the resources to make a distinction between theory-change and meaning-change, so long as that distinction is plausibly understood. The plausible version of the distinction that I have shown this for is one which makes no concessions to the analytic-synthetic distinction. By that I mean: I have not shown that I can make a general distinction between theory-change and meaning-change, but rather that in any particular case about which we already have a conviction that it is a case of one rather than another, the conviction is cashed out, in my belief or description-oriented picture, in terms of the existence of the shared beliefs in the changing theories. To insist that this is not enough, to insist, that is, on preserving a more general way of drawing the distinction, is to demand one of the fruits of the more fundamental analytic-synthetic distinction. It is like asking in a general way to distinguish between what is a matter of meaning and what is a matter of fact or theory, and then applying that to the question of change in these matters. But if there is no tenable analytic-synthetic distinction, then there is no general way of drawing the distinction about change. There is no general test which we can apply to any case of change presented to us and which will tell us what sort of change is involved. That, as Quine has shown, is a matter of decision and if that is right it is not a very important thing to have a strict general distinction. It is not, in general, terribly important which we say it is. This does not mean that if in a particular case we feel strongly that it is a case of one rather than the other change that we can have no more to say than that it is a strong feeling. Something more can be said and it is that further thing that my appeal to shared beliefs consolidates. It spells out with more resources what is initially expressed as an intuitive conviction that we often have.

Thus we find ourselves intuitively saying "Surely the Greek astronomer and the contemporary astronomer are talking about the same thing!" In fact, that is precisely what the wide-content theorist says in order to then show that we cannot avoid invoking some causal-theoretic and direct-referential account of the concept "star" in order to give ourselves the right to say it. In this wide-content theoritst's argument, I am prepared to grant that there are convictions we have of this kind; but the causal-theoretic or direct-referential account of concepts is not necessary to spell out what the conviction is based on. I am further saying that the wide-content theorist invokes something stronger than shared beliefs because he is not just interested, as I am, in spelling out what the intuition in particular cases is based on. He wants a general way of making the theory-change/meaning-change distinction and in doing so reflects his unconscious commitment to an implausible analytic-synthetic distinction. To the extent that the latter distinction is implausible, the general way of making the theory-change/meaning-change distinction is unnecessary. In other words, by a short step, wide content is unnecessary.

If my picture of things is correct, then meaning is specified by those beliefs that are invariant between changes (or disagreement) in belief. And that I find a very intuitive picture of what one notion of meaning is. This notion of meaning fixes the subject for belief-change. If there is nothing invariant then there is no preservation of meaning, and the change must be counted as a case of meaning-change. I submit that our convictions about which sort of change it is, walk in tandem, not with some conviction about a causal chain which lies altogether outside the ken of our beliefs, but instead with our conviction that there are some invariant beliefs. More will be said about theory-change in chapter 4, after discussing the question of the connection between intentional content and the notions of truth-conditions and reference. But we do not have to wait till then to draw the general conclusion that my more fine-grained way of drawing intentional content is in no danger of collapsing all change of belief into change of meaning.[79] I take the foregoing discussion to have established this conclusion.

To sum up, I have tried to defend the notion of intentional content I proposed in chapter 1 against the following three inter-related objections which issue from what, I believe, are the deepest motivations for orthodox externalism. They are, first, that my view of content fails to capture an essentially social element in content; second, that it fails to capture an essentially normative element in content; and, third, that it does not allow us to retain an intuitive distinction between theory-change and meaning-change. The first objection was answered in the first section, but the answer remained tentative pending a response to the other two objections. I have answered the second and third objections at length in the rest of the chapter.

In the discussion of all three, I have tried to distinguish between what is is worthwhile in these objections and what is not. I have identified the conception of the social and the conception of the normative that is worth capturing, the sort of distinction between theory-change and meaning-change that is worth retaining. And I have tried to show how my unified notion of content does capture and retain these things. I have been critical of those conceptions of the social and normative, critical of that conception of the theory-change/meaning-change distinction, that only wide content can capture. To the extent that I have succeeded in doing so, I have shown that orthodox externalism is not a compulsory way of thinking of intentionality

# 4

# Truth and the Locality of Content

## WHAT IS THE FUNCTION OF TRUTH-THEORIES OF MEANING?

So far, much has been said about the external constitution of content but not much about the commonly held idea that content is individuated by truth-conditions. It is widely thought, and it is natural to think, that the question about whether or not external facts constitute content is the flip side of the question, whether or not content is individuated in terms of truth-conditions. And since contents are composed of concepts, and reference contributes to truth, this pair of questions will have its pair of analogues: the question whether concepts are, in general, fixed by external causes is the flip side of the question whether concepts are individuated in terms of reference. It shall be assumed throughout that there *is* something, at least initially, natural about thinking that each of these pairs contains questions which are interdependent, questions which are flip sides of a single idea. And given this assumption we can consider what, if any, connection a unified view of content should take to hold between externalism and truth-conditions. We can consider the connection in response to an objection to my unified view of content and the externalism on which it is based.

Is my insistence on imposing a rather serious constraint on the external element not going to have the effect of spoiling the idea (the flip-side idea) that content is individuated in terms of truth-conditions? Now, obviously, the answer will be that it all depends on what one takes truth-conditions to be. If one insists that the external factors which are involved in the notion of truth-conditions are unconstrained by an agent's beliefs or descriptions, then one will convict my position of having divorced content from truth-conditions. Insisting on this is, of course, a matter of terminological decision and we cannot quarrel with that, except to say this. Even if, making a terminological decision, we did convict my position of such a thing, we must pause a little to notice that truth-theories of a certain kind may still be used to specify our concepts and, therefore eventually, our contents. Truth-theories of what kind?

Davidson has, famously, invoked Tarski-style truth-theories (with modifications to handle indexical features) for precisely these purposes.[1] However, it is not going to be possible to work with the Davidsonian truth-theories if we want from truth-theories a way of putting a theoretical face on (i.e. a way of representing the flip side of) the deliverances of an externalist and unified account of content, with the crucial constraint I have proposed. To begin with, two crucial modifications must be made in order to match what the constraint imposed by the account is bound to deliver.

In order to make the modifications, there is no need to spell out the details of Davidson's project here since they are not relevant. I shall assume knowledge of the rudiments of Tarski-style theories and assume that the reader is familiar with the entrenched idea, entrenched since Frege first proposed it, that truth-conditions individuate meaning and content. The idea of exploiting a Davidsonian version of a Tarski-style truth-theory is, of course, just one prominent proposal for elaborating the relevance of truth-conditions for meaning and content. There are a variety of other proposals for elaborating it, with which I will not engage. The orthodox externalists all take it for granted that meaning and (wide) content are individuated in terms of truth-conditions and take it for granted that there will be some version of truth-theoretic and denotational semantics. As will emerge in the next section, there is a great deal of difference between their view of referential semantics and the Davidsonian version of a truth-theory. It will also emerge there that my way of seeing the point of truth-theories in the study of meaning and belief differs from both Davidson's and their versions.

But first the modifications to Davidson. Since a good deal of the point of my account and its constraint comes out clearly in the puzzle cases, let me explain the modifications with the case of Pierre in Kripke's puzzle. Recall that an account of Pierre's contents, which makes those contents psychologically efficacious, has to make it come out that he has two London-beliefs and therefore, two London-concepts. This is what imposing the constraint will, in general deliver, despite my general commitment to externalism. (For the twin-earth puzzle it will, on the other hand, deliver a *single* water-concept, despite my commitment to externalism.) In order to represent these two concepts in the truth-theory, the first modification will have to be our ways of talking about the object language; it will have to introduce a term to capture Pierre's second conception of London. In the example, we do actually have two terms *"Londres"* and "London" so we could just adopt them both. This may give the impression that we are scrambling languages; but that impression is superficial once we remind ourselves that it is idiolects we are accounting for. After all variants on Kripke's puzzle can be raised which do not involve two natural languages like French and English. (Kripke himself offers an example of this kind – the case of "Paderewski" – in the paper in which he raises the puzzle about London and *Londres*.) In such variants it would be clear that we would still need two terms to keep track of the agent's two concepts and there would be no impression of scrambling languages. Agents' terms in such variant puzzles will have to be treated as having unpronounced subscripts and the theory will then explicitly represent their terms and the concepts they express with two terms (e.g. "Paderewski$_1$" and "Paderewski$_2$." ) Just in order to avoid misunderstanding about scrambled languages in Pierre's case too, we might as well proceed in this first modification, by introducing two new terms to capture Pierre's two concepts of London, "London$_1$" and "London$_2$" . The examples where only one natural language is involved show us vividly, anyway, that if one is going to have a theory (and a truth-theory in particular) representing agents' concepts, and if the theory is to represent the concepts as constituted by an externalist account with my constraint, then such neologisms will inevitably have to be introduced. Let me call this the "left-hand side modification" to mark the fact that we may have to fiddle with the left-hand sides of the clauses of the theory, by introducing neologisms which may never have been on the agent's lips.

But there is just as crucial a modification that must be made on the right-hand sides of the clauses. And here, invoking a proposal made by John McDowell(1976)[2] (in an only slightly different context from Kripke's puzzle), one must insist that there is an enrichment in the language of the theorist, in order to make clear that Pierre indeed does have two different concepts, even though there is only one city. There must, therefore, be *different* specifications (or entries as we might have said if these were translation rather than truth manuals) on the right-hand sides for the two terms introduced on the left, despite there being only one city. That is, we must respectively put down London$_1$ and London$_2$ on the right-hand side, even though *we* think that Pierre's different conceptions are different conceptions of the same city. The theory after all is a theory for Pierre. Thus equivalent truth-theories may not be equally good as theories of concepts and contents for different agents. A theory which contains the axioms "'London$_1$' refers to London" and "'London$_2$'refers to London" , or, for that matter, a theory which contains the axioms "'London$_1$' refers to London$_1$" and "'London$_2$' refers to London$_1$" while fine if it were a theory about us and all agents who know of the identity, would be no good as a theory about Pierre since it would fail to capture his different conceptions.

There is no obvious mistake involved in insisting on this scruple about keeping the right-hand sides of such truth-theories distinct, since there is no reason to think that truth-theories have to prove identities. We should not be misled by the extensional nature of truth-theories and our own knowledge of the relevant identities to abandon scruple about what to put on the right-hand sides. This, then, is the second or right-hand side modification.

I just said that though a theory which did not have distinct right-hand sides may be fine if it were a theory about us, it will not be fine as a theory for Pierre. But is it really fine as a theory about us, if we are interpreting Pierre? Let me briefly say something against even this concession; and in doing so let me also address the obvious worry that there is a certain artificiality in thinking even of the *left* hand sides as containing two separate terms in theories for *us*–the first modification–since *we* do not have two different concepts.

The seeming artificiality of this disappears as soon as we realize that *we* have to imagine that there are two cities in order to produce the appropriate empathy needed to be theorists about Pierre's idiolect. But quite apart from that, this seeming artificiality is a decisive advantage. A reason for saying (despite our belief that there is only one city) that a theory for us too should treat "London" and *"Londres"* as terms expressing different concepts is that such a theory will serve better in contexts where belief *revision* or theory-change is an issue. In these contexts more than empathy for what we take to be a convicted geographical ignoramus is at stake. If it turns out, fantastically, that we are wrong in thinking that London is *Londres* and that Pierre is right after all, then my more fine-grained way of doing things will make clear the direction in which belief will have to be revised. That is to say, unlike a theory of truth and reference in the strict sense which posits only one concept rather than two, this more fine-grained truth-theory will display much better *both* directions in which theories could change, our's *or* Pierre's. We would appreciate this point much more vividly if we had a case in which we were not so confident that the agent was wrong (as we are when the agent is Pierre who does not believe that there is only one city). If the case involved an issue on which we were not as clearly convinced that the agent was wrong, then we may well want to entertain the possibility that we too may be wrong; in which case it would be a real advantage if a theory for us also attributed two different concepts. In many contexts of attribution of concepts and contents to agents (i.e. in many contexts of interpretation of agents) we may, through a consideration of the beliefs and conceptions of the agent being interpreted, come to open our minds about identities and a host of other things; we may begin to think it is an open question as to which of us is right; and in those contexts both the first and the second modifications may be necessary in theories representing our own concepts and contents. Such theories for us and the agent involved will display much better the possible directions in which belief can be revised, in our favour or in his. The theories will give us a common base from which doubts can be expressed about both parties' beliefs, and revisions can be made by either. We should not be misled by examples such as Pierre's, in which we are absolutely convinced that the interpreted agent is wrong, into ignoring this advantage of these modifications even for theories about us, the interpreters. (Incidentally this point about the advantage of these fine-grained truth-theories in thinking about theory-change is a corollary of the point made at the end of chapter 3 that shared beliefs rather than orthodox notions of reference are needed to account for disagreement or change in theory. There too, those who insist on the orthodox notions have allowed themselves to be unnecessarily dominated by examples where one of the theories in the disagreement or in the change is considered obviously wrong.)

I am now in a position to say what a unified account of content like mine should take the function of the clauses in a truth-theory of meaning or content to be. Concept-specifying clauses in a truth-theory for Pierre such as "'London$_1$'

refers to London₁" "'London₂'refers to London₂" tell us that the terms "London₁" and "London₂" in his idiolect respectively summarize such beliefs of his as the belief that London₁ is the city which his nanny told him of and the belief that London₂ is the city in which he is now living. This is what makes it possible to say that when he says *"Londres est jolie"* he is saying (and thinking) that the city which his nanny told him of is pretty and when he says "London is not pretty" he is saying (and thinking) that the city which he is now living in his not pretty. Descriptions can substitute for the names in contents once one sees that the clauses specifying the concepts an agent has do nothing other than specify the beliefs which he associates with the relevant term. And this is true not just for names but for terms such as "water" and "arthritis" as well.

I have concentrated on the puzzle case of Pierre but the point about the function of truth-theoretic clauses is perfectly general. The general lesson is that truth-theories serving as theories of meaning are not quite what their simple-seeming clauses suggest, i.e. they carry with them information that they do not explicitly state. Thus if we say that it is (partly) in virtue of tacit knowledge of such a theory that an agent says what he says and does what he does, we are suggesting that the agent knows what these clauses *implicitly* state; we are suggesting that he has the beliefs that are crystallized in these clauses. These clauses summarize certain beliefs of the agents for whose meanings and contents these theories are devised.

This, I will eventually claim, is an absolutely essential way of thinking of truth-theories which represent the deliverances of a genuinely *unified* notion of externalist content. This claim, with some justice, may be viewed as an abandoning of any claims to a deep connection between meaning and truth for that connection surely demands that the clauses of truth-theories do more than merely summarize certain beliefs of agents. If all the term "refers" is brought in to do is to summarize certain beliefs of agents, it has nothing much to do with any standard view of reference. From the standard and official perspective it will not seem like reference at all. This is true. In the study of concepts and contents I have given up reference for beliefs or descriptions.

It might at first sight seem like a version of description-theoretic or belief-theoretic account of reference, but even to say that would be false. It is true that I have talked of, and will talk of, descriptions mediating reference but by that I will only mean that there is no way to think of external elements determining concepts, there is no way to think of concepts being individuated by external objects, except as constrained by an agent's beliefs. Crucially, moreover, for me there is no way for the objects to come apart from the constraining beliefs in the determination of concepts. This suggests that it would be quite false to say that my account and the orthodox causal theories are different and competing accounts of reference. Mine is not an account of reference at all. It is not even an account of reference as it enters in the specification of meaning. I do not think reference does enter into its specification. It is an account of meaning which appeals to certain clauses in theory of truth which use the term "refers" and it appeals to them with a very specific and limited function: the clauses summarize and therefore implicitly convey the beliefs and descriptions an agent associates with his various terms (in the way described a few paragraphs ago) and in doing so the clauses specify the concepts of the agent. If calling my view a description-theory gives the impression that it is a description-theory of reference, I must warn against calling my view that. No doubt, for me, descriptions or beliefs play a vital role in the individuation of concepts, but for the reason just given it would be misleading to think of my account as a description-theory of reference. No doubt my belief-or description-oriented account and the causal account of reference are competing accounts, but they are competing externalist accounts of concepts or the *meanings* of terms. They cannot be competing accounts of reference because mine is not an account of reference at all, whereas the causal theory is.

For me, there is no way for the external object to come apart from the constraining beliefs in the determination of content. Let me return to Pierre to drive this point home. Though the different sets of beliefs about London that Pierre has, in virtue of which he has two different conceptions of London, are not stated by the clauses for "London$_1$" and "London$_2$," the *different* clauses (the difference being ensured by the modifications) for "London$_1$" and " London$_2$" nevertheless implicitly convey these different sets of beliefs. Many beliefs may overlap in the two sets but the fact that he does not know of a certain identity forces us to put down two distinct right-hand side specifications. On the right hand, then, we are using two distinct terms in our own (now) enriched language. It is theory for Pierre, and as far as he is concerned, i.e. from his point of view, there are two cities. Moreover, for me, there is no way *within the theory* to decouple the city from the beliefs or descriptions, there is no way, from within the theory for him, to say that there is one city and he has two differing sets of beliefs about it. We could do that if we used the same right-hand side specifications. But the way I intend the second modification, that is forbidden. A second attributor giving the meaning of the term "London$_1$" as it is used by the *theorist* of Pierre's idiolect on the right-hand side in a clause for Pierre, will not, *in the context of the theorist's use*, see it is as summarizing a set of beliefs which includes the belief that London$_1$ is London$_2$. This identity belief is not one of the summarized beliefs. The context of that use is one of giving a theory for Pierre, and the theorist is capturing Pierre's conceptions in the clauses. Even though the theorist happens to believe in the identity, in the context of that use, the identity-belief is not relevant to the theorist's use of that term.

So it can be insisted: even though the externalism on the flip side of these theories ensures that these clauses are meant to capture Pierre's conceptions of *things*, still in my way of thinking of the clauses, one cannot see the things as decouplable from the conceptions; within the theory one can only say that the two clauses capture his London$_1$-conception and his London$_2$-conception; one cannot say that they capture two conceptions that he has of London. Just the idea of imposing my constraint on externalism to capture agent's conceptions of things may not have made it clear that this is what I meant by "agents' conceptions of things." I will show why this is essential to retaining the unity of content in the next section. And I will show that thinking it essential in no way compromises externalism.

This undecouplability of the city from the beliefs (of course, from a position within the truth-theory for Pierre) demonstrates vividly that my talk of beliefs or descriptions which these clauses summarize does not amount to a description-theory of reference. If description-theories are theories of reference, i.e. of something that is characterizable as something neutral which description-theories and causal theories are competing theories of, then mine is not a description theory of reference. Reference in that sense is not playing any role in the individuation of Pierre's or any other person's concepts. The undecouplability is a symptom of this fact.

I should warn against a certain misreading of my claims that reference clauses have only a summarizing function regarding beliefs of agents and that they are not specifying reference in the official sense. This claim is not to be confused with a claim of Davidson's to the effect that reference, in the sense given by causally or physicalistically pinned down reference relations as one finds suggested in the writings of Hartry Field and others, is unnecessary (see Field 1972; Davidson 1977). In making his claim, Davidson argues that if one thinks of the idea of reference relations between terms and items in the world as tested only indirectly via their consequences for specifications of truth-conditions of whole sentences, then there is no reason to think of the reference relations as themselves pinned down causally or physicalistically. But my claim is more radical. I deny not only that the clauses specifying reference are tested directly, I am denying that there is anything more to these clauses than the function of conveying (implicitly) the beliefs the agent associates with the term on the left had sides of the clauses. Two questions immediately arise about my view.

*First*: an eyebrow may be raised about why the beliefs or descriptions (which, on my view, individuate concepts) have to be implicitly conveyed. Why do we have to have these beliefs summarized by reference-clauses such as "'London' refers to London" or "'water' refers to water." If all the reference clauses do is summarize beliefs, if all they do is make the specifications of concepts merely implicitly, why not instead lay all the beliefs out explicitly and abandon the reference-clauses?; or, at any rate, abandon them (and the idea of a truth-theory) as a way of specifying agents' concepts (and contents). What good is a theory which merely summarizes the information that eventually goes into psychological explanations, and what prevents us from *stating* the information in the theory, thereby showing it to be something quite other than a *truth*-theory?[3]

There is nothing, in itself, wrong with a theory that does not explicitly state all the information it carries, if there are strong reasons to think that that cannot, in any case, be done. Let us take an example. I drink some water from my kitchen faucet. This is explained by my desire that my thirst be quenched and my belief that drinking water will quench my thirst. What is the concept of water in this belief or this desire which is attributed to me to explain this action? I claim that it is specified by a reference clause which summarizes certain beliefs I associate with my term 'water'. Which beliefs? It need not summarize all the beliefs that I associate with the term 'water' because in this context, or locality as I have called it earlier, not all of them are relevant. But many are relevant and the fact is that it is foolish to think that we can explicitly state them all. There is, of course, the belief that water is the liquid that comes out of the kitchen faucet, but there is also the belief that water will not poison me, that it will not be boiling hot, that I will not have to pay an unaffordable sum of money for it, and so on and on. I do not, of course, have these beliefs in the forefront of my mind but if I am prompted by questions I will assent to all these beliefs, so it is not as if they are irrelevant to individuating my concept of water which composes the explanatory belief-content or desire-content.

Hence, in most localities or contexts of explanation where a belief is attributed, the concepts of which the belief is composed will be individuated in terms of other beliefs which it is not going to be possible to list explicitly. If the problem is bad in localities, imagine what it is like at what, in chapter 1, I called the aggregative or meaning-theoretic level, where no particular context of explanation is involved. At this level all the beliefs a person associates with a term individuate his concept. If we found it hard to explicitly list the selection of beliefs involved in a particular explanatory locality, imagine how hard it would be to explicitly list *all* the beliefs an agent associates with a term.

So whether in localities or at the aggregative level, the beliefs can at best be conveyed implicitly. Not only are they too many to list but they have inter-relations which make for an integrity that is impossible to disentangle in a list of explicit statements. There are very serious limitations on how much we can verbalize and intellectualize *all* the intentional states being summarized in these truth-theoretic clauses; and any effort to do so will only impose an arbitrary and distorting neatness on the highly messy variety of states that go into our possession and exercise of concepts. Any single belief or any manageable set of beliefs is, of course, the sort of thing that can be explicitly stated. But, unless one believed in analyticity and in definitions at the meaning-theoretic level, there is no single belief or select set of beliefs that is essential to answering the question: what is the meaning of term *t* for this agent? and therefore there is no single belief or set of beliefs that individuates the concept in all localities. For this reason I have said that if there is any point to the traditional idea of "a theory of meaning" at all, it is only to specify the aggregate of beliefs that a person associates with his term and then we can select from these aggregates to specify the local concept which composes a content attributed to him in a particular locality. But, we have seen that at both levels the beliefs are too many and too integrated to list explicitly. The theories whether at the aggregative level or at the local level, thus, sensibly make no effort at making such an explicit statement but instead merely put a summarizing face on it, and claim only to convey the information implicitly.

In any case, I do not see why there should be such a fuss about my not specifying the meanings of terms explicitly, since truth-theories serving the orthodox externalist positions on meaning also convey information implicitly. They, too, make substantial specifications with the insubstantial-seeming reference-clauses. Of course, there are differences between us. Some of those who proceed without my constraint on externalism deliver up truth-conditions as conceived by God, or by society and its experts, or by experts at the end of inquiry, or even just by the radical interpreter. But how are truth-theories better off in these settings than they are in mine on the question of imparting information implicitly? After all even there the base clauses of these truth-theories if they are going to do their job at all, presumably impart some information or other. The only difference is that the information is not going to be merely the beliefs of the agent to whom the concept is being attributed. It is no good saying that clauses of the truth-theories in the hands of these philosophers, unlike as for me, state or convey nothing over and above what is explicitly stated by the clauses. One cannot just hide behind the disquotation in the clauses. We need to know what the right-hand side tells us and just saying (say) "'water' refers to *water*" does not *explicitly* tell us anything. It conveys implicitly the scientific expert's conception or the radical interpreter's conception or whatever. Hence the worry about my summarizing function of truth-theories only implicitly imparting all this further substantial information should also be a worry for the view I am opposing and *their* use of truth-theories. It is a perfectly general problem for anyone hoping to exploit truth-theories for a specification of meanings and contents.[4] No doubt if, like some of them, one appeals to what is taken to be the scientific essence (i.e. to the expert's belief that it is $H_2O$, or whatever,) rather than appeal to all the beliefs an individual agent associates with terms like "water," the information conveyed will be much more minimal and less messy than the sort of thing I have in mind by what is imparted by the clauses of a meaning-theory. But the principled point is that the clause of *all* truth-theories of meaning convey some substantial information or other implicitly.

*Second*: the next obvious question which arises is this. I have said that any account of content which respects the unity of content and which therefore imposes my constraint must also see concepts as being individuated by the beliefs of agents. I have said that clauses in a certain sort of truth-theory may be exploited to specify implicitly what these concepts are by summarizing these beliefs. But why any longer, given that the reference-clauses of the theory implicitly carry all this *other* information, should one continue to think of these meaning-theories as theories of *truth*? Truth and reference cannot, after all, be equated with an agent's beliefs. But, for me, it is precisely an agent's beliefs that clauses in a truth-theory are supposed to summarize. Why then call it a "*truth*" -theory ? Why persist in calling them "*reference*" -clauses ?

To being with, it is not at all uncommon in our general practice, quite apart from matters of meaning and content, to resort to terms which will convey things implicitly when they cannot be conveyed explicitly. A good analogy to bring out this point (though I warn that it is merely an analogy and is not meant to suggest any further parallel than bring out this point) is our use of the demonstrative in certain contexts. We often say things like "a person is in pain when he wears *that* sort of expression." We do this precisely because we know we cannot possibly make explicit all the different information, even just information about the different expressions, that would tell us when somebody is in pain. The use of the demonstrative has the summarizing function made necessary by the forced implicitness. Now, even though they do not point to examples, I think words like "refers" and "is satisfied by" which occur in the clauses of a truth-theory which specified our concepts should be seen as having a similar summarizing function and for similar reasons. So if it is true that the clauses of a meaning-theory cannot state all the information that goes into most of the concepts an agent has, if it would not be possible to state all the beliefs she associates with most of her terms, the summarizing function of the word "refers" may be invoked just as the demonstrative invoked in the analogy.

But this does not answer the question why have I chosen the particular form of words "refers" and "is true" to carry out the summarizing function. My response is that this is a matter of nomenclature. We need not do so. There is no reason for anyone to lose much sleep over matter like this. I will even admit that perhaps we should not do so because it is bound to mislead people into thinking that I am still committed to a view of concepts which is based on an official notion of reference, even if in a description-theoretic form. Perhaps I should have used some other form of words in the theory which specified meanings. One reason why I have nevertheless allowed myself the use of words like "is true" and "refers" is that, for all my denial of the relevance of reference to content, I remain an externalist and I do not think that concepts and contents can be constituted independently of our relations with external things. It is easy to lose sight of this in all the talk of summarizing beliefs and the denial of reference playing any role for me. The point remains that, on the flip side of the truth-theories, there is still an *externalist* view of concepts and contents. All the talk of the belief-summarizing function replacing the official view of reference ought not give the impression that one has surrendered all externalism. The replacement of reference in the official sense comes from constraining the externalism, not from abandoning it. A constrained externalism in the service of a unified notion of content should be represented in truth-theories whose clauses do no more than summarize beliefs of agents.

The constraint in my externalism makes clear that it is not reference (in any standard sense) to things which individuate concepts but agents' conceptions of things which do. So another way of stating the reason why I have persisted in calling it a truth-theory is that its relevance to our notion of truth is surely not *wholly* lost just because the judgments of truth that are involved now are of truth as the agent conceives of it.

No doubt, one could say that if it is merely an agent's conceptions of the truth that these truth-theories convey then they ought not to be thought of as truth-theories. Of course one could say that. That is a matter of decision. I have made a different decision. I have stuck with talk of "truth" -theories because, even if they do not have the full official prestige, these truth-theories do get one to agents' conceptions of *truth* after all. I do not doubt that there will be those who insist that truth as the agent sees it is not truth; only truth as God, or the end-of-time inquirer, or the radical interpreter, would write it down, is truth; they will say I should not call theories which serve my externalism truth-theories. Against such an insistence I can, obviously, have no quarrel. All the facts and issues are out in the open and the words may fall where one wishes. The notion of truth-theory I have been promoting is of a theory which, like any truth-theory, connects an agent's concepts with the external world; the fact that there is an externalism on the flip side (whose deliverances regarding concepts these theories are representing) ensures that the beliefs that the clauses summarize describe objects and events and states of affairs in the world external to the agent for whom it is a theory. This gives it some right to being thought of as having something to do with the concept of truth; after all, this is just what the natural intuition, which I mentioned in introducing the flip side at the beginning of the chapter, demanded. However, because these theories are representing the deliverances of a unified externalist account they have the effect of taking us to the truth-conditions (to the external states of affairs) as the agent conceives of it (them). For me, the concept of truth is relevant to truth-theories of content only in the sense of truth as an agent (whose contents are in question) conceives of it. Thus it has similarities and dissimilarities with the sort of theories that will count as truth-theories in the orthodox externalist picture of the flip-side of their externalism. When deciding which terminology to adopt, if one finds the differences more significant than the similarities, then one will withhold the label "truth-theory" from it; if not, one will not.

By pursuing the consequences of my constraint on externalism in a way that allows for the unity of content, I have rejected a referential specification of concepts and meanings. I have committed myself instead to specifying concepts implicitly in terms of beliefs and descriptions with the use of a truth-theory. In order to add more detail and fortification to my unified account of intentionality, I will, in what follows, take up three large issues. These issues must be addressed if my constrained externalism and its flip-side conception of truth-theories is going to carry conviction. They may be posed in the form of questions about my view. First, does my constraint on externalism and my way of seeing the role of truth-theories bring in a crippling holism into the study of content. Second, does not the fact that reference is doing no work for me (not even in its description-theoretic form), that it is beliefs and descriptions which are doing all the work, amount to my really having abandoned externalism? Third, if one gives up on a referential account of content and on all versions of orthodox externalism, how can one account for the fact that the attribution of content partly has the function of communicating information *about the world*, and how can one any longer see the point of the very notion of content as lying partly in its ability to explain our success and flourishing in the world? The next three sections will be devoted to answering these three questions respectively.

## HOLISM AND THE LOCALITY OF CONTENT

The first question posed above can only be answered by introducing the thesis of the locality of content from chapter 1. The issue of holism will first be raised in a sharp way by invoking some recent criticisms of holism in the study of content by Jerry Fodor (1987, ch. 3) The issue will then be addressed by elaborating on the locality of content and finally, the section will conclude by sketching some details of my view of content which flow as a consequence from the locality thesis.

In recent years, holism for Fodor has become something akin to what Carthage must have been for Cato: he lets no opportunity pass for saying that it must be destroyed utterly. His primary reason for such hostility seems to be this. If the content of an agent's belief turns on the contents of his other beliefs, as holism about meaning or content requires, then no two agents are ever likely to have the same belief since at least some of the beliefs which surround it are bound to have different contents. Things will be even worse than that. No single agent is likely to have the same belief-content from one waking moment to the next since its surrounding belief-contents are presumably changing due to new perceptions or reasoning that he has or undertakes. This is disastrous for any idea of content since it will have as a consequence that we will not be able to make any generalizations about beliefs over people, not even make generalizations about the beliefs of an agent over time. This will put into doubt the explanatory efficacy of content since presumably beliefs explain behavior in virtue of some generalization, however low grade and qualified. And if beliefs and intentional content do not pull their weight in explanation that will put into doubt their very existence as real states of an agent. Fodor himself presents holism as such a threat to realism about intentional states.

How does all this have relevance to my unified, externalist position of content? The answer should be obvious. My externalist position imposes a constraint upon the description of the external causes that fix the concepts of an agent, a constraint which brings into consideration the other beliefs which one has attributed to the agent. This just is holism, in one clear and widely accepted sense of the term. That it is external causes which are involved does not, in any way, soften the holistic implications of the constraint imposed on the descriptions of those causes. For me, external causes are not thought of in the way they are presented in some of the more orthodox externalist accounts. As Loar puts it in one place, describing my position before he attacks it, external "causal factors are determinants of contents when and only when embedded in holistic cognitive facts "(Loar 1985b, p. 122).

(This should not give the impression that the sole point of the constraint (C) is to add holism to externalism. Though it does add holism, it does not merely do that, nor is that the chief motivation for the imposition of the constraint. The imposition is motivated by the desire to redeem externalist content for psychological explanation by not allowing externalism to leave out the agent's conceptions. Holism is a necessary consequence of imposing the constraint. Imposing the constraint entails holism but not vice versa. Holism can be embraced without imposing my constraint and without taking my view of truth-theories, as for instance in Davidson's position which has all along been holist in this sense which Fodor is opposing.)

All the same holism is a consequence of my position and so the question arises: does it follow that my view of how externalism enters content makes content subject to the crippling criticism Fodor makes against holistically conceived content?

I would deny it. Fodor's worries about holism flow from a deeply mistaken, though almost universally held, conception of the relation between a "theory of meaning" and content. The point of content lies in the role it has in the commonsense explanation of behavior. It is very important to understand the exact relationship between the theory of meaning or the theory of concepts, as I have (interchangeably) been calling it, and the contents which explain behavior.

Let me reintroduce from chapter 1 and elsewhere in the book a distinction, and some terminology I have used to make the distinction. The point that needs to be stressed to make my case against Fodor's anti-holism is that it is quite wrong to think that the deliverances of a "theory of meaning" (which consist in the specification of an agent's concepts) are exactly what compose the contents which explain behavior. Thus, a distinction needs to be made between two levels, the level of a theory of meaning on the one hand and the level of contents at which behavior is (commonsensically) explained on the other. I describe the former level as "agregative" and the latter as "local." Here is the idea from chapter 1 again.

A "theory of meaning," if one wants such a thing at all, summarizes, in the base clauses of a truth-theory, all the beliefs an agent associates with each of his terms. So at this meaning-theoretic level, a theorist of meaning producing a theory of meaning for me will have sample clauses such as "'Bombay' refers Bilgrami$_{it}$ to Bombay." My claim is that, by this, all he means is: the term 'Bombay' in Bilgrami's idiolect summarizes all Bilgrami's beliefs about Bombay at a given time. When the theorist says that the clause summarizes all Bilgrami's beliefs "about Bombay," the *use* of "Bombay" is of course, in the language of the theorist. The subscript is necessary on the assumption that no two people, and no one person at different times, share all their beliefs about anything, and we need some indication, therefore, that the clauses are summarizing different beliefs. The claim is not restricted to proper names but covers predicates as well. These clauses thus specify, by summary, the concepts an agent has. This is what I call the "aggregative" level.

If anybody needed convincing that theories of meaning are not significant what I have just said should have convinced them. That a theory summarizes all the beliefs that an agent associates with each term in his idiolect should be proof that such a theory can be of no specific interest or use at all.

However, not all the beliefs that are aggregated (by summary) at the meaning-theoretic level in the specification of a given concept are relevant to the other level, where actions are explained by the attribution of contents. In the explanation of an action, belief-contents (along with the content of other intentional states) are invoked, and these belief-contents are, of course, composed of concepts. But the concepts which compose contents at this level where actions are explained are not exactly the concepts that are specified at the aggregative level of meaning theory. To say that, would be to get quite wrong the relationship between meaning-theories and content; it would be to confuse two levels. Rather, what happens is that in citing beliefs (and desires) of agents at the level of the explanation of some piece of behavior, we are distilling some beliefs out of the aggregate of beliefs summarized in any given clause or clauses at the meaning-theoretic level, and we are citing contents which are composed of concepts that are to be understood in terms of these selected beliefs. I call this level where actions are explained, the "local" level.

The point of the distinction is to mark the fact that explanations are always in a locality and that meaning-theories which specify concepts in general have no *direct* relevance to particular localities.

The example given in chapter 1 should make this abstractly drawn distinction between "aggregate" and "local" clearer. Imagine two agents, one knows chemistry, the other does not. Thus one's concept of water is different from the other's since one's aggregative level beliefs about a certain substance are different from the other's, i.e. the clause for "water" for one summarizes, among other things, beliefs regarding the chemical composition of water etc., while the clause for the other does not. Meaning-theories will, therefore, attribute different concepts to them. But now imagine that we are explaining actions of these agents. Suppose that we are explaining why they each picked up and drained a glass full of some substance and suppose we say that they did so because they each desired that their thirst be quenched and they each believed that draining a tumbler full of water would quench their thirst. This sort of thing (explanation) happens only in a locality. In the locality of explaining these particular actions we have to distil out whatever we need from their respective aggregate of beliefs that go into their respective and different concepts of water as specified by the meaning theories for them. However, in this particular locality, we find that in distilling out what we need for the concepts that go into contents which explain their respective actions, we do not need to select those beliefs that one of them has about the chemical composition of water in order to explain his action. In this locality, the selections for the two of them *can* certainly coincide, even though, at the aggregative level, they do not coincide. To put it very loosely, those contents which explain this action of the chemically knowledgeable agent will be composed of a concept different from one which will compose the contents that explain some action of his, say, in a chemical laboratory. The chemical beliefs will be irrelevant to the contents in the former explanations. (This admittedly is a very loose way of putting things because obviously even in the chemical laboratory, a chemically knowledgeable agent may commit some action for which it is not necessary to select his chemical beliefs. For instance he may just be drinking a glass of the substance for the same reason that he does in the kitchen. So, by locality, I obviously do not mean locality literally in the sense of kitchen or laboratory; I mean rather the particular contexts created by particular explananda.)

It may seem that, for all my desire to see the mind and intentionality as unified, I have generated a version of bifurcation of content of my own; that I have produced a bifurcation of levels: aggregative and local. I think that would be to miss the point behind both the unity thesis and the locality thesis. For me, there is only one notion of content which is externally constituted and explanatory of action. There are two notions of concepts: aggregative and local. But there is only one notion of content because the aggregate level of concepts does not compose any contents at all. They are trumped-up posits, only there to acknowledge a larger pool of resources from which local concepts (which do go into contents) are selected. The idea of a level of meaning-theory is not the idea of a level at which there are beliefs with a different kind of content than at the local level. Of course, concepts at the meaning-theoretic level are aggregates of beliefs with content. However, these beliefs have the same kind of content, unified content. The very same kind of contents are to be found at both levels. But the only level at which any serious work is done by the notion of content is at the local level. So the distinction between levels does not amount to different notion of content at all.

It might also be objected that this picture, of selecting or distilling beliefs from aggregates in localities, will make all beliefs in localities analytic. Suppose I say to you "Water is good for the kidneys" and, in doing so, express that belief of mine in this locality of utterance and communication. Now, if the term "water," in this expression of my content, summarizes a selection of my beliefs from an aggregate which (being an aggregate) contains my belief that water is good for the kidneys, will it not seem that I have uttered something which, given my idiolect, is analytic? If the meanings of terms are to be spelt out in terms of beliefs, then any utterance expressing a belief which contains that term as a component will seem to be expressing something which is already contained in the meaning of the term. The trouble seems to lie in thinking of concepts or term-meanings as being spelt out in terms of beliefs. Only thinking of concepts as primitive, and denotational, it will seem can avoid this sort of problem. Only then will all statements which are manifestly non-analytic count as non-analytic.

But this is not a serious problem. In the locality of my utterance, I am communicating some information to you which I think you do not know. So my use of the term "water" in that sentence in that locality summarizes beliefs which I take you to share with me. You do not, according to me anyway, share the belief that water is good for the kidneys. Those beliefs which I take you to share with me fix the subject, about which I am then trying to say something that will be informative for you. But that means that the belief that water is good for the kidneys is not selected as going into the meaning of the term "water" in that locality. So the utterance is not analytic. The locality thesis precisely rules out its analyticity because it insists on selecting for the term "water" in that locality only those beliefs which fit in with my communicative purposes.

A deeper objection against my view raised by someone with Fodor's anxieties might be that I do not have a clear principle according to which we can decide what to distil out of the aggregate level into the local level.[5] That is, at least so long as one has given up on the analytic-synthetic distinction (and Fodor agrees, indeed insists, that one must give up on that distinction),[6] it is not clear what such a principle should be.

But there cannot be a general problem about saying that what is to count as relevant to the explanation and what is not, at any rate no more than it is a problem to say what it is that is to be explained. If we know what it is we want explained (and everybody, Fodor and everybody else, has to grant that at least that is known) then we know when some information is redundant to explaining it. One could only deny this if one denied that we know what we want explained and even Fodor, cannot be denying that, because if he did, he presumably could not raise his initial worry (about how holism destroys explanation of behavior that generalizes over people) at all. Everybody has to make some judgment about the explanandum before any such worry can be raised at all. There is no avoiding it. It is not to lapse into the analytic-synthetic distinction to say that we have to make some judgment about what the explanandum is. In general it cannot be to say anything wrong to say what we cannot avoid, viz., that we must judge what we need explained before we raise problems for what goes into the explanation. Once we have a judgment about what is to be explained, then we can tell what is redundant or superfluous to the information needed to make the explanation. Of course, like all judgments, we may revise these judgments about what the explanandum is, if we find we are not getting an overall coherent local account of the agent in question. But the point is that, relative to a decision about what the explanandum is, we know what to distil or select and what to leave out. The situation on this front is no different in psychological explanation that it is in explanation in the "strict sciences." Hempel (1962) once made clear that deductive-nomological explanations will not be spoiled, where some redundant information is introduced which is not necessary to the explanation, because he assumed that it is unproblematic that we can know what is redundant and what is relevant. My claim is that in psychological explanation, the generality over people that Fodor wants is preserved in particular localities when we notice, as in the case we considered, that an agent's chemical beliefs are redundant in explaining his behavior.

The protest that there is no principle for deciding what the relevant beliefs are in the local level, is, therefore, exaggerated. All one needs to do in order to fasten on the right explanandum and the right explanans, at the local level, is to see what beliefs the two agents will agree on. Imagine them communicating in this local context of drinking water and see what they agree on and what beliefs puzzle and throw them off. If one of them says that the substance that they wish to drink will not poison them and the other agrees, then that belief may be counted as relevant to this local concept "water" which goes into the explanation of their actions. If one of them says that the substance has the chemical composition $H_2O$ and the other is puzzled by that, count that belief as irrelevant in this locality. There is no serious obstacle to finding out which the relevant and irrelevant beliefs are.

Fodor's anti-holistic worry is that two agents will very likely never have the same contents if holism is granted and therefore we will never get explanations that generalize over people (or a person over time). My picture of things removes that worry. It is true that, in my picture, no two agents are likely to have the same concepts at the general and aggregative level of meaning-theoretic specifications. Yet in my picture this does not have any consequence for contents and therefore for the explanation of the behavior that contents effect. Holism may thus be granted at one level but if one understood that the relevance of that level to the other, where contents are cited and explanations are given, is of a very specific kind, one would not see holism as having this crippling consequence. I have already said what this specific relevance is. Meaning-theoretic specifications which are made at the aggregative level are relevant to content and explanations only in that they provide resources which one selectively exploits at the local level where explanations take place. At this local level, as we saw in the example above, two agents may be said to have the same contents if we think that the explanations being given need not exploit in the concepts which compose those contents, those beliefs of theirs which at the aggregative level reflect that their concepts are different. Since explanations only take place in particular localities there is thus no bar to explanations holding for or generalizing over people,[7] just because the concepts specified by meaning-theories are different for those very people.[8] Fodor's mistake is to have failed to distinguish between the two levels. His conception of a meaning-theory is that it specifies concepts which go directly and exactly into contents i.e. into what explains behavior. Since as we have admitted concepts specified by holistic meaning-theories are never likely to be shared by agents, he therefore concludes that no two agents will ever be likely to share contents. He gets wrong the precise nature of the relevance of meaning-theories to contents.

This is a very widespread mistake in the philosophy of language and mind. We cannot stop to uncover the ways in which philosophers have found themselves in insoluble difficulties and puzzles by making this mistake; but if one sees this point about the relationship between meaning-theories and content, and if one realizes the importance of what I call the thesis of the "locality of content," then one will see that the theory of meaning cannot have the central and pivotal place that philosophers have been giving it for many years.

Indeed, as stated in chapter 1, the notion of concepts which "theories of meaning" have standardly been said to specify has no psychological reality at all. It tries to answer the question "What are an agent's concepts?" But since this question has bite only in particular localities where one has a specific goal in mind (such as to explain an action by citing contents, or to compare a person's theories – about stars, say – with another's), the answer one usually wants is an answer that is more specific than the aggregate level answer to the question. So once one takes my belief-oriented line on concepts and once one gives up on the idea of analyticity which demands that there is a single set of beliefs that defines a term or concept, the traditional idea of a meaning-theory's specifications of meanings or concepts is shown to have no psychological utility and, therefore, no psychological reality. We may posit such specifications as idealized aggregates (produced by an idealized method which pretends to have surveyed "all possible evidence" as Quine said of the radical interpreter). We posit them as an innocuous gesture to acknowledge the fact that when we attribute local concepts we make selections of beliefs, and the selections are selections from somewhere, from some larger pool of resources: so why not these aggregates ? (If someone denied the need to posit this larger pool to select from, if someone thought that one could attribute local concepts without thinking of the beliefs they summarize as being selected from some aggregate resource, I would have no objection since it only underscores my view of the idleness of the "theory of meaning." My idea that it summarizes *all* a person's beliefs was meant precisely to make vivid that idleness.)

If this means that the idea of a theory of meaning is much less interesting than we have taken it to be in the past two or three decades, then let us acknowledge that that is so. We should not be disappointed that it is so uninteresting because it is always very interesting to learn, and no easy thing to learn, that something that we thought was terribly interesting was not as interesting as we thought it was. No doubt philosophers will think that to localize content and meaning in this way is to promote a skepticism about them. But equally one can say the orthodox externalist theories avoided this "skepticism" by artificially foisting on us a notion of content and meaning that was, as I have tried to establish, unmotivated or badly motivated; and, in any case, they have had to appeal to a second notion of content to do various tasks that this badly motivated artifact is incapable of doing. Tasks which, from my perspective, are only done in localities by the *only* notion of content there is.

Once the locality thesis is in place, it is not hard to see why it is unnecessary to follow Fodor on the path of a naturalistic reduction of meaning and reference in terms of the sorts of causal-informational externalism he offers,[9] nor in the highly convoluted attempts he makes in order to account for such things as errors once he follows that path. For him, since concepts as specified by meaning-theories go directly and exactly (as specified) into contents and since contents must be the sorts of things that two or more people can often be said to have in order to have some generality in the explanations they figure in, it follows that the concepts as specified by meaning theories must not be holistic. This is because holism forces that no two people are likely to have the same concept. He therefore proceeds to characterize concepts that meaning-theory specifies along the causal-informational lines criticized in chapter 2. So, if one gives up the first of his premises viz. that meaning-theories specify concepts which go directly and exactly into the composition of contents and if, instead, one embraces my thesis of the locality of content, then one can deny the causal-informational, denotational account of meaning and replace it with my externalism with its holism-entailing constraint.

Lest there is confusion about the terms "local" and "locality" , I should point out that Fodor also uses the terms "local" and "locality" to talk of the nature of content. For him locality of content is something that issues from his denying holism as being a property of meaning-theories. Thus, for him, localism is afforded by atomism about meaning. It should be clear that this use of the word "local" is not mine at all. I am granting holistic meaning-theories and then denying that meaning-theories are relevant to content because, contents and the concepts they contain are always local. For him, like for me, content must be local. But for him this means that it must be non-holistic in the sense that it must be the product of a non-holistic theory of meaning. For me it is "local" not because it is the product of a non-holistic meaning-theory but because it is not a product of a theory of meaning at all, in any direct sense. The term "local" for me marks something by way of a *contrast* with a level in which holism is legitimately involved. For him it simply marks *anti*-holism.[19]

Some time has been spent criticizing Fodor's positive criticism of holism because it seemed to me a clear and vivid way of seeing the significance of an absolutely crucial feature of my account of content: its "locality." However, Fodor has also made some weaker remarks against holism, arguing, not positively, that it is false and that it has untenable consequences, but also negatively that no good argument has ever been given for it. He says that one tends to slide without justification or argument from an epistemological holism (which he does not contest) to a meaning holism (which in his more positive criticism he has contested). But this slide is not justifiable and so there is no argument for holism about meaning, he says. The criticism he makes will not be spelt out here; this is not the place to address these negatively expressed qualms and produce a general argument for holism. I am not sure that I have a general and independent argument for holism. The holism that enters with my constraint is argued for to the extent my constraint is argued for. My constraint was argued for in chapters 1-3 and most specifically in chapter 2. The main underlying point was that, without it, one cannot have an externalism which constitutes content as the sort of thing that is relevant to psychological explanation. If one wants a unified account of content, that is, if one wants the very content that is externally constituted to be what explains behavior, then one needs no further motive or argument for the constraint, or the holism it entails. So holism as it enters into my picture is not subject to the negative critical remarks Fodor makes against Quine, Davidson and Putnam when he accuses them of sliding from epistemological holism to meaning without noticing the slide.

I have granted that there may not be a general argument for holism. Holism may, all the same, be indispensable. The only thing for philosophers to do, who do not like it, is to try to give a treatment of content and belief that is not holistic and see if they succeed. I do not believe anybody has. Fodor tries to give precisely such an account in his book – his denotational semantics based on a casual-informational externalist account. But, as we saw in our discussion of Fodor in an earlier chapter (see objection B in the last section of chapter 2), this account too needs to solve the puzzle about Pierre and Frege's puzzle, which we grappled with there. He proposes to solve them by positing a notion of belief over and above belief-content, a notion cashed out by pure causal roles which, he grants, must be holistically characterized. So he too brings in holism. And there is no point in pretending, as Fodor does, that this is not holism about *content*. Anything that solves these puzzles does work that matches the work of "modes of presentation" and, therefore, *is* agents' conceptions. If it is agents' conceptions, it *is* content, whether one calls it that or not. Thus even Fodor's account does not avoid the holism he detests.

### Some Consequences of Locality

The thesis of the locality of content is an absolutely fundamental supplement to the idea of the unity of content, which has been nursed through this book; and it removes certain obvious difficulties for the notion of unified content. We have already seen that it removes the difficulty that holism poses for content. But it is relevant to some other difficulties as well.

One such difficulty which can be addressed by the locality of content has to do with the thesis of the linguistic division of labor, and how it too might spoil the unity of content. In chapter 2, I said that it is a very strong intuition that if I and my twin-earth *doppleganger* were chemically ignorant, then we have the same water-beliefs which explain many common actions of ours, however different the chemical composition of the relevant substance might be in our relevant environments. For example, the action of drinking a certain substance when we were both thirsty, and desired the cheapest available drink. So long as we did not know any chemistry, it did not matter, whether the environment was different in this respect. My constraint made it possible to stick with this intuition and stick also to the unity of content. That is, the constraint made it possible to say that our respective contents may be determined by the environment without surrendering this intuition and without moving to another notion of content to retain the intuition. However, in chapter 2 I also admitted at another point, while discussing Putnam's thesis about the division of linguistic labor, that ignorant agents may, as a matter of fact, have built into some of their concepts, their reliance on experts in the community. Though this way of thinking of the division of linguistic labor avoided Burge's conclusion which attributed the expert's concepts to those agents (it avoided it because such reliance is not part of the expert's own concept), it nevertheless has an awkward consequence for the intuition that I and my *doppelganger* share the same content. The intuition was that I and my *doppelganger*, if we do not know any chemistry, may have the same water-beliefs. But now if we rely on different experts who have different chemical beliefs, then it should follow from my treatment of the reliance, that the water-concepts should be different. His reliance-belief that water is what the expert (on twin-earth) calls "water" will make sure that his water-concept will be different from mine. It seems, then, that I cannot have both the intuition and give my gloss on the reliance that comes from the division of labor thesis.

However, if we keep in mind the locality thesis, then it is perfectly possible that, even though at the aggregate level our concepts of water are different because we have different reliance-beliefs, in a particular locality, those respective reliance-beliefs may be irrelevant to explaining some commonly describable action of ours, such as the action of drinking water in order to quench our thirst in the cheapest available way. To explain this common action we do not need to appeal to contents that are composed of water-concepts which are the product of selecting from the aggregate level any reliance-beliefs at all. Our reliance-beliefs are irrelevant to explaining either of our actions. So it does not matter that our reliance-beliefs and, therefore, our water-concepts, are different at the aggregative level. In this locality the water-concept that enters the explanatory belief need only be comprised of quite other beliefs (beliefs such as "water is the substance that is now flowing out of the kitchen tap" etc.). Thus, despite relying on different experts we may still retain the intuition that our action here is explained by the same beliefs. Therefore one has not abandoned individualism about content for social externalism about content by admitting that, at the meaning-theoretic level, one's reliance on experts with crucially different beliefs about something amounts to having different concepts at that level. The locality of content ensures that.

The locality of content was also relevant to the discussion, at the end of chapter 3, of how a desire to preserve the meaning change/theory-change distinction gives apparent support to orthodox externalism. It is worth sparing a word to make explicit the relevance of the locality thesis in my argument against orthodox externalism on the question of how to preserve this distinction. There is no need to invoke wide content to preserve the distinction. The desire to preserve it in advance of (or independently of) specific intuitions that the distinction holds in particular cases is to hanker for the fruits of the analytic-synthetic distinction. Where there is an intuition, in a particular case, that we have a case of theory-change rather than meaning-change, there is no need to bring in the notion of wide content and direct reference to explain the intuition, since the intuition can only be based on the existence of an invariance (however slender) in the *beliefs* between the earlier and later theories or theorists.

The insistence on not worrying about providing a philosophical basis for a general meaning/theory-change distinction, but only providing it in particular cases, is part of the commitment to the locality of content. For it has the effect of saying that content depends on the particular case involved. What we need in order to say that theory-change has taken place is just this: some sub-set of the set of beliefs which goes into a concept of a theorist at an earlier time are retained at a later time. However, a theory of meaning which works only at an aggregative level will attribute two different concepts to the theorist at these different times because, at the aggregative level, the beliefs which comprise the concepts will, *ex hypothesi*, be different. At that level one looks at aggregates not sub-sets of aggregates. Any change is going to mean that the aggregates are going to be different at the different times. So a theory of meaning cannot give us what we need to say that it is a case of theory-change, because we need there to be constant meanings in order to say that it is a theory-change. If we look just to the aggregate level there are no constant meanings. This is just to underline that a theory of meaning is not the central thing that philosophers take it to be. Its function is relatively minor because all it does is to track the very general resources we must then select from in order to do the specific things we are interested in, when we are interested in content, i.e. explain behavior, revise theory or belief in principled ways, compare theories etc.

In the case at hand, we need to say what makes for the conviction that we have a case of theory-change. That means looking in this locality in which we are comparing temporally distant theorists for an invariance or commonality between beliefs at earlier and later times. (In the case of explaining an action we look in a particular locality to the beliefs that are needed for the explanation of that particular action.) In both cases the notion of meaning or concept that emerges is at a local level. Just as with action where we ask, how shall we explain this action, here we ask, how shall we establish the conviction that this particular change is a case of theory-change? And in this locality we give the answer by looking to the shared beliefs which establish what the shared subject-matter (say, "star" ) is. At this local level, the theory of meaning does not have any direct answers to offer at all. It only provides a pool of resources from which local answers are selected.

This view of how to preserve theory-change has the consequence of sometimes denying transitivity over a series of changes of theory (see chapter 3). Once we are clear about the locality of content, there is no need to be alarmed by this consequence. It is easily explained. There can be shifts of locality which spoil the idea that something like transitivity should be preserved, and only a refusal to keep track of the shift in locality makes one want transitivity, even so. So, there may be an invariance between a theory I hold at times $t_1$ and $t_2$ and another invariance between the theory I hold at $t_2$ and $t_3$. Let us say that the first invariance gives us the conviction that I have changed my *theory* (rather than changed my subject or meanings), so we may say that I now have a different theory about $x$. But the invariance between my theories $t_2$ and $t_3$ may be in a different locality and the same beliefs are not shared in this locality, so there is no temptation to say that this too must be a change about $x$. It is a different invariance. However, there would be a temptation to say this if we had adopted an orthodox causal theory of reference, and there was a common unmediated causal external link for the relevant concepts in all three theories. That is, on this scenario in the wide content picture, both instances of theory change are cases of theories about $x$ changing, since the fixing of the concept $x$ is not via shared beliefs but some alleged causal underpinning independent of all beliefs and descriptions.

One can imagine a tolerant orthodox externalist going along with my view of concepts, for the sake of argument, but then saying, with disappointment: "The view would be fine but for the fact that it can destroy the transitivity in theory-change. That is surely a sign that something is wrong with the view. In the end you must come around to some causal-theoretic account, to preserve transitivity." If I am right, however, intransitivity in such situations of theory-changes will only be taken as a sign that something has gone wrong, if we fail to fully appreciate the locality thesis. If we merely adopt my belief-oriented view of concepts without adopting the locality thesis, we will see the failure to preserve transitivity as an embarrassing consequence of my view. Thus my response to such disappointment can only be to point out that the locality has shifted from one change to the other change, and the assumption that it must must be $x$ that both changes are about is based on a failure to see this shift. One fails to see the shift in locality only if one has no place for locality of this kind in one's theoretical framework. The insistence that it is $x$ that both changes are over is precisely the result of missing the fact that questions about theory-change are questions that arise only in local contexts and not at the general meaning-theoretic level. And, in turn, it is missing this fact that makes philosophers think that the general meaning-theoretic level must, in the end, be chased out by some orthodox version of the causal theory of reference, rather than as in my more innocuous idea of theories of meaning where it is cashed out in terms of aggregates of beliefs.

What has been said about theory-change and transitivity, applies generally to questions of inference, where different premises may invoke concepts which, despite appearances, are different due to shifts in locality; yet being caught in the wrong picture of concepts one insists that the inference must go though. Often the inference ought not to go through and only being in the grip of the wrong picture of concepts and contents makes one think that something has gone wrong if it has not gone through.

This point applies as well to questions of communication and the reporting of beliefs where three agents may be involved. Imagine Norman who does not know that a man he knew as "Cassius Clay" went on, in his maturity, to become a Black Muslim. I report a belief held by Norman, the belief that Cassius Clay was a Praxiteles in chocolate, to Mailer, who knew what Norman did not know, but did not know something Norman knew, viz. that someone that he, Mailer, knew as "Muhammad Ali," was once a youngster from Louisville who was born a Christian. I report it by saying that "Norman believes that Muhammad Ali was a Praxiteles in chocolate." I see no reason to deny that, in doing so, I have failed to report accurately what Norman believed. The locality in which this communication took place was quite different from the one in which Norman communicated his belief to me. In the latter a hearer's ignorance of a boxer's future religious developments is crucial, in the former a speaker's ignorance of a boxer's past is crucial (as is, presumably, my impatience in not explaining it to him); and once one sees that, one is not tempted to say that what was believed by one was exactly communicated to the other. It is only refusing to see the local contexts of such questions that makes us think that what was communicated to me by Norman was exactly what was communicated by me to Mailer. Once again the causal-theoretic conception of concepts or meaning will allow us to say that exactly the same things were communicated in both cases but that picture of communication is based on a wrong conception of the relation between the theory of meaning or concepts and the content of beliefs that enter communication (and enter other such things as the explanation of behavior, belief revision and theory change etc.).

There is, of course, more to be said about the subject of how belief-reports communicate information about the world as opposed to just information about a person's beliefs. It may be that what I wanted to communicate to Mailer was not exactly what Norman communicated to me. Perhaps what I wanted to communicate by citing what Norman believed was not what Norman exactly believed but some information about the world, as Mailer conceived of it. But in that case, the right and honest thing to say is that I achieved these communicative purposes but failed to (indeed, *by* failing to) accurately say what Norman believed.

In the final of this chapter, I will say more about this function of belief-reports where information about the world is conveyed by them. Here I only wanted to show the relevance of the locality thesis to the question of communication.


## TRUTH-THEORIES OF MEANING AND THE UNITY OF CONTENT

This section will address the second of the questions posed above: since I have abandoned a referential account of concepts (even in its description-theoretic form), since I do not think that the "reference" -clauses of a truth-theory of meaning do anything else but summarize certain beliefs of agents, why is mine an externalist account of content? I will show how and why I am still an externalist. But that would not be sufficient for the purpose of establishing the main claims of this book. I will also show why this way of thinking of truth-theories of meaning allows for the only externalist view which is compatible with the unity of content. I will argue this by elaborating on some subtle but important differences between my view of truth-theories and those of other non-orthodox externalists like Gareth Evans, John McDowell and Donald Davidson. It will emerge that the version of externalism I espouse is, by contrast more distinctly "Kantian" in one rather special sense of that term.

The entire issue of the usefulness of truth-theories in the study of content is an issue of how to represent externalism about content and the particular sort of individuation of content that exernalism brings with it. Truth-theories with certain modifications are useful in representing my particular externalism, and I have admitted that these will not count as truth-theories in any official sense since the point and function of such truth-theories and their clauses, for me, is very different from that of other externalists who have also found truth-theories useful in representing their externalism.

## Externalism without Russellian Thoughts

It is particularly important to note significant differences between my conception of the point and function of truth-theories and John McDowell's, because it is McDowell's suggestion I have adopted for the second modification. It may seem that since Mcdowell and I are agreed on the usefulness of a particular truth-the-oretic representation of externalistically conceived content, that we must also share the same externalism about content and share the same idea of what work the truth-theory is doing. But that is not so. The concern that is indeed shared by us is to make the truth-theories sensitive to how an agent conceives of things. It is this concern that prompts McDowell to formulate the modification he proposes and it is this concern that makes me follow him in adopting this modification. But, in fact, there is serious disagreement about the nature of externalism, and there is only a limited agreement on the point and function of the truth-theories formulated along the lines of these modifications. In other words there is disagreement, first, on what the truth-theories are representing (the externalism). And, second, though there is agreement that truth-theories serving as theories of content should remain sensitive to agents' conceptions of things and agreement on the form of the theories which will preserve this sensitivity, there is still serious disagreement on how exactly it is preserved and what the function of such modified truth-theories is. The two disagreements are closely related and they will not always be kept separate in the discussion that follows.

McDowell's view of the role of truth-theories in the study of content, in effect, denies what I claimed in the last section: that the function of the clauses of the truth-theories is to summarize beliefs of agents.[11]

Even though McDowell modified the theory in the way we mentioned in order to keep faith which agents' conceptions, he still thinks that in the case of Pierre, for instance, the clause in each case simply states which city Pierre's name names. For him the sensitivity to agent's conceptions emerges in the context of interpretations (in the context of assigning concepts and contents to agents), but the context of interpretation does not make any difference to what the clauses of the theory say, whether explicitly or implicitly. In interpretation we select a particular clause rather than another, but the selected clause in virtue of its selection does not say or imply more than that Pierre's name is a name of the city in question, it does not say or imply what his conception of the city is. Instead, McDowell thinks that the theory would not be interesting if it were not usable in interpretation, and wanting it to be usable in interpretation puts constraints on how we would express it, over and above the constraint that its deliverances should be true. For Pierre we would have to express it along the lines suggested by the modifications. Hence, according to McDowell the truth-theory does not even implicitly convey anything about content. He calls this conception of truth-theories and the clauses in them an "austere" conception. An austere conception of truth-theories does not deny that something about content is conveyed – quite explicitly – by a claim *about* a truth-theory, to the effect that it can be used in interpretation. The modifications are necessary because being careful about how we fix extensions (i.e. which right-hand side expressions we use to do so) is desirable in the context of the use to which we want to put truth-theories. But the theories themselves are austerely conceived. They themselves do not explicitly or implicitly convey the information I claim they do.

One wants to ask, however, how they are so usable in the context of interpretation unless the clauses implicitly convey the agent's conceptions? McDowell would say, and has said (in correspondence with me) that "the context has the point of enabling us to use the truth-theories *as if* they specified content [my emphasis] in a way that is sensitive to agents' conceptions and to the fineness of grain necessary for the psychological efficacy of content." They do not, therefore, have to be seen as implicitly conveying the content, so the clauses do not carry or summarize any extra information.

The idea of using truth-theories *as if* they specified content is a little fishy, and not particularly illuminating, in the way that almost all philosophical talk of "as if" is fishy and unilluminating. It seems to me that such talk with respect to truth-theories here is no advance whatever on my talk of summarizing or implicitly conveying information. In fact, it is much more mysterious. No doubt, one avoids the messiness (in one's truth-theory) of all that information implicitly conveyed if one takes his ("austere") view rather than mine about the function of the clauses. But one trades messiness for obscurity. And in any case the mess will have to be somewhere in the picture, as we shall see, even for McDowell. It is just that by this obscure talk of "as if" he avoids the messiness in the specification of the concepts.

Notice that I am not for a moment saying that McDowell, in effect, capitulates to a view of content that is not sensitive to agents' conceptions. I also acknowledge that he sees the role of an agent's beliefs in the task of getting around the sort of puzzle Pierre poses.[12] I only worry how one can, without obscurity, pursue the idea that truth-theories representing a unified view of content can be sensitive to agent's conceptions without seeing the role of the agents' beliefs in the way I do. I see them as being what the clause of truth-theories summarizes. He denies that.

Why is it so important to him to deny it? It cannot just be that he thinks that the use of terms like "truth" and "refers" are inappropriate for something that merely has the function of summarizing beliefs. That is a terminological matter. The question before us is a substantive one and can be rephrased as follows with different terminology: why, despite his sensitivity to the need for capturing agents' conceptions, does he want a theory of reference and truth to capture them; why does he not instead work, as I do, with a theory which specifies (implicitly or, if it were possible, explicitly) the beliefs of agents which comprise these conceptions? This question does not present my view of how to specify meaning and concepts as involving truth-theories at all. I want to make clear that from now on this will be the real question under discussion. Even if I often put the question in the terminology of our opposing view of truth-theories, this is the real question.

One answer to this question might come from the thought that his "austere" theories specify such minimal information that that information is more likely to be within the ken of the speaker or thinker's own awareness. To specify anything richer or more substantial may explain a person's linguistic capacity but it would appeal to things which an agent might have no self-knowledge of. McDowell himself makes this charge against less austere visions of such theories than his own, accusing them of what he calls "psychologism." He explicitly singles out Michael Dummett's view of how one must go beyond these austere truth-theories which merely tell us such things as what objects names name to theories which specify less austere "implicit knowledge" such as speakers' "ways of knowing" the objects; and he also very likely has in mind to attack the sort of tacit linguistic knowledge posited by recent linguistic theory.[13]

When McDowell attacks the idea of "ways of recognizing" he says this: "one can have the ability to tell that a seen object is the bearer of a familiar name without having the slightest idea how one recognizes it. The presumed mechanisms of recognition might be neural machinery – its operations quite unknown to the possessor" (1976, p.167). McDowell also criticizes the idea of implicit linguistic knowledge comprising the notion of sense or meaning, saying that to postulate inner cognitive mechanisms is to be guilty of the psychologism that Frege detested. He says: "There is no merit in a conception of the mind which permits us to speculate about its states, conceived as states of a hypothesized mechanism, with a breezy lack of concern for facts about explicit awareness" (McDowell 1976, p. 148).

But it should be clear that whether or not these criticisms hit the targets they are aimed at, they cannot be relevant to the view of theories I am promoting. When I claimed that the theory's clauses summarize beliefs I did not have in mind anything like the "ways of recognizing" which are being criticized here. The beliefs that would handle Pierre's case, for instance (beliefs such as "London is the city my nanny said Oscar Wilde lived in;" "London is the city my nanny grew up in;" perhaps, sometimes, beliefs such as the metalinguistically specified

"London is the city my nanny called 'London'" etc.), do not amount to different "ways of recognizing" a city. And if they did, i.e. if that is all that Dummett had in mind when he talked of "ways of recognizing," then it does not seem to me that he should be the target of these criticisms. Even in cases where perceptual beliefs are being summarized by the clauses, that would still not amount to anything like what McDowell finds objectionable. Once we are clear that it is beliefs which are in play, and not neural mechanism of recognition nor some non-intentional cognitive counterpart to the neural mechanisms of recognition, McDowell's criticisms are not relevant.

It is true that the beliefs summarized by the theory's clauses are not always beliefs that we have at our fingertips or at the forefront of our minds but they are all the same beliefs that we could, on reflection, recall and would assent to if we were asked if they were true. It is also true that not all specifications of such beliefs will get us uniquely to the object that we or Pierre have in mind to think and talk about, and when that is so and when we do have a unique object in mind, we may need to appeal to the sort of metalinguistically specified belief just mentioned. If we cannot come up with beliefs that get us uniquely to an object, then perhaps we are not using the term as a singular term. (Perhaps, in some scenarios, which some philosophers ask us to imagine, all we can be meaning by "Godel discovered the proof for the incompleteness theorem" is that some man discovered the proof of the incompleteness theorem.) The point is that nothing other than beliefs of this kind comprise the idea of sense or meaning or agents' conceptions, and psychologism would be a quite unfair charge to bring against an idea comprised of such things. Positing such things is by no means to show "a breezy lack of concern for facts about explicit awareness."

This makes clear also that the idea of implicit knowledge or belief operative here is not at all on a par with the sort of tacit knowledge of language one finds posited by recent linguistic theory. Much of linguistic theory which posits that kind of knowledge concentrates not on the lexical aspects of language which is our primary concern (term like "London," "water" and so on) but on more structural aspects of language. Even when these theories are concerned with semantics and not syntax, they are concerned with more structural aspects of meaning than we are. There is a clear sense in which the mind as described by these linguists, in the domain of their primary interest, is often unrecognizable to agents. None but a very few scientists of language and its mental structures may ever be able to apprehend the details of the sort of tacit knowledge posited by these linguists. But implicit knowledge of the descriptions that one believes as holding of a star or a city or of a natural substance or a disease is not like that. I have admitted that agents often cannot verbalize these beliefs and list them all explicitly, but nevertheless these are the sorts of items that can be recalled by agents upon reflection; and I mean can genuinely be *recalled* as opposed to *acquired* via an education at the Department of Linguistics at the Massachusetts

Institute of Technology. For, it is out of the question that the sort of tacit knowledge often posited by linguists can be recalled.[14]

I took up these anti-psychologistic considerations just to make sure that there was no temptation to think that McDowell's appeal to them in his attack on Dummett and others carries over into a plausible attack on my vision of what theories specifying an agent's concepts should be doing. These anti-psychologistic considerations, then, do not provide an answer to the question about McDowell's "austerity" and I turn now to a much deeper set of considerations to answer it.

A fundamental part of the answer to our question is that McDowell is committed to a very different externalism from mine. This disagreement has consequences for the way we see the work that the theories which specify concepts are supposed to do. The disagreement flows from McDowell's commitment to the idea that singular thought is, in essence, what he calls "Russellian thought." This idea is the cornerstone of his and Gareth Evans's externalism about content, but there is no reason for an externalist conception of mind to make any such commitment.

Evans (1980) and McDowell (1976, 1984a) are as sympathetic as I am to an anti-internalist, anti-Cartesian conception of mind and are as opposed as I am to multiplying notions of content. (As an important terminological aside I should point out that they use the term "Cartesian" to cover all internalism, i.e. it is meant to cover more than phenomenological versions of internalism and includes more modern materialist and functionalist notions of internalism as well. I will follow them in this use.) But this convergence of sympathies between us does not cash out in the same strategies for repudiating Cartesianism. Our externalisms are very different.

They claim that we must turn our backs on Cartesianism by viewing singular thoughts as being "Russellian," in the sense that if there is no object that the singular thought is a thought about, then, strictly speaking, there is no singular thought at all. What is added to Russell by Evans and McDowell is that this thesis also covers singular thoughts about objects in the world external to agents, whereas for Russell it was restricted to sense-data.

Speaking of singular thought which involves demonstratives (and the point is extended by him – and McDowell – to cover proper names), Evans says: "For example, an internal state can be ascribed the content that *this table is round* only if there is a particular object it is about and on which it is causally dependent" (Evans 1980, pp. 79-80).

The motive for saying this is to deny a second notion of content. He says, "There is no neutral or 'existence-independent' specification of this content to which we can retreat if the subject is hallucinating." Thus, for Evans, one should refuse to move to a second notion of psychological content that is shared by hallucinator and veridical perceiver, not because the already available content *this table is round* is perfectly adequate, but because, as he says, "If there is no object (whether or nor the subject believes there is) there is no content – no thought." Evans concludes this passage with an anti-Cartesian sentiment: "and this means that if the ideal description of mental life... is one which carries absolutely no commitments about the nature of the organism's environment, then it is an unattainable ideal."

I entirely concur with this last sentence as I do with the denial of a second notion of content. But I disagree with all that Evans says in leading up to these conclusions. There is little reason to deny what is intuitive and obvious: that a hallucinator and a veridical perceiver do share a thought, a singular thought;[15] and it is the shared thought that is of interest in psychological explanation, for it will explain common actions of these agents. It is fairly intuitive what I intend by "common" actions here. One way of conveying what is intended is to contrast their actions in this situation with their actions in some other situation, in which one of them thought that that table was square and the other thought that that table was round, or one thought that that chair was round and the other that that table was round. In these other situations, we would expect their respective beliefs to explain not common but different actions on their part, in an intuitively understood sense of "common" and "different" .

The important point is that, for me, the insistence that there is a shared thought between veridical perceiver and hallucinator requires no retreat from externalist content and is no concession at all to Cartesianism. But, for Evans, the insistence reflects a surrender of externalism. It requires retreating to a second non-externalist notion of content shared by the two agents. This can only be because he thinks of externalism very differently from the way I do.

Where does the difference between Evans's opposition to Cartesianism and mine lie? It lies partly in the fact that, for me, the external contributions to content come by an indirect method, in which it is concepts that are first attributed to agents on the basis of observing correlations between utterances containing particular terms and external items in the manner described in chapter 1. The point to be stressed is that mine is not an externalist theory of *content* in any direct way. The causal relations between external states of affairs and whole utterances of sentences are necessarily the evidence we look to for the attribution of *concepts*.[16] That is what makes me an externalist. That is where external things enter into the study of content; and content can itself be analyzed in terms of composition, by some routine method, out of concepts. It is hard to stress enough this two-stage process by which externality enters content (see chapter 1).

It results in the connection between external objects and contents being a very general one, by which I mean that there is no demand that for any particular singular thought, where an external object does not exist, there is no content of the relevant kind. Since it is concepts, generally, ("table," "round," "water,"' etc.) which are fixed by looking to certain external relations (under the appropriate constraint), any particular content is still in place, if the objects that it is about is missing. So we can, on occasion, hallucinate tables, see patches of water where there is nothing but a stretch of highway, and there is no externalist bar to having these perceptual contents reported as "This table is round" or "That's water ahead.' But admitting this does not spoil the idea of the general externalist connection, viz. that we only have such concepts as table, highway, etc. because we stand in external relations to things, i.e. because we are *not* in some Cartesian scenario of the First Meditation.

One consequence of this is that my opposition to Cartesianism is on much more general grounds (see my discussion of internalism in chapter 5). What I am stressing here is that those grounds are much more general than Evans's, so the whole anti-Cartesian strategy is very different. Here is what I mean by "more general grounds." Allowing the intuition that in particular cases of hallucination, hallucinators and veridical perceivers share contents, my repudiation of Cartesianism comes by denying that these particular cases can be generalized. I deny, on the basis of an argument (to be sketched in chapter 5), that there can be comprehensive hallucination or that all our beliefs about the external world can be false. This denial of the possibility of comprehensive illusion implies that I am an externalist, as I defined externalism at the very beginning of chapter 1, and as everybody else defines it: our contents cannot be thought of as being altogether independent of the causal relations in which we stand with the external world. If, as Descartes implies in the First Meditation, all our beliefs about the external world, could be episodes in a sustained dream, could exist even if there is no external world, that would imply that we could have all the contents we have independently of the external world. Since externalism, for me, comes in, merely via a denial of the coherence of such comprehensive error, and since my externalism about content is indirect in the sense mentioned in the last paragraph, I can say: in particular cases of hallucination, singular contents may still be attributed without compromise of the externalism. And I can say of these contents that they may be the same singular contents as the contents of veridically perceiving agents.

Evans's externalism repudiates Cartesianism much more brutally and straightforwardly because it denies even the initial intuition that there are shared thoughts between hallucinating and veridically perceiving agents. I claim, however, that psychology, however anti-Cartesian a discipline it is, still operates with that initial intuition and if an externalist view of content can accommodate the intuition, there is no reason why it should opt for something more radical. The externalism I favour thus stands distinguished from Evans's externalism.

(I should point out that I have deliberately taken care to say that Evans and McDowell repudiate Cartesianism rather than that they offer a demonstration of its falsity. That is because all that they offer is a way of thinking about content which does not allow Cartesianism to be true only if there are singular thoughts.

Since all they say is that singular thoughts require a referent for the singular term, Cartesianism may still be true if all our thoughts were non-singular. A Cartesian skeptic could respond to their view of singular thought not by rejecting it but by saying that there are no singular thoughts. If Cartesianism is to be shown to be false by their strategy, they will also have to show something that their strategy by itself has not established, viz. that we have singular thoughts.)

It may be objected that I have focused too much on their anti-Cartesian motives and that there may be other related motives, having to do with the nature of demonstratives, which make them favor the Russellian thesis. Many philosophers, even those who find Cartesianism perfectly acceptable and therefore are opposed to Evans and McDowell, may nevertheless find their negative point that the hallucinating agent lacks a *singular* thought convincing. They may find it convincing because of the nature of demonstratives. They may say that my intuition that the hallucinator and veridical perceiver share the relevant psychologically explanatory contents can be accommodated by saying that what they share is not a singular thought but a general thought. Thus they would join Evans and McDowell in denying that what these agents share is thoughts specified as "*That* table is round". They would deny that the intuition demands a singular specification of the shared thought; in fact, they would object that it is odd to say that the hallucinator should be attributed the content "*That* table is round" since there is no table there and the attributor knows that. There is no table for the "that" in the attributor's attribution to get a grip on. (These objectors are assuming a view of content-attribution, due to Davidson, in which the attributor has to be able to make a saying of his own by uttering the content sentence.)

The objection first mislocates the special nature of demonstratives in an agent's psychological economy and, second, it fails to see my point that one can come to have mastery of certain *concepts*, including demonstrative concepts, on the basis of standing in external causal relations without requiring that *each content* in which that concept occurs must have an external object as referent in order to be a singular content.

Recall that we are attributing contents which are supposed to get right an agent's psychology and therefore we are supposed to get *his* point of view, his conception of things. And surely from the agent's point of view, his content *is* the content "*That* table is round," and not some non-singular surrogate for it. As far as he is concerned, as far as he conceives of things, he is having a singular thought and not the rephrased general thought that this view is suggesting. And by his "conception of things" I do not mean anything phenomenological. So I cannot be accused of old-fashioned Cartesianism. The intuition that the hallucinating agent has a singular thought and that he has the same thought as the verdicial perceiver is not a phenomenological intuition at all. The point is rather that the semantic or inferential role of the thought in his psychological economy is the role of a demonstrative thought.

What makes something have the psychological role of a demonstrative thought? Not the fact that an external object is involved, because if the agent is hallucinating it is *not* involved. Rather, the fact that in his psychological economy there is an element of reflexivity, even though there is no external object. And, in particular cases, that is perfectly possible. That is, it is perfectly possible, in particular cases, that the reflexive element essential to demonstratives indexicals can exist, without there being an object there. Demonstratives, in those particular cases, can continue to play the psychological role which is peculiar to them and which comes from their special reflexivity. This special role they have makes them ineliminable. To say that indexicals are ineliminable in this way is to say that they have a reflexive role which no non-indexical paraphrase of them can capture. No indexical in a judgment is paraphrasable without appeal to some other indexical. "I" can only be replaced by the "thinker of *this* thought;" "That" can only be replaced by "the object of *this* demonstration" or by "the object in front of *me*;" and so on.

The crucial point is that this ineliminable role has nothing necessarily to do with the Russellian claim about the object-dependence of each demonstrative thought. One can instead diagnose that ineliminable psychological role of indexicals along lines that are now familiar from the writings of John Perry (1979)and David Lewis (1979). Their diagnosis is that a proper understanding of agency requires us to see indexicals as playing an ineliminable reflexive role. I would not be an agent, I would not produce actions such as drinking a glass of water on grounds of thirst, if I did not think such things as that it was *I* who was thirsty or that *that* glass of water would quench my thirst. As this diagnosis makes clear, the reflexive role of indexicals disallows rephrasing these indexical thoughts in non-indexical terms. It disallows attributing thoughts such as "the only Indian in the Columbia Philosophy Department is thirsty" and "the glass of water on the kitchen table will quench my thirst" because these may not be enough to account for action and agency. I need to know that I am the only Indian in the Columbia Philosophy Department and that that is the glass of water on the kitchen sink. These points are well known and will not be rehearsed here. My claim is only that it is these points about motivational forces and agency which capture the special and unique psychological role of demonstratives in an agent's psychological economy, and one does not need to posit Russellian thoughts over and above them to capture what is special about demonstratives. There is no need to demand that each singular thought must be object-dependent in the Russellian way. Hence I conclude, contra Evans, that since this ineliminably reflexive psychological role can exist even if, on occasion, there is no object present (no glass of water or table), it can be shared by hallucinator and veridical perceiver.

It is true, of course, that causal (sensory) relations with an external world are necessary, in general, to have the special reflexive element in one's thought at all, i.e. the scenario of Descartes's First Meditation, where there is comprehensive independence of thought from the external world, leaves mysterious how we could ever have demonstrative thought with its special reflexive element. This is a point that someone should be willing to grant to Evans. But granting it does not mean that we cannot find intelligible that that reflexive element exists in the psychological economy of an agent *on a particular occasion*, when he has a hallucinatory demonstrative thought. That hallucinatory thought can still have the special psychological role of demonstrative thought in his psychological economy.

In conceding the point granted to Evans in the last paragraph, we would, of course, be rejecting any account of the special reflexive nature of demonstrative thought that is purely internalist. John Searle (1983) offers such an account and proudly announces it as an account of demonstratives that would allow brains-in-vats and other such imaginary Cartesian agents to have demonstrative thought. The point granted to Evans contradicts Searle's account. But if I am right, internalism and the Russellian thesis version of externalism are not the only two options on the special character of demonstrative thought. One does not have to take the Russellian view if one does not like Searle's view. One can explain the special nature of indexicals along Perry's and Lewis's lines having to do with their unique role in accounting for agency, thereby finding Russellian thoughts unnecessary.[17] One can accept that one would not, in general, have a grip on the special nature of indexicals without being the sorts of creatures who stand in causal and sensory relations with the external world, thereby rejecting Searle's internalist account. One could nevertheless insist that the externalism this rejection of Searle brings is not Evans's and McDowell's externalism to which the Russellian thesis is central.

Hence the grip on demonstratives that an attributor must generally have in order to attribute demonstrative thoughts certainly comes from, among other things, relating utterances of others (initially, his linguistic trainers) to objects in the external world. But once he has such a grip there is no problem in his attributing demonstrative contents, on occasion, to agents who are hallucinating.

So, though the attributor may know that there is, in fact, no table there, he will find it odd to ascribe the thought "That table is round" only if he allows *his* conviction about its non-existence to dominate his task of capturing *the agent's* psychological contents; and only thus will we look for a rephrasing in non-singular terms. To do so misses the context in which contents are to be ascribed and within which I make claims for my own anti-Russellian intuitions, the context of capturing an agent's conceptions of things.

Someone may persist and say that I still have not answered the objection that the fact that the attributor has to use an utterance of his to attribute the content in a that-clause and the fact that the attributor knows that the agent is hallucinating, makes it impossible to attribute the singular content "*S* believes that that table is round." My answer is that the objection betrays a prejudice we have encountered before, a prejudice which makes it virtually impossible for an attributor to put oneself into the shoes of an agent. Actually to produce sufficient empathy for the agent in order to accurately report his thoughts, it is *not even* required that the attributor has to put himself in the shoes of the agent. In order to capture agents' conceptions he does not have to empathize so much with the agent that he momentarily adopts the agents' thought that there is a table there. Even if he were to just entertain the faintest possibility that the agent is right (i.e. that the agent is *not* hallucinating) and that he himself is wrong, then the problem posed by the objection disappears. The objection is biased by the choice of examples just as the orthodox externalists were by the Pierre example in which the attributors are sure that Pierre is wrong in denying the identity of London and *Londres*. Similarly, here too there is strong conviction that there is no table. Other examples where there is not such strong conviction of the wrongness of the attributee would silence the objection. But the fact is that in *any* given thought one might have, there is some room for doubt: we just may be wrong and Pierre may be right that there are really two cities, we just may be wrong and *S* may be right that there is a round table there. If so, this objection should be silenced in the example under discussion as well. If there is a chance at all that the attributor is wrong and *S* right, why should the attributor withhold the demonstrative thought from *S*? It is that demonstrative thought, after all, that *S* may just be right in holding.

Of course, here too it is relevant that the attributor has to have a general grip on the special nature of demonstratives and that, in general, comes from standing in relations to external things which provide sensory input. So there is no abandoning of externalism. But once he has the grip, he can produce the requisite empathy on the occasion on which he is working on what he takes to be a hallucinating agent, an occasion on which there is no object for his own (attributed) demonstrative utterance to take a grip on something.

I have argued against Evans's and McDowell's thesis that non-referring demonstratives in hallucinatory thoughts are not genuinely singular thoughts. They also extend this Russellian thesis to singular thoughts containing vacuous or non-referring names. My argument is highly relevant for this extended thesis also because proper names in some eventual sense contain a hidden demonstrative element.

Just as with demonstratives, McDowell wishes to deny that a thought with a non-referring proper name is a genuine singular thought. For me there is no bar to thinking of it as a singular thought. For me the clauses in a truth-theory for a non-vacuous proper name summarize an agent's beliefs. The clauses for a vacuous or non-referring name will also summarize a set of beliefs, except of course there is no such object in the external world. The question McDowell worries about is, why a content (say, "Pegasus was swift") which contains a non-referring singular concept, if it is thought of along the lines I am suggesting for these latter clauses, should be called a singular thought at all? That is, it will be demanded that I owe a general statement of what the singularity of thought consists in.

Now, just as with demonstratives, there are surely ways other than Evan's and McDowell's for answering this question, ways which do not require that the purported object of reference itself must exist for the thought to be a singular thought. I am inclined to make the difference between the beliefs summarized in the two sorts of clauses (clauses for referring and clauses for non-referring names) by reminding ourselves of the analogy with demonstratives. It is more than just an analogy. If the name has a bearer, then we may say that the beliefs summarized are about that object. The demonstrative here is (eventually)[18] something that can be thought of as a demonstrative in the strict sense of pointing in the presence of an object (and, as always for me, there will be some minimal belief involved even in the identification of the object being pointed to, over and above all the beliefs about the object which are being summarized). In the case of a name without a bearer, what makes it a singular concept which goes into genuinely singular thoughts, is that a demonstrative is involved here too. What makes it different from the name with a bearer is that the demonstrative involved is not one in the strict sense of pointing in the presence of the object, not even eventually so. It is a different sort of demonstrative, one which gets its point merely from the context of the agent's beliefs. Thus, for instance, an agent may have all sorts of beliefs about a horse such as that it had wings, it caused a volcano to well forth with a stroke of the hoof, etc., and he believes of *that* horse that it is swift. The demonstrative here gets, in this way, its entire point from within the context of such beliefs. I have already dealt with the objection that the attributor of the content and concept does not have a grip on the demonstrative unless there is a horse there. I do not deny that mastery of demonstratives, in general, requires one to have been in appropriate relations with external objects. But this does not entail that one cannot attribute the hidden demonstrative element at work (in non-referring proper names) in the manner just suggested, when there is no object present (not even eventually) to which a strict demonstration can be made.

In the case of fictional non-referring names the beliefs of the agent that the attributor will invoke in order to fix the hidden non-strict demonstrative are really *make*-beliefs. So the clause "'Pegasus' refers John Doe to Pegasus" will summarize all John Doe's make-beliefs about an "object", an "object" of a non-strict demonstrative fixed via some of those make-beliefs along the lines just mentioned. When the attributor says that the clause summarizes his beliefs about *Pegasus*, his use of that term will be the use of a term in his own language. And the hidden non-strict demonstrative here too will be fixed (by another attributor) in the same make-beliefs which we will assume the (first) attributor shares with the agent. Things are a little trickier in the case of non-referring names which are not fictional names, i.e. when the agent really *thinks* that it is a referring name but the attributor does not. Here the beliefs invoked to fix the hidden non-strict demonstrative will *not* be make-beliefs of the agent. But when the attributor says that the relevant clause summarizes all the beliefs the agent has about..., this use of a term in his language will have to be understood (say, by a second attributor) in terms of beliefs that are make-beliefs of the attributor, since the attributor knows that the name is a non-referring name. The attributor is make-believing what the agent is believing.

And so the clauses for both sorts of names (referring and non-referring) summarize a set of beliefs and they both involve a demonstrative and that is why both sorts of names play the *same* sort of role in the agent's psychological economy. They are both, therefore, genuinely singular terms. Thus there is no reason to say that only one of them deserves a clause in a truth-theoretic formulation and only one of them contributes to singular thought. As far as their *meaning* goes, the meaning of both referring and non-referring names is given by these beliefs which are implicitly conveyed by summary in the clauses for them. What makes them different is that only one of them *refers* to an object and that fact is captured in the distinction between the demonstrative groundings just sketched. Since the distinction in the grounding does not make different the psychological role of the singular thoughts in which these two sorts of singular concepts occur, it does not cripple any particular singular thought containing a non-referring singular concept from genuine singularity. Both non-referring demonstratives and names can figure in the characterization of genuinely singular thought.

We have concentrated on Evans's and McDowell's discussion of the defective cases (hallucinations and non-referring names) to bring out the thrust of their Russellian view. But quite apart from the defective cases, the nature of demonstrative contents in the context of *veridical* perception may be thought to favor Evan's and McDowell's externalist position. For instance, it might be said, on their behalf, that there is an intuition that two agents who perceive two different tables, even where both are veridical perceivers, must have different contents. Thus, for instance, I and my *doppelgänger* on twin-earth must have different thought-contents since the contents are about two different tables and the actions they psychologically explain (say, of our both placing our feet on our respective tables because we are tired) are actions upon two different objects: he acts upon his table and I act upon mine. And so the contents that explain those actions must be different. When each says "It would be restful to put my feet up on *that* table" , it is intuitive that these express different contents because there are different tables that the demonstratives pick out.[19] This may be thought to be an intuition favoring the specific way in which the Russellian view emphasizes the external object in specific demonstrative contents.

I deny that the fact of there being different tables can be of any interest, if one takes the idea of intentional content as something that is essentially connected to psychological explanation. If the alleged difference is supposed to come from the fact that there are two different tables in the respective environments, a reason has to be given why this should make any difference to psychological content. As far as the agents' psychologies are concerned, it is the same thought; and I am insisting that it is the same *singular*, not general, thought, with the same inferential and ineliminable reflexive roles; and, again, as far as our interest in psychological explanation is concerned, it is the same sort of action which is being explained. As it happens there are different table in the environment but that makes no difference to the structures of practical reasoning and the actions and contents they work upon, which interest the psychological explainer. So even though there is a sense in which the explananda and the explanans *could* be described differently for the two agents, as far as psychological content is concerned that difference is trivial and uninteresting.

To say that this difference is uninteresting is to agree with many philosophers. But to say that it is uninteresting is not at all to say, as many of these philosophers have, that the demonstrative and indexical elements themselves are not interesting or relevant to psychological content of the thoughts in practical reasoning. I am not saying that psychological explanation need only appeal to general thoughts. These elements cannot be replaced by non-singular specifications, they are essential and ineliminable from the practical reasoning that goes into acting. On this I am in agreement with Evans and McDowell. The point of disagreement is that I am arguing that the role of the demonstrative is exactly the same in the two agents. It plays exactly the same role in their respective putting of their feet on their respective tables. And I have already said something about what that common role is. Hence, all that I find uninteresting is that there are different tables. That fact is trivial to and makes no difference to psychological content, nor to demonstrative content and its special role. Therefore, even if one grants the importance of demonstrative thought to psychology and psychological content, there is no reason to think that, in the example mentioned, I and my *doppelgänger* have different contents.

I suspect Evans and McDowell have claimed greater importance for a difference I call trivial because they think that if we downplay the difference, we will make content susceptible to a Cartesian characterization.[20] As a description of the way philosophers of mind have thought of this issue, they are perfectly right. Philosophers, having pointed out the irrelevance of the fact that there are two different tables in the *external* environment to psychological explanation, go on to posit an *internalist* notion of narrow content for the task of psychological explanation. This pendulum swing from an implausible and unintuitive externalism to internalism is unnecessary. One simply does not follow from the denial of the other. One can grant the irrelevance of the difference and still resist internalism and Cartesianism on general grounds. There is no need, therefore, to succumb to narrow content. One can point to the irrelevance of there being different tables and yet insist that if there were not, in general, such things as tables with which we stand in causal relations we would not have any of the concepts or thoughts we have. Hence, Evans's and McDowell's position is not the only way to make the case against Cartesianism. My externalism turns its back on Cartesianism just as much as theirs does, but it does so without making any unintuitive assumptions about how our singular psychological contents must be Russellian. To think that resistance to the Russellian thought thesis as being unintuitive *must* stem from an internalist prejudice is quite simple to have overlooked the fact that one can repudiate internalism on much more general grounds than theirs. The unintuitiveness of the Russellian thesis stems rather from our most ordinary thoughts about what is of interest and relevance in the commonsense explanation of human behavior, thoughts which an externalism ought to try to respect.

A passage from McDowell should help to drive home some of the points just made. Talking about his Russellian view of singular terms, he says this:

Opposition to this [the idea of Russellian thoughts], on behalf of Frege, involves, I believe, a suspect conception of how thought relates to reality, and ultimately a suspect conception of the mind. The Fregean view would have to seek its support in the idea that thought relates to objects with an essential indirectness: by way of a blueprint or specification which, if formulated, would be expressed in purely general terms. Whether the object exists or not would then be incidental to the availability of the thought. Underlying that idea is the following line of argument. When we mention an object in describing a thought we are giving only an extrinsic characterization of the thought (since the mention of the object takes us outside the subject's mind) but there must be an intrinsic characterization available (one which does not take us outside the subject's mind) and that characterization would have succeeded in specifying the essential core of the thought even if extra-mental reality had not obliged by containing the object. From this standpoint the argument for the non-Fregean [Russellian] view outlined above goes wrong in its principle that a thought expressed by a sentence containing a name, if there is any such thought, is correctly describable as a thought, concerning some specified object, that it satisfies some specified condition. That would be a merely extrinsic charac- terization of the thought expressed; it succeeds in fitting the thought only if reality obliges. If reality does not oblige, that does not show, as the argument suggested, that no thought was expressed after all. For the real content of the thought expressed would need to be given by an intrinsic characterization; and that would specify the content of the thought without mentioning extra-mental objects, and thus in purely general terms.

The conception of mind which underlies this insistence on not mentioning objects, in specifying the essential core of a thought, is the conception beautifully expressed in Wittgenestein's remark, 'If God had looked into our minds, he would not have been able to see there whom we were speaking of'. It is profoundly attractive, and profoundly unsatisfactory. Rummaging through the repository of general thoughts, which, when we find the remark plausible, we are picturing the mind as being, God would fail to find out, precisely whom we have in mind. Evidently that (mythical) repository is not the right place to look, but god (or anyone) might see whom we have in mind rather by–for instance–seeing whom we are looking at when we speak. That sort of thing–seeing relations between a person and bits of the world, not prying into a hidden place whose contents could be just as they are even if there is no world–is, in part, what seeing into a person's mind is. (McDowell 1976, pp. 153-4)

There are two comments to be made on this passage by way of disagreement.
*First:* McDowell argues that a denial of the Russellian view flows from a commitment to an internalist picture of the mind. (In this he seems to share with diehard internalists like Searle the conception of the available choices.) That is the point of his second quoted paragraph, the last sentence of which says that to fail to take his view amounts to saying that to find out the contents of the mind one has – if one could, and I suppose only God could – to pry "into a hidden place whose contents could be just as they are even if there is no [external] world." It is precisely such a picture of the mind that I think an externalism repudiates but, as I just argued, it is wholly unnecessary to adopt the externalism of the Russellian view in order to repudiate it. My argument turns on two factors:

(1) The internalist picture of the mind is false, if it is false, not because the Russellian thesis is the true but because even if particular errors about the external world (described in singular contents with singular terms and concepts) are conceded to be thoughts with genuine singular contents, one ought not to allow the generalization from these particular errors to comprehensive error; one ought not to allow that there is any coherence to the thought that such error is comprehensive. In other words, conceding genuine singular contents for erroneous thoughts is not to allow that a mind is the sort of thing, to use McDowell's words, "whose contents could be just as they are even if there is no world," the scenario of Descartes's First Meditation. And the crucial point I want to insist on is that not to allow it is all one needs to be an externalist. This is admittedly a rather indirect way of establishing externalism: it does so merely by denying, on the basis of a general argument, that it would be incoherent to think that all our thoughts could be the thoughts they are even if there is no external world. This is akin to the general indirect strategy by which Kant argues against idealism. And I take this indirectness to be a virtue because one can be an externalist without embracing either orthodox externalism or the unintuitive idea of Russellian thoughts.

(2) Externalism about *content* should be seen as having an indirect route in

another, not unrelated, sense. It is *concepts* (or at any rate many concepts) that are externally constituted out of the causal relations that we have with external objects. This gives rise to an externalism about content because these concepts are what contents are composed of.

Once we see the point in (2) about how externalism is primarily a doctrine about the possession of concepts and only indirectly about contents, the point being made in (1) above becomes much clearer. That point was that externalism could be maintained even if not every singular content has the requisite object, demanded by the Russellian thesis. Well, if externalism is merely the doctrine that we would not possess such concepts as "table," "chair"... unless we stood in causal relations with the external world, there is no reason for an externalist to deny that, on occasion, I could have a singular content like "That table is round" without there being a table there. One does not automatically become an internalist or Cartesian if one does not deny it. (2), thus, explains how (1) is possible.

*Second*: In the first cited paragraph, McDowell attacks a certain idea of "indirectness." He attacks the view that treats non-referring singular terms in a non-Russellian way and says that any such view "would have to seek its support in the idea that thought relates to objects with an essential indirectness: by way of a blueprint or specification which, if formulated, would be expressed in purely general terms. Whether the object exists or not would then be incidental to the thought."

Now, both (1) and (2) above admit that the way external objects are relevant to content is very indirect. But notice that this indirectness of the relation between contents and external objects one finds in my view is not the indirectness McDowell would find in anyone who opposes the Russellian view. I agree with McDowell that when we look to find out what the contents of a person's mind are we should not, even if we could, look to a mythical repository of non-singular or general thoughts inside of him. There are, as I keep insisting, *singular* thoughts with their special ineliminable psychological role. As an externalist, I also agree that the idea of the mind as an "inner repository" is also unnecessary. Where we disagree is how we look to the relevance of the outside of his mind and this is where the indirectness of *my* view comes in. This indirectness makes no concession the idea that the relation of thought to the external world has the essential indirectness "by way of a blueprint or specification which, if formulated, would be expressed in purely general terms." It is the quite different indirectness of (1) and (2). Thus, though I am sure that he is right about how many others are happy to move to the non-singular blueprint, I reject the accusation that my denial of the Russellian thesis would make me committed to the indirectness he has in mind.

Having said something about the difference between our externalisms, I return now to our differences on the question of the clauses in truth-theories: it does seem as if McDowell would want to deny the belief-summarizing role I wish to give them because he fears that it will result in this picture of thought relating to external reality with the indirectness he has in mind. Only if one restricts the function of the clauses to telling us what objects the names on the left-hand sides name will avoid the indirectness he has in mind.

It has just been shown that even if one takes my view of the function of the reference-clauses, one does not imply anything which is susceptible to McDowell's charge of indirectness – though I have granted a sense of indirectness in the way my view sees the relevance of external objects to content.

But there is also the question as to what exactly his own positive view is, of how a truth-theory achieves sensitivity to an agent's conceptions of objects. What exactly does that amount to if we restrict the function of the clauses in the way McDowell wants? He does not deny that an agent's beliefs are relevant to the project of making a truth-theory sensitive to agents' conceptions. (Nobody can deny it because nothing but beliefs can comprise agents' conceptions.) He does not, however, want to allow my idea that the clauses themselves summarize the beliefs. Where, then, do the beliefs of the agent enter into his picture, if not as what the clauses summarize? I have no clear answer to this question. Beliefs are somewhere in the offing providing for the conception-sensitive work that the modified clauses are supposed to do. But they are not what the clauses themselves implicitly convey. The singular term simply names the city but nevertheless somehow the beliefs are hovering somewhere in the picture so as to account for Pierre's different conceptions.

Why should not someone rightly conclude from this that it is an implicit concession to bifurcation? Not, of course, to bifurcation into wide and narrow content as orthodoxly conceived, but all the same into two notions of content.

There is, *on the one hand*, the singular "concept," which each of Pierre's two names expresses, which applies to the one city. This means that looking to the clauses, despite the modifications of them, will not by itself get us what we want, viz. that, from his point of view, there are two cities. If the clauses of a truth-theory are not allowed to summarize or implicitly convey his beliefs, the fact of there being two distinct right-hand sides in the clauses will not, by itself, ground the claim that there are two different cities from Pierre's point of view. Something else will be needed to ground it. This will be his beliefs. So there are, *on the other hand*, the different "conceptions" of the city given in his different sets of beliefs about the city.

In other words, there are *concepts* and *conceptions* obtained from looking at the truth-theories and at the beliefs respectively. How can one deny that this amounts to bifurcation, with one notion of content containing the concept and the other, the conceptions?

So, unless one sees the clauses for the concepts or terms as themselves conveying the beliefs, the concept and conceptions cannot be yoked together into a unity. If you believe in unity you had better find a way of representing it *in* your truth-theories and I do not see how you can do so unless you see the function of the truth-theories along my lines rather than McDowell's. Introducing the "as if" conception of truth-theories and their clauses is of no clearly discernible help in achieving unity. McDowell wants the beliefs or descriptions to do the agent-sensitive work without embracing a belief - or description - theory of sense or meaning. I do not see how the work these beliefs or descriptions, then, do is not a case of smuggling in through the backdoor a second notion of content.

I claim instead that agent-sensitivity and unity of content are only achieved by adopting a sophisticated version of a description-theory of the meaning (not reference) of terms, which is, unlike standard description-theories, externalist, and which, because it is subject to the locality thesis, brings with it no smell of definitions or clusters that description-theories are contaminated with. To take the view I do of the clauses in a truth-theory of meaning is precisely to adopt such a theory.

I have charged McDowell's refusal to take my line on the function of the clauses as leading to a hidden bifurcation. Let me sum up my reasons for doing so. I cannot find a way of putting together three different things that McDowell believes in: the sensitivity that truth-theories must show to agents' conceptions; the refusal to allow that the clauses of truth-theories implicitly convey the beliefs of agents; and the refusal to bifurcate content. The obscure talk of truth-theories functioning "as if" they specified content is of no help at all with this problem.

The passage cited from McDowell brings out how the resistance to seeing the clauses as I do might come from a fear that all singular terms (and, therefore, singular thought) will be eliminated if clauses for them are seen as merely summarizing beliefs. We will be left with non-singular rephrasing of singular thoughts. And that is the "indirectness" that fills him with horror. The cited passage also makes clear that McDowell's fear of loss of singularity and the indirectness that that would entail, in turn, stems from the deeper fear of a loss of externalism, a fear that these would render the external world as "extrinsic" to the mind.

Given that my view retains certain forms of indirectness and given the non-Russellian way it retains singularity, this fear may seem to be justified about my view. I have given my reasons for denying this. The fear is based on a widespread, longstanding and dogmatic assumption that one does not have an externalist conception of language and thought unless one has direct link-ups between language or thought and the world. It is this assumption that lies behind McDowell's disallowing the clauses of a truth-theory to summarize the beliefs of an agent.

I do not mean to suggest that McDowell's Russellian view is not also a Fregean view which allows that the relations between an agent's singular terms and the external world is mediated by an agent's conceptions. He certainly allows for this, indeed insists on it, and it is what makes his view different from some of the other externalists I have been opposing in earlier chapters. So when I say it is the fear of the loss of direct link-ups I do not mean to suggest that he is anti-Fregean.

I have said that there is no other function of the clauses which specify concepts but to summarize certain beliefs of agents. And I have said this of all concepts, even of singular concepts such as names. These are not specified by stating what object a name names. It is specified rather by merely summarizing a selection of a set of beliefs that an agent associates with the name. A question, then, arises, as to how externalism enters into this way of thinking and theorizing about language and thought. Why can an internalist not also take this view? This is a perfectly fair question. I repeat the point about my indirect way of establishing externalism made in (1) above and give the following answer to this question. For an internalist to take this view he would have to say that we could have all these summarized beliefs, and be in possession of all the concepts being specified, whether or not there is an external world with which we had causal relations. This is how, in chapter 1, we, following Putnam and others, defined internalism (or "methodological solipsism," as Putnam and others sometimes call it). And it is the denial of this doctrine which defines externalism. It is also this doctrine that Evans and McDowell set out to oppose when they oppose Cartesianism. My claim is that we can deny what the internalist is saying by producing an argument to show that one cannot have all the beliefs and concepts one has unless one stands in causal relations with an external world. I hope to produce such an argument in chapter 5. In the present chapter I only want to say that whether I succeed in producing it or not, to try to produce an argument of this kind is to strive for an externalism very different from McDowell's and Evans's.

Now, why do I describe this difference between us as issuing from a refusal on my part to admit to direct link-ups between language and the world? One might think that all I mean by denying direct link-ups is already implied in my constraint (C). The constraint denies that external things can fix an agent's concepts except by appeal to other beliefs she has. But that is not all I mean by denying direct link-ups. If that is all I meant I could not distinguish my externalism from McDowell's because McDowell is clear that he wants to appeal to an agent's beliefs in order to capture the agent's conceptions of external things.

It is the way I see through the consequences of adopting this constraint which distinguishes my position from his and which with some right may be called a denial of direct link-ups. The constraint allows one to capture an agent's conceptions of things. But, for me, as I have said earlier, the conceptions of things are not to be seen as decouplable from the things. That is why mine is not just a description-theory of reference serving as a theory of sense or meaning. Mine is a description (or belief) theory of sense or meaning. This is why I say that the clauses of a concept-specifying theory do no more than specify the beliefs than an agent associates with his terms, including singular terms such as names.

McDowell insists that concept-specifying theories do not do that. In the case of names, they simply say what object the name names. One assumes that this means that he does not take my "undecouplable" view of agents' conceptions of things. The "undecouplability" of the conceptions from the things is not a commitment he needs to make given the way he conceives of these theories. For him, the theory just takes one to the things referred to and the beliefs or descriptions which comprise the conceptions of the things are not summarized by the clauses of the theory at all, but are nevertheless somehow in play. The advantage of his view it would seem is that despite the fact that it is *conceptions* of things that are specified, despite the fact that reference is mediated by *descriptions* as Frege demanded, it is really the *things* we are taken to in the clauses of theory and it is really *reference* that the clauses specify. Despite his commitment to senses and agents' conceptions, it is *de re* senses that he wants (see McDowell 1984a). This is what I mean by direct link-ups. He has it both ways. He has direct link-ups and he has the conceptions and mediating descriptions or beliefs.

I do not have it both ways nor do I want it both ways. I do not believe that one can have it both ways without a hidden bifurcation and I have tried to show that. I insist that all the clauses of a concept-specifying theory do is summarize beliefs. I am happy to say, therefore, that the agent's conceptions can not be decoupled from the things they are conceptions of and happy to say that the concept-specifying theory does not specify the reference (not even description-mediated reference) of terms. This is what I mean when I say that I deny direct link-ups.

But, then, of course the menancing question we posed above looms large. Why am I, despite all this, an externalist? This is the question I answered above. The answer was frank about the indirectness with which it establishes externalism. This indirect way of establishing it allows me my denial of direct link-ups which I have just sketched by contrast with McDowell's view of truth-theories. It also makes it totally unnecessary to embrace McDowell's and Evans's externalism which depends on the unintuitive thesis about Russellian thoughts.

McDowell's and Evans's insistence that opposition to their externalism based on the idea of Russellian thought must ultimately be diagnosed as flowing from internalist commitment betrays a prejudice that their externalism and internalism are the only available choices. This prejudice blinds them to the possibility of another way, a non-Russellian way that an externalist may capture agents' conceptions. I have, with some risk, called this other way Kantian partly because it does seem to me that their prejudice is the sort of thing that blinds one to strategies of argument against idealism long available in the history of epistemology. Kant himself saw the prejudice as the basis of a widespread refusal to countenance the Kantian position (what Kant himself called "empirical realism") which was an alternative to both Berkeleyan idealism and Lockean direct realism.

Here I intend to bring attention to only one strand of Kant's anti-idealist strategy, his argument to refute Berkeley's idealism. I do not mean to draw attention to his positive alternative doctrine of "transcendental idealism" with its particular conception of the place of space and time in our overall epistemology.

What I find sympathetic in Kant is his idea that there was a general (problematically described by him as "transcendental" ) argument for concluding that Berkeleyan idealism was false. He believed that there were general reasons having to do with the presuppositions of what he called "objective time-determination," (say, the determination of the duration of an event) which would show idealism to be an untenable doctrine, which would show that our experience was necessarily, though not of course exceptionlessly, experience of objective things external to us.[21] Because he claimed to have such a negative argument against the idea that none of our perceptions involved things external to us, he found it altogether unnecessary to swing to the other existing realist positions, which he found as problematic as idealism. His position was a realist one because it denied Berkeleyan idealism on the basis of an argument which showed that all our judgments could not be characterized in the idealistic terms that Berkeley described them.

It is this strategy against idealism that parallels my strategy against internalism. I stress that in pointing to this analogy with Kant's way of establishing "empirical realism," I do not intend to follow him in other details of his "empirical realism." Kant was primarily interested in epistemology and most of those details would more naturally lend support to Putnam and others who have recently invoked Kant to redefine the notion of truth along more epistemic lines and to propose a notion of realism called "internal realism." This is not my interest in invoking Kant. My point is restricted to the use of the notion of truth in the study of content. It is not clear to me that having done so, I have to redefine truth itself along Kantian lines. I may want to but I do not have to just because I have denied that there need be direct link-ups in the study of content and that standard notions of reference and truth-conditions have any role to play in the study of content. My point is only about content. I could still say that an agent's contents are true only if they coincide with God's contents. Presumably to say this would be to reject Putnam's "internal realism" . I do not actually want to say anything of the kind but the point is that if I actually did say that unKantian thing, it would be compatible with my "Kantian" strategy against internalist views of content.

Hence despite the large differences in context, aim, and subject-matter, the one point of analogy that I want to make with Kant abstracts from these differences to highlight a common strand of strategy about how to think of the external element and its relevance to content. The common strategy is simply to try to establish a certain doctrine (for me externalism, for Kant "empirical realism") by repudiating the coherence of some opposing doctrine (for me Cartesianism or internalism, for Kant "empirical idealism") on the basis of a general argument to the effect that all our thoughts (judgments) could not be of the sort that the opposing doctrine took them to be.

Chapter 5 has more to say about the general argument against Cartesianism, though I will resist the idea that it constitutes a transcendental argument. Here, I only mention this sort of argument as a possible way of establishing externalism despite thinking of theories specifying concepts as merely summarizing beliefs; and as an answer to McDowell's prejudice that we have no choice except between the externalism of his Russellian thesis and Cartesianism, a prejudice which echoes a familiar blindness to certain strategies of argument in the history of epistemology.

### *Davidson's Conception of Truth-theories of Meaning*

At the beginning this chapter I said that truth-theories, if they are to cope with the constraint on externalism I have introduced, will have to make two modifications to the sort of truth-theories we are familiar with from the seminal writings of Donald Davidson. This section will examine Davidson's truth-conditional account of meaning and his externalism, and diagnose briefly why, despite his externalism, he has neither imposed the constraint I insist on nor seen truth-theories of meaning as having the function I take them to have.

There is much that my overall perspective on belief and meaning owes to Davidson's overall vision. It would be a much easier step for Davidson's externalism, and for his conception of the relevance of truth-conditions to meaning, to adopt the constraint and the conception of truth-theories I propose than it would be for the orthodox externalism. Nevertheless, it would be a measurable step, for there are substantial and interestingly revealing differences between his view and a view of a content which is governed by the two theses of the unity and locality of content; revealing of the theses themselves as well as the nature of Davidson's vision of language and human action and the role of truth in their study.

Much of the details of my externalism and its truth-theoretic flip side flow from the difficulties posed by certain puzzles. Davidson has nowhere written on the sorts of difficulties that arise out of Kripke's puzzle or, for that matter, the puzzle that vexed Frege and forced him to introduce the notion of sense. It was interesting and instructive for me to ponder whether he would agree to impose my constraint on externalism, whether he would have then made the ensuing modifications and, above all, whether he would have then also embraced the merely summarizing role I have given to truth-theories.

But his response (in conversation)[22] to these proposals was quite different and it is easier to put it together with his classic proposal that a meaning of a sentence is to be understood in terms of the concept of truth. The response was this. His way of dealing with the question of sense and the difficulties of Kripke's puzzle is not to admit to truth-theories specifying some notion of an agent's "conception of things", as I have done. He, therefore, does not see the role of truth-theories as I do, he does not see them as summarizing an agent's beliefs. He sees them as having a somewhat different role. The idea of agents' conceptions was to capture the basic point of intentional states, to capture what goes into the psychological explanation of action. It is not that, in denying a basic place to the idea of such conceptions as what truth-theories specify, Davidson, in the end, fails to produce an account which is satisfying for psychological explanation. Rather, like McDowell, he simply sees no need to give special place *in truth-theories* to the idea of such conceptions, in order to provide an overall psychologically satisfying account of agents. He worries that to do so will introduce an idea which is caught up with a murky, traditional, conception of meaning and analyticity that Quine successfully repudiated.

Davidson, from the outset, has always said that his overall account has two components. He calls one the "meaning" component and the other the "belief" component. The first component is a theory which yields as its consequences truth-conditions for the sentences of a person's speech, and the second is a list of a person's beliefs. (Actually, he has more recently started emphasizing that there are three components. I ignore the third, which is a desire component, a list of a person's desires, since that is not crucial to my making the comparisons between his view and mine that I want to make.) Together these two components are an interpretative theory for the person. In this double-barrelled theory, Kripke's puzzle is not to be accommodated by tampering with the idea of a truth-theory, as I have suggested. His view of the solution to such puzzles is somewhat different. Putting aside for now the superficial worry about scrambling languages, let us see how his view works out for Pierre's two words (or concepts) "London" and "*Londres.*" [23] For Davidson, it is not necessary to represent in the truth-theory itself (by the discriminating right-hand sides in the axioms) the different sets of beliefs Pierre has associated with "London" and "*Londres.*" That would be, unnecessarily, to pursue the murky idea of an agent's conception of things. The relevant clauses that a radical interpreter (who believes in the identity of London and *Londres*) would produce in a Davidsonian truth-theory for Pierre, are as follows: "'London' refers to London" and "'*Londres*' refers to London."

Now, to the protest that this would make Pierre (in Kripke's original puzzle) come out to be a logical idiot when he is not one, come out as contradicting himself when he is not doing anything of the sort, Davidson's double-barrelled account can offer the following reply: that outcome will only follow if one ignores the other component, the belief component, where Pierre's beliefs are given. But, if one keeps it in mind, one will notice that in this component, in this list of Pierre's beliefs, there is the belief that London is not *Londres*. (To deal with Kripke's original puzzle, one does not even need to positively say that the belief that London is not *Londres* is present in the belief component, merely that the identity-belief is missing. But in some of the variants on the Kripke puzzle, discussed in chapter 2, Pierre's behavior suggests that it must be present in the belief component.) Once one pointed out that the crucial identity-belief is denied or missing in one component of the overall theory for Pierre, then the overall theory cannot be accused of making Pierre out to be a logical idiot since the appearance of contradiction suggested by looking only at one component is removed when one looks at the other as well. If Pierre assents to "*Londres est jolie*" and to "London is not pretty," he is not, as it might seem if one looked at just the truth-theory, contradicting himself. The puzzle thus disappears. Similarly, his puzzling inactions or actions in the variant puzzles are also explained away.

So, it is only a combined theory giving truth-conditions *and* a list of beliefs that will provide psychological explanation of behavior. There is no specific place in this picture for meaning in the sense I have been promoting, which is an agent's conceptions of things. The overall theory is supposed to do the job that an agent's conceptions are supposed to do for me, but without giving a specific place to agents' conceptions in the way that I do. Davidson thinks that it is a positive advantage to give an overall account which is satisfying from the point of view of psychological explanation but which has no particular place for something murky like agents' conceptions. If one can achieve what these murky things are for without finding a place for them, that is all to the good, he thinks.

The truth-theories and the truth-conditonal account of meaning just sketched are not, in the end, going to be able to avoid the bifurcation of content. When Davidson insists that it is not the truth-theoretic or meaning component but the belief component which will handle the puzzle, he is, implicitly, committinghimself to one notion of truth-conditional content generated by the consequences of the meaning or truth-theoretic component, and a second notion of content which is suggested by the more agent-sensitive belief component. These are two quite different ways of treating concepts. Of course, this is not bifurcation into wide and narrow (or internalist) content but it is a bifurcation into concepts which go into the explanation of behavior (which solve the puzzles) and concepts which do not.[24]

If the belief component has the belief that London is not *Londres*, we know that that belief has, as component, two concepts which are not identical, the concept of London and of *Londres*. These are the concepts which compose the content of the belief being appealed to in the belief component that excuses Pierre from logical idiocy. But the concept which is attributed by the meaning or truth-theoretic component is being claimed to be just the one concept of London.

The bifurcation is obvious: the two components are thinking of concepts quite differently.

Even if we are dealing with the case where the identity belief is missing in the belief component, one would have the same bifurcation as soon as one realized that Pierre could dissent from the identity-belief when prompted, and the principle of disquotation would put into the belief component the bifurcation-forcing belief.

Though I have also charged McDowell with bifurcation for very similar reasons, it is interesting to notice the delicate points of difference among Davidson's, McDowell's and my position on truth-theories of content. McDowell does not agree with me that the modified truth-theoretic representations should be seen as implicitly conveying beliefs of agents and, therefore, as capturing agents' conceptions. As we saw, he thinks that agents' conceptions are captured by looking to their beliefs, and by seeing the modified truth-theories doing their work as theories of content in some "as if" mode. This, however, creates, as we also saw, a worry about what exactly this mode is. Now, if one took this worry seriously, one would have two choices. One could take the line I am taking and see the clauses of the truth theories as implicitly conveying beliefs. Or one could eschew the right hand side modification of the clauses of the truth-theory, so that there is no such worry, and instead see the puzzle solved entirely by appeal to the belief component, i.e. to agents' beliefs. This latter option is Davidson's notion of a double-barrelled theory of meaning and belief for a person. If one took his view one would get out of the worry which only is a worry if one sees the clauses as modified. If the clauses do not have the right-hand side modifications there is nothing to work in the "as if" mode. The agent-sensitive work is done by appeal to the beliefs of the agent and there is nothing in the (unmodified) clauses which even mimics the work. But I am claiming that the worry should be avoided by taking the former option. It can be avoided without giving up on the modification of the clauses. I do find the idea of the modified clauses working in the "as if" mode obscure, but I nevertheless retain the modifications, insisting that they be seen as conveying the very information that amounts to agents' conceptions. Taking my way out of the obscurity, one avoids bifurcation of content altogether, taking Davidson's way out, one falls into a bifurcation of the kind I mentioned in the last paragraph.

These last comparative points should make clear that these are not three equidistantly removed accounts here. In fact, the differences between Davidson and McDowell are minor compared to the differences between either of them and me. McDowell himself explicitly presents his own view of truth-theories as a way of elaborating the Davidsonian conception of them, an elaboration of it which brings it explicitly into line with the Fregean ideal of understanding the notion of *sense* in terms of the notion of *truth*-conditions. Though, Davidson would probably reject the Russellian thesis about singular terms that McDowell avows, and though Davidson has resisted accepting the right-hand side modification McDowell proposes, their view still share the idea that beliefs constrain the role of the specifications of reference in order to do what agents' conceptions are supposed to do. It is a very small step, therefore, for Davidson to simply embrace the right-hand side modifications. It would be a much larger step to see the modified clauses as having the function I claim for them. Contra both McDowell and Davidson, I see no reason why Fregean sense should come in a double-barreled theory of this kind. I see no place for a truth-theory that is not itself conveying the information that amounts to the sense of terms. If a truth-theory, itself conveying this information, could be convicted of conveying something which was non-externalist, then I could see a point in an externalist wanting some other notion of a truth-theory to bring in externalism. But I have been at pains to deny that it can be convicted of any such thing. It thus offers externalism and agents' conceptions without the concealed bifurcation of content we detected in McDowell and Davidson.

If there is a hidden bifurcation in Davidson's view, a question arises about what the difference is between his view and the orthodox externalists I have been attacking; why have I not classified him with the others since he too encourages bifurcation? The answer to this question involves more than one layer of consideration.

There is, of course, the difference (see n. 24) that there is no commitment in Davidson to internalist or narrow content at all. But the more subtle and interesting difference between Davidson and the orthodox externalists is that the relation between his two components, the belief and the meaning components, is not the same as the relation between the two notions of wide and narrow content; and this relation is not same because of the very different ways in which Davidson and these other externalists view the idea of a truth-conditional notion of meaning, i.e. the truth-theoretic or meaning component in Davidson, for all its differences from my view of truth-theories, nevertheless still works with a different notion of truth-conditions than these other externalists.

Where one orthodox externalist stresses the essences in nature or the initial episodes of baptism to fix reference, Davidson who insists on the interpretative stance of radicial interpretation, stresses the things and events in the world, as seen by the radical interpreter's lights. Reference is thus not the intensely metaphysical notion that it is for such a causal-essentialist position. Also, since he stresses the interpreter's lights he does not think either that there is some direct causal-informational channel between nature and an agent, in a way that makes the interpretative position of the radical interpreter unnecessary. So truth-conditions are quite different for him from what they are for Fodor and Dretske as well. This may give the impression that he takes reference and therefore truth-conditions to be socially mediated in Burge's sense but that impression would also be wrong as Davidson (1987) has explicitly argued. The Davidsonian interpreter does not see the agent, i.e. the interpretee's social fellows, as being crucially constitutive of the interpretee's thought and meanings. The interpreter fixes reference by his lights and that is by no means the same as the social view in Burge, as we saw at various points in chapter 3. It is true that Davidson thinks that the interpreter's lights cannot deliver judgments about the world around him that are very different from the interpretee's judgments or for that matter from anybody else's judgments. Nevertheless, the emphasis is on the interpreter, who need not look to other members of the interpretee's community as Burge demands nor even be a member of the community of the interpretee. Hence Davidson's notion of truth-conditional content is different from all the three orthodox externalist positions.

One way of putting the difference is to say that, even though he does not abandon reference for a belief-summarizing function for the clauses of a truth-theory, his view of its place in the study of meaning is still radically different from the way it was viewed before him. In the recent history of the place of reference in the theory of meaning, Davidson's main advance (as I see it) is that he takes the metaphysics out of reference by stressing the interpreter's role in fixing reference. His more recent repudiation of the Burgean social element adds the further advantage of not replacing the metaphysics with a social *ersatz*. Truth-conditions are fixed by the interpreter's lights and not in these other ways which, in one form or another, encourage a metaphysical conception of reference.

This contrast in how truth-conditions are viewed leads to another striking contrast: the relation that holds between Davidson's two components on the one hand and that between two notions of content that many orthodox externalists are committed to, on the other.[25] The relation between Davidson's two components is a fluid dialectical relationship. And it is this fact that forms the basis of his particular way of rejecting the analytic-synthetic distinction. It is also this fact which generates Davidson's particular and, I believe, extra brand of Quinean holism.[26] There is no echo of these things in the relations between wide and narrow content. The chief underlying source of the difference is that in stressing the interpreter's role in fixing the truth-conditions, he also stresses that the interpreter has a certain amount of flexibility in trading the attributions in one component with those made in the other. (This flexibility is not to be had if one adopts the more metaphysical stance of the other externalists.)

The flexibility in Davidson is something like this. Reference and, therefore truth-conditions (one of the two components) are not fixed by the essential articulations of nature, nor by remote baptism ceremonies, nor by the information that nature channels out to agents. It is fixed by the interpreter's conceptions of the world. But because it is not fixed in these other ways, "fixed" or "fixing" is too strong a word for what the interpreter does. Because reference does not depend on these sources defined by things ulterior to human lights, it is possible for the interpreter to allow for a certain amount of play between the truth-conditions assigned to the words of the interpretee and (the other component) the beliefs attributed to him. As Davidson puts it in one place, the interpreter assigns truth-conditions by placing weight on the beliefs he considers more important than others to a particular concept or term. Thus, if we are considering the concept of "malaria" (this is his own example), the belief that it is accompanied by high fever is less important than the belief that it is caused by the bite of an anopheles mosquito.[27] This may seem as if the analytic-synthetic distinctions is at play or, to use Wittgenstein's terminology, the distinction between criteria and symptom. But Davidson is careful to add that he sees no need for being very rigid here; though weights are placed, they need not deaden the relation between the two components. In this he follows Wittgenstein who also insisted that there is a fluctuation between criteria and symptom. This allowing for the fluctuation between the two components is Davidson's way of embracing Quine's holism and Quine's rejection of the analytic-synthetic distinction. One can change things in one component, if one makes corresponding changes in the other. And such a dialectic of fluctuation between the components is what he sometimes calls the "inextricability" of meaning and belief, the "interdependence" of the two components of his theory. If the truth-conditions were fixed by the orthodox externalist's more ulterior sources (nature's essences for example) this would not be possible; and that is one of the advantages of the interpretative stance.[28]

So much for the comparison between Davidson and the orthodox externalisms. Let me return to the differences between him and me. My way of rejecting the analytic-synthetic distinction is different from his and it does not presuppose that there are these two components. This point can be brought out by looking to the different roles Davidson and I give to truth-theories.

Davidson, even though he wants an overall theory that is sensitive to what is needed for psychological explanation, nowhere emphasizes the idea that the clauses of a truth-theory themselves specify agents' conceptions. Sensitivity to the need for a psychologically efficacious notion of content, which captures agents' conceptions, therefore, leads him to the hidden bifurcation I detected and made explicit above. For me, sensitivity to the psychological aspects of content need not, in any way, lead to any hidden bifurcation. For me, this sensitivity comes from keeping an eye open for agents' conceptions and specifying these in the clauses of the truth-theories themselves. Agents' conceptions are not reflected in the constraining of the truth-theoretic component by another belief-component, rather agents' conceptions *are* meanings and are nothing but the beliefs that it is the task of the truth-theories themselves to summarize. For me, conceptions just are individuated by beliefs, which are gathered and summarized in aggregates and then, more selectively, at the local level.

This makes it possible for me to rest my rejection of the analytic-synthetic distinction entirely on my insistence (spelt out above) that meaning is thoroughly local and contextual. There is no fixed meaning or analyticity because meaning changes from locality to locality, as the discussion of theory-change and of explanation in localities showed. There is no canonical local selection of beliefs from the aggregates. Thus, armed with the locality thesis, one may introduce the idea of meaning as agents' conceptions (and truth-theories of meaning as themselves capturing agents' conceptions) without any fear of falling into the murky picture of meaning and analyticity that Quine was attacking. The basis of the contrast with Davidson's way of rejecting the analytic-synthetic distinction is now obvious. Because he emphasizes a truth-theoretic component which does not merely summarize beliefs but stands in separate status from a belief component, a fluidity between two components alone can avoid the analytic-synthetic distinction.

This brings into his view an extra holism, something over and above the holism which says that any given content is what it is because of other contents it is inferentially and conceptually related with. It is the additional holism of meaning-belief inextricability and interdependence. There is no place for such holism in my thesis since I do not have two components. In my way of doing things there is no component which is characterized in such a way that such fluidity has to be brought in to resist the analytic-synthetic distinction. It is not as if I am denying such fluidity, but rather I am saying that its question does not so much as arise. The very idea of such fluidity presupposes that there be a truth-theoretic component characterized in a way other than merely as summarizing agents' beliefs and therefore other than itself capturing agents' conceptions of things. No such component exists in my picture. The "truth"-theoretic aspect of my view, therefore, does not require this sort of dialectic relation with the beliefs of an agent. Instead, for me there are only aggregates of beliefs summarized in the "truth"-theories and selections from them that compose concepts in the contents in particular localities. It is the stress on localities by which I deny the analytic-synthetic distinction, not by fluidity between two separate components. There is no other holism in my picture over and above the holism defended against Fodor, and required for any conceptual role semantics.

This difference suggests a related and interesting difference between my view and Davidson's on the nature of meaning. Davidson's way of denying analyticity consists in allowing that for any one of his double-barreled theories, there can be another, which specifies something different in one of its components so long as it makes corresponding changes in the other component. This raises an alarm because it may seem like a meaning-nihilism which comes from the attack on analyticity. There are no meanings at all, there is only arbitrary choice between different equally good double-barreled theories of meaning-belief. Davidson denies that this is cause for alarm since there will be an invariance between these different double-barreled theories. That is, there will always be a way of going from one double-barreled theory to another. Such invariances are what meaning must be thought to be in the post-Quinean era where there are no analyticities.[29]

Now, for me too a sense of meaning as a form of invariance can quell alarms about meaning-nihilism. But the idea of invariance is not Davidson's. The meaning-theoretic or aggregative specification of concepts for agents summarizes an aggregate of beliefs they associate with a term. Now here too, as we saw above, an alarm is raised as to whether any two people or one person from one time to another, ever have the same concept or meaning. They almost certainly will not have coinciding aggregates for any concept, so there is, as Fodor points out, the spectre of meaning-nihilism. The response to this alarm is to point to the possibility of invariances in localities. In localities one just selects different beliefs from these aggregates of beliefs for different purposes. There is no commitment to a canonical selection which might smack of analyticity. But there is sense of meaning which survives because in the same localities there could (and very likely would) turn out to be invariances in the selected beliefs attributed to different people or to an agent at different times. This notion of invariance is not defined over a truth-theoretic and a belief component. It is just defined over belief in localities. It is, thus, a wholly different idea of meaning as invariances from Davidson's.

The difference between Davidson's view of a truth-theoretic conception of meaning and mine has been sketched, and I have tried to show why it is that a commitment to a *unified* conception of intentionality can only be captured by truth-theories with the point and function that I proposed at the beginning of this chapter. But it is not just that I think that my way of thinking of truth-theories is to be preferred to Davidson's because his involves a hidden bifurcation. I do not see the point of a truth-theory of meaning and content other than the point of summarizing an agent's beliefs and thereby capturing his conceptions. It seems to me that once one sees via the locality thesis that there is no fear that agent's conceptions amount to definitions or analyticities, there is no reason to see truth-theories as doing anything more than what I suggest for them. There is no point that Davidson could have for truth-theories as a special kind of component, separate from an agent's beliefs. What point could there be? Here are two speculations.

Can it be that he is, after all, interested in a general distinction between theory-change and meaning-change as the orthodox externalists are. If he were, one could see some point in thinking of truth-theories as other than a device for summarizing beliefs. The truth-theories (meaning component) would provide the anchors which would give us the stable meanings over which beliefs or theories (belief component) could change or diverge. The speculation does not, at first, seem quite right. The desire for a general (as opposed to my localized) distinction between theory-change and meaning-change is just a desire for one of the fruits of the analytic-synthetic distinction. But, as we saw, the fluctuation Davidson allows between the two components is intended to, and has the effect of, rejecting the analytic-synthetic distinction. But, on a second look, it is possible that he wants to find a way of having some of the fruits of the analytic-synthetic distinction without the distinction itself. That is, despite his rejection of the analytic-synthetic distinction, perhaps he thinks that unless there was some component genuinely deserving the name "truth"-theoretic, there would a total collapse of theory-change and meaning-change. And, finding that undesirable, he proposes a truth-theoretic component which, unlike my truth-theories, preserves something of the idea of a general distinction between theory-change and meaning-change; and yet because of its fluid dialectic relation with the belief-component, it avoids the analytic-synthetic distinction.

Can it also be that he worries that without truth-theories, which form a separate component from a belief-component, one will have no direct link-ups with the world of the sort we discussed in the last section? That again, at first sight, does not seem quite right either. One would have thought that the point of devising the interpretative approach was partly to avoid the direct link-ups demanded by other externalisms. But perhaps, despite his advocacy of the interpretative approach and his rejection of causal theories of direct reference, he (like McDowell) thinks that beliefs or descriptions should be brought in merely as mediating reference so that they do not give up altogether on direct link-ups with the world – for else there would be no genuine externalism. My view brings them in a way that altogether gives up on direct link-ups because the beliefs are not just constraining the reference clauses, they are being summarized by those clauses. Reference is playing no role. So the second speculation is that a lingering desire not to give up direct link-ups for fear of giving up externalism might explain why Davidson does not see the clauses as merely summarizing beliefs or descriptions in this way.

Both these motivations might explain why he holds on to his notion of truth-theories which do not themselves specify agents' conceptions. I, however, do not share either of those qualms cited by these speculations. First, I am happy to let go, not merely of the analytic-synthetic distinction, but also of all its fruits, including the idea of a general distinction between theory-change and meaning-change. My locality thesis combined with my belief-oriented view of concepts allows me a localized (not general version) of the latter distinction, and that is all I think we need once we have abandoned the analytic-synthetic distinction. And, second, I am happy, also, to let go of the idea of reference and direct link-ups with the external world because I think we can get an externalism without such link-ups so long as we, on general grounds in the Kantian style, resist the idea that content is independent of the external world, as Descartes's First Meditation suggests.

Without these qualms I can take the view that truth-theories themselves specify agents' conceptions. But my taking this view should not give the impression that the interpreter of the agent will usher himself and his conceptions out when he comes up with a truth-theory for the agent. Nor am I necessarily denying Davidson's claim that the agent's conceptions will to a large extent coincide with the interpreter's. The interpreter's lights are relevant because they are taken to be the arbiter of *truth*. It is they which assess the conceptions and beliefs of the agent for truth. But it is *not* relevant in the sense that the truth-theory which the interpreter comes up with for the interpretee is something more than, or other than, a theory which specifies the agent's conceptions of the truth. One does not need another component to help see the truth-theory as taking us to agents' conceptions. The truth-theory itself conveys the agent's conceptions. No amount of conviction in the claim that the lights of interpreter and the agent cannot be all that different should allow us to see a greater relevance than that for truth-theories.

Can my insistence on how truth-theories must themselves specify agents' conceptions be described as a genuinely Fregean conception of sense? In one straightforward sense it can. Agents' conceptions are what solve the puzzles in the examples that exercised us and that is clearly a Fregean achievement. But, in this book, a solution to these puzzles has been only the occasion for elaborating an externalism and a unified conception of intentionality. In this elaboration, agents' conceptions emerge as quite unFregean, at least if Frege is seen as many contemporary philosophers see him. Though the general relevance of Frege's notion of sense to intentionality has not been missed by philosophers, the relevance has been advanced in way which do not square with my view of intentional content. There are three things I have warned against in particular.[30]

First, in Searle (who is not a bifurcationist) and in many orthodox bifurcationists, the Fregean idea has been developed as providing an internalist notion of content. It is precisely this that McDowell and Evans fear about the Fregean ideal and it is why they offer their own notion of a Russellized Frege, of *de re* senses. My notion of sense avoids both these contemporary Fregean trends, and provides an alternative way of developing the relevance of Frege's notion of sense for intentionality, a way which might with some caution be described as Kantian in the specific sense I mentioned earlier.

Second, philosophers have worried that the appeal to descriptions or beliefs in the study of meaning or sense is a surrender to the idea that meanings must yield analyticities, that terms must have definitions (whether strict definitions or definitions which come from a weighted majority within a cluster of descriptions).[31] The undesirability of this has led some to think of terms and concepts – at any rate, some terms and concepts – as primitive things, with no descriptive sense. It has led others, like Davidson, to posit two interdependent components in the study of an agent's intentionality, neither of which specifies the undesirable element of agents' conceptions or sense, but the dialectical combination of which helps capture what sense was traditionally supposed to capture. Both these ways of avoiding the undesirable element promote one or other form of the bifurcation of intentionality. My view, with its emphasis on the locality of intentional content, avoids the undesirable element of definitions and analyticities, without any hint of bifurcation of content. It captures Fregean sense without surrender either to definitions or to the bifurcation of intentionality.

Third, there has been much focus on the claim that Frege gave a description-theory of reference. My appeal to beliefs and descriptions, as what "reference" -clauses traffic in, may seem to be Fregean in this sense. That is not so. Reference, as something that a description-theory or a causal theory are competing theories of, is not something that plays any role in my picture of intentionality. Mine is not a description or belief theory of reference but a description or belief theory of Fregean sense or meaning, which is given in the "reference" -clauses. It is thus a "truth" -theory of meaning which gives no place to semantics in the familiar referential and truth-conditional sense of semantics;[32] not even a place supplementary to the idea of agents' conceptions, which most others will allow. I cannot allow that because, as I have shown, it would be to surrender the unity of content. I do not allow it because it is not needed.

## THE INFORMATION-COMMUNICATIVE AND SUCCESS-EXPLANATORY FUNCTIONS OF CONTENT

The third question raised in the first section was how, if one gave up on the essential connection between content and truth-conditions (in the standard sense) could one capture some of the functions that are essential to our concept of content?. It is often claimed that there are certain functions which content has, which cannot be retained if one adopts my notion of externalist content and my notion of a truth-theory. They cannot be had if one adopts my constraint on externalism and if one thinks of such theories as doing no more than summarize an agent's beliefs. Wide content and genuine, official truth-theories of meaning alone can speak to these functions. There are two such functions, in particular, that seem to be in jeopardy.

*First*: Brian Loar states things well when he says that attributing truth-conditional content has the function of displaying how agents can be "conveyors of more or less reliable information about the world around them" (Loar 1985a, p. 62). (This is supposed to contrast with the function of explaining action, a function carried out by narrow content. Recall Loar is a bifurcationist.) In saying this he speaks for a lot of philosophers.

The question before us should, therefore, be: is attributing truth-conditional content in some sense over and above an agent's beliefs and conceptions or, more strongly, is attributing wide content over and above unified content, the only way to see agents as conveyors of more or less reliable information about the world?[33] The answer might seem obviously to be "yes" because if all that truth-theories do is summarize beliefs of an agent, then the attribution of truth-conditional content in my impoverished sense will at best have the function of conveying information about the agent's beliefs and not about the world.

But, to begin with, one should be clear about what exactly is meant by saying that attribution of wide content "conveys more or less reliable information about the world." The idea, crudely, is that, if one assumes that agents are functioning normally (e.g. they are not hallucinating) and if one assumes that attributors are speaking sincerely and literally etc., and if one then attributes aloud wide contents to agents, then someone could infer what the world is like. For instance, I tell you, who are sitting in the deep interior of a large room that John, who happens to be standing near the window, believes that it is raining. Assuming that John is not hallucinating etc., and that I am being sincere, literal etc. (assumptions which from now on I will cease to mention) and given that wide content is externally constituted, you can infer that it is raining.

Notice, however, that this example, given all we have said about it, does not place wide content in any particular advantage over unified content. My notion of content is also externalist and its attribution would yield the same inference on the assumption of the agent's normal functioning. The only kind of content whose attribution will not carry out this function of conveying information about the world is internalist narrow content. (And that is not surprising since internalist narrow contents are defined so that the world could be wholly different and yet those contents would be exactly the same – no wonder they need convey nothing about the world.) It is only because Loar and almost everybody else who has written on the subject assume that the only contrast with wide content is given by internalist narrow content, that they jump to the conclusion that attribution of wide content alone can show how agents can be seen as conveyors of information about the world.

But perhaps we are not seeing Loar's point sympathetically enough. Loar's general point about this function of wide content attribution can be adapted towards a slightly different point, which may do more damage to unified contents. This adapted point is better brought out in a different example where the nature of the special externalist commitments of "wide" content are spelt out.

We attribute to an agent the belief that there is water in front of him. The argument would now be that it is only if someone took this attribution to be an attribution of wide content, that she would learn from it that there is a substance in front of him which has, among other things, the property of having a certain chemical composition. Hence on twin-earth someone would get quite different information from the parallel attribution to his *doppelgänger*, information about a substance with a quite different chemical composition. The example certainly brings out that attributing unified content – for all its commitment to externalism – will not necessarily convey *this* information. In particular, if unified content is attributed to an agent known to be ignorant of chemistry, then we will not infer that piece of information about the world. And moreover we would, on unified content attributions, get the *same* (impoverished) information from parallel attributions to similarly ignorant agents on twin-earth. So Loar's point, now reflecting the full and very specific stretch of externalism involved in wide content, would be that only attribution of wide content can display how agents are conveyors of full and specific stretches of information about the world around them. Attribution of unified contents, for all their externalist constitution, would convey nothing as much or as specific. And since we often do learn the fuller and more specific information from attributions of content to agents, those contents must be wide rather than unified. Unified contents fail to carry out an important function essential to content-attribution.

My answer to this claim to advantage of wide over unified content is not to deny that we often learn a lot about the world from content attributions but to insist that, in the cases in question, we learn it not just from the attributions of content but from the attributions of content plus our knowledge of various things. This allows that the contents attributed are unified rather than wide. Take again, the example of the belief about the presence of water attributed to an agent known to be chemically ignorant. We may often learn from this attribution that there is a substance with a certain chemical composition present, but this is not so on the basis just of the content attribution. If it were just on that basis, the content attributed would have to be wide content, i.e. we would have to attribute to him a content which contains the concept of water that we, his social fellows, and the experts have. Rather, we learn that information on the basis of the attribution of unified contents plus our knowledge (or belief) that what the agent only takes to be a substance which is, say, colourless, thirst-quenching and so on has, in fact, a certain chemical composition. The concept that enters the unified content of a chemical ignoramus is merely the concept of, say, a colourless etc. substance assuming obviously that being colourless etc. are the properties he conceives that substance to have. However, *we* may know that what he takes water to be has a certain chemical composition. Thus, adding that on, we conclude that a substance with a certain chemical composition is present. There is an extra step in the inference by which we acquire that information from content attributions. But with the extra step in place it should be clear that attribution of wide content is not necessary to see agents as conveyors of reliable information about the world. Attribution of unified content will do so just as well.

*Second*: The other function of wide content that is not carried out by unified content is supposed to be this. Attribution of wide content has the function of explaining why agents who possess content meet with a considerable measure of success in the world. Attribution of unified content could not do that, and so, if we just had unified content there would be no good explanation of this success.[34]

What is meant here by "success" and "explaining" success? Can it mean that agents' success in the sense of satisfying their own desires can only be explained if their beliefs and desires are given wide contents. Clearly, that cannot be right. A chemically ignorant agent's desire to quench his thirst is satisfied by acting on his belief, with the *unified* content, that drinking water – the liquid that comes out of his kitchen tap etc. – will quench his thirst. There is no need to attribute a content containing the concept of water which experts have or which tracks the essential articulations of nature. Of course, if the agent is not chemically ignorant, sometimes his desires themselves – say, his desire to do something in a chemical laboratory – may have to be specified in contents containing the concept of water conceived as $H_2O$; and so also would his beliefs. But for this agent, these would be unified content since they keep faith with how he conceives of the world, conceives of that substance. The subsequent success of his actions in satisfying his desires would be explained, therefore, entirely by these unified content attributions.

So this cannot be what Putnam and others have in mind when they talk of success. Rather, by "success," they must have in mind the phenomenon of the agent's capacity to survive and flourish in his or her particular environment as opposed to some other. Take twin agents on earth and twin-earth. The argument really suggests that attribution of wide contents alone explains why one succeeds in one environment and his twin in the other. Wide content's sensitivity to the full and specific stretch of the external environment keeps their respective contents relevantly distinct at all times. Unified content which only has highly limited and constrained, only a very general sensitivity to the external environment, will often attribute the same contents to both. It would not, therefore, explain our survivals and flourishings in our *respective* environments. It would not explain why we are best fitted to cope with out own environments.

To begin with, it is a *prima facie* sign that an argument for a conclusion is seriously flawed when somebody can exploit it for a virtually opposite conclusion. I say this because in a well-known paper, Daniel Dennett (1982) invokes considerations of being best fitted for an environment in order to justify and elaborate a commitment to narrow contents, while here we are being told that only wide contents can be tied to the idea of an agent's successful fit in his environment. What is especially bizarre is that in that paper Dennett is invoking these considerations not even for a notion of unified content that is externalist like mine. If he were doing that it would perhaps be a little more intelligible that the same considerations can be invoked for different notions of content since at least both notions would externalist. But Dennett's question in the paper is: how can we tell from just the *internal* workings of an organism, what environment it is best fitted for? It is not necessary to go into the details of his view here because they are not relevant to the point at issue. I want merely to stress that he is invoking considerations of successful fit with the environment to ground a notion of *internalist* or narrow content. And now we are being told that these very same considerations justify the introduction of wide content. It is enough to say that, *prima facie*, this does not bode well for these considerations about success establishing *either*.

I am, in fact, highly skeptical that Dennett's effort at grounding and elaborating narrow content via consideration of success in one's environment is at all effective in doing so. But the present concern is to evaluate these considerations as an argument for the necessity for wide content. And it seems to me that as such these considerations fare very poorly. This is not because I have concluded that ignorant agents (whether their ignorance is about the chemical structures in their environment or about all sorts of other things in their environment) are as likely to survive and flourish in the environment as knowledgeable agents. Not at all. Such a conclusion about flourishing does not follow from an insistence on unified contents. It does not follow because the conclusion does not even speak to the issue about how to specify (widely or in any other way) the *contents* of an agent's beliefs, but rather the conclusion speaks to whether the agent has a sufficient number of beliefs which are *true*, so as to allow the agent to flourish in it. I am quite happy to concede, with obvious qualifications which we need not stop over now, that agents who have more true beliefs about the features of their environment have more of a chance of succeeding in that environment. This concession, however, says nothing about how to individuate and specify the contents of agents' beliefs. Unified contents, in my sense, are just as capable of truth and falsity, and so all one has to say is that the more true (unified) contents one has the more likelihood of success. Wide contents need not enter into the picture at all. All one needs are true beliefs and beliefs specified with unified contents can be true.

It is only if one thought that unified contents, unlike wide, are not capable of truth and falsity in a genuine sense, that one might think that wide contents must be introduced to account for success in given environments. But there is no reason to foist such a preposterous position on the unified content theorist. Just because he claims that belief-contents are individuated by how the agent conceives of things (rather than by how the expert or God or the end of inquiry or the radical interpreter conceives of them) it does not follow that beliefs, so individuated, cannot be true or false. Surely it should be possible to say that they are true when the world is how he conceives it to be. Or, if one prefers, one can say that an agent's belief is true if that belief is also believed by the expert, or by God, or by the radical interpreter, or if it is sanctioned by the end of inquiry, depending on one's favorite way of bringing in the point of view that has a hold of the full articulations of nature's essences. Hence, there is no problem about unified contents being true; and since that allows us to say that it is the extent of his *true unified* contents that account for his success in his environment, I repeat that wide content is unnecessary. Neither the fact of information-conveyance, nor the fact of agents' success in the world, requires one to give up on, or add to, that idea of externalist content, which is sufficiently specified on the flip side by my unofficial versions of "truth"-theories.

To conclude, I have now completed my defence of an externalism and a truth-conditional account of content which may be contrasted not only with the orthodox externalisms but with the less orthodox externalisms and truth-conditional notions of content we find in Davidson and McDowell. Only this way of thinking the nature of truth-theories and the truth-conditions they specify will allow for the notion of content which is defined by the two theses of the unity and the locality of content.

In chapter 5, I finally turn to the question I have been putting off throughout the book: why should we be externalists at all, even in my constrained sense? Neither the unity thesis nor the locality thesis would have any point if it were not for the fact that they were theses defined upon a non-standard externalist, nevertheless, *externalist* position about content. But why be externalist at all?

# The Case for Externalism

This book has proceeded with two assumptions: first, that the content of intentional states explains behavior (in the sense of commonsense psychological explanation) and, second, that this content, specified in that-clauses, is externally constituted. The problem of the unity of content was the problem of reconciling these two assumptions about content in a single notion of content. In the explorations of the last three chapters, I have not really questioned these initial two assumptions but instead looked at the diverse implications for the philosophy of mind and language that emerged from the form of reconciliation that I offered for them in my externalism of the first chapter.

In this last chapter, I want to say something about the assumptions, in particular about the second assumption which is much the more controversial. Defending it is to attack internalism about intentionality, and that is much of the aim of this chapter.

The first assumption is not as controversial as the second but it has not gone without criticism. It is sometimes said the function of explanation cannot be the essence of the intentional states on the ground that an intentional state can only play an explanatory role in conjunction with other intentional states, but a subject may have only one belief and yet be a genuine believer. This atomism about beliefs is a subject that has come up earlier in the discussion of Fodor's anti-holism, and I have had my say against it there. I will only repeat that the arguments against holism which lead Fodor and others to embrace such an atomism are finessed by my locality thesis and there is no need to adopt his atomism which brings with it a host of questions and problems of its own.[1]

It is also said that the first assumption encourages an attitude of instrumentalism about intentionality. The idea, apparently, is that one would be ignoring the fact that a belief is a real thing if one stresses too much its instrumental role in explaining behavior. In itself this objection is shallow and unconvincing, as unconvincing as being told that if one emphasized in one's characterization of the concept of a knife that a knife's point and rationale is to cut things, then one will be ignoring its status as a real thing. This objection to the first assumption cannot be that there are beliefs which can exist without explaining anything. The first assumption only makes a general claim about the point and rationale of our talk of intentional states. That there is an intentional state which can be said to exist without it actually explaining anything does not spoil the general point about the connection between intentional states and behavior. These points are too obvious and do not need elaboration.

Often this latter criticism of the first assumption comes embedded in a criticism of the second assumption. It is said that, in stressing the explanatory role of intentional states (first assumption) one takes too much the external (second assumption), or third person, or explainer's, point of view. In doing so, one leaves out the agent's or the first person or the *internal* point of view. Without this we would leave out what is intrinsic to beliefs and desires and look only at their role and usefulness to explainers. This question will be discussed toward the end of the chapter. It is raised here to indicate that a defense of the second assumption against internalism may be caught up, in part, with a defense of the charge of instrumentalism brought against the first assumption. In other words, a quick dismissal above of the objection to the first assumption may not be fully justified until a full defense of the second is made, since, apparently, part of what is supposed to be bad about the second assumption is that it promotes and is encouraged by what is bad about the first. Rejecting the charge of instrumentalism, therefore, requires not merely to defend a form of realism about intentional states but a position which might be called "realism without internalism."

To begin, then, with the more controversial second assumption, i.e. externalism, one way of approaching this question is to ask: what do internalists have against externalism?[2]

One argument against externalism, which we have considered at length and rejected, is that it produces a notion of content which gives up on the first assumption. Some externalisms do do that and I have criticized them. I will no longer be concerned with that since in the last four chapters, assuming the truth of externalism, I have probed and come up with what I take to be the right externalism, an externalism which does not give up on the first assumption. My question will now be what motivates my externalism: why must I even have *my* externalism, why is not internalism true?

The question is a little complicated since there are internalists, like Searle, who oppose externalism in the sense of rejecting it altogether, and internalists – too numerous to mention again – who oppose it in the sense of wanting to supplement it with a second internalist notion of content.[3] Both may give the same reasons against externalists, saying that there are things worth doing or capturing that externalism content cannot do. The latter does not go on to say, as the former must, that there is nothing worthwhile that externalist content serves which cannot be served by internalist content. The latter, unlike the former, does not reject the second assumption that is now under discussion, he only rejects my idea of the unity of content. Since my case for unity has been made, it is the former and stronger and more exclusively internalist position that I will dwell on when I defend the second assumption itself. This should not, however, give the impression that the arguments against the very idea of internalism given here have no relevance against the weaker position which wishes to supplement internalism with "wide content." If the arguments have force they should have force against the very plausibility of the idea (even despite the supplementation) that there is a notion of content which is independent of an agent's relations with the external world.[4]

The stronger internalism must proceed by rejecting the motivations of externalists as either not good ones or, where good, capturable within internalism. To some extent that is how Searle (1983) proceeds. He asks himself: What is it that externalists want from their externalism which they think that internalism cannot capture? He then answers this question and argues that internalism can have it too. In this section I will argue that he misses the deepest motivation and arguments for externalism, and later spell out what those are by showing how internalism cannot fulfill those motivations.

Searle gives the following answer to his own question. Internalists have often been charged with conceiving of our thoughts as wholly general and as not having a special particularistic element. Externalists complain that many of our thoughts, especially our perceptual thoughts, are not general. This is a charge which Searle thinks is worth repudiating, for perceptual contents should take in particularity, and internalists should be able to specify thoughts about particular objects. He sets himself a problem. For most internalists the content of my perception of a yellow station wagon and your perception of a different, but qualitatively identical, station wagon is the same content. One would only accept this, most externalists say, if one leaves the particularity out of perceptual thinking and see all such thoughts as being general. Searle agrees with those externalists. And he sees this in the form of a problem or a challenge: how can internalism make it come out that in the example above we have two different thoughts? He calls it the "particularity problem."

He says that those who have lodged this complaint against internalism assume that there can be no response an internalist can make without giving up on the internalism, or at least giving up on his own stronger internalism by supplementing it with an externalist notion of content. They think that only externalist conceptions of content which appeal to external causes of content will make it come out that we have two different contents. He brings this point out, as externalists themselves often do, with examples of twin agents on earth and twin earth. So, for instance, the agent on earth sees his wife Sally and the agent on twin earth sees his wife twin Sally. Externalists make it come out that there are two different contents by insisting that what determines their respective contents is that Sally causes the perception of the agent on earth, and twin-Sally causes the perception of the agent on twin-earth. Searle's objection to this is that it is a solution from, as he calls it, a "third person point of view." What we need or, at any rate, what an internalist needs, he says, is a solution from the "first person" or perceiving agent's point of view. I will return to the question of the first-and third-person points of view later in the chapter. For now, let us look at this claim that an internalist can offer his own solution to the "particularity problem'"

His solution apparently must be from the first-person point of view. And this, Searle says, must consist in an answer to the question: what is it about *my* perception that it requires that it must be satisfied by the presence of Sally and not by any woman with various features type-identical with her?[5] The answer is roughly this. Perceptual episodes and experiences have intentional content and these are, in the usual way, specifiable in a that-clause: "I have a visual experience that there is a yellow station wagon there." Such simple specifications may be all right for many other sorts of beliefs, beliefs that do not involve particularity. But for beliefs which do, such as perceptual beliefs, they are insufficient. The satisfaction condition for perceptual beliefs must contain a complication; they must include the condition that the visual experience "must itself be caused by the rest of the conditions of satisfaction of that visual experience." So we get contents of the following sort: I have a visual experience that *there is a yellow station wagon and that there is a yellow station wagon there is causing me to have this visual experience.* So also, in the twin cases, we have: I see that Sally is there and *Sally's being there is causing me to have this visual experience.* And we have my twin's content: I see that *Sally is there and Sally's being there is causing me to have this visual experience.* This is described as the causal self-referentiality of perception.

The content is specified above by the italicized words. Notice that the casual element is part of the content of the perceptual belief. Searle has no objection to the solution appealing to causality, so long as there is no concession to externalism. The element of causality is not external because it is part of the agent's perceptual content itself. Thus no external causes are constitutive of content even though we might be thinking of external things. It is not the actual cause (external) that accounts for the different contents of mine and my *doppelgänger*, but rather that component of the content itself which is about the cause of the particular visual experience that the possessor of the experience is undergoing. It is part of my intentional content that it is my wife Sally that is causing my visual experience and it is part of his that it is his wife causing his visual experience. So even if the twins have phenomenologically identical experiences, we can say that their contents are different, and we can say it without appealing to any thing external. The causal self-referentiality sees to that. Proof that externalism is not necessary to solve the particularity problem, he says, lies in the fact that neither Sally nor twin-Sally need be there, and yet we may have our respective contents. One could, whether one was veridically perceiving or hallucinating, have those contents. All that would be different is that in the case of the hallucination the satisfaction or truth conditions of the content would not have obtained.

As it happens I reject the very idea of the "particularity problem" as being well posed. Even if I did not, I do not think Searle's solution to it is satisfactory since it does not account for two people who are seeing the same station wagon. Searle allows himself to be too dominated by the context of the twin-earth examples. In that context the particularity problem is one of showing that there are different contents forced by particularity. Searle's solution shows how causal self-reference allows that. But this solution implies something very counterintuitive about another example of two agents (on this earth) where perceptions are not always and necessarily of different things as they are in the twin-earth puzzles. Here Searle's solution would seem to attribute different contents when it ought not to, i.e. when different perceivers are undergoing different perceptual episodes of the same thing. The solution, invoking self-referentiality, attributes different contents so long as the perceivers and perceptual episodes are different (so long as there are different selves referring to themselves or different perceptual episodes whose contents are referring to the perceptual episodes themselves). But if the perceptions are of the same thing, the content should be the same. The very same idea of particularity that required him to find the twins as having different contents should require him to find these two agents as having the same contents, i.e. the twins were seeing different station wagons but these two agents are seeing the same station wagon. His solution delivers the right result (different contents) in the twins example but the wrong result (also different contents) in the second example. This is proof that his solution delivers the right result in the twin example for the wrong reason.

Does this criticism of Searle amount to my saying that I take his particularity problem seriously but that I think that externalism, in the sense of externalism that he describes and finds unnecessary, is the only position that can capture the particularity he thinks is worth capturing? No, instead I reject the way he thinks of the particularistic element in perceptual thought because I do not think the twins need be required to have two perceptual thoughts in order for those thoughts to have the particularistic element. In chapter 4, I showed how one could capture the special psychological roles of the singular, particularistic element in those thoughts, without claiming that the contents are not shared by the two people. The quite just demand that we should not think of perceptual contents as being purely general should not, therefore, be presented in terms of the "particularity problem."

I argued in chapter 4, that the following two claims are compatible. (1) You and I, even my twin-earth *doppelgänger* and I, can look at different station wagons and have the same perceptual thoughts. (2) These thoughts would be singular thoughts, i.e. they would have a particularistic element. I also said there that (1) was not a concession to internalism because it could still be true that the singularity, insisted on by (2) was something we had a general grip on only because our thoughts were, in general, constituted by external things. That just is externalism and it is argued for by saying that internalism cannot make sense of our general grip on singularity and demonstrative thought. This form of externalism is not at all the externalism that is the target of Searle's attack. It is different because it makes no demand – as both Searle and his target do – that the twins have different singular thoughts.

All this suggests that I am bound to reject the problem that Searle poses for his own internalism – and tries to solve with his causal self-referential analysis – as being a hard problem for anything. Neither internalism nor externalism need or should want to say that the two perceptions of the twins must be different.

But even if the "particularity problem" does not threaten internalism, it does not mean that internalism has a satisfactory account of the fact that we have singular thoughts at all. The problem of how one can have a grip on demonstratives and singularity at all, without externalism, is a different problem from his "particularity problem," and Searle nowhere addresses this question. Externalism (even if of a kind different from the one he attacks) may still be the only thing that can account for the general possibility of possession of singular thought at all.

It is this sort of externalism, and roughly this sort of line of argument against internalism, that I want to pursue in this chapter. (I say "roughly" this line of argument because I will not exactly retain the special concern with singular thought and particularity.) The line of argument will all the same proceed as above, without making demands about the external determination of any given thought, but nevertheless claiming that without externalism some basic features of thought – singularity being just one example – cannot be account for. It is a line of argument which brings with it certain epistemological considerations.

I began with this critical discussion of Searle because it is important to point out that internalists should not impute the wrong motivations to externalism and then argue against it. Internalists need to be more scrupulous and consider the best motivations and arguments of their opponents, otherwise their internalism will not be properly justified. Searle's work so far on the subject of internalism has suffered from this flaw.[6] It is a flaw one finds in many attacks on externalism. I want now to give what I take to be the best motivations and arguments for externalism and show that internalists have no counter to these arguments. I repeat that these will not be motivations for externalisms such as those of Kripke, Putnam, Burge, Fodor et al. I have over the past two chapters rejected various motivations for one or other of these externalisms that I have been opposing. What I will now give will be motivations and arguments for my externalism.

## THE BEST MOTIVATION FOR EXTERNALISM: PUBLICNESS

We do believe that meaning and intentional contents must be thought of as public phenomena. They are properties of agents that other agents can, in principle, discover. This epistemological conviction is commonly accepted, quite explicitly by many philosophers, ever since Wittgentein's mature work; but it was implicitly held in the thought of anti-Cartesian philosophers well before Wittgenstein, as well as taken for granted (though of course with major exceptions) by a longstanding tradition of thought prior to Descartes. Let me, then, for the moment, follow most others, in taking for granted that meanings and intentional contents must be public. (For those who will not allow me to take it for granted, I will provide a different argument for externalism turning on different epistemological considerations, in the next section.)

A good question to raise at this point would be the style of question made famous by Kant: What makes this publicness of belief and meaning possible?[7] What about belief and meaning makes them such that they are publicly available properties of agents? The only correct answer to this question lies in externalism.[8] It is only because an agent's meanings and beliefs are, in general, constituted by a world external to the agent that those meanings and beliefs are available to others who live in that world, to others who can experience the same environment.

Of course, all this needs a great deal of qualification.

There are qualifications about what is meant by publicness itself. First, obviously not every thought is publicly known since agents might successfully conceal many of their thoughts from others. This in no way undermines the claim of publicness, which only claims that thoughts are, in general and in principle, publicly available. Second, when Wittgenstein talked of the publicness of meaning, he obviously did not mean to point to the fact that you and I who know English pretty well find each other's meanings available to one another. Publicness is not facility of communication and understanding. He had in mind a more principled notion of publicness, where anybody's meanings could, in principle, be available to any other, who had the capacity for meaning and intentionality.

Then there are qualifications about the externalism and the nature of its connection with the publicness which it makes possible. Here again, clearly not everything one means and believes needs to be externally constituted if it is to be publicly available. But that is no problem for me since my externalism itself is not the sort of externalism that demands that all concepts or contents, not even all singular contents, have to be externally determined. I have already said this while discussing Evans's and McDowell's views. There will be all sorts of thought on occasions that are not caused by external things even if they purport to be "about" existing or occurrent external objects and events. There will also be all sorts of highly theoretical concepts whose links with external causes will be more indirect than others. There will, as stated in chapter 1, be all sorts of fictional terms and mathematical concepts which are not externally determined. Nevertheless, our thoughts will in general be determined by external things. By "in general" I just mean that if someone said that it is possible that none of our thoughts or concepts are externally determined, they would be saying something false. This allows that particular thoughts and concepts need not be externally determined. Since the Kantian question about what makes publicness of thought is itself a general question is this sense, the externalist answer to the question need not sustain itself for each given thought or concept.

The answer, therefore, can be: externalism must, generally, hold for publicness to, generally, be possible. Without it holding, we will have no answer to our Kantian question about publicness. With it, publicness becomes unsurprising and unavoidable. A common external world which we experience, in general, determines our thought. How, then, can our thought, in general, fail to be, in principle, available to one another?

Let me say something by way of elaborating and justifying this externalist answer to our Kantian question. In giving the answer, I have deliberately done something less obvious and simple than might seem necessary. For, after all, why not just take the simple stance of saying that the publicness of thought and meaning can be secured by the more immediately obvious claim that they reveal themselves in our action? The inner process is necessarily revealed in outer behavior. That is the only stance warranted by the question. It is also the first thing that occurs to one when confronted with the question. This simple stance, however, though not false, is insufficient. And it is insufficient because it fails to speak to the right level of theoreticity of the phenomena of meaning and content.

I will explain this by considering two answers to the Kantian question which are alternatives to the externalist answer I have given. Neither of these two answers invokes externalism but they are compatible with the simple stance I have just cited and accused of insufficiency. I will argue that these alternative answers are unsatisfactory because they fail to capture the appropriate level of theoreticity at which notions like meaning and content stand.

The first alternative answer to our question about publicness appeals to certain versions of functionalism. There is a fairly widespread conviction among contemporary philosophers of mind and language that the propositional attitudes, even if they cannot be gathered into types which reduce to the types we gather our physiological states into, can nevertheless be reduced, holistically, to types of functional states. And these functional states can be defined in terms that are strictly non-externalist. The terms in the definitions do not involve anything more external than inputs described non-distally (peripheral stimuli) and output described as bodily motions; and, of course, the view is also committed to physiological states which carry or "realize" the functional states that are defined as mediating between these inputs and outputs. I do not here want to take up the question of the general viability of such an internalist functionalist reduction,[9] I only want to consider its relevance to the question I have raised about publicness.

This first answer appeals to this version of internalist reduction and says that it has a perfectly good way of dealing with publicness since all the items such functionalism appeals to are perfectly public items: peripheral stimuli, neural states and bodily motions. There is nothing epistemologically problematic about them, they are not inner or hidden in the despised traditional Cartesian sense. Externalism is not, therefore, necessary to ensure publicness.

This is strictly speaking correct since there is no gainsaying the public availability of the states appealed to by functionalism of this sort. What is wrong with it is that is fails to see the spirit in which the question about publicness was raised. It fails to see that it was not publicness strictly speaking that was being demanded. The fact is that the items which functionalist reduction appeals to (in particular the first two items) are public in a way that is irrelevant to the force of the question. When one talks of the publicness of language and mind, one means their availability literally to a public and not merely to those who, armed with relevant instruments and with a reductionist theory (yet to be forged) can examine these items in an agent. A notion of publicness which was only defined upon such a more restricted public, in possession of such a theory, would make "meaning" and "content" theoretical terms at the wrong level of theory. Only public items in the external environment are available to a public, in the requisite unrestricted sense that we were interested in, when we raised the Kantian question; which is why those who live in a shared environment and have access to such external items can have access also to the thoughts and meanings of others, which are, in part, constituted by those items.

This criticism of the first alternative answer – that it makes the notion of meaning too remotely theoretical – may give the impression that I am denying that "meaning" is a theoretical term altogether. I do not mean to give that impression, and I will correct the impression by turning now the second alternative answer, which, I believe, does make the mistake of denying all theoretical status to "meaning." I, thus, take meaning to be a theoretical notion, and in order to get the right account of its public nature it is necessary to find the right level of theoreticity.

The second alternative answer is suggested by a view of McDowell's, even though, he happens to be, as we have seen, an externalist. The answer, however, is independent of his externalism. McDowell argues that skepticism about other minds[10] can only be answered if one takes the right view of what he calls "the epistemology of understanding." [11] In particular, he argues that we must think of understanding others as a form of *direct* perception of their meanings and he intends that analogy to be taken quite literally. By it, he means that we must think of understanding as simply perceiving *in* the bodily motions and sounds of others, their meaning and their thoughts. To such a view, my answer above will seem quite false; false because my answer will seem, from the point of view of this commitment to directness, too round about, since it takes meanings to be theoretical posits, constructed partly out of the relations in which their possessors' sounds and bodily motions stand to their environments. (I contrast theoretical posit not with commonsense posit, but with the idea that there is something directly perceived and which is not to be viewed as a construction out of a theoretical procedure which involves an essential appeal to an external element in the constitution of what is constructed.) At the very least my answer will seem quite unnecessary, since the direct availability of meaning and belief to perception will make the more round-about strategy redundant. Hence, even if externalism is true, it will be irrelevant to the question about public availability; which explains why McDowell could reject my answer and yet be an externalist.

This direct or "naive" realism about others' thoughts and meanings is perfectly all right as a piece of descriptive phenomenology of speakers of the same language, since it is usually the case that our understanding of such others is non-inferential. But McDowell presents his thesis not as a point about the phenomonology of understanding others but as a thesis about the epistemology of understanding, as a way of refuting skepticism about others minds. And there is no reason to think that the two are the same. It is as an epistemological thesis that it is to be faulted for leaving out the theoretical nature of meaning.

The idea of directness of perception – whether the perception of meaning or anything else – when presented as a piece of epistemology (rather than phenomenology) presents an old and, it seems, unsolved, problem. And that is the problem of having to account for the manifest and widespread fact of perceptual error – in the present case, of error in the sense of misunderstanding of another's meanings. All the efforts by naive realists to deal with this problem so far have not been very compelling. Even if some effort were successful in accounting for error, the complications that it would have to introduce in order to do so can only be justified if the naive or direct realist had a good positive argument for saying that a direct realism is necessary for the epistemology of understanding.

McDowell's positive argument is that it alone can account for the publicness of meaning, it alone can account for the availability of other minds. I am denying that. I think that an externalist strategy *alone* accounts for it. The phenomenological matter is irrelevant to it. The only argument one could get from a position like McDowell against something like my externalist strategy is that, because of its indirectness, it falsifies the phenomenology of understanding others. The claim will be that only his direct perception view keeps faith with the phenomenology. But since the externalist strategy is not intended to speak to a phenomenological question, this cannot count as an effective argument against the externalist strategy. A reason has to be given for collapsing the phenomenological with the epistemological. I have no quarrel with his phenomenological description of understanding so long as it is granted that epistemology sees the possibility of understanding others as something which is grounded in the external constitution of meaning and content. And if McDowell is prepared to grant that, then it is altogether unnecessary for him to have boosted the phenomenological point as having the deep epistemological relevance he sees in it, viz. that it provides the only answer to the skeptic about other minds. The "direct perceptual realism" (in McDowell's hands, an epistemological doctrine produced by this unnecessary boost) is irrelevant to the skepticism. He would have granted that the real anti-skeptical work is being done by the externalism.

McDowell says that without direct realism one is reduced to lame arguments against the skeptic such as the argument from analogy which, as Wittgenstein pointed out, was a complete surrender to the skeptic. It is a surrender to the skeptic because it makes understanding others a very indirect affair, it only allows self-understanding the privileged directness.

It is interesting to see why philosophers have fallen prey to the temptation of thinking that direct realism is the only anti-skeptical strategy. The temptation arises from wrong and misleading views about what it is one must be committed to if one rejects the direct realist picture. This point needs exploring a little further because it is a fairly common temptation and is not restricted to the epistemology of understanding.

The point emerges well in a recent brief commentary on Kant's views on skepticism by Barry Stroud (1984, ch. 4).[12] The subject is skepticism about the external world, but the issues are not essentially dissimilar to those we are considering in the differences between McDowell and my views on skepticism about other minds. Speaking of Descartes and many contemporary epistemological theories, Stroud says: "For Kant they all fail because they all represent our knowledge of things outside of us as in some way indirect or inferential... For skepticism to be avoided, then, all accounts of our knowledge of the world as inferential or indirect must be rejected... For Kant our perception and therefore our knowledge of external things is direct, unmediated and unproblematic "(Stroud 1984, pp. 130-4). He also says: "If objects in space are never perceived directly and yet we know of them somehow indirectly, it would seem that we could know of them only by inferring their existence from something else we are directly and unproblematically aware of" (p.130). And he identifies these unproblematic things as sensory experiences, which, he says, Kant rejects: "This general gap between appearance and reality is an expression of what can be called 'the epistemic priority' of sensory experiences, perceptions, representations or what Descartes calls 'ideas', over those independent objects that exist in space... Kant holds that any view according to which one's experiences or appearances are epistemically prior to external things in this way must be rejected" (pp. 140.1). He then sums up Kant's argument against what he calls "skeptical idealism" or, in other words, Kant's argument for what he calls "realism." Realism he correctly describes as the idea not that every experience of objects is veridical but that it is, in general, veridical, i.e. in general it is experience of objective things.

In summing up the argument, however, he says two quite different sorts of things without making them explicitly distinct. He first says that the argument establishes that "inner experience in general is possible only if 'outer experience' in general is possible" (p.145). But, second, he also says that Kant's strategy involves showing that experience of outer objects is unproblematic and directly available, and to do so Kant presents his famous doctrine of transcendental idealism in which space and time are said to be forms of our sensibility, thereby making objects in space themselves available to us with the requisite directness.

While not wishing to deny that Stroud faithfully reports Kant's strategies and arguments to avoid skepticism and idealism, it is possible to detect, or at any rate impose, two genuinely different strategies of argument in all this, which Stroud does not notice. If the goal is to show how our experience is in general veridical or experience of objective things, then it seems perfectly all right to stop at having established the first of the two things. It is enough to have established that one could not have inner experiences in general if one did not have outer experiences in general. This would in itself show, in one sense, that there is no epistemic priority to inner experience. Inner experience would be dependent, in a clear sense, on outer experience. Now if this first strategy could reach such a realist conclusion by some argument (transcendental?) as Kant suggests it could – and he actually offers one – then there would be no need to adopt the second strategy, viz. a very specific doctrine of idealism (transcendental!) by which one would place objects in space and time as it were "in us" by making space and time forms of our sensible powers. The directness of this latter form of "realism" [12] (achieved by adopting a certain form of idealism) is not necessary to overthrow skeptical idealism. It is pre-empted by the first strategy.

Having said that the appeal to the first strategy amounts to a denial of the directness of outer perception, the question now is whether the *in*directness of outer perception is in any way a bad thing. There is no reason any longer to think so since it does not make any commitment to (indeed it denies) the primacy of the inner Cartesian objects of experience. The first strategy could not be an anti-skeptical strategy if it allowed this primacy since it is this primacy that encourages skepticism. This shows it is false to think that indirectness of outer perception *has* to be described as the indirectness of something outer known indirectly and problematically because there is something inner known directly and unproblematically. Stroud describes Kant as thinking it has to be described this way but he fails to see that the first of Kant's strategies undermines the compulsoriness of the description. One alternative, though anachronistic, way of describing the indirectness might be to say that the assertibility conditions for our perceptual thoughts about the external world would always be different from their truth conditions, i.e. there is always a logical gap between an agent's reasons for asserting his perceptual thought, say, that there is a table in front of him, and the conditions that would make his assertion true. This does make the epistemology genuinely indirect but it involves no commitment to Cartesian epistemic priorities involving "ideas" or sense data or representations or other such objects of thought. (Nor does it imply a commitment to the more modern dress surrogates for them: a canonical set of assertibility conditions, a sort of foundation out of which truth-conditions for perceptual sentences and contents are built up.) We can conclude, then, that the choice need not ever be between commitment to objects such as sense-data etc., which make for some epistemic priority, on the one hand, and direct realism, on the other.

It is true that my insistence on seeing the possibility of two anti-skeptical strategies in Kant would involve a reading of Kant that stressed much more certain parts of the "Transcendental Deduction B" and "The Refutation of Idealism" over the "Transcendental Aesthetic" and the "Transcendental Deduction A," but others have already advised that,[13] and in any case the whole matter is quite outside the province of this discussion. I raised it only to show that there is a temptation to adopt McDowell's direct realist strategy against skepticism about other minds in the face of bad indirect views (such as the picture encouraged by the argument from analogy which promotes rather than thwarts skepticism by making our own inner states epistemologically primary). And to show that this temptation has been felt before in the tradition of general anti-skeptical thinking. And finally to show that, here as well as in the general tradition, there are alternative strategies like mine which allow for an indirectness that is perfectly acceptable. In the tradition where the question was skepticism about the external world, bad forms of epistemological indirectness (the primacy of sense data or inner representations which also promote skepticism) have also tempted philosophers to adopt direct realist views (promoted by the second of Kant's strategies), where there were perfectly good indirect views (implied by the first of Kant's strategies).

The analogy is not going to be perfect obviously because I do not want to accuse McDowell of some analogue of Kant's "transcendental idealism" in some obviously bad sense. But the analogy should drive home the following point. A commitment to indirectness is not, implicitly, a concession to skepticism about other minds at all. It does not leave us with no better appeal than the argument from analogy which, it is true induces an unsatisfactory indirectness in one's thinking about other minds. The externalist answer that I give to the question of publicness offers an indirect alternative to his direct realist view without falling into the undesirable indirectness of the argument from analogy.

These two alternative answers – the functionalist's and McDowell's – to the question "What makes publicness possible?" are poor answers because they fail to capture the appropriate theoreticity of the notion of meaning and content. But notice that the contrast of my externalist answer to these two alternative answers is slightly different in each case. I have said, against McDowell, that meaning and content are not a matter of direct perception. They are theoretical notions. On this the functionalist of the first answer and I are agreed. Just as meaning and content are the central notions of a functionalist theory according to the first answer, they are products of a another kind of externalist theory of attribution according to the externalism of my answer. My gripe against the functionalist answer, therefore, is not that it takes away from the theoretical nature of these notions, as McDowell's answer does, but rather that it makes meaning and content theoretical notions at the wrong level of theoreticity, because it invokes things which are not available to the wider public. The sense in which the externalist answer makes them theoretical notions gets one to the right level of theory because it invokes items that are available to a wider public.

I had promised to show how the wrongness of these two specific alternative answers would explain the insufficiency of adopting the simple stance of saying that our thoughts and meanings are public because they are available to others via our behavior. If the availability is not *additionally* routed through the element external even to our behavior (that is external even to what carries our behavior, our bodily motions), then the stance will inevitably have to rely on one or other of these two unsatisfactory answers. It will have to rely on them to say how our bodily motions, themselves, can be said to reveal our thoughts to others capable of understanding thoughts. In the one case they would reveal them by forming part of a functional system which reduces intentionality to a system of inputs, mediating states and outputs; but, as we saw, this, by appealing to public items hidden from general view, would secure publicness in the wrong, and much too strict a sense. We could, then, move to the other case, and secure the right and broader publicness, within the stance's restriction to behavior, but we would have to say, with McDowell, that the more general public can see directly in the bodily motions (in the displacement of limbs, production of sounds etc.) the thoughts and meanings of agents. The criticism of this is not that the simple stance is insufficient, because by its stress on bodily motions, it fails to appeal to intentionally described behavior. No, the simple stance, which goes back to Ryle and Wittgenstein (see n. 14 below), clearly does appeal to bodily motions only as genuine carriers of intentional behavior. It is not some strict behaviorism. The point is rather that because it appeals to nothing more than that (nothing external to that, as I insist we should), the intentionality has to be see *in* the bodily motions *directly*.

Taking the simple general stance that behavior makes available our thoughts, therefore, leaves us with two unsatisfactory answers to the question of the epistemology of understanding; unsatisfactory, because they make meaning and content for too theoretical or too little theoretical. It is only making the stance more complex by connecting the behavior with the external environment, that will give us publicness of the right kind, and will, at the same time, give us more than a phenomenology of understanding. It will give us a satisfactory epistemology of other minds.[14]

Having argued that meaning and content are theoretical notions and that externalism is essential to its theoretical constitution, someone many protest that its theoretical status does not have to have an essential externalist constitution. Why can we not just simply see them as the only theoretical things that we can attribute in order to explain the highly complex and inter-related patterns of bodily motions and sounds that human being produce? – assuming, surely correctly, that physiological and purely causal-dispositional attributions are not going to give satisfactory explanations of the patterned and systematic complexity of those productions. It is true that doing this means redescribing the bodily motions in intentional terms but why do we need to see intentionality as being constituted by the external environment? We should just simply say that meaning and content are established as theoretical simply on grounds of inference to the best theoretical explanation of these explananda. In short, the protest is that my criticism of McDowell is correct in that I insist that intentional attributions must be seen as attributions of a theory, but incorrect in thinking that it needs any further grounding in something external, once we understand that intentional attributions are the only theory we have for what we want explained.

But the question arises as to what the protestor's answer is to the question about publicness? No doubt intentional attributions are the best theoretical explanation of the complex physical output of certain creatures such as human beings or persons, but what allows one person to come up with such a theory for another? The protest just assumes that we can make the sorts of intentional attributions we do without the external connections I insist on. But it does not say how it is one does so. How does one come to attribute beliefs to another on the basis of observation of his physical output, thereby explaining that output? In conceding that it is theory he is presumably saying that we do not just directly perceive the meanings and thoughts. But then what makes it possible to come up with such a theory? If the protestor does not answer this question, the concession to the idea that meanings and thoughts are theoretical notions, is no genuine or significant advance on McDowell's direct perception epistemology.

If the best theory we needed to account for our complex physical output was physiological theory, it is perhaps possible to see why the protestor would not worry about our question about publicness and why he would be indifferent to the externalism that any answer to the question must bring. The physiological states of an agent are perhaps something we can have access to and specify *without* appeal to external items constituting them. But the protestor is saying that intentional attributions of thoughts and meanings, and not physiological states, provide the best theoretical explanations of such complex physical output. In making intentional attributions we say things like "Searle believes that that is a yellow station wagon," "Evans believes that that table is round," "Putnam believes that water quenches thirst," "Descartes believes that he is sitting in front of a fire," and so on. We use concepts like table, fire, water, station wagon... to state the concepts and contents of agents. And the question is how can we do this, how do we have access to these concepts of an agent without giving the sort of externalist answer I give. I will return to this question later. The point for now is that it is not even to have taken up the question about publicness, to say, as the protestor does, that an agent's thoughts are publicly available simply because it is only attributing *thoughts* which will satisfactorily explain his complex pattern of physical output. This ignores the question, what is it to attribute thoughts, what makes possible that we attribute those things with those sorts of specifications rather than, say, just physiological states? And once we bring this question in, externalism must be brought in, to answer it.

Before leaving the defense of my externalist answer against alternative answers to the publicness question, let me mention that it is sometimes thought that Platonism also offers yet another answer. It is an alternative apparently not because it is internalist, but because it is not externalist in anything like the sense I have insisted (where the environment enters to determine content). The idea is that content and meanings are neither internal nor external but objective and real things, possibly of an abstract sort. As far as one can tell, however, this view is not on a par with any of the views we have been discussing. It is an assertion of objectivity in these matters which amounts to saying that if two subjects believe or mean the same thing, then there is something objective that they both believe or mean. In itself that does not say on what basis they understand each other or others understand them, so our question is not so much as being addressed. It is true perhaps that meanings and contents must be objective if they are public; but our question was about what makes publicness possible, what ensures that one's thoughts and meanings will be, in principle, available to another. A mere assertion of their objectivity says nothing to answer that.

## Why Publicness?

So far in this section I have argued for externalism as the best among various answers one might give to the question about what makes publicness possible. The argument, obviously, turned on accepting a widely accepted claim about meaning and thought, the claim that they are necessarily public. The argument, even if it persuades those who accept the claim, will leave those who do not, cold. Let me discuss what is involved in rejecting the claim about publicness and why one ought not to reject it.

Though it has had its detractors, in much of the philosophical culture influenced by the mature Wittgenstein the publicness thesis is taken for granted. This is often so even after an acknowledgment by many that the so-called anti-private language argument is less than successful in establishing the thesis. What could underlie this confidence? What could justify the publicness taken for granted in my argument for externalism?

The publicness of meaning and thought is a special case of very general thesis which has nothing in particular to do with meaning or thought. This is the thesis, as one might crudely put it, of the knowability, in principle, of any truth that is there to be known. If this thesis is acceptable, then so should a thesis of the knowability of thought and meaning, since it would just be a specific instance of it.

Naturally, the more general knowability thesis comes with qualifications. For instance, it is surely to be allowed that it fails to hold in those cases where an impossibility theorem can be proved; that is, it fails to hold where it can be shown, and therefore known, that something is unknowable, proved that something is unprovable. Godel showed that for a certain truth, which gives us some idea of the standards to be met before we deny the knowability thesis. Short of showing that sort of thing, the thesis claims, with Peirce, that there is no need to put "unnecessary roadblocks on the path to knowledge." Another obvious qualification or, rather, clarification ought to be that "knowability" need not amount to verifiability in anything like the sense that verificationists have insisted on. There is no canonical set of procedures involving assertibility conditions rather than truth-conditions in terms of which the knowability of facts expressed in sentence is to be cashed out.

The overall point is that the publicness assumption, essential to my argument for externalism, is a specific case of the general knowability principle; and it is justified to the extent that the principle is true and acceptable.

There is (and has in the past been) resistance to the knowability thesis as one finds it in Peirce and others. It comes from those who are committed to a radical form of realism. A clear recent example of such resistance can be found in the chapter entitled 'Thought and Reality' in Nagel's book *The View from Nowhere* (1986).

Nagel claims that there can be aspects of reality which may be completely unknowable and tells the following sort of story to make it vivid. There are lots of things known to advanced scientists and even many of us who are not advanced scientists, which are not known to children and cannot be known by people with severely restricted mental capacities. Might there not be a species of knowers who have capacities of mind and knowledge that are in advance of ours, in ways analogous to the ways ours are in advance of retarded people. We simply lack the capacities to know what they know. This is intuitively, Nagel says, a manifestly conceivable thing. He argues that a genuine realism should conclude from this analogy that knowability in principle is a false ideal; the analogy shows that the ideal *is*, despite my denial above, a form of verificationism or idealism, which underlies the more specific and more restrictive idealism and verificationsms. For it too would, in a general rather than specific way, restrict the notion of truth with epistemic constraints flowing from human capacities. It is a false ideal because it cannot entertain the possibility of such a community of super-knowers, and the analogy has shown that we have as much right to deny its possibility as children (even adults arrested as mental children) would have to deny that advanced scientists know what they know.

Something like the intuition Nagel captures in this analogy is, no doubt, the source of certain versions of a strongly realist philosophy. This is not the place to argue in detail about whether this realism is defensible and which, if any, should replace it. It would be enough to stop here and say that it is this general issue of realism which underlies, and which is at stake in, the question of publicness. The plausibility of the publicness thesis, for those to whom it is plausible, is derived from an underlying commitment to the implausibility of this strong version of realism. This is, as I said, because the publicness thesis is a special case of the knowability thesis, which is denied by this realism. However, though it may be enough to stop with having said what is at stake, let me say just a little bit more so as to force those who agree with Nagel to see that they owe us a little more philosophical work than the mere appeal to the intuition that his analogy brings out.

Why does Nagel feel the need to raise the analogy? The analogy is bruited by him in order to respond to the objection that his strong realism announces a notion of reality (possibly unknowable) which is simply that, an announcement. An announcement that there is such a reality without any clear or specific idea of what it is that we are granting when granting it, the objection claims, is not yet to have granted anything. This is surely a fair demand for more substance in the strong realist thesis. The analogy is bruited, in response, to bring out the intuitive substance of what is being granted.

The analogy is between the sort of incomprehension congenital nine-year olds have towards advanced scientists and the sort of incomprehension we might have towards that understanding and thoughts of the species of super-knowers. There is a specific point in the analogy, however, that needs explicit clarification. Congenital nine-year olds have a partial understanding of advanced scientists; they understand their talk of hamburgers and houses, if not their talk of room-temperature fusion. One may, therefore, ask whether there is a partial understanding that we have of the super-knowers. If there *is* an admission of partial intelligibility, then that allows for the possibility of an, in principle, understanding of the limitations that prevent greater comprehension. It allows for it because it allows that there is more of the same *kind* of thing that one, due to contingent limitations, cannot grasp. This understanding of limitations can be more and less specific, more and less vague, but its possibility is there insomuch as partial intelligibility is there. And if there is a sense of limitations that can exist for members of a species when they compare themselves to other members of it, then surely there can be in the inter-species case. There, too, partial intelligibility can give one a sense of limitations to be overcome if reality is to be fully knowable. Thus, it does not seem as if the analogy quite establishes the unreachable-in-principle reality of Nagel's realism, so long as partial intelligibility is allowed by the analogy. It no more establishes Nagel's ultra-realism than my realizing that I would have to be retrained and educated in a way that mortality does not permit (or perhaps even that I would have to be born all over again) before I understood the advanced thoughts of my colleagues in the Physics Department, establishes his ultra-realism. Thus, allowing partial intelligibility in the Nagelian analogy would imply a surrender to the knowability principle, and would undermine the ultra-realism the analogy is meant to support.

So if the analogy is to be fully convincing it must envisage a species of super-knowers whose thoughts are not even partially intelligible to us. But now this raises again the very sort of demand voiced by the objection and to which Nagel's analogy was supposed to have provided a response. We may now demand (with as much fairness as we demanded an elaboration of the notion "reality" in the bald announcement that there is a possibly unknowable reality) what is your notion of "thought" in the announcement: the super-knowers may have thoughts which we cannot (even partially) understand. The use of "thought" in the conclusion of the analogy now seems as much part of a mere announcement as the notion of "reality" did in the announcement prior to the analogy. Why should we think it is thoughts that super- "knowers" have? The lack of even partial intelligibility removes any clear and specific idea of what it is for super-knowers to have *thoughts*. The analogy breaks down just at the point it should hold, once partial intelligibility is withheld. (And not to withhold partial intelligibility, to allow partial intelligibility is, as we saw, to give Nagel's opponent the wedge he needs to insist on knowability, at least, in principle.)

The problem is this and it is not a new one. Nagel quite rightly notices that objections to his ultra-realist view cannot be dismissed by him as verificationist or idealist in the ordinary and undesirable sense. But the more general idealism or verificationism that he wishes to charge his objector with would only be a fair charge if he gave himself the right to the use of concepts like "thought" in the conclusion of his analogy. For surely a mere rejection of verificationism does not mean one is not constrained by any standards of intelligibility. His use of "reality" in the announcement of an unknowable reality seemed, by his own acknowledgment, to be *a prima facie*, violation of an intuitive principle demanding a non-verificationist intelligibility. The analogy was supposed to give or at least hint at a way of removing this *prima facie* unintelligibility. But, if I am right, by the same general demand of non-verificationist intelligibility, the analogy too falls short because it introduces another unintelligible notion, of the super-knower's "thoughts."[15] Without getting a further response from him on this, we need not concede that his analogy has given him the right to charge his opponents with idealism or verificationism.[16] I suspect all further responses will be subject to the same worries.

To conclude, then: if I am right that publicness is a special case of knowability in principle, and knowability in principle is acceptable unless shown to be wrong by a strong version of realism, and right that this has not yet been shown, then publicness is with us. And if I am right that publicness is only explained by externalism, then so is externalism.

## A SECOND EPISTEMOLOGICAL ARGUMENT FOR EXTERNALISM

In putting forward the argument of the last section I introduced for the first time explicitly *epistemological* considerations into the matter of internalism versus externalism in the study of content. Epistemological considerations which affect the study of content can be of, at least, two (inter-related) sorts. On the one hand, they can be about the nature of one mind's access to another's mind and its contents. It is these considerations which were relevant to the issues of publicness discussed above. On the other hand, they can also be about a mind's access to the external world.

Since a good deal of discussion of internalism emerges from a discussion of the Cartesian conception of the mind, it tends to explicitly revolve around the latter sort of epistemological considerations and only implicitly about the former. That is to say, discussion of an internal or Cartesian conception of mind, partly because of the focus of Descartes's own interests, concentrates on how the mind might be independent of the nature of its external environment. Such a conception of mind cannot avoid having to deal with the question of the mind's accessibility or inaccessibility to other minds, as we have seen in this chapter, but that was not a question that Descartes himself took up explicitly. His gaze, and the gaze of those more contemporary philosophers who find Cartesian intuitions compelling, is on epistemological considerations of the latter sort.

It should be obvious how epistemological considerations of both sorts can be used to promote or oppose internalism. I have been arguing that the former sort, involving publicness, oppose internalism. But, as we have seen, those who do not think public access is a necessary feature of content, may use it to promote internalism. Similarly, those who think that skepticism about the external world is a conceptual possibility have used the latter sort of epistemological considerations to promote internalism, arguing that internalism alone is compatible with such a conceptual possibility. Therefore, those who oppose internalism must resist this line of argument and offer instead a reason for thinking that the latter sort of epistemological considerations, if anything, promote externalism. Let me turn to that task.

### Question-begging Thought-experiments

Skepticism about the external world is usually expounded by arguments and thought-experiments such as the argument from illusion, or the argument from dreaming in Descartes, or more recent arguments asking us to imagine brains-in vats. The internalism is supposed to issue intuitively from the plausibility of these arguments and thought-experiements. I will argue briefly that things are the other way around. These arguments and thought-experiements come to the conclusion they do about the conceptual possibility of skepticism regarding the external world only because they presuppose internalism. It thus misdescribes things in a very misleading way to say that internalism issues intuitively from the plausibility of these arguments and thought-experiments.

Let me quickly take up brains-in-vats. The point of appealing to them is to intuitively consolidate a metaphysical claim about the supervenience of intentional contents on interior states, i.e. states of the brain (including functional states that are definable as second-order properties upon such states). To make a familiar story very brief, we are told to imagine that a mad scientist, with the use of a computer, simulates a brain in a vat of nutrient fluids to have the same interior states as mine, including the same peripherally described inputs, and the same verbal output or "utterances," described as physical inscriptions or sounds. It is concluded that it is intuitive that its utterances and thoughts must be the same as mine. So, it too thinks, and says, such things as that there is a depressing amount of snow falling outside the study window in New Haven. If one concedes that this is intuitively so, then one is supposed to have conceded that the external world makes no difference to the contents of thoughts and utterances, since the environment of the brain is not New Haven and has no snow, but instead is a vast computer to which it is hitched and which the mad scientist is manipulating in order to simulate these interior states in the brain. Skepticism about the external world, at least in the sense of radically *false* belief, if not radically *unjustified* belief, is said to follow from all this because clearly all such beliefs *are* false of its environment.

Many externalists have resisted the claim to an intuition of shared thoughts here, saying that one should say instead that the brain's utterances and thoughts do not have contents about New Haven, snow etc., but rather about events in the computer in *its* external environment. For them, my contents are about snow because there is snow in my environment, whereas it contents are about changes in the computer to which it is hooked up for that is what is happening in its environment. It has by and large true beliefs about its environment and I about mine. For externalists, the verbal output of the brain is the same as mine in a sense that is purely physical and, therefore, too restricted to amount to being the same language. The languages and thoughts are quite different because the environments are quite different. The internalist will reply that this is highly counter-intuitive, given that the peripheral inputs, interior states and peripheral outputs and "utterances" are the same.

It seems to me that this entire dispute is about intuitions that are not pre-philosophical at all, and the internalist is quite wrong to think that the intuitions it appeals to are not tinged with its own philosophical position. My own intuition is to agree with the internalist on this much. My intuition in such a case is also that the brain and I have the same mental and linguistic contents because it would be too much of a coincidence that our utterances are exactly the same. (Thus I would deny what many externalists say.) But I would also deny that my intuition – which I share with the internalist – has anything to do with the fact that the internal descriptions for both are the same. I would be inclined to think that, in general, if one wishes to say that the brain's "utterances" are the same as mine and are correlating very well with an environment in New Haven and not in its immediate vicinity (where there is nothing but a computer), then those utterances may indeed get the same contents as mine – only this would get a quite different explanation from the internalist's, it would get the explanation that the brain has a highly non-standard "perceptual" apparatus (involving the mediation of a mad scientist) connecting it with events in distant New Haven. Thus the intuition is the same as the internalist's without any concession to internalism, i.e. it is not an internalist but an externalist intuition. It is externalist because the work underlying the conclusion that the contents are the same lies in noticing correlations between utterances and an external environment, however distant. In general, an externalism is merely committed to content being attributed to an organism by looking to correlations with external causes. If those correlations are better made with causes in a distant rather than the immediate environment, then if one had a "perceptual" theory connecting the organism with that environment, there is no bar to the contents being about objects and events in it.

I do not at all insist, however, that this is a pre-philosophical intuition and I concede that the internalist may stick with her intuition that the contents are the same for quite different philosophical reasons having to do with sameness of interior descriptions. Both opposing intuitions flow from our respective philosophical positions and cannot therefore by used to promote those positions.

In order to show up my response as still pre-philosophically counter-intuitive and to show her own to be pre-philosophically intuitive, the internalist, at this point, might raise the example of the miraculous brain-in-a-vat, which is exactly like the other, except that it is not controlled or constructed by any mad scientist. There are simply miracles occurring on its periphery. The claim will be that it cannot be talking about New Haven on intuitively externalist grounds because there is no link via the mad scientist connecting it to events in New Haven. So if I still have the intuition that it has the same contents as I do, then that can only be on internalist grounds of sharing the same internal descriptions. I deny it. I still have the intuition about there being the same contents, I say, only to the extent that I am *committed* to their being *some* non-standard perceptual apparatus (even if not anymore the one via the mad scientist). If we still have the intuition that its thoughts are the same as mine, then we must keep looking for such non-standardness in the perceptual links because our view of content is committed to finding them. Insistence on shared contents and failure to have come up with a perceptual theory making the appropriate external causal connections, no more forces us to cave in to the internalist intuition, than insistence that there is a specific disease called cancer and failing to have come up with the a theory about what causes cancer forces us to concede that the disease has no cause.

And it would be unfair for the internalist to complain that the insistence on such a non-standardness of perceptual apparatus to consolidate the externalist intuition is an insistence on something miraculous and itself unintuitive; unfair because the non-standardness of the perceptual apparatus I am insisting must be there, only matches the non-standardness of the miraculous brain-in-a-vat we are being asked to imagine.

Thus the externalist can dig her heels in and say that there is and can be no other basis for the continuing intuitive claim that the contents are the same than an externalist basis, even if it means positing highly non-standard and, as yet undiscovered, perceptual apparatus of the brain.

I repeat that the externalist digs her heels in with an intuition that is *within* her externalist position and, therefore, this has no power of argument against opposing internalist intuitions. I am not, therefore, claiming, as some externalists have done, that externalism itself provides the best argument against the idea of skepticism about the external world generated by these thought-experiments. No, the aim of the preceding discussion was only to bring out that the internalist intuitions are equally post-philosophical, are just as question-begging as the externalists. The point was only to reveal how the internalist's appeal to skepticism about the external world via arguments such as those invoking brains-in-vats have not yet made any effective and non-question begging case against the externalist. Does all this mean that the externalist cannot, herself, produce any arguments which justify externalism against internalism in the context of epistemological considerations having to do with the external world? Things may not be quite that bleak.

## Modest and Ambitious Arguments for Externalism

Tyler Burge (1985) has argued that internalism is not something that follows upon Cartesian skepticism in the sense of radical and comprehensive error about the external world. But by this he means not what I have just argued, viz. that it is presupposed by Cartesian skepticism rather than follows upon it. Rather he means that one may concede the epistemic possibility of Cartesian skepticism and, at the same time, withhold a concession to internalism,[17] i.e. one may, for the sake of argument, grant that one is radically mistaken about the external world without granting that one's thoughts are internally determined. He says that internalists who involve epistemological considerations about the external world have a tendency to make a false "move" or "conflation." The conflation, in his words, goes roughly like this: "It begins with: 'Things [in the external world] might have been radically otherwise... and relative to these imagined circumstances our actual thoughts would be subject to numerous and radical errors.' It concludes with: 'Things [in the external world] might have been radically otherwise and our thoughts and minds would remain just as they are.'" (Burge 1985, p. 67).

I do not see that this is a false move in the sense that Burge claims because, as I tried to show, a claim to radical error about the world presupposes independence of thoughts from the world. So if one concedes the first step, then the "move" to the second has already been made in the concession.

But Burge's paper has more than the negative point I am disputing. The positive part of Burge's paper gives an argument to show that internalism about (perceptual) intentional contents is not plausible. However, it is an argument which begins with frankly externalist premises. And Burge is open about the limited ambitions of his positive argument. There are three premises. To put them briefly, they state, first, that perceptual judgments are about objective entities; second that they are specified as being about them ("That's a *crack*," "That's a *shadow*"); and, third, that such perceptions are formed because of the causal and law-like relations in which perceivers stand to the objective entities they perceive. From these premises he argues the following.[18] Something we attribute as a misperception to an agent, in which one kind of objective entity is judged by him to be another ("That's a shadow," judged of a crack), will not be attributed to him as a misperception in a counterfactual world, where there are no objective entities as shadows, even if he is internally unchanged. In such a counterfactual world, we will specify the content of the perceptual state as "That's a crack" because there are only cracks and no shadows in this world.

The argument is impeccable and it brings out very well the fact that the idea of a certain kind of misperception in the actual world, the possibility of which is inherent in the first premise (perception of objective things entails the possibility of misperception, entails the possibility of a gap between what we take things to be perceptually and what they are), cannot be captured in the counterfactual case, given the third premise. That is why the states in the actual and counterfactual world must be different. The externalist third premise makes clear that the misperception in the actual world cannot be attributed in the counterfactual world. If one gave up externalism one could not attribute a misperception in the actual world or the counter factual world. In that case we could attribute the same state in both worlds because the internal states are, *ex hypothesi*, the same. But in that case we would also have to give up on attributing a misperception in the actual world. And that would mean giving up the first premise.

Burge is open about the fact that his argument is modest in the sense that it only shows that the anti-solipsist first premise sanctions a very particular notion of error in perception, which cannot be captured by an internalist position which works without the third (or the second) premise and substitutes for them some internalist versions of them for individuating content. It is modest because what it really does is go from one aspect of anti-internalism to another. But the project of the argument is very worthwhile since in doing so he not only shows the interconnections of important aspects about our intuitions about perception, but he also sheds light on how much the internalist is denying that we may want to have. The modest goal may be partly a consequence of his having conceded, for the sake of argument, that he is not going to quarrel with the conceptual *possibility* of comprehensive Cartesian error; the idea of his argument can thus be seen as a way, nevertheless, to bring out why, *in fact*, our perceptual intentional judgments are most plausibly seen as externalist. (I think that this way of putting the point behind his positive argument, the modesty of its aim and how it flows from a concession to the conceptual coherence of Cartesian skepticism, makes it unnecessary for him to make his negative point against the internalist's appeal to that coherence in the form that I earlier disputed, i.e. it makes it unnecessary for him to say that even if comprehensive Cartesian error occurred, that would prove nothing about internalism in content.)

But the question remains: is this the sort of modest effort that an externalist must be content with in the context of these particular epistemological considerations regarding our access to the external world? Let me briefly try to present a case for saying something a little more ambitious against internalism in this epistemological context.

The whole question of how strong an argument we can produce against internalism in this context is a delicate one and is historically ridden with a great deal of discussion about the viability of "transcendental arguments" against skepticism. I do not want to enter in detail into such a discussion. I do not want to open a can filled with debates about empirical versus transcendental arguments since those debates assume that there are certain clear distinctions which have long been challenged. Perhaps those challenges can be answered but I will not try to address that here. Instead, I will proceed from the modesty of the sort of thing Burge says, and see what stronger conclusions we might be able to approach.

Burge, if I have correctly represented his main argument and its point, asks the question: what can we say against internalism about the content of perceptual episodes, given that these are, in general, about objective things and can be erroneous in a specific sense that flows from this, admittedly already, anti-solipsistic claim that they are about objective things? His answer assumes a further anti-internalist premise that such contents of perceptual episodes about objective things are in fact formed and explained by the causal relations (and optical laws) holding between perceivers and objective things, and then it comes to the conclusion I mentioned above. The fact of these externalist premises makes clear that someone who is a determined internalist will insist that this begs the question. And Burge admits this.

The point is not merely that determined internalists can dig their heels in no matter what anybody says. The point is not that they can repudiate Burge's further anti-internalist premise and insist on internalism by invoking various miracles[19] as alternative internalist explanations of the contents of perceptual episodes. If that were the only point, then not even so-called "transcendental arguments" would establish externalism and anti-skepticism. There is no arguing against an absolutely sophomoric insistence on internalism and skepticism. The point is rather that more sober internalists can insist that Burge begs the question against them because there may be *non*-miraculous, that is to say not supernaturalist but naturalist, internalist explanations of the contents of our perceptual episodes. Such an internalist will admit Burge's further externalist premise probably states a more likely explanation of perceptual contents than the naturalist internalist alternatives to it, but that cannot, she will say, be a satisfying argument against her since skeptics never claimed to say that radical error is the case, only that it cannot be ruled out as a coherent possibility. And if that is so, then internalism alone, with these alternative explanations, can allow for that coherence. Such a sober internalist, as opposed to a sophomoric one, is a worthy opponent of an externalist who wishes to say something more ambitious than Burge.

Let me therefore propose the following criterion on the subject of modesty and ambition in the matter of anti-internalism in the context of these epistemological considerations. An argument against internalism is *maximally ambitious* if it can trump even what I have called the "sophomoric" skeptic and internalist, that is if it can show to be wrong an internalist who is going to appeal to miraculous internalist explanations whenever explanations are crucially required of him. An argument against internalism is *maximally modest* if it appeals to the greater plausibility, on empirical grounds, of externalist explanations over non-micarculous internalist ones, i.e. naturalist internalist explanations. And, finally, there is an *intermediate level of ambition* one can exhibit against internalism by showing that there is no naturalist internalist explanation available when explanation is called for, i.e. by showing that internalists must *always* fall back on miraculous explanations.

Transcendental arguments are usually intended as maximally ambitious. Since I do not quite know how to explicate the nature of such arguments and since I doubt that there is anything that can satisfy the sophomoric skeptic and internalist, I will not make any claims of the maximally ambitious kind. The maximally modest aims – such as the one we find in Burge's argument – may be the best we are going to get but I think it would be premature to rest with that conclusion. It is worth giving a fair run to a line of attack at the intermediate level of ambition against the non-sophomoric internalist.

Remember that an internalist who is the target of these "intermediate" level arguments is a sober philosopher, not a Cartesian ideologue, and will always be prepared to respond to the challenge which demands alternative internalist but, always, non-miraculous and naturalist explanations of him, even if these explanations are not as likely (empirically) to be true as the rival externalist accounts. And the intermediate level externalist argument against him will try to deny that these responses can ever be successful. It will try to show that all these responses must fail and that the internalist has no appeals to anything but miracles. If the externalist can pull off this intermediate strategy against the internalist, he will have pulled off something that deserves a better name than the somewhat dismissive and derisory "inference to the best explanation strategy." That name is more apt for the maximally modest strategy which allows the internalist non-miraculous explanations and says merely that the externalist has better explanations than these internalist explanations. One can understand someone saying contemptuously of this strategy, "Ah, but that's *merely* inference to the best explanation." The intermediate strategy, however, not only says that the externalist explanations are better than these respectable, naturalist internalist explanations, he says that these respectable internalist explanations are only at first sight respectable and hide an underlying appeal to miraculous explanations. He says that the internalist, on scrutiny, will always, given his internalism, be driven in the end to make an appeal to miracles. This leaves the externalist in a position, which it would be exaggerated understatement to describe as "inference to the best explanation."

Thus the intermediate strategy, if successful, will give the externalist something worthwhile and not too unambitious against the internalist. I will try to show how the strategy might be successful. I will try to present an argument which shows that even though the internalist seems to be producing a respectable naturalist alternative to externalist explanations, he, ultimately, must resort to a miraculous explanation if he is to remain an internalist.

### An Argument of Intermediate Ambition against Internalism

Let me float the intermediate strategy by moving away from the contents of perceptual episodes to the concepts which are invoked in the specifications of such contents. For many philosophers, the failure of externalism to prove its case lies in the possibility (even if not plausibility) of alternative internalist naturalist explanations of why we perceive and judge what we do on particular occasions. The internalist assumes the supervenience of content on the *inner* physical and functional features of perceivers and thereby is prepared to countenance radical Cartesian error. The externalist making no such assumption does not. The debate, at this point, appears, as we saw earlier, to be a stand-off. Let me try to show why it is not, by moving to the level of concepts rather than the contents that they compose in particular perceptual episodes, in order to tip the scales in favor of externalism via the intermediate strategy.

Let us assume to begin with that everybody in this dispute, including the internalist, is agreed that phenomenalism is a failed programme in philosophy. We know now as well as we can know anything in philosophy that we cannot reduce the vocabulary by which we talk of the external world to the vocabulary of sense data or sense impressions. And this is so even if we are prepared to entertain as a conceptual possibility that we are radically wrong about the nature of the external world, even if we grant the conceptual possibility of Descartes's First Meditation. This is an uncontroversial assumption because even the most fierce internalist in our midst, John Searle, will assent to the assumption. His internalist specifications make full use of phenomenalistically unreduced concepts such as "station wagons" and there is no evidence that he thinks or desires that his internalism should await a phenomenalist reduction of them before it will be fully justified. We and he would be less inclined to take internalism as seriously as we do if it turned on such an eventuality. And this is not due to the empirical unattainability of the reduction of one vocabulary to another. Rather we know that "brownness, squareness, hardness," for example, does not capture what we intend by "table."

To accept the failure of phenomenalism is to accept this. We cannot even as internalists deny that, in the specification of contents, we must indispensably use concepts which purport to refer to the external world and not to inner sense data. These concepts will not, in the Cartesian eventuality, succeed in doing what they purport to do because there is nothing to refer to. But the indispensability of the concepts in the specifications must be granted by the internalist, even for the scenario of the Cartesian eventuality.

Now here is a curious thing. Why is it that a position should find itself indispensably using a conceptual vocabulary, whose precise point is to refer to the external world in the specification of contents, when it is the chief point of the position that contents are precisely not determined by anything in the external world? This is a curiosity that needs some response. It raises an important challenge for internalists. The challenge is: with what right do internalists help themselves to this vocabulary or these concepts? With what right do internalist like Searle ("There is a yellow station wagon in front of me") or Descartes ("I am sitting in front of the fire in a dressing gown") specify the contents in their examples of beliefs with concepts such as "station wagons," "fires" and "dressing gowns"? Whence this elaborate conceptual repertoires if not due to (causal) relations between possessors of the concepts that this vocabulary expresses, and the external world? – the very relations that internalists wish to deny as being constitutive of meaning and content.

Searle and other contemporary internalists have not troubled to set themselves this challenge and respond to it. Phenomenalists were internalists who did try to meet this challenge honestly and thus tried to provide an alternative to the externalist explanation. Instead of appealing to the sort of externalist explanation of perceptual contents in Burge's third premise above and distilling from it an externalist account of the concepts that go into the specification of those contents, phenomenalists tried to reduce these concepts by construction from a set of more primitive inner objects which they called sense data. We have seen that this internalist answer is not inferior to the externalist on mere grounds of lesser empirical plausibility but that it is a non-starter because it fails to capture what it is supposed to. But what else can an internalist say by way of response? There does not seem to be any alternative explanation to externalism and phenomenalism.

At this point a host of issues arise concerning nativism in the philosophy of language and mind. For an alternative to the empiricism in externalist explanations might just be to appeal to the other Cartesian idea of innate ideas.[20] If these concepts were innate there would be no need for the externalist explications which rely on the causal relations that agents often stand in to the objective instances of these concepts. Now Searle's and others internalists' silence on the matter of this challenge can only be taken as an implicit commitment to the idea that, for all we know, there is no external world, and the indispensability of our using these concepts in the specification of our thoughts is explained by the fact that we were either just born with them or they grew in us as we grew biologically. Something like this internalist response is explicitly given by Chomsky.

Nativism, as is well known, has powerful arguments in favor of it when applied to certain features of syntax, but our question is about the lexicon. Similar arguments from considerations about learning have been applied to the lexicon by Fodor (1979) and also by Chomsky (1966). But nativism in this extended sphere is a very controversial matter and there has been very widespread skepticism about it (see especially Putnam 1967). This is not the place to enter the controversy. However, I do want to argue that even if nativism can be extended to the lexicon, its appearance as an alternative to externalist explanation to our question about these concepts is, in the end, illusory. If the appeal to nativism is not to appear wholly miraculous and thereby disappear from view as a target for the intermediate anti-internalist strategy we are pursuing, then it must introduce considerations that promote, rather than substitute for, externalism.

One way I put my question about the concepts of objective things was to ask with what right do internalists employ them in the specification of concepts. In response to this sort of question, Chomsky appeals to something like the implicit commitment I was pinning on the internalist in the paragraph before last. He says:

> Take Descartes. [Bilgrami says] he has to explain what right he has to the concept of fire or dressing gown. It's a funny question to start with. Does he also have to explain what right he has to his circulatory system or his left arm? These are certain things that grow in a certain way in his body (putting aside Cartesian dualism, untenable as well as necessary) on the occasion of experience. There is, of course, a further task to explain why certain concepts in the mind/brain grow rather than others, given that experience. The problem here is the same, in principle, as explaining why his circulatory system or his left arm grew, given the nutritional environment of the cell, not something else (wings, etc.). That's a problem for science, not raising any fundamental question in the case of concepts that doesn't arise for arms and circulatory systems. (Chomsky 1989, p. 12)

The question I asked was with what right do *internalists* (like Descartes or Searle) *employ* concepts of objective, *external* things. The question cannot be too odd since phenomenalism gives an answer (an unsatisfactory answer but nevertheless an answer) to that question on behalf of internalists by saying that internalism need not invoke anything external to justify the use of concepts about external things because it reduces these concepts, without remainder, to simple inner objects of experience. The question I asked was not a general question about the *right* "he" in the sense of *anyone* has to *have* these concepts, but rather the right he has to the use or employment of them, given *his* internalist philosophical commitments. The question of "right" and the question of "whence the possession of these concepts" are not the same question.

One can paraphrase the, or one, point underlying my raising my question for the internalist, as being to ask: how is it that we (anyone) are in possession of concepts of external and objective things; and as being to claim: that internalists like Descartes do not have a satisfactory answer to this, and, therefore *they* (internalists) do not have the right to employ the terms expressing these concepts in the specification of contents.

So much for the question. Let us look hard at Chomsky's answer. Chomsky says this sort of question is not interestingly unlike a question about how we come to be in possession of our left arms or our circulatory system. And he says the answer is similar. Like arms and circulatory systems, concepts of objective and external things "grow in his body on the occasion of certain experience." The appeal, then, is to a combination of biology and experience. I would not deny that. But in itself that does not say anything against the externalist answer. If it turns out that the experience required is the experience of objective and external things, then externalism is still true.

Things are different, however, if the relevant role of experience in Chomsky's answer is not experience of external things but something more analogous to the surrounding facts about nutrition, as one sentence from the quoted passed above suggests. In this case, it would seem that the biological considerations are playing the main role (rather than experience) in the answer to the question. If so, one assumes that the claim must be that the genetic endowment does much to explain the possession of the various such concepts we have. The appeal to genetic endowment is an appeal to a respectable, naturalist, internalist explanation. It explains how the concepts grew in us, given, of course, experience thought of analogously with nutrition rather than experience of the external world.

But this just *is* a respectable naturalist version of nativism about these concepts. Giving a more diminished role to experience suggests nativism; and the rejection of dualism and the stress on biology rescues the nativism from being a non-naturalist, miraculous doctrine. Thus we have an alternative to externalism which is still within the sights of non-miraculous, naturalist explanation of our possession of these concepts. This is a genuine response to the (intermediate level) challenge posed to the internalist by this question about concepts, a response that shows that the intermediate strategy I am pursuing against the internalist has not yet succeeded against him. This cannot, however, be the resting point.

Any nativist claim about such concepts if it is not to be miraculous (God just put those concepts there in us!) presumably must make an appeal to genetic endowment. I do not not want to enter here into the debate between Fodor and Putnam on the question of the superiority of nativism over empiricism in that domain of language that has to do, not with syntax, but with the lexicon (which is our primary concern in being concerned with these concepts). On the other hand, I do not want to make my case against internalism by just assuming that the most sophisticated case for nativism (due to Chomsky and Fodor) is false either. What I do want to say is that I do not think that this respectable version of the nativist answer to our question about concepts can in the end bring any succor to internalism. The reason for this is simple. The answer appeals to biology and to genetic endowment. And a question arises now for the species, as it did for the individual agents within it, a question about what explains the possession of these concepts. What, in the evolutionary story, explains this fact about innate conceptual structure that the species is endowed with. There can be no answer to this other than that which invokes adaptability to an external *environment*. The externalist can, of course, exult in this. If the nativist story attributes to us a panoply of concepts about various features in the external environment on the grounds that we have it in virtue of the fact of belonging to a certain species in the scale of evolution, and if that itself is explained in terms of the adaptability of the species to its environment, then it must surely be that the explanation must invoke as part of the explanation the causal relations that have held between members of the species and those objects in the environment to which it has adapted. Externalism, in the sense I have been insisting on, is, therefore, a core, an essential component, of the explanation that even the *nativist* is committed to. It is this core which is a necessary condition for the possession of these concepts. So even if nativism is true, externalism is still in the picture.

On the other hand, if nativism were false and a more empiricist story about the possession of these concepts were true, this core (no longer a core in an *evolutionary* explanation but rather a core in our description of ordinary experience) would still be the only satisfactory non-miraculous answer we have to our question about where our concepts of external items come from (on the assumption that phenomenalism is wrong).

And if nativism were claimed to be true and it did *not* appeal to a biological and evolutionary explanation (which, if I am right, in the end relies on externalism,), then it would be a completely mysterious and non-naturalist answer to our question. Mysterious and non-naturalist in the way creationism always is.

The intermediate strategy thus seems to have found that right level of argument against internalism. We have trumped the internalist in the sense of forcing him to appeal to miracles at the crucial points in his dialectic.

It is not the strongest thing it is possible to say against the internalist because it falls short of a providing a "transcendental argument." But it does seem to have brought out how utterly implausible internalism is in a satisfying way. It is stronger than the modest aims Burge set himself and achieved. And it is distinct progress on the question-begging responses that externalists might make to brain-in-vat examples.


## CAN EXTERNALISM CAPTURE THE FIRST-PERSON
## POINT OF VIEW?

So far in this defense of externalism against internalism, nothing has been said about the first-person point of view. This may seen both artificial and unfair since many of the arguments in favor of internalism turn on the claim that externalism cannot capture the peculiarly first-person point of view so essential to the mind, and hence to intentionality in particular.

The expressions "first-person point of view" "first-person perspective" (which are supposed to stand for the essential thing that externalism leaves out) are highly omnibus expressions and contain diverse strands and themes. Much philosophical confusion comes from not sorting them out and many unconvincing arguments in favor of internalism depend on leaving them unsorted.

What are these first-personal elements and themes in intentionality that are allegedly being ignored by externalists? I can detect several, some of which we have already considered at length in the course of the book. Let me make a stab at sorting them out and saying why none of them really succeeds in overturning the externalist position of this book.

First, we noted in chapter 2 that it has been said that an externalist ignores that agent's point of view in ignoring her conception of things. This sort of idea emerged in the Kripke puzzle and the general discussion of the fineness and coarseness of grain of content. I have shown how my constraint on externalism, despite externalism's third-person perspective, allows externalism to capture the first-person point of view in *this* sense of that term.

Second, it is repeatedly said that externalism leaves out the special authority that an agent has over her own thoughts and indeed often puts into doubt that she knows her own beliefs. I have shown here too, after my criticisms of Burge and Davidson in chapter 2, how imposing the same constraint allows for the self-knowledge of thoughts that an agent has, even if her thoughts are externally determined.

Third, it is said that in asking questions about knowledge and skepticism from a third-person point of view, one begs the question against the skeptic, since the possibility of skepticism is only vivid if the question about knowledge is raised from the first-person point of view. And since internalism is presupposed, as we saw, by skepticism in the sense of the conceptual possibility of Cartesian error, we have begged the question against internalism as well by posing things from the third-person point of view.

But the plain fact is that not all ways of describing either internalism or the related arguments for the possibility of skepticism about the external world have to be from the first-person point of view. Permitting a vagueness about terms like "outside,"[21] internalism is merely the doctrine that intentional states are not determined by anything outside of the agent who possesses them. This doctrine, as just stated, is stated perfectly intelligibly without mention of the first-person element. The first-person point of view and internalism do not coincide.

The first-person element was not discussed in the last section, not because it is unimportant for the overall internalist argument, but only because the particular internalist argument from the possibility of skepticism about the external world need not include any strand of the first-personal element in order to make its case. I say "need" not because it is often, in fact, made from an angle in which the first-person point of view and the special authority of first-personal knowledge of intentional states play a central role. For instance, in Descartes's first two Meditations, it does seem to play such a role as it does in much of John Searle's writings on this subject. Yet internalism, as we saw, can be the presupposition of an epistemological view which allows for the possibility of radical error without in any central way invoking the special authority that an agent involved in such error has over his thoughts. We may speak of what we are committed to (internalism, the idea that a person's intentional states are not determined by his relations with the world) in allowing for a person who can be in such a state of radical error, and we may speak of it without mentioning anything about first person authority.

While we are entertaining the possibility that an agent is in radical error we, of course, assume that he is not wrong about what thoughts he has, which are possibly so erroneous. This is so even if we are entertaining the possibility of own thoughts beings in radical error. But that is a mere assumption that makes no assertion that there is such authority. It is just that we have to hold the thoughts steady while we consider their falsity; we cannot doubt that we have the thoughts whose falsity we are allowing, while we are allowing it. In itself that does not amount to a philosophical claim about first-person authority. It merely says we cannot doubt that we have those thoughts while imagining those thoughts to be false. That does not mean that we assert anything positive like that we do have first-person authority over them. Even Descartes's own narrative order in the Meditations makes the claim to such authority in the Second Meditation after having raised the possibility of radical doubt in the First.

However, narrative order is not everything and Descartes did raise the possibility of radical error by setting a test for knowledge that involved first-person authority. His test for knowledge was very demanding: one knows, only if one knows that one knows, and the dreaming argument is supposed to show that the test is devastating to claims to knowledge. And even quite apart from the test, Descartes at all points raises the question of radical error from the first-person point of view ("My belief that I am sitting in front of the fire in a dressing gown might be false and so might all such beliefs that come from the senses") and in doing so he gets us to think how differently and how much more our thoughts are accessible to us than the world which many of them claim to represent.

But what is not at all clear is that radical Cartesian error requires the Cartesian way of raising its own possibility, and certainly modern ways of raising it via brains-in-vats do not always raise it that way. And certainly none of the considerations which internalists have been invoking, and which Burge's and my own intermediate strategy have been arguing against, depend on an essential first-personal element.

There is a fourth, more phenomenological interpretation we may give to the expression "first-person point of view." This has not come up earlier in the book, so it needs to be discussed in some detail here before I can fully repudiate the charge that I have left out something essentially first-personal. It has been the focus of much recent philosophical work on intentionality. Let me approach this view of the first-personal by looking in close detail at the most sophisticated elaboration of it that I have seen.

In recent papers Brain Loar has argued that externalism fails to capture '*subjective* intentionality' because it fails to ask the crucial question about concepts and contents from the first-person point of view (Loar 1985b, 1987). Loar rightly points out that the real issue here is not just externalism but the third-person point of view more generally. He argues that the representational properties of content cannot be captured by any externalist accounts because they all ask the philosophical question from the third-person perspective. He actually even argues that they cannot be captured by those internalist accounts, which leave out subjective or first-person perspectives, and take third-person and objective perspectives on the internal states – accounts such as functional role theories, for example. I will restrict my defence to the externalist accounts. Loar says:

> But non-phenomenological attempts to account for our conception of psychological content (whether anti-individualist, functionalist or causal-reliabilist) are misguided. Something similar has increasingly become evident about non-phenomenological theories of our concepts of phenomenal states. Despite the past half-century's tradition, nothing terrible results from acknowledging that aspects of our concept of pain are due to "ostensive definition" , i.e. derive directly from what we notice of pain in experience. Similarly, our view of psychologically explanatory states as *ways of conceiving things* is not unconnected with our first-person awareness of our own conceptions and the role they apparently play in our behavior. Just as our ascriptions of pain to others involves a projection of subjectively apprehended properties, so with psychological content.

> If from a third-person perspective internal properties are correctly seen not to determine representational properties of content, how might changing the perspective make a difference? Here a more cautious formulation of the basic phenomenon helps. Commonsense psychological explanation appeals to *content-like* properties, to states that somehow *appear* representational. But it is not to be taken for granted that psychological appeals to properties will still appear representational with a shift from the introspective/projective perspective on those properties to an objective third-person perspective.

> When I attend to my own thoughts, I find them intentional, apparently independently of any judgment I might make about, say, causal chains leading back from them to their putative references. In judging that a thought of my own is about Freud... I do not have to make hypotheses about the external contingent connections of that thought. Suppose then that when I attempt to understand the specifics of how another is conceiving things, I try out a thought (foreign perhaps to my preferred way of thinking) and project it: "this is how it is with that person." Then the internal intentionality I find in the thought as I experimentally entertain it will appear to carry over when I project it. (Loar 1985b, pp. 135-6)

This is a "Golden Oldie," unblushingly sung.

Notice that this passage first discusses some of the earlier senses of "first-person point of view" we mentioned, before it fully brings in the fourth sense under discussion now. I agree with Loar, and have argued myself, that some externalist accounts do not capture the agent's own perspective on things (first sense) and have argued further that they even make impossible first-person authority of many intentional states (second sense). Indeed, the very externalist accounts he mentions and considers, the standard causal-theoretic accounts,[22] are the very ones that fail in this regard. But my own externalist account does not fail, as I have argued.

My own externalist account makes his internalist, projective account unnecessary, since his internalist, projective account is prompted by the false perception that *no* externalism can capture the "first-person perspective" in the first two senses of that expression. In order to demonstrate this, however, I must contest a claim he implicitly makes in this passage. Recall that he says, "When I attend to my own thoughts I find them intentional, apparently independently of any judgments I might make about, say, causal chains leading back from them to their putative references." This brings in an essentially phenomenological test (the "When I attend to... I find..." test) for deciding whether internalism or externalism is true. It is a test which introduces the fourth sense of first-persons point of view that we are now discussing. My claim will be that Loar's initial reasons for bringing it in are not justified because those reasons turn on a dissatisfaction with certain very specific externalisms – but not all externalisms, not mine – for not capturing the first sense of "first-person perspective." It is because he finds externalism unsatisfactory in this regard that Loar turns to this test. But my externalism is not unsatisfactory in this regard.

I agree with him that my finding my own thoughts intentional (when I attend to them) does not require me to judge anything about the causal chains leading back from my having those thoughts to the originally baptized objects. But I agree with this not merely because I find that those chains insisted on by the standard causal-theoretic externalist are irrelevant to content. I agree with it because in attending to a thought of mine I need not judge anything about external causal links even if there were such causal links that were relevant. So I would deny that in attending to the intentionality of one of my thoughts, I have to make any judgment or attend to any kind of causal links that I might have to the external environment, even the highly constrained causal links insisted on in my own externalist account. This does not mean that my thoughts could be what they are independent of all causal links with the environment. I have given arguments in this chapter to show that they cannot be. But we need to be told why it is that the appearance of intentionality of those thoughts must take in those relations in the attendance of those thoughts, in order for those relations, in general, to determine what intentional contents those thoughts have. I see no reason why they should. I agree that if my concepts and contents are determined by things which I do not know at all (the chemical composition of substances which, in my ignorance of chemistry, I do not know) then, there is a real question whether my point of view (first sense) is being respected when a thought determined by such facts, and as being about such facts, is being attributed to me. But that is a quite different point from the claim that in attending to my thought and the appearance of its intentionality, I do not judge anything about the links of that thought with the chemical composition of the substance. I do not judge such links in such attendings even if I had full knowledge of chemistry. In the latter case, all that are involved and may be judged if I am reflecting (attending to them) are the chemical beliefs or descriptions. No external causal links need to judged.

The phenomenological test Loar urges on us would indeed exclude all externalisms, even mine; but we have been given no reason to impose the test. Loar leaps from his attack, earlier in the passage, on the inadequacy of certain externalist accounts in capturing an agent's point of view (in a perfectly straight-forward sense of agent's point of view, i.e. the first of the first-personal themes mentioned above, an agent's conceptions of things) to talk of how any satisfactory account of an agent's point of view must take on what is involved in an agent's attendings upon his own intentional states. But an agent's attendings are going to involve a sense of first-person point of view in a quite different sense (the fourth sense) from what was found missing in the inadequate externalisms (the first sense). However, if the inadequacy can be remedied by embracing a better externalism such as mine, then all this further talk of what goes into attendings need not be brought into the study of intentionality. It is true that no judgments about external links whatever go into these attendings, but why should we care about that, if no convincing reason has been given to make relevant these attendings in the first place.

Loar, in this passage, however, offers another and different reason for the importance of the fourth phenomenological sense of "first-person perspective" from the failure of externalism to account for agents' conceptions in the first specific sense mentioned above. He thinks his phenomenological point about what is involved in attending to one's thoughts is also forced by a failure of a certain "objectivism" in the study of content. (Though I am not happy with the term "objectivism," here, I will follow him in his terminology.)

He is quite right to point out that many externalist, and many "objectivist" internalist, accounts leave out something essential, which might, if we insist (though equally unhappily) be called the "subjectivity" of intentionality. By appealing merely to external causal chains, or internal causal (functional) roles etc, they see intentionality in purely "objective terms.

But, I will argue that the notion of objectivity that makes for the trouble here need not be replaced by a first-person point of view which has to be characterized in Loar's terms involving attendings to one's thoughts and then projecting on to others. It need not lead us to the fourth, phenomenological sense of "first person point of view." Indeed, the notion of objectivity does not even stand in strict contrast to the idea of first-person point of view, so characterized – thus my unhappiness with the terms "objectivist" and "subjectivist." The trouble with the objectivity involved here has to do, as Loar himself points out, with a sort of reductionist thinning of an intuitively richer representational notion of content. In Loar's view the richness and the irreducibility can only be recaptured by looking at what goes into our attendings to our thoughts and the phenomenological appearance of intentionality there. But I claim instead that the irreducibility, the essentially representational nature of intentional states, lies elsewhere. It can be captured in the obstacle my constraint (C) places on all efforts to reduce content to the more purely "objective" features that causal and functional theories appeal to. My constraint does not allow that content can ever be exhaustively explained by features that do not invoke content itself.[23] It does not allow that one may determine content by causes which are not constrained by further contents. This was my criticism of certain orthodox externalism in chapter 2. Externality and causality by themselves, without an appeal to other contentful states cannot account for content. Thus there can be no thinning or diminishing of content, no reduction of content to something entirely devoid of content.

I would resist calling this (C)-induced irreducibly representational aspect the "subjectivity" of content or "first personal" content because of the possible association with Loar's own positive view that we are now discussing. But that is a purely terminological matter. If somebody insisted that it was a kind of subjectivism, we might in a concessive way say that this (C)-induced irreducible representational element was a fifth specific interpretation to the first-person point of view idea. It is quite different from the fourth phenomenological interpretation. The important point is that a dissatisfaction with the "objectivist" third-person accounts in capturing the representational properties of content need not force one into Loar's view or the fourth and phenomenological version of the first-person point of view idea. If it is insisted that it nevertheless is properly described as a special first-person point of view, that is all right by me, so long as it is distinguished from Loar's phenomenological angle. It points to a distinct fifth sense of that phrase.

Loar does not give any argument for why the shunning of "objectivity" should force us to the phenomenological picture. He makes a dig at the trends of the past 30 years on the related theme of phenomenal states and then, without argument, assumes with a long previous tradition (which in any case is having something of a revivalist trend of its own in the past ten years or so) that an appeal to the subjective phenomenological point of view will allow for the irreducibility he finds missing in the standard causal theories. My alternative appeal to an external causal account, which is filtered always through an agent's beliefs, establishes the irreducibility of content despite the reliance on external causal underpinnings. The unavoidability of the filter ensures the ineliminability of content itself in the philosophical analysis of content. There is no thinning out of content into something else. This is all that an account of the representational element of content needs.

My way of accounting for the irreducibly representational feature of content, I have said, makes no appeal to the phenomenology that come from the sort of attending to one's own thoughts that Loar demands. It comes rather from the fact that any concept which is externally determined for an agent is always so determined under some other beliefs and descriptions that the agent has, which are relevant to describing the external determining cause. This makes it impossible for the externalist determination to lead to a notion of concept and content which leaves out their representationality. This also leads as I said in chapter 4, to something like a description theory of concepts. Loar (1985b) has explicitly criticized my view (Bilgrami 1985) and, in doing so, has invoked the same arguments and examples – like the one about the Freud-thought – as he does in this passage. Even in this paper, he considers a description-theory as a possible alternative to his phenomenological answer to the first-person question about what my Freud-thought is, and he attacks it. I must respond to the attack if my repudiation of the relevance of the phenomenological sense of "first-person perspective" is going to stick. He says:

> A reply may go like this. My conception of Freud is descriptive – I conceive of (say): the famous psychologist referred to as "Sigmund Freud" in my social group. Then my knowledge that my thought refers to Freud is simply knowledge that my thought refers to the famous psychologist referred to as "Sigmund Freud" in this social group, whoever he is... Now this reply merely postpones recognizing the basic point (i.e. that one can have knowledge of the references of one's own thoughts that is not ostensibly knowledge of externally determined relations), postpones it in the following sense. The description-theoretic interpretation would exclude Freud from (as we might call them) the *basic references* of my thought, references that are not via descriptions. But you can't do that indefinitely. Certain demonstratives, predicates and logical connectives must be basic, in the sense of not implicating definite descriptions; they correspond to Russell's constituents (although Russell notoriously had an overly narrow view of those constituents)....(Loar 1987, p. 97)

Even though I have resisted posing this first-person question – what is my Freud-thought a thought about? – in terms of attendings and what they contain, I believe a version of this description-theoretic rival will do perfectly well exactly what Loar thinks it cannot do: account for the irreducible non- "objectivist" representational property of my content about Freud. The description-theoretic reply Loar considers in this passage is not exactly my view since it makes no mention of a constraint in an externalist method of theoretically accounting for concepts and content; it makes no mention that the concepts in the descriptions themselves are also determined externalistically (of course, under the same constraint). More likely, since he is a bifurcationist, Loar thinks that this description-theoretic rival position he has imagined is a (misguided and, as he tries to argue, unsuccessful) effort to add the wrong internal notion of psychological content to the only externalist content he countenances (orthodox causal-theoretic and social): misguided and unsuccessful because it tries to provide an internalist notion that can never really take the place of his phenomenological/projective internalist account.

But what is his argument for saying that all description-theoretic views will be unsuccessful in this task of capturing the representational element? It is that they merely put off acknowledging that sooner or later there will be some basic terms of my idiolect which will not be description-theoretically treatable. And then one will only have introspection to appeal to since the non-descriptive externalist elements of these basic predicates will not be found in the attendings to our thoughts, and so the representational property of the thoughts will be lost. So he seems to be granting that the irreducible representational properties would be captured by a description-theoretic view, if the view could avoid eventual appeal to non-descriptive elements. It is just that he thinks it cannot avoid this and that is why his own version of the phenomenological picture of the irreducibly representational properties of intentionality is forced on one.

I do not know what his imagined internalistic description-theorist will reply to this. But I deny here, as I have elsewhere in the book, that there is a gound floor of basic terms which are accounted for by external causal links that are unconstrained by the agent's other beliefs. This is not even true of the demonstrative terms, as I have argued. There is no getting away from the constraint (C) on externalism, even at the ground floor, as I argued in chapter 2. One indeed postpones indefinitely what Loar thinks cannot be so postponed. It is precisely this which allows for the irreducibility of the representational content in my view. Loar gives no argument against it, whereas my argument for it has all along been that it alone allows for both externalism and the explanatory power of content. No doubt those who want a strict naturalist reduction of content like Fodor and many others will object to the indefinite postponement. No doubt there will those who think that there is no genuine externalism but only an internalism manqué, if the belief constraint is applied indefinitely. But I have addressed these objections elsewhere in the book.[24] So I will allow myself to rest with the claim that the description-theoretic rival considered by Loar makes quite unnecessary his phenomenological alternative.

Before leaving this discussion of the accusation that externalism has left out the fourth phenomenological sense of first-person point of view, I must look at an argument for it other than Loar's. It is very likely that there are philosophers[25] (Searle) who think that Loar's stress on phenomenology and introspection is forced on us for reasons other than Loar cites, i.e. not merely forced by the inability of externalism to capture the first sense of the first-person point of view, nor merely by the inability of "objectivist" accounts to capture the irreducibly representational nature of intentionality mentioned in the fifth sense of first-person point of view. For such philosophers, the phenomenological question about what goes into attendings is forced on more positive grounds, on the grounds that an answer to it alone will tell us what it is like to have any particular thought.

This view thus introduces an essential element of consciousness in thought. Not just consciousness in the innocuous sense of self-knowledge, but in the phenomenological sense being discussed. The view is that it is this element of consciousness which must be brought in in answering Loar's question about what goes into the attending our thoughts. And once the question about what goes into attendings of our own thoughts is answered in this way, we can then project the thought on to others and say, by analogy: this is what it is for them to have this thought. (So, on the matter of attending or introspection, as well as on projection, Searle and Loar might agree, even if the arguments by which they lead up to this point are very different.) And the anti-externalist claim now will simply be that even if the externalist imposes my constraint and thus captures the "agent's point of view" in the first, second and fifth senses, externalism will still not capture it in the fourth sense. It will not capture it in this more strictly phenomenological and introspective sense (the "what it is like to have that thought" sense) of that expression.

I must confess, following others who are influenced by Wittgenstein, that I do not find the question "What is it like to have this thought?" entirely clear. Not that I do not have any sense of what questions of this general form mean. Rather I do not quite understand why this form of question (what is it like to have...) is specially significant about thoughts. Whatever this form of question in general and intuitively means, why is it what it raises something especially difficult about the nature of intentionality and thoughts? Why is the question what is it like for me to have a knee any less significant than the question about a thought? And I am certainly not even slightly tempted to say that in coming to understand the nature of knees one must attend to one's own knee and then project on to others. So then why this procedure for thoughts? It simply will not do to reply that it is thoughts (and other mental states)[26] alone which involve agents' conceptions and which involve a special first-person authority that agents have. Those are things that are specified in the first two specific senses of the first-person point of view and, I have argued in chapter 2 that they pose no problems for externalism properly conceived; so they raise no motivation for this further, obscure, strictly "phenomenological" sense of first-person point of view.

The projective conception of understanding others and attributing content outlined by Loar is a natural step once one insists on his essentially introspective or phenomenological first-person version of internalism. It is akin to resorting to the argument from analogy once one grants the essentially skeptical position on other minds. I have tried to show by way of two arguments in earlier sections of this chapter why we need never be in a position of having to resort to either of these things and in this section I have argued that, as far as I can see, Loar and Searle have not given any arguments to show that we must.

## REALISM ABOUT INTENTIONAL CONTENT

There is a sixth sense that is often given to the idea of the first person perspective. I take it up separately because it might be seen to have special relevance to a dissatisfaction with not merely the externalist assumption of this book but also the book's other assumption about the role of content in explanation.[27] Here the complaint against externalism is that, because it is too caught up in the third-person point of view and in the interpreter's or attributor's explanatory and other such interests in the attributions of content, it will turn out that such attributions will fail to get right what contents an agent "really" or "intrinsically" have. In effect, the complaint is that in adopting the third person or interpretative point of view, externalism leads to instrumentalism or anti-realism about intentional content. It does so because if one sees intentional content as constituted by what another (an interpreter) attributes to an agent with explanation in mind, then the interests of the interpreter will enter in a way that reduces intentionality to a mere *stance* that one adopts towards subjects whose behavior we want to explain or interpret. The only way to get at the states they really have, the only way to get to intrinsic intentionality, is to approach the general philosophical issue from a first-person point of view. This sixth or intrinsicalist sense of first-person point of view actually appeals to, and rests on, some of the other senses, as we shall see, but it is special because it makes explicit the implications for intentional realism, of taking the first-person point of view.

A recent example given by Dennett (1987) may help clarify the idea underlying this sixth sense. (It is explicitly directed against "intrinsicalism" or realism about intentional states as it is found in various writings of Searle.) Take a machine in New York City which accepts quarters and hands out chocolates. As far as the machine is concerned, the Panamanian balboa will do just as well – its physical shape and contours are acceptable and exchangeable for chocolates. However, one can imagine that while in New York City and in the charge of some local owner, only quarters are acceptable – the exchange upon being fed a balboa would count as a mistake. In Panama ("the poor man's twin-earth" as Dennett calls it), under a quite different charge, things would be just the other way round.

Though, because of its limited abilities, no one will think this machine has intentional states, an instrumentalist is supposed to take the view that human beings are just like this machine in a crucial respect. What counts as an intentional state with one content rather than another is a matter of the social and interpretative context in which the human beings (machines) are lodged. One thought or utterance might count as a mistake in one such context, another in another. This is an instrumentalism that Dennett has often espoused and, while doing so, has often listed several prominent philosophers of mind as being on his side. Searle and other realists reject the idea that the situation with human beings is at all like it is with the machine. For them, our talk of this machine accepting coins or makings mistakes is mere talk, not only because the machine's abilities are very limited, but also crucially because intentional states are not up to the interpreter and to the social context in which agents (to whom they are attributed) live; they are intrinsic to agents. The only way to get a true characterization of them therefore, is to respect this intrinsic nature i.e. their point of view.

This way of drawing the antagonism between realism and instrumentalism about intentional states, it seems to me, is much too simple. In fact, it had better be so since neither Dennett's nor Searle's position seems very attractive. What complicates things is the fact that taking an interpretative or, what Searle calls, "a third-person point of view" need not by any means have the consequence that the intentional contents attributed to human beings will be interest-relative in anything like the sense suggested by Dennett's analogy with the chocolate machine. There are surely constraints one may place on attributions by a third person which do not leave out the agent's point of view. Take, for instance, the early disputes over the nature of radical interpretation where it was thought that meanings and beliefs were to be attributed to an agent by an interpreter with the constraint that overall agreement between agent and interpreter be maximized. It was justly protested that this view would leave out the agent's point of view and thus the agent would be said to have propositional attitudes she did not really have; so a quite different constraint was proposed – first, I believe, by Richard Grandy (1973) – which sought not to maximize agreement but to minimize unexplained error. As I say below I doubt that it is this constraint exactly which is necessary, but quite apart from the question of which other constraint would be necessary to capture the beliefs an agent really has, the point I want to make immediately is this. In the sentence before last, I raised a genuine question about realism regarding intentional states and the first-person point of view. And the question is raised *within* a *third*-person characterization of intentionality, i.e. within the context of an interpreter's attributions. This suggests that though some version of the opposition between the first- and third-person points of view is relevant to the dispute between realism and instrumentalism about intentionality, it is not the version we find in the dispute between Dennett and Searle. The version which is relevant turns not upon intrinsicness in the sense of internalism and the Cartesian perspective but rather on what constraints to place on attributions of content to an agent, even within, if need be, a third-person point of view. Only some constraints will lead to attributions which capture the point of view of the agent to whom the contents are being attributed. Others will impose too much the interests and point of view of the interpreter.

This means that, in this context, there is an ambiguity in expressions like "first-person point of view." If one applied the right constraints, one may work with a third-person point of view and not first-person point of view (one sense) without distorting things in a way that fails to capture the first-person point of view (second sense). And it is the second sense, and nothing but the second sense of "the first-person point of view" which is necessary to achieve a realism about beliefs. To get what beliefs an agent really has one has to impose the right constraints that keep the interpreter's interests out when they distort his attributions, as, for instance, when he works with the constraint of maximizing agreement. If, instead of maximizing agreement, he constrained himself to attribute those beliefs and concepts that he thought the agent must have, given the agent's other beliefs and concepts, then the distortion that comes from the mere desire to maximize agreement is removed.

It is true that an externalism may be insensitive to the right constraints, in which case externalism would indeed be guilty of the charge of failing to capture the agent's point of view and, therefore, failing to get right what the agent really believes. The example considered in chapter 1, of how not to describe the external determinant as a clutch, but rather, perhaps a pedal, if the agent does not have rudimentary beliefs about the workings of automobiles, is a good example of how these constraints would help the third-person point of view in extertanlism, to get to the concepts and contents the agent really has. Notice that the constraint applied in this particular example – my constraint (C) – is not Grandy's "minimize unexplained error" constraint. There is no error on the agent's part if we interpret him as thinking "That's a pedal" in front of what we knowledgeable interpreters think of as a clutch. Hence, leave alone "maximize agreement," I am not prepared to commit myself even to "minimize unexplained error" in the attribution of concepts and contents. The constraint operative in this example is just my constraint (C), and, I believe, it is what we indispensably need in content and concept attribution from an externalist and third-person point of view. The point here is that there is no more to realism about beliefs than the imposition of a constraint of this kind on belief attribution.[28]

An interpreter who attributes contents meeting the right constraints tries to attribute the contents that the agent really has. He is no different from anyone else trying to describe any other feature of the world. He may not always succeed. He may make some false attributions. But we do not always succeed in getting things right in many things we say. The point is that, once we are sure that he is working with the right constraints, there is no philosophical bar to thinking that he is striving to get what the agent really thinks. Realism about intentional states is just the claim that attribution of intentional states is attribution of the sorts of things that one can be right and wrong about, say true and false things about. Interpretation or third-personal attribution of intentional states *under the right constraints* ensures that we are thinking of intentional states in this realist way.

There is no reason to look for intrinsicness in any further sense in order to establish realism; and so there is no need to worry that if we think of beliefs as what a third-person attributes with a view to explaining behavior, we would be abandoning intentional realism.

## *Realism about Content and Indeterminacy*

None of what I have been saying so far in this section, at least in its general form, should be surprising to anyone who is committed to the necessary publicness of meaning. That is, none of it should be surprising so long as those who talk at length about the "first" person point of view do not degenerate to so strict a Cartesianism that they surrender the publicness of meaning and content. Since an agent's thoughts are discoverable by a public, by a third person, there cannot be any wholesale wrong doing or thinking in taking a third-person point of view on an agent's thoughts. This last point, and the points earlier in this section which led to it, have obvious implications for the threat indeterminacy is supposed to bring to intentional realism.

If these points are right, there cannot be anything to Searle's (1987) recent attack on Quine (1960) and Davidson's (1973a,b) commitment to the indeterminacy of meaning and content.[29] He argues that indeterminacy can be avoided if one shuns the third-person point of view of radical translation and interpretation.

This brings an uncessary opposition between a third-person point of view and first-person authority. If what an agent believe and means is publicly discoverable then a radical interpreter working, as I keep insisting with the right constraints, may presumably discover them. So if a radical interpreter's discoveries here are ineradicably subject to indeterminacy, then thumping the table with the authority an agent has over his own thoughts and meaning will not eradicate it at all. (Not unless the authority implied a denial of the necessary publicness of meaning.) What one should conclude, therefore, is that indeterminacy is in the end harmless and leaves unthreatened the notions of meaning and content over with we have first-person authority. Such authority is undeniable, but it does not have the significance Searle sees in it.

In expressing the harmlessness of indeterminacy, Davidson has sometimes said that the indeterminacy, consisting of empirically (behaviorally) equivalent sets of assignment of beliefs and meanings to an agent, is like the different assignments of numbers by different scales for the measurement of temperature. The two sets of assignments in both the case of belief and temperature encode the same information. One can go from one set of assignments to the other without loss of overall information, even though at the level of specific assignments of number, even though at the level of specific axioms in a truth-theory and specific assignments of content to beliefs, there will be differences. But since the differences will be systematic as the temperature example suggests, there will be a way of going from one to the other, thereby reflecting the invariance between them. This analogy was intended by Davidson to convey the harmlessness of indeterminacy.

One can also use it to convey the unthreatening nature of indeterminacy to realism about intentional states by saying that one is no more tempted to ask which of two beliefs or meanings does an agent really have, no more than one is tempted to ask is it really 32° F or O° C.

Dennett (1990) has recently objected to this analogy, saying that it fails to do justice to the hard cases of indeterminacy and he suggests a different analogy. He offers an elaborate example of differences between perceivers in the recognition of patterns seen through noise in a series of samples of distribution of dots. One perceiver may see noise at some place where another sees pattern. I will not sketch the example in detail because the moral we are to learn from it is simple and does not require the details: the differences in pattern recognition between perceivers is a matter of the interests perceivers bring to their recognitions. Belief attribution and interpretation is similarly a discernment of patterns in agents and is subject to similar indeterminacy from similar sources. There may be a level of descriptions that describe what is really there in both the perceptual and the interpretative cases, but pattern recognition and content attribution are at a level that is indeterminate in a way that makes talk of things really being there inappropriate. Too much depends on the interpreters. Dennett concludes that the analogy with rival temperature scales trivializes indeterminacy in a way that the analogy with pattern-recognition does not. Indeterminacy is not as trivial as Davidson is saying. There is a genuine complexity and non-triviality to the indeterminacy in the attribution of meaning and belief which the temperature analogy belies, but which the pattern analogy respects.

Dennett thus supports Searle against Davidson on the harmfulness of indeterminacy by insisting on its non-triviality. But, unlike Searle, he is not willing to say that there is a solution to the indeterminacy problem. He is not prepared to appeal to some intrinsic notion of meaning and belief content which will get rid of indeterminacy by telling us which of the different sets of meanings and contents that get assigned by the theories are really possessed by the agent. What he shares with Searle is the conviction that meaning and belief seen from the third-person, non-intrinsic point of view are interest-relative in a way that gives rise to non-trivial indeterminacy. But not being an intrinsicalist, he is happy to live with the interest-relativity and the indeterminacy which it gives rise to.

I do not here want to defend Davidson and the analogy with the measurement of temperature. I am inclined to think that it does fail to convey some of the non-triviality of indeterminacy, though since it is merely an analogy I do not think is a matter of great significance. The important point is that there is an invariance between different empirically equivalent theories or assignments of meaning and belief to a person, whether or not the analogy is exactly what captures it. I think Dennett's complaint against the trivializing of indeterminacy by the analogy is a fair one but, for reasons I have already given, I do not think that is due to any distorting interest-relativity of the interpretative approach. The problem of interest-relativity for me, is handled by imposing the right constraints. Dennett's paper does not even consider the question of what the right constraints on interpretation should be (constraints akin to Grandy's or the constraint (C) on interpretation); and nowhere in the paper does he offer an example of indeterminacy that is in explicit violation of explicitly imposed constraints of this kind.[30]

I think that the temperature analogy is not always helpful on somewhat different grounds. Indeterminacy of meaning and belief, in the Davidsonian framework, can come in two quite different forms. There is one sort of example in which two truth-theories may assign systematically different references to the terms of an agent's language. Davidson, following Hartry Field (1975) and John Wallace (1977), gives examples of this sort of indeterminacy by asking us to consider examples of permutation where for every singular term assigned an object by one theory, the other assigns the shadow of that object, or assigns an object 3 ft to the left of that object, and so on. In such cases of indeterminacy, the belief component in a Davidsonian theory,[31] *automatically* shifts from one theory to another in order to march in step with the permutation of reference. There is no special difficulty or complication about the beliefs that the belief component will attribute, since there will be a systematic way of keeping pace with the differences in the meaning or truth-theory.

However, there are cases of indeterminacy which are not so trivial. There are cases of theories which differ from these trivial cases because *they distribute the weight between meaning and belief differently*. In these cases, there is no automatic way of making changes in the belief component in order to calibrate with the differences in the meaning component. Does Ancient Athens fall within the extension of "democracy"? – that depends on all sorts of things such as whether you believe that women are citizens, whether you believe that slaves are citizens.... Different theories can make different assignments of reference or extension for a number of such terms in this way, but, in these cases, the corresponding changes in the belief component will have to be much more complicated and messy then in the trivial cases of indeterminacy of reference. One way of describing the difference is to say that, in the more complicated indeterminacy, there is a genuine shift of weight between meaning and belief. In such non-trivial cases of indeterminacy, it does seem to me that the invariance between indeterminate theories is not best conveyed by an analogy with different scales for the measurement of temperature.

But, equally, on the other hand, there is no reason to think that the inability of the analogy to satisfactory capture this distributive shift in weight of meaning-belief has anything to do with the ineradicable and distorting interests that the interpreters bring to their respective theories. I see no reason to deny that despite the failure of the temperature analogy there is something invariant between two such non-trivial indeterminate theories.[32] It is just a much more complicated invariance than the invariance in the trivial permutation cases of indeterminacy. This more complicated invariance is all one needs in order to be able to say that the two theories are identical up to an incommunicable difference. And if meanings and beliefs are public, what cannot in principle be communicated, cannot be believed or meant. Thus indeterminacy, an inevitable consequence of the third-person point of view which rejects the Cartesian or Searlian version of direct first-person awareness of intrinsic meaning, and insists on the constructibility of meaning on external evidence, is still no threat to realism about beliefs or meanings.

I conclude that the sixth sense of "first-person perspective" which sees that perspective as alone capturing the "intrinsic" or "real" nature of intentional states is spurious. Intentional realism is not threatened by the third-person perspective of externalism. These arguments for the compatibility of intentional realism with externalism have obvious relations to the arguments by which I established and defended externalism in the earlier sections of this chapter. But since the connection is susceptible to misunderstanding, I will assert it all the same. It is often said that externalism puts the focus on the process by which an interpreter (a third person) discovers content and therefore it cannot illuminate what is discovered about an agent; the former, being of epistemological interest only, cannot give us the nature of the states themselves. That is why the third-person point of view of externalism cannot capture what intentionality really or intrinsically is. But, if my dialectic in this chapter is right this puts the emphasis altogether in the wrong place. It is not that interpretation constitutes content. Rather it is because content is externally determined that it is a public phenomenon. And because it is a public phenomenon, the third personal or public's point of view of externalistic interpretation (of course, with crucial constraints) will help shed light on intentionality, as it really is.

I conclude, then, that none of the six different specific glosses we have given to the idea of the first-person point of view gives the internalist any case against the externalist's general commitment to a third-person perspective on content. Externalism does not leave out any essential subjectivity nor does it succumb to an instrumentalism about intentional states just by stressing the role of their attribution by a third person in the explanation of behavior.

If, in addition, the arguments in this chapter for externalism have been effective we may, now, conclude that both the assumptions of externalism and the explanatory rationale of intentional states have been justified. Taking these two assumptions for granted. I have defined, elaborated and defended the unity and locality of content over the previous four chapters. At the end of this fifth and last chapter we are able to say that the unity and locality of content are finally and firmly secure, now that the assumptions on which they had been defined and elaborated have themselves been justified.

# Epilogue

It may seem that the anti-internalist arguments of chapter 5 were pushing at open doors. After all, has there not been a powerful trend in this century's philosophizing about mind and knowledge – both in Continental Europe and in Britain and America – in which Cartesianism is treated as a philosophical leper? Is not anti-Cartesianism, by now, banal? All the same, I must admit internalism still gives me bad nights. I do not think this is just a neurosis. It is not just that one continues to run across an occasional stubborn Cartesian philosopher such as Searle;[1] internalism is a hidden commitment of the widespread belief in the necessity and viability of a notion of narrow content,[2] and as such it is constantly showing up in a variety of modern guises. The anti-internalist arguments of chapter 5 were aimed against this widespread implicit survival of Cartesianism.

The arguments are not perhaps utterly decisive. The first argument from publicness is based on a principled rejection of an ultra-realism, but it will not convince those for whom ultra-realism is a form of religion. The second argument, though not at all as lacking in ambition as the maximally modest anti-internalist arguments (the "inference to the best explanation") arguments – was not the product of what I called the maximally ambitious strategy, either. It still lacked the knockdown force that those who have endeavored with "transcendental" strategies against Cartesianism have hoped for. I have no illusions that these arguments will completely silence the internalist. Consequently, Cartesianism will no doubt still cause me to sweat and stamp about at night. However, I believe, the arguments have gone some distance towards justifying the governing assumption of this book, that some version of externalism about content has got to be true.

The well-springs of chapter 5's arguments for externalism have been in epistemology. It is because of this that externalism, as I see it, need not take the shape of the orthodox externalist doctrines criticized in chapters 2 and 3. Those doctrines sought the sources of externalism in a variety of quite other places than in epistemology: in normativity, in society, in scientific essentialism, in Russellian singular thought, in the mechanisms of theory-change, in the communication-imparting function of belief reports, in the explanations of our flourishing in our specific environments etc. I have devoted chapter 3 and parts of chapter 4 to countering these motivations for the externalisms I have rejected. From the point of view of the externalism proceeding from the epistemological arguments of chapter 5, all these alleged sources for externalism are barren.

Once one sees clearly that the best arguments for externalism against internalism are epistemological, the form of externalism one adopts need make no commitment to traditional causal and social externalist theories of reference. The space is open now to develop a constrained externalism that is free of those features which threaten the unity of content; one is free to develop an externalist view of content which leaves unspoilt the power of content to explain or rationalize behavior. To put it slightly differently, one is free to develop a view of externalist content which walks in tandem with Frege's notion of sense. In chapter 1, I sketched such an account and, in chapter 2, I showed how it does not threaten the unity of content in the way that the orthodox externalisms did. But chapter 1 provided only a sketch of the unity of content. In chapter 3, I elaborated the individualistic and non-normative aspects of my externalism and my unified view of content. In chapter 4, I elaborated its relations to the idea of truth, truth-conditions and truth-theories, as well as its relation to holism and its distance from standard ideas of the point and scope of theories of meaning. By this time, it had become apparent that the unity of content, which I had established in chapter 2, could only really be supported if one also saw content as thoroughly local. In localities one could redeem all the features that orthodox externalists wanted from content: its resistance to holistic excess, its capacity to allow for error and for theory-change, and the respect any notion of content must show to the fact that agents show deference toward and reliance upon other agents. But in these local settings those features lacked the ulterior properties of Norm, Society and Essential Natures in the full-dress, blue-chip, high-profile sense that philosophers have often wanted from them.

So, in a way, the three middle chapters of the book can be seen as a struggle to sedate the doctrine of externalism. But despite sedating it, it should be clear from the first and last chapters, that I have also tried to nurse it devotedly. There is no vestigial notion of narrow content in my unified view. Chapter 5 should have made it clear that internalism, even in its weakest, tattiest form has not taken root in my externalism, though there will be a misguided temptation to think that it has, because I have constrained externalism by an agent's own beliefs, and I have argued for externalism on the basis of a very general and negative argument, which made no demands for direct link-ups with reality. With some right, therefore, I have described my version of a Fregean notion of content, as also being "Kantian."

The philosophical account of intentionality that comes through at the end of its all is at odds with every existing view of content, at the same time that it tries to retain various seemingly conflicting features of these opposing views. The account, therefore, is fraught with the danger of being multiply misunderstood. From the perspective of any one of these views it will be susceptible to misunderstanding due to the prejudice of association with some other despised view. Thus: if it is Fregean it must be either internalist as in Searle or externalist as in the neo-Fregean doctrine of Evans and McDowell; if it appeals centrally to descriptions and beliefs, it must be a description theory of reference; if it takes concepts and the meanings of terms to be given in terms of agents' beliefs, then it must have allowed content to lose touch with the external world; if it appeals to truth-theories it must be committed to some standard and official notion of reference or to a Davidsonian conception of truth-theory; if its externalism amounts only to a denial of the scenario of Descartes's First Meditation on the basis of a general and negative argument, it cannot really be a genuine externalism;[3] if it gives up on the social element in meaning, it must slide into a privacy about meaning; if it gives up on truth-conditions in the official sense, it must be basically some form of verificationism; if it gives up on reference in the study of content, then it cannot possibly account for theory-change or for the possibility of any kind of falsehood; if it makes content local, then it is nihilistic of content; if it gives up on normativity, then it is dispositionalist and naturalist about content; if it gives up on norms intrinsic to meaning, it must give up on all linguistic intelligibility; if– with its constraint (C) – it gives up on naturalism, it must be some retrograde unscientific view of content; if – with its constraint (C) – it accounts for concepts and contents by always appealing to other contents, it must be circular and unilluminating; and so on and on.

I have said why my account specially invites such misunderstandings, but this really is a familiar problem for all efforts at providing a positive philosophical treatment of a subject. A high susceptibility to misunderstanding is built into any genuinely philosophical account of anything, higher, I believe, than is to be found in any other sort of account. For good or ill, that is one of the perverse ways in which philosophical discussion seems to sustain and perpetuate itself. I could not do better than to try to be scrupulous by warning against some of these misunderstandings when they were likely to arise at various points in the text. My hope has been that an unreactive reading of these chapters, watchful of these misunderstandings, will have reached through to the unity and locality of intentional content.

# Appendix: Self-knowledge and Intentionality

In chapter 2, I showed how to reconcile our self-knowledge of our intentional states with an externalism about them. But I did not say anything more general about the nature of self-knowledge once it was seen to be compatible with externalism. In chapter 5, I rejected all phenomenological conceptions of intentional states, conceptions which saw their essence as partly lying in their subjectivity, in their special availability to one's own introspective attendings to oneself. Once this phenomenological picture of intentionality is rejected, our automatic assumptions about the nature and the very possibility of self-knowledge dissolve. But there, too, I did not say anything positive about how one might alternatively explain and justify self-knowledge.

In this Appendix I will only be able to state in the briefest of terms what the special problem of explaining and justifying self-knowledge is and, then, again in the briefest outline offer an explanation and justification. The brevity of this discussion is particularly regrettable not only because the problem is a deep and vexing one and deserves a more elaborate treatment, but also because the solution I offer is so obviously controversial and has irritated so many people when I have presented it in talks and conversations, that it would have been useful to take the chance to spell it out with all the qualifications it needs, and with an eye to answering fundamental objections against it. But this is only an Appendix, and, in any case, when I did set out to discuss it in detail, it became obvious that the subject would need a book-length treatment of its own.[1] It would have been irresponsible, however, to complete this book on intentionality, uncommitted though it is to any effort at comprehensiveness, without even a whisper toward a solution of a problem, which is so central to its subject, and which arose at crucial points in its dialectic. Here, then, is the problem and the whisper of a solution.

Crispin Wright has stated the problem succinctly.[2] The chief advantage of my solution is best seen in the light of what I take to be an inadequacy of his own solution. In a short space, I must present the problem that Wright sees and his solution only in the barest outline, without most of its more subtle details. Here is how he states the issue:

A central preoccupation of the *Investigations* and Wittgenstein's other later writings on the philosophy of psychology, is with the concepts which – like meaning, understanding, intending, expecting, wishing, fearing, hoping – seem to hover, puzzlingly and unstably, between two paradigms. To the left, as it were, stand genuine episodes and processes in consciousness: items, which like headaches, ringing of the ears... may have a determinate onset and departure... To the right, by contrast, stand qualities of character, like patience, courage... which are naturally viewed as constituted in the (broadly) behavioural dispositions of a subject, are fully manifest in the things he is inclined to say and do, and advert to no inner phenomenological causes of these inclinations. Descartes' conception of the mental tended to draw everything toward the left pole. The Rylean reaction, by contrast, tended to colonize as widely as possible on behalf of the right. And the difficulties raised by the concepts with which Wittgenstein was preoccupied is that we are pulled in both directions simultaneously. Their first-person epistemology pulls us to the left – since explaining it seems to call for a construal of such states as objects of consciousness. But as Wittgenstein... effectively argue [s], nothing strictly introspectible has, in the case of any of these concepts, the right kind of characteristics. We cannot, honestly, find anything to be the intention, etc., when we turn our gaze inward; and anything we might find would have no connection, or, at best, the wrong kind of connection with those subsequent events – what we go on to count as fulfilment of an intention, etc. – on which the correctness of the earlier ascription of an intention, etc., depend. But if we, accordingly, allow overselves to be pulled towards the right hand pole... we find ourselves in difficulties with normativity and with saving ordinary first person epistemology. We need, accordingly, some account of or perspective on these concepts which is conservative with respect to the features which give rise to the difficulty – the combination of first person avowability and 'theoreticity' – yet dissolves the temptation to assimilate them to cases which they do not fundamentally resemble. (Wright 1989c, p. 237)

In short, the problem, on the one hand, is that there is a special character to self-knowledge of intentional states which cries out for a Cartesian treatment of it, a treatment in terms of a model of inner observation of intentional items in consciousness. But to think of self-knowledge along these lines blots out the distinctively dispositional or "theoretical" character of intentional states. The problem, on the other hand, is that respecting the distinctively dispositional character of intentional states would threaten the special nature of self-knowledge of these states – it would make self-knowledge of them an inferential matter, in the sense that Ryle problematically suggested, and, thereby, make it nothing special at all, like all other knowledge. (I am ignoring his claim that it would also threaten the normativity of meaning and intentional states because of my conviction that I have removed that threat in chapter 3.)

The Cartesian view has something right in that it saw the need to acknowledge that self-knowledge was more direct, in some way, more a matter of "avowability," than the inferential paradigm allowed. The inferential view has something right in that it respects the dispositional features of intentionality. But they both also have something wrong. So, neither the inferential nor the observational paradigm fits self-knowledge, and these seem to be the only two paradigms for knowledge.

Should we then conclude that we do not have self-knowledge of intentional states because neither of the paradigms for knowledge fits it? That would be a frivolous conclusion to come to. But then what? Wright suggests – as have Davidson and Burge, and very likely Wittgenstein, before him – that self-knowledge is not a "*cognitive achievement*" at all, so the epistemological paradigms do not have to fit it. Rather it is *constitutive* of the very notion of intentionality that we by and large have self-knowledge. And by this he means that intentional states are "judgement-dependent." Intentional states are the kind of states which, under ideal conditions, if the possessor of a particular such state judges that he has it, then he has it. It is not as if, under these conditions, he is particularly well placed epistemologically to "track" the independently constituted facts of intentionality. No, under these conditions, his judgments constitute the facts of intentionality.

Now this will seem, at first sight, to be a superior form of sheer intellectual laziness. We have found that the intellectual work expended on giving an epistemological justification of self-knowledge on the basis of the only two epistemological paradigms that we know of came to nought, so let us stop work and make self-knowledge a primitive fact which comes with the very idea of intentionality!

But Wright, in fact, does a lot of philosophical spadework to make the idea less of a cheat. He fully realizes that there are exceptions to the sway of self-knowledge due to considerations like self-deception. He realizes that these exceptions would have to be ruled out in the ideal conditions mentioned above. And he worries that ruling them out will take place by stipulation of triviality-inducing "whatever-it-takes" formulations of the ideal conditions. However, in response to these difficulties, he askes us to reflect on the fact that the ruling out of something like self-deception is, as he puts it, "positive-presumptive."

> By that I mean that, such is the 'grammar' of ascriptions of intention [and other intentional states], one is entitled to assume that a subject is *not* materially self-deceived, or umotivatedly similarly afflicted, unless one possesses determinate evidence to the contrary. Positive-presumptiveness ensures that, in all circumstances in which one has no countervailing evidence, one is a priori justified in holding that the 'no self-deceptions' condition is satisfied.... (Wright 1989c, p. 237)

Upon this point, Wright rests a further claim. That we will not see someone as self-deceived unless there is positive evidence to the contrary, or that – lacking positive evidence to the contrary – we are not agnostic about the fact that he is self-deceived, suggests to Wright the following claim. It seems *a priori* reasonable to say, lacking positive evidence about self-deception, that an agent believes he has a certain intentional state (say, a certain intention), if and only if, he does.

And so, finally, he poses the question: why does this seem *a priori* reasonable? This is the question that the judgment-dependence thesis is supposed to answer. This question, which Wright describes as a question about the *a priori* reasonableness of a certain claim, is just a question about, what was more traditionally called, the presumption of "first person authority." Since I think the phenomenon is more neutrally described without talk of "a priori," I will stick with the latter description.

The judgment-dependence of intentionality, according to Wright, explains our presumption of first-person authority. It is because intentions and beliefs and other such states do not comprise a realm of independent facts which our judgments or opinions about them (expressible in iterated formulations such as I believe that I believe..., I believe that I intend...) track, that we may presume a special authority over them. Or, to put it more positively, it is because it is the nature of such states that our judgments (made under conditions treatable along the "positive presumptive" lines just mentioned) constitute those facts, that we may presume a special authority over them. This is his way of glossing the idea that self-knowledge is constitutive of intentionality and not a cognitive achievement. And the gloss is an explanation of why we presume first-person authority, an explanation of why it is that we find (given the positive presumptiveness of the "no self-deception proviso") the claim that an agent believes he has a certain state, if and only if he had it, an *a priori* reasonable claim.

I do not want to deny that there is something positive-presumptive about the ruling-out of something like self-deception, nor do I want to deny that that, in turn, promotes a presumption of first-person authority. But I do not think that the explanation Wright offers is substantial enough as an explanation of this phenomenon. It does not seem enough to offer the thesis of judgment-dependence. Unless the thesis is fortified by more substantial considerations, someone more skeptical of claims to constitutiveness in these matters may offer an alternative answer to Wright's question.

One can imagine the following alternative answer. The presumption of first-person authority is to be explained along reliablist lines to the effect that, crudely put, every time we ask ourselves what we intend or believe, and give an answer, it tends to be the right answer. This inductivist justification of the presumption of first-person authority and of the apparent *a priori* reasonableness of the claim Wright is explaining, rules out the constitutiveness of self-knowledge for intentionality, and it makes unnecessary the thesis of judgment-dependence. Self-knowledge can now, under this explanation, remain a "cognitive achievement." It is still possible to say, given the reliabilist treatment, that intentional facts about an agent are an independent set of facts which he is especially placed, epistemologically, to track with authority.

This Appendix cannot possibly take up the question as to whether Wright is mistaken in insisting on the constitutive thesis or not. That is a complicated question which needs extensive and detailed discussion, and needs to be carefully formulated in a way that cannot be done in a short space. So I will, here, simply assume that the constitutive thesis is true, in some form or other.[3] My claim is that it needs substantial support from further considerations if it is going to have any way of opposing the alternative reliabilist approach to the same explanandum: the presumption of first-person authority. It is not possible for Wright to express dissatisfaction with the reliabilist answer on the ground that it is too insubstantial. Precisely the same is true of his own answer. Without some substantial grounding of the idea of constitutiveness, things can, at best, be seen as a stand-off between the two explanations.

Here then, with appalling crudeness, is a proposal in four steps to ground the idea that self-knowledge is constitutive of intentionality, thereby making the idea, itself, more substantial.

First, it is not a cancellable fact about the kinds of creatures we are that we react to each other in moral terms. That is, we praise and blame each other, punish and reward each other, for our actions. If we ceased to do this then it would be a serious question whether we should think of ourselves as *persons* in anything like the sense we now do. So I am appealing to a fact about the kind of creatures we are, a fact of philosophical anthropology which cannot be repealed without changing the subject of both philosophy and anthropology.[4]

Second, these reactions presuppose that we hold each other responsible. That is, we only praise and blame each other because we take it that we are responsible for what we do. There is no purchase to the general idea of praise and blame unless those praised and blamed are, in general, responsible, and take themselves to be responsible, for what they are being praised and blamed for.

Third, it is a presupposition of the general idea of being responsible for something we do, that we know what we are doing. If, in general, we did not know what we were doing, we would not hold ourselves and each other responsible for what we did.

Fourth, if, in general, we know what we are doing, we must, in general, know our beliefs and desires and our intentions because it is these states which bring about and explain our doing. That is, we have self-knowledge of our intentional states.

That is the conclusion we wanted when we were seeking an account or justification of self-knowledge. We now have it, only we have it from considerations having to do with moral responsibility rather than epistemology. That is to say that we have explained the phenomenon that Wright wanted explained with his talk of constitutiveness. But that talk comes through as less dogmatic and less easily silenced by alternative explanations and ways of talking. It will not, for a moment, pretend that the appeal to these considerations has automatically repudiated the reliabilist explanation. But these considerations need an urgent response from anybody who wishes to deny the constitutive thesis.

It is possible also that these considerations and their bearing on self-knowledge can be reconciled with such knowledge being a cognitive achievement. In one sense there had better be such a reconciliation because there are clear cases of self-knowledge where introspection and inference are involved. It is just that there are far too many cases where they are not involved, so the reconciliation had better also pay attention to that fact. At the end of this reconciliation, I believe there will still be something to the constitutiveness of self-knowledge and the judgment-dependence thesis. The thesis that self-knowledge is constitutive of intentionality need no more be overturned by clear cases of cognitively achieved self-knowledge than the thesis that the external world is constitutive of belief can be overturned by clear cases of hallucinatory perceptual belief. The idea and ideal of "constitutiveness" in such cases need therefore to be carefully elaborated. But, I believe that once they are elaborated and once one fully sees through the implications of having self-knowledge fall out of these moral philosophical considerations, the very notion of judgment-dependence will have to be at once looser and richer than in Wright's less substantially grounded way of thinking of it.[5] These are some of the issues which need a much more extensive discussion than I can give here.

But that is not the end of it by any means. There are literally a score of qualifications to be made to my proposal, and an equal number of difficulties with it that have to be addressed. To take just one example, there is the obvious fact that we are often subject to praise and blame when we lack self-knowledge – culpable ignorance – and reasons will have to be given why that does not undermine the proposal. The reasons would bring in the notion of intellectual or cognitive responsibility, something not mentioned explicitly in the proposal, but which is willy-nilly implicitly in play.[6] That is also a very big subject and, as I said, just one among a vast number of issues that need addressing before the proposal will satisfy.

I hope to be able to present a much more through development of this proposal in a longer work soon, where these difficulties are addressed, where vital refinements are made to its crude formulation here, and where I also compare it with the views and proposals of other philosophers such as Wittgenstein, Davidson, Burge and Wright who have written on self-knowledge. My reason for having presented it here at all was to make an honourable stab at staving off a threat issuing from the special character of self-knowledge to the externalist and anti-phenomenological view of intentionality that I have presented in this book.

If I am right, it is not enough that we take self-knowledge out of the clutches of epistemology and make it constitutive of intentionality. Unless we go on to

situate self-knowledge in the larger context of moral philosophy, broadly conceived, we will never fully think our way out of the oscillation that has held sway
between Descartes and Ryle, or at any rate between sophisticated contemporary
versions of Descartes and Ryle.[7]

The threat from self-knowledge to sensible views on intentionality has been
an artificial product of a very long period of philosophizing, in which the obvious
and yet deep connections between different philosophical notions were kept
invisible, due to monolithic conceptions of what is central in philosophy. The
post-Cartesian obsession with epistemology, and then the post-Fregean obsession with a narrowly conceived project of a theory of meaning which replaced
it in reaction, have prevented us from seeing self-knowledge of meaning and
mind in its proper and larger context. They have distracted us from the obvious
connections between ourselves as linguistic agents on the one had and, on the
other, as the sorts of creatures who hold each other morally responsible.

# Notes

*Chapter 1    Belief, Meaning, and the External World*

1   I will try to use the term "content" with as low a profile as possible, leaving it open
    whether these specifications of content should be cashed out in terms of "sets of
    possible worlds," "propositions," "thoughts," "inscriptions in a language of thought,"
    or "meanings of sentences in a public language of one who specifies these contents."
    However, I have a prejudice in favor of the last of these which may emerge from time
    to time in the focus of the discussions of certain points. But those points could be
    reformulated with a different focus by someone with a different prejudice, without
    loss of the points themselves.

2   Two points ought to be made clear about this integrity. First, it does not suggest the
    conceptual primacy of intentionality over meaning and it certainly does not hold out
    the promise of the reduction of the latter to the former. In this respect it does not follow
    John Searle who thinks agents' meanings are *derived* from the intrinsic intentionality
    of the mind (Searle 1983, 26-9). Nor, obviously, does it follow the more fierce
    reductionist path of those who take Grice's (1957) analysis of meaning to be stressing
    the conceptual primacy of an agent's intentional states over his or her meanings, and
    then further reduce intentional states themselves to a system of purely causal or
    functional roles. See Loar 1981) for a sophisticated effort at such a reduction. Grice's
    famous analysis of meaning was first given in 1957, and I suspect there is a real
    question about whether by it Grice had in mind the conceptual primacy that is often
    attributed to him or whether it was a piece of neutral conceptual analysis.
    Second, there is the vexed question of whether creatures who lack language can have
    intentionality or not. I will have nothing to say about this question in the book. My
    assumption of "the close connection" and the integrity of meaning and intentionality
    does not prejudice the case against an affirmative answer to the question. For the
    purposes of this book, the assumption of the close connection can be put in conditional
    form such that it is taken to apply to only those creatures who do possess language.
    (In making this assumption about such creatures I am, of course, in numerous
    company.)

3   This general formulation and characterization of externalism is the standard one in the
    literature and was perhaps first formulated as a definition of externalism in Putnam
    1975), where he contrasts externalism with a doctrine he calls "methodological
    solipsism" and which, in this book, will be called "internalism." Internalism is
    sometimes spelt out in terms of the idea of the supervenience of intentional states on
    the inner states of agents, and externalism is then defined as a denial of such
    supervenience. I prefer to stay out of discussions of supervenience so I will continue
    to characterize externalism and internalism in the terms of the First Meditation as I
    have above.

4   The reader must forgive me the clutter of signposts in this chapter which will alert him or her to those places in other parts of the book where there are detailed discussions of points mentioned here only in passing.

5   Though I will start with the repudiation of bifurcation into wide and narrow (or internalist) content, I will, in chapter 4, also reject the more subtle and unconscious bifurcations I detect in McDowell and Davidson which are not into wide and narrow contents but are nevertheless bifurcations.

6   This may seem a little arbitrary, but I ask the reader to be patient until the non-arbitrary point behind the stipulation emerges. My claim will be that there is general definition of externalism – already given above – which it is not compulsory to then develop in the specific ways these orthodox theories of reference and concepts develop them. I offer another way to think of externalism (this chapter) and I discount the role of "reference" as it relates to content (chapter 4) and once I have done that it will be clear why "wide" as a label could be restricted to something more specific than "externalist" content. We need more than one label because there is a principled difference between these externalisms I oppose and my externalism. Since the externalists I oppose coined the term "wide," I retain the term for their specific externalist doctrines.
    The classic formulations of these externalisms are in Putnam (1975), Kripke (1972) and Burge (1979). Burge nowhere calls his notion of content "wide" because he does not believe his externalism forces a distinction between two notions of content. In the next chapter I will argue that his externalism does force a second notion of content and in doing so will justify my thinking of him as being committed to "wide" content. See also Loar (1985a) for an argument leading to the same conclusion. Kripke also does not talk of "wide" content and, in fact, until 1979 had not followed through the implications of his view of reference for intentionality (Kripke 1979). See Loar (1985a) again for an argument that two notions of content are forced by Kripke's view of reference. Given the unwillingness of both Burge and Kripke to acknowledge a distinction that, I think their views necessitate, I will simply define my own use of the term "wide" content throughout this book as follows, even though the definition will not make full sense until the reader has read a few more pages. I will call any externalist notion of content that fails to impose my constraint (C), "wide" content. I spell out this constraint in this chapter. Chapter 2 will show how all these philosophers have in one way or another failed to impose it.

7   Fodor's position was formulated well after the others (1987), and is in many ways quite different from theirs, but in the context of these themes the differences are not relevant since, as I will argue in chapter 2, it has the same destructive effect on the unity of content as the others. The externalist position of Davidson (1986) as well as the different position of Evans and Mcdowell (Evans 1982; McDowell 1984a) are separable from the orthodox positions I have mentioned. They are nevertheless distinct from the externalism I propose below and the differences between them and me are on a different level. I discuss these differences at length in chapter 4.

8   On some of the points that follow, up until the heart of my externalism which is the constraint itself, I will be working with points that may be found explicitly or implicitly in one or other of their notions of radical interpretation.

9  See a little later in this chapter for a qualification of this notion of concept to deal with two levels of the use of the notion.

10  This fits in with the general definition of externalism given at the very beginning of the chapter and commented on in.3.

11  The impression may come from such superficial things as my use of expressions like "ground floor" and "points of entry into another's mind," and less superficially from the fact that more traditional *internalist* foundationalist views, such as Russell's Logical Atomism, also stress the indexical utterances, but with an accompanying stress on correlations with inner experiential items rather than with external items in the environment.

12  I stress this qualification to distinguish the holism I intend by my constraint from other well-known doctrines such as Davidson's. In chapter 5, while discussing the differences between Davidson and my positions, I say more about the differences between these holisms.

13  I do not there *argue* for the irreducibility of content since that would have taken me into themes at some distance from the thread of dialectic I have set up for this book. In my (unpublished) "Unity and Autonomy of Content," I do argue for it, claiming that the naturalistic irreducibility of the mental is forced by the difficulties with externalisms that fail to impose my anti-foundational constraint.

14  This point about looking at whole utterances in the correlations as being mere evidence ought not to give the impression that I am in any way giving up on Frege's "Context Principle" which stresses that it is only in the context of the sentence that a term has meaning. Not at all. I can grant that principle and still say that term-meanings are constituted by external items, and sentence-meanings are constituted by external items only in the sense that they are composed of term-meanings which are. The latter in no way implies that term-meanings are self-standing and independent of sentence-meanings. It does not imply it because it is possible for term-meanings to depend on sentence-meaning without sentence-meanings being constituted in the same way as term-meaning. The dependence stated by the principle merely says that terms would not have meanings if terms did not occur in sentences with meanings. Why should that require anything as strong and specific as: terms get their meanings in ways that are dependent on the ways sentences get their meanings?

15  Of course, the evidence can only be thought of as being gathered from observation of particular localities.

16  Indeed, if one could think of the beliefs that go into the specification of local concepts as not being selections from somewhere, as not being selections at all, I would be perfectly happy because it would downplay the importance of meaning-theory even more: it is the locality thesis I am really insisting on.

## *Chapter 2    The Unity of Intentional Content*

1  Thorought this book, I use the words "psychology" and "psychological explanation" to mean only commonsense psychology and commonsense psychological explanation. I will not spend time sketching the basic nature and structure of such explanations

since it is well known and oft-repeated. But if at any stage the details are necessary for the discussion of a particular issue, I will expound them. It sometimes goes by the name of "rationalization" in order to mark a contrast with explanation as it is found in the fundamental realms of physical science. This contrast with strict scientific explanation is itself the focus of much philosophical interest today but it will not be a central interest of the chapters that follow. The contrast does not affect the idea that these rationalizing explanations are theoretical in nature (even if not fully "scientific" ) and, ever since Aristotle, philosophers have grappled with the details of the sort of theory that is involved. The theory begins with simple codifications of the implicit practical inferences involving beliefs and desires which are attributed in the commonsense explanation of agents' behavior; but it has, of course, been considerably sophisticated by the refinements of the apparatus of the theory of decision.

2   By the "general form" I mean to contrast it with specific versions of externalism, such as those I am opposing as well as my own specific version.

3   Indeed, the examples were first introduced by the orthodox externalists themselves to intuitively argue for their specific externalisms, and they play an essential role in that argument. Once the orthodox externalisms were in place, the examples were subsequently exploited – quite rightly in my opinion – to bring out the bifurcatory implications of these externalisms. I will take it as a sign of bad faith if someone, faced with the charge of bifurcation, suggests that the examples and the orthodox externalisms that they are intuitively supposed to lead to are not essential to these philosophers' general commitment to externalism. Since these philosophers proceed by making the examples central to their dialectic, I am going to take seriulsy the orthodox externalist intutitions they have claimed as issuing from these examples. This is justified all the more when, on moving from examples and intutitions to their motivations and arguments for externalism, in chapter 3, we find that they are indeed motivations and arguments for the orthodox externalisms attributed to them in this chapter on the basis of the examples.

4   It would be quite wrong to think that the view of reference being assumed here (which is essential to these examples raising the problem for unity they are intended to raise) leads to *de re* attributions of content. The problem for unity is not that content is to be bifurcated into *de re* attributions and *de dicto* attributions. One can see a temptation to think that that is what is at issue: externalism forces *de re* attributions, explanation requires *de dicto* attributions. But that is not the issue at all. The issue is rather entirely about *de dicto* attributions. The problem is that the assumption of a certain view of reference forces a bifurcation of *de dicto* attributions into an externalist one and an action-explanatory one.

5   In his paper, Kripke (1979) explicitly mentions only the translational and disquotation principle as two assumptions governing the raising of the puzzle. But he spends the first several pages of stage-setting trying to rule out what he calls "Fregean" and "Russellian" views on reference which may be thought to overturn his own view of it. Clearly the stage is fully set for him only after these have been ruled out and after his own view of reference can be taken for granted. For that reason I am treating his view of reference as a third governing assumption for raising the puzzle. The rest of the discussion of the puzzle below makes clearer how the assumption crucially lies behind such puzzles and examples.

6 To generate a flat contradiction, Kripke introduces what he calls a "strengthened disquotation" principle. See Kripke (1979, p. 258).

7 This bifurcation is fairly widely accepted by philosophers who embrace this externalism about content. When it was first made by Putnam (1975) and in immediately succeeding papers, it was made more in terms of meaning; it was only later that it became explicitly connected with issues in the philosophy of mind.

8 There is, of course, a trivial sense in which the psychological explanations of their actions must be different since there is a trivial sense in which their actions are different: one is drinking his water, and the other his. I will return to this point about indexical elements in explanation in my discussion of the externalism of Evans and McDowell in chapter 4.

9 I must remind the reader once again that I am concerned only with the apparent inability of externalist content to be efficacious in *commonsense explanation* of behavior. There are, in the philosophical literature, other motivations for positing a second notion of internalist content. One such motivation is that it alone will be efficacious in a *bona fide* science of psychology, where one goes beyond commonsense explanation of behavior. Another motivation for positing internalist content is derived from a metaphysical intuition that we need a second notion of content which is supervenient on the inner physical and functional states of agents. I am not going to discuss these other motivations for bifurcating contents. And it will be part of my complaint against those who are rightfully dissatisfed with the inability of the contents mentioned in the discussion of these examples to commonsensically explain behavior, and who turn to a notion of internalist content to explain it, that they often run together *that* motivation with one of these other two. If they did not run these together, they would be less quick to insist that only turning to an *internalist* content commonsensically explains behavior. But all this lies ahead. For now, I am restricting myself to a specific philosophical use of these examples: to prove that externalist content fails to capture what is necessary if content is to be efficacious in commonsense explanation of behavior.

10 In many articles subsequent to Burge (1979), he often discusses and embraces a non-social externalism as well. What is a little confusing is that he often speaks of externalism in a very unspecific way, in the way I did when I first introduced the general idea in chapter 1. And his label for the position which it opposes is "individualism" rather than internalism. And individualism, for him, accommodates any view which opposes not only social externalism but non-social externalism as well.

In all subsequent discussions of Burge in this book I will concentrate on his specifically social externalism as specified in Burge (1979) and as sketched below in the text and in(the cuucial) notes that follow, especially. I will restrict the term "individualism" to a position opposed to social externalism alone. Thus, for me, there can be a position which combines individualism and externalism. Indeed, that is my own position. Note 37 mentions the pitfalls of not keeping track of the different strands in Burge's omnibus use of the terms "externalism" and "individualism" .

11 I use the word "often" deliberately. Burge does allow for some concepts of an individual to be idiosyncratic and not the same as his community's. I will take what he says about the "arthritis" example as a basic and paradigmatic commitment of his

social externalism, despite his careful qualifications issuing from other sorts of examples. It is enough for me that he says what he says about this arthritis case to find myself in serious disagreement with him. His insistence that Bert has his community's concept, his disallowing of the reinterpretation of Bert as saying and thinking something along more individualistic lines (i.e. as having his own idiosyncratic concept of arthritis) is quite wrong enough for me. No qualification will remove my disagreement with that claim since I will be arguing that there is no harm, and that indeed there is overall theoretical advantage, in the individualist reinterpretation of Bert.

12 Two caveats: first, the beliefs cannot be widly divergent or else Burge's position has not even an intial plausibility and Burge and others are frank to admit that there is no strict way of saying what counts as wild and what not. But, clearly, if Bert thought that "arthritis" was a word, not for any kind of medical condition but rather for a piece of furniture, say, that eould count as wild. He must at least think, let us say, that it is a disease. Second, I have talked in an unspecific way about an "agent's fellows" to mark the social environemnt. This could mean the experts on some particular phenomenon, such as, in the arthritis example, the doctor; but clearly it does not have to be experts.

13 Recently, in a discussion after a paper he gave on "narrow content" at Rutgers University, Putnam himself identified his thesis with Burge's. But there is nothing in his writing that suggests it and, as I say, the two theses are in fact quite separable.

14 I am being careful to say "when they rely on them" because I do not think that the principle of division of labor should be seen as operative without it being *in fact* the case that an agent is relying on another. Such reliance is a fact, a fairly widespread fact, and when it is a fact any account of an individual's concepts needs to take it into account. In this sense the *facts* about an individual agent make appeal to her social environemnt necessary. But it is not to be assumed to exist *on general theoretical grounds* in the use of all terms on all occasions by non-experts, even if the individual agent concerned, on reflection, denies that she was relying on the expert in a given locality of thought or linguistic usage. (See chapter 1 for my notion of "locality".) On many occasions a medically ignorant agent may use a term like "arthritis" and not be relying on anyone. For instance, suppose she was talking to someone about her mother and suppose that that someone knew that her mother had arthritis. Here her use of the term could be the non-relying use of a term to talk about a disease that her mother had. In this "locality" we need not attribute to her the concept cashed out as "the disease that my doctor knows more about and calls 'arthritis.'" In this locality she simply is not relying on the doctor. Her concept here is just simply cashed out as "the concept of a disease that my mother has."

15 The phrase has been made familiar by Kaplan and a number of philosophers who have anti-Fregean views about reference. It is not surprising that such a view is relevant here since the notion of psychological content is the philosophy-of-mind counterpart, as it were, to the philosophy-of-language notion of Fregean sense. My own overall view can be seen as an externalist conception of sense. In this it goes against most conceptions of sense. There is, however, another externalist view of sense, that of Gareth Evans and John McDowell, and I will mention the differences between my view and theirs in chapter 4.

16 In the vast literature on this subject, there is a distinction between a causal theory of reference in this sense and a position which makes no effort to ground the idea of direct referenc in such a causal story. This would, as I said, leave the idea of direct reference rather mysterious. Sometimes the term "direct reference" is used in a restricted way for this mysterious position and the term "causal theory of reference" is used for the former. The point, however, is that both reject conceptual mediation. The former has causal mediation in the sense just sketched; the mysterious position lacks even that, but neither will have anything to do with conceptual mediation.

17 It would in any case be odd to think of such descriptions as conceptually mediating the reference of most contemporary speakers' concept of London since most speakers are unaware of these descriptions that went into fixing the reference of "London."

18 Fodor asks the question about mental representations in the head and he has very specific reasons for doing so, but of course the question can be raised more generally about terms and concepts even if one does not share his views about beliefs and concepts involving such representations.

19 It is worth noticing, therefore, that this determined commitment to denotational semantics on Fodor's part makes absolutely clear that the use of the term "information" in characterizing his position is a very special use. For normally one would have thought that information is precisely what would get rid of the Kripkean and Fregean puzzles. But the term is strictly embedded in an ultra-naturalistic account where information itself is characterized in strictly causal terms (the causal covariances) which have no place for the notion of sense. So in Fodor's picture the denotational aspect is primary and the use of the notion of information does nothing to spoil it.

20 Astonishingly, in the passage just quoted from Loar, he is making this criticism of me. My position could not be further from positions like Kripke's and Putnam's and was introduced by me via a criticism of such poitions. I suspect that he falls into this misinterpretation partly because in Bilgrami (1985) I may have misled him by using terms like "causal" externalism to describe my position, something I have consciously avoided here so as to avoid being confused with these other positions; but partly also because he, like so many others, have not entertained the possibility of a position within externalism which rejects the social and the non-social positions described above, and they cannot quite believe that someone could be arguing for something like that.

21 Remember, this is how I too, following Putnam (1978) who first explicitly raised all these issues about content, defined externalism at the beginning of chapter 1. Putnam defines it as a *negation* of what he calls "methodological solipsism" and which, in turn, he defines in Cartesisan fashion, as the doctrine that content is wholly independent of the external world.

22 In chapter 4, I will explain why I use the word "reference" at all in describing my view. It will be clear, when I do, that it is "reference" by courtesy only.

23 There is admittedly a slight oddity in speaking of their content as "wide" content if they do not admit to another notion of content which is "narrow." But it is not hard to live with the oddity if one keeps in mind that I have defined "wide" content more neutrally as a product of an externalism which does not work with my constraint.

24 That is exactly the phrase Donald Davidson used in making the complaint to me; John McDowell has also made the same complaint. I suspect that it is not merely that the

complainer worries that I am positing something that is not necessary. There are two further points to the complaint. First, there is the thought that, of course, there *all sorts* of descriptions of the twins' actions which are going to be the same but that is of no great significance to explanation. I will discuss this point when I discuss Evans and McDowell's externalism in chapter 5. Second, and this is the deeper point, there is also the anxiety that insisting on a common element in the twins' will lead inevitably to an internalist view of their psychologies. That anxiety is made wholly unnecessary by my externalism. My externalism shows that an externalism can acknowledge that the explanans and explanandum of the twins can be the same.

25 There is, of course, the difference that the Pierre example involves two natural languages but that is a superficial feature of the example. The problem that we want to raise and even the problem that Kripke wants to raise is about concepts as well as terms and can be raised within a single natural language.

26 Thereby showing that he does not even have unreflective or "tacit" knowledge of what social externalism sees as constituting his concept. If he did ever articulate it it would be because he had acquired *new* knowledge, not dredged up by reflection, knowledge that he tacitly held. It is admittedly true that this last point may seem to hold of other forms of knowledge sometimes allowed as tacitly or unconsciously held by agents, such as knowledge of the further recesses of grammar posited by psycholinguistics. Even Burge, however, is clear that he does not see Bert as possessing the knowledge of experts in this tacit or unconscious way that these other forms of knowledge are possessed. And he is surely right to find no temptation in seeing things that way. Yet, I would submit, if one scrutinizes *why* one is *not* so tempted, the plausible diagnosis for it is that tacit or unconscious knowledge is only tempting as a posit when the states posited are indispensable to the explanation of the behavior of the individual.

27 It is not coincidental that Burge should call the notion of meaning which is tied to concepts which are individuated by reference, "translational meaning." I think the thought behind this is exactly the thought behind Kripke's principle of translation in his formulation of the puzzle about belief. Recall that the principle said that translation preserves reference (and truth), thereby forcing a translation of "London" into "*Londres*," despite Pierre's explication of the meanings for the two terms being quite different.

28 The idea of metalinguistic specifications of concepts or term-meanings in an agent's idiolect are, for various reasons, held in suspicion by many philosophers. One reason is that if our concepts were all metalinguistically specified, then there is no sense in which our concepts or thoughts would be about anything in world. They would only be about other peoples' (the experts') opinions and habits of speech. But this kind of alarm is highly exaggerated. There is no reason to think that the metalinguistic specifications should be given for all concepts in all utterances. I must invoke my thesis of the locality of content to make this point fully clear. One only need introduce metalinguistic specifications, if in fact the reliance of the agent on the expert for a given concept is relevant to any particular content that is being attributed to him in any particular locality of content attribution. So, to take the example given earlier in n. 14, suppose I say to you that arthritis is painful in the context of discussing my mother and you know that my mother has arthritis, then in this context, it is perfectly

possible to attribute a concept of arthritis to me that is not metalinguistically specified. In this locality there is no need to bring in my reliance on the expert; my concept here is exhausted by such beliefs as "the disease my mother has," "the disease which we talked about when we last discussed my mother" etc. Hence, at many localities there will not be metalinguistic specifications. Of course, if I am utterly ignorant and rely on the expert without any other beliefs about the thing in question, then I do not have any beliefs other than metalinguistic ones. In such cases, in every locality in which the concept in question is attributed to me, it will *have* to be the metalinguistic belief which characterizes the concept. I think it is safe to say that we are not so ignorant with regard to most of our concepts, so this ought not to generate any serious alarm. Another source of worry about metalinguistic specifications is that we will not be able to say of agents speaking different languages that they have the same concept of, say arthritis. This is because the metalinguistic specifications will mention particular terms in particular languages ("What the experts around here call 'arthritis,'" "what the experts around here call 'arthrite'"). This is a version of Church's well-known problem. But here the worry is exaggerated because most of our concepts are not exhausted by such metalinguistic specifications and will get specifications of other non-linguistic beliefs for which no such problem will arise. These are the beliefs on the basis of which translations will be made. Of course here again, in cases of total ignorance, where the concept is only metalinguistically specified there will be a problem. But the fact is that when an agent is relying on experts from a position of such wholesale ignorance, such a problem *should* arise. There is every reason, in such cases, not to translate their terms into one another, when they are from different linguistic communities, because their concept *is* merely linguistic in the problematic sense.

Yet another source of worry about metalinguistic specifications is that they make meanings contingent since they depend on what, in fact, is called something or other in particular societies. This worry only comes from a commitment to a notion of necessity, which is hardly compulsory in the study of meaning. It is perfectly possible to work with a notion of meaning or concepts which accepts that particular concepts or terms' meanings are fixed by contingent facts and regularities of an agent's behavior, and then once fixed thus, we take them to define the concept or term for that agent. Such a notion raises no particular problem for the metalinguistic specifications.

29 Burge himself does not accept this metalinguistic ploy. In Burge (1979, pp. 96-7) he very explicitly rejects these metalinguistic specifications as a way of avoiding his social externalist conclusion.

30 Recall what Burge says about "tiger" when he is talking of the "translational" concept in the first long quotation cited during the discussion of the first objection.

31 Actually, even if Burge denies that he is privileging the expert's belief over the other beliefs, the fact is that so long as the expert's belief is one among the several beliefs that go into a "cluster" rewrite, the inconsistency (of the first horn) will still get attributed to the agent who says or thinks "I have arthritis in my thigh."

32 In cases, that is, where there is no evidence of self-deception or other psychological Freudian phenomena which are obstructive of self-knowledge. See n. 26 and also the discussion of Objection A in the final section of this chapter for more on this point.

33 It is hard to imagine anybody who would be so complacent as to embrace the conclusion about lack of self-knowledge on externalist grounds and also at the same time insist on the unity of content, i.e. insist that there need not be – for each externalist content not known to the agent who possessed it – a non-externalist counterpart which is known. Such a position would be tantamount to the claim that one should altogether give up on the intuitive conviction that we have self-knowledge of our contents on grounds that are highly abstract, grounds such as an externalism about content. But, as said in n. 32, our intuitions do not allow us to give up on this conviction unless there are very specific reasons having to do with much less abstract psychological phenomena like self-deception and so on. Externalism about content is simply not a reason of this specific kind and we would, therefore, at least want the non-externalist counterparts so that we can retain the conviction in some form.

34 It is tempting to have concluded from Burge's own admission of the fact that an agent often only has partial knowledge of his concepts (such as Bert's knowledge of his concept of arthritis), that he too is bifurcating content into two: one notion of content containing those parts of his concepts which he does know, a second notion containing those parts of his concepts he does not know. It would then be possible to say that the former contents are known to the agents and the latter not, the former explains actions and the latter does not. But that view is not Burge's. Not only does he deny any need for bifurcation but, as we shall see below, he provides an account of self-knowledge of one's contents which does not allow externalism to thwart our knowledge of our own intentional states. For him, the fact that we have only partial knowledge of many of our concepts (a fact entailed by his version of externalism) does not force partial knowledge of one's own contents at all. His account of self-knowledge makes that clear. So we cannot use his admission of such partial knowledge of concepts to force a bifurcation of two notions of content on him, without considering his account of self-knowledge.

35 In Davidson (1987, 1991), he says no more than we have in setting up the *prima facie* problem that externalism poses for self-knowledge. See Bilgrami (1991a) for a detailed criticism of Davidson's own way of reconciling self-knowledge with externalism, where I argue that the reconciliation fails because he does not set up the problem and the need for reconciliation in the right way.

36 I can hear someone protesting: but he is not, on your view, even thinking something false. On your view there are no false thoughts, only idiosyncratic true ones. That is not true at all and I establish that in chapter 4 when I discuss the implications of my externalism for the question of the normativity of content and the question of theory-change and meaning change.

37 This is a common tendency in some of Burge's papers written after Burge (1979). In them he has written with the intention of defending the bold and interesting social externalist position he first formulated in Burge (1979). However, in these discussions he very often ends up offering plausible defences of a much more generalized externalist position of the sort we defined at the beginning of the book (so general that it could even be compatible with individualism). So one has to be careful in reading these more recent papers to insist that he also provide a defence of the specific position he first formulated in Burge (1979).

38 Things are, in fact, a little more complicated in a way that does not much concern us here, so I will put the complication in this note. It is not that Fodor, in general, is against any idea of bifurcation or of a second notion of content. He is in fact a bifurcationist. But he does not think that the need to capture the fineness of grain or more specifically the inferential role and agent's conceptions is what forces the second notion. His motivation (Fodor 1987, ch. 2) for positing a second notion of content is one that we decided to put aside in n. 9, the motivation that demands that contents supervene on the interior of agents so as to allow for an ultimate reduction of content which makes possible the stricter kind of scientific psychology. He thinks the twin-earth examples favor Putnam's and Burge's views and, therefore, threaten such supervenience. The second notion of content which he introduces is thus intended to provide for the commonsense explanation of action. The second notion that he favors for that purpose is one that derives from Kaplan's idea of "character", introduced by Kaplan initially to deal with indexicals. This is a notion first sketched in some detail by Stephen White in his influential article 1982. Since I am not interested in the supervenience motivation I need not sketch those details here. But there is a serious question whether that notion of content is well suited to fulfill the motivation that I am interested in, which is to capture inferential role and agents' conceptions that will explain action. White and Fodor nowhere argue that it could do so. In White (1991), he explicitly concedes that it will not do so and suggests another notion of narrow internalist content to figure in action-explanation.

39 Fodor makes this point and explicitly discusses it in the context of the Pierre example in his very interesting paper (Fodor unpublished manuscript).

40 A few points about the term "conceptual role." The idea it expresses is just the same idea that I have been informally sketching as "conceptions of things" and "inferential roles," i.e. as the sorts of things needed to explain actions, only for me they are not, as they are for everyone else, internally characterized. As a result, for me they do not stand in contrast to a notion of externalist content. I have not troubled to characterize the idea of "conceptual role" fully and have talked rather imprecisely of "conceptions of things" and "inferential roles" only because there is an abundant literature on this subject already available. A full characterization of intentional states and their contents as conceptual roles (or, more strictly, as being determined by conceptual roles) would characterize them not merely in terms of their place in a system of intentional states of an agent which are related to one another, as I have been doing so far when I talked of inferential roles. What would have to be added is the functional relations they bear to non-peripheral intentionally described perceptual inputs, on the one hand, and to motor outputs described as actions, on the other. The meaning of a sentence and the content of an intentional state would now just be the place (actual or potential) which it had in such a system or conceptual scheme. There is a question about how tightly such a system can be defined for given agents since the the system is not merely mechanistic (causal relations between his or her intentional states) but conceptual and inferential, and therefore, normative. There is fair amount of literature on the idea of conceptual role and the view of meaning and content it promotes. All of it, however, assumes that it is an internalist view of meaning and content, (though see the discussion of Harman below). The view goes back to Sellars (1963) and has most recently been defended by Block (1987a).

41 I use the word "objects" here innocuously to talk vaguely of the things that our thoughts are about (London, water) and not the "objects of thoughts" I have rejected in the discussion of Objection B above.

42 Fodor has in some places (Fodor unpublished, p. 13) written as if something more than pure causal role might be involved in dealing with the examples but that it still does not amount to conceptions and content. In these places he suggests that the differences in causal role are really determined by differences in the form and not the content of inner representations. But here too it does seem to be an unjustified restriction on how to think of (and what to call) the feature that gets us out of the difficulties raised by his examples. And it is unjustified for exactly the same reason. The work this feature does in getting us out of the puzzles is too powerful to receive these restricted formal descriptions. The descriptions of form will be at the wrong level. the work is not done at the level of the causal medium or vehicle of the explanatory states, as it were, which is where the formal characterization of the differences puts it; the work is being done at the level of the rationalizing elements and therefore to think of what is doing the work as getting purely formal descriptions is seriously to mismatch the descriptions and the work they describe. In saying this I am not making a dogmatic *externalist* claim. The point now is not that contents capturing conceptions of things cannot be internalist. Brian Loar (1985a) offers such an internalist notion of content and there are other offerings in the literature. And though, of course, I am eventually denying that a notion of content which captures agents' conceptions should be internal, I would still grant that at least an internalist notion of content which goes beyond formal descriptions to genuine conceptual roles, would at least not be guilty of the serious mismatch I just mentioned.

## *Chapter 3   Society and Norm*

1 There ought to be no whiff of tautology in this since the general idea that content and meaning are social is perfectly compatible with them not being social in the sense of social externalism, as defined and discussed over the past many pages. Hence individualism about content which is to be defined in contrast to social externalism may well capture whatever social features are rightly thought of as relevant to content.

2 The social element Kripke introduces in this work (1982) is not emphasized in his early work on reference, discussed in chapter 2.

3 See Taylor (1975) for some useful historical material on this tradition of thought. It is an interesting project to clearly work out the different historical figures and strands in this tradition, and to uncover the points where something like social externalism is implicitly taken for granted in so much of its thinking about language (especially) and mind.

4 This tradition–along with other views–will also be an implicit target of my discussion of norms in the next section.

5 This is partly why it is so hard to keep apart those arguments in Burge which are supposed to support his social externalism from those which support Putnam and Kripke's position or, for that matter, those which support a very general notion of

externalism, compatible even with my externalism. See chapter 2, nn. 10 and 37 on this point. It is his social externalism as presented in Burge (1979), however, which is his most striking and original contribution to this field and in my discussions of Burge I am restricting my attention to that.

6  It is perhaps because he did not see this that Loar (1985b) made a number of criticisms of Bilgrami (1985), which really should be addressed to Kripke and Putnam's causal-essentialist externalism. See particularly his criticism of what he takes to be my view of natural kind terms and his criticism of my notion of the reference clauses in a truth-theory which he takes to involve a notion of rigid designation.

7  See Bilgrami (1985, 1987) for a discussion of the distinction between the public and the social with regard to meaning and content.

8  Of course, one needs to qualify this with the point about reliance on others in the community (and the linguistic division of labor) made in chapter 2. But that point, as I have stressed more than once, is compatible with individualism.

9  The ultimate dispute between Burge and me is over this very last point. It is, therefore, more emphatically about idiolects than sociolects. It is a dispute about whether idiolects should be thought of as constructed after the construction of and dependent on sociolects or whether they should be thought of as fully describable independent and prior to the construction of sociolects as mentioned a little earlier.

10 See n. 11 of chapter 2 where I pointed this out and went on to say that the disagreement between me and Burge may nevertheless persist since individualists will disagree about the paradigmatic cases Burge fastens on, such as Bert and "arthritis," where Burge disallows attribution of an idiosyncratic concept. Incidentally, Burge himself is also very clear that he is not raising the questions we have just listed. He is clear that his anti-individualism is a doctrine about idiolects. See especially Burge (1989).

11 It is quite possible that Chomsky does not have in mind to say anything as strong as I have been representing him as saying and as his rhetoric sometimes suggests. It is possible that the rhetoric exceeds his intention which is to present the less radical critique of social externalism, requiring only that we do not eventually rest with the assumption for agents like Bert.

12 From now I will not keep bringing up these two implausible alternatives of these two horns and will assume that no one is prepared to embrace them. I will, therefore, proceed as if it has been established that social externalism and the other orthodox externalisms disrupt the unity of content.

13 Loar (1985b) makes this protest explicitly against my view. Burge (1979) makes a similar point.

14 See especially nn. 1 and 9 of chapter 2.

15 I do not want to suggest that this is a wholly contemporary pursuit. It issues from its own tradition which goes back at least to Hobbes.

16 See Paul Churchland (1981) and Patricia Churchland (1987) for the stress on neuroscience. In Stich (1983) and various writings by others there is a stress on purely syntactic characterizations of content so as to suit states which possess them for cognitive science.

17 In chapter 4, I will also show how the idea of bringing in these descriptions should

not raise an alarm about how content will become too messy and too rampantly individualistic to ever be shared by individuals.

18 This point may lead someone to want to say something stronger on behalf of individualism than I have said. She may want even to deny that our everyday reports are social externalist rather than grant, as I have, that they are. She may want to say that the ordinary unreflective report of Bert as "believing that he has arthritis in his thigh" is really an abbreviation of the more careful tracking of what I am calling the more theoretical notion of his content. I suspect, however, that Burge and Loar are right in saying that except in specific contexts when those making the reports are in fact being careful, this stronger claim for individualism belies the facts of reportage.

19 Russell (1951) was responding to Strawson's (1950) attack on his theory of descriptions.

20 A brief bibliographical note. It should be pointed out that though Burge has with great subtlety and elaborateness spelt out and argued for social externalism in the form in which I am discussing it, Dummett (1978) is the first philosopher to have explicitly stated and argued for it, including intimations of the argument from deference discussed below. The Hegelian and Wittgensteinian antecedents cited by Burge and others are, of course, much less specific than anything in Burge or Dummett. And if I am right about the linguistic division of labor as being compatiable with individualism, then Putnam's view cannot really count as an antecedent to Burge's, even though it seems to have been intended as such. Loar (1985b) explicitly criticizes me (Bilgrami 1985) for insisting that deference has to be accounted for along the pragmatic and historical lines I mention below instead of along Burge's social externalist lines.

21 In private correspondence. Part of his reason for saying that I should not grant the fact of deference in the specific form I am granting it is because he thinks we often may defer to some who does not speak the same language (in the sense of sociolect). He writes: "Suppose the expert happens to speak a variety of Cockney that I can barely understand? Is that part of my sociolect? I can perfectly well defer to my Italian gardener with whom I share only the Latin names for elms and beeches. Is his Naples dialect part of my sociolect?" These are certainly important points to consider in clarifying the argument from deference. All the same, but for the complication involving translation that is introduced by the second example (and I assume that so long as we are talking about concepts, and not merely "terms," the idea of deference can be retained across translations), this repeats Chomsky's skepticism about sociolects, which I have already commented on in the text earlier.

Another part of his reason for not granting it is that deference is not as widespread as I concede it to be. He writes: "I've lived in Boston for 38 years, and I speak with a Philadelphia accent. In fact, all these things are clear and uncontroversial with regard to pronunciation, plainly rule-governed behavior if anything is, and no one seems to be troubled by the facts which seem to be something like this: our biological constitution (Universal Grammar) determines to quite close detail how the mapping between words and sounds is organized; there are some options left open, which are fixed by evidence from the environment; after that, we speak in accordance with the internalised rules, not caring very much what anyone else does, or even being aware of it, though there is a small amount of adaptation around the edges – thus my speech is no longer precisely that of people who stayed in the neighbourhood where I was brought up. I doubt that anything is fundamentally different at the level of meaning or syntactic form." I do, in fact, have doubts that in the mater of meaning (especially the lexically oriented meaning – rather than the syntactically determined aspects of meaning – which we are discussing in the example of "elm" or "arthritis" ) Universal Grammar fixes very much at all. This does not mean that I do not think there are very many cases where we resist deference. I go on to discuss such cases in the text. But they involve sorts of consideration much less abstract and theoretical than those from Universal Grammar. I will not deny that one may turn out to be wrong in thinking that Universal Grammar determines much less in the domain of meaning that Chomsky says. After all it is an empirical matter. And if Chomsky is right on that matter, he would have derived his denial of the fact of deference from what is established about the sway of Universal Grammar. Yet for the immediate purposes of the dispute with social externalists, it may be a shrewd strategy, anyway, to grant them the fact of deference in the interim and show that it does not amount to an argument for their thesis.

22  The publicness constraint speaks to epistemological demands which cannot be accommodated and explained in other ways than by imposing the constraint on the constitution of content. In chapter 5, I argue for the necessity of imposing this publicness constraint. Here I am denying that deference is similarly unexplainable and unaccommodatable except by imposing the stronger social externalist constraint.

23  What I am straining to draw attention to is that the fact that we do not defer in these exceptional circumstances is itself explained along the same pragmatic lines as deference is explained. In my example, I did not defer precisely because I wanted to be understood without strain. This makes vivid how basic and comprehensive the pragmatic explanations are.

24  Though see my skepticism in chapter 1 about different individuals having the same concept outside of a locality.

25  That there should be an agent and attributor at least is already implicit in the idea that meaning is publicly discoverable. One could, I suppose, even deny the need for an actual attributor since discoverability does not strictly require one, but it may be a handy device to have him in order to keep us honest against an unconscious slide into privacy. See below in the next section's discussion of Robinson Crusoe for more on this point.

26  It goes without saying that citing this aspect of Quine does not mean that one finds the other aspects of his methodology, such as the extreme behavioristic naturalism acceptable. Quine's views on meaning and belief are deeply torn and the fierce naturalism and eliminativism is detachable from the (or one) general idea behind radical translation. That is, it is possible to use the idea of radical translation to get to the essentials of meaning and belief without embracing this naturalism. Donald Davidson's use of it in various papers presumably intends to put it precisely to that use of since Davidson is so explicit about the irreducibility and indispensability of the intentional idiom.

27  Indeed my individualist reading of the very idea of radical translation may run afoul of Quine's own subsequent definition of "observation sentence" in social terms.

28  Quine might resist the "must" since he takes charity to be merely a "supplementary

methodological canon" of radical translation. Davidson is very clear that it is not an option but is part of the very idea of interpretation.

29  I return to this topic at length in the discussion of the Robinson Crusoe case in the next section.

30  Our concept of arthritis is not the best example of the sort of natural kind term which the causal-essentialist view makes so much of and which would help distinguish his view from the social externalist view. Unlike the concept of water, which one thinks of as a substance which experts could get wrong, the concept of arthritis is the concept of a disease which one thinks is more or less wholly fixed by our experts' view of it.

31  It may be thought that neurophysiological and inner functional states are perfectly public, despite being inner, and so if there is a reduction of meaning to such states then publicness at least is not threatened. This would be to totally miss the point underlying the insistence that meaning and content are public. I take this up while considering more refined reductions of meaning and content in the context of arguments of publicness in chapter 5.

32  This anti-internalism does not amount to what I am calling externalism, since one can oppose this anti-internalism without insisting that the outward criterion explicitly involve the world external to the agent whose inner processes are in question. They could possibly involve just his behavior and that is all that Wittgenstein himself explicitly stresses. I do not mean to suggest that he would exclude the external, only that the very specific and explicit way of bringing in the external that we have been discussing in these chapters is nowhere mentioned by Wittegnstein. I take this distinction up in chapter 5 also.

33  Kripke has other criticism of the dispositionalist answer but I will focus only on this criticism invoking normativity since my interest is primarily in the relevance of normativity in motivating a certain externalist view of content. Kripke himself is very explicit that it is this criticism which he take to be the deepest and the one that is ultimately devastating of the dispositionalist answer.

34  Kripke sometimes characterizes the "skeptical solution" as a position which gives up on providing truth-conditions for sentences attributing meaning and rules, a position which resorts to providing only assertibility conditions for them. By contrast a "straight solution," if there was one, would be a position which succeeded in giving truth-conditions for them. This way of putting things does not, for me, add anything of interest to the distinction between the two kinds of solution. My primary interest in the skeptical solution is that it is a solution which appeals to the community of the agent. That one should go on to see this in assertibilist rather than truth-conditonalist lines adds nothing to that primary interest. See Bilgrami (1986) for a skepticism about the possibility of making out a viable distinction between truth and assertibility conditions in the study of meaning.

35  Actually though I am stressing social externalism in this passage, it is not just the social externalist but all the other orthodox externalist views of content which afford us the normativity that is demanded by Burge and Kripke. All of them allow us to say that Bert and KWert are mistaken in the sense required. Indeed causal-essentialist externalism allows us something stronger than social externalism since it allows us to apply norms that are not even part of the practice of the community, but which flow

from the objective nature of the kind involved whether historical communities in the past have had knowledge of it or not.

It is important, however, to keep in mind the fairly obvious fact that in the contrast within orthodox externalism between social externalism and one or other of the orthodox *casual* externalisms, these latter are causal externalism *about reference or sayings or thoughts*. Norms could not arise for us if we were just causally embedded in nature because a mountain is causally embedded in nature and it is not subject to norms. So these orthodox causal externalisms import normativity not in so far as they are causal but in so far as they purport to be causal accounts of our thoughts and concepts.

36  As Kripke puts it: "Is not the dispositional view an equation of performance and correctness?" (1982, p. 24). We might add the following to make his point explicitly relevant to the view under attack: is not the view an equation of projections based on the regularities of performance with normative rules for correct performance?

37  This way of treating the individual need not imply a denial of the claim that one needs a second person or interpreter to have thoughts and meaning at all. It only implies a denial of Kripke's skeptical solution and to Burge's social externalist views. See the discussion of Davidson below for more on this.

38  Though I have not read them, I am perfectly aware of the fact that there are a number of authors (and co-authors) out there who have written on what exactly Wittgenstein intended. I also have the sense that there is very little agreement between them. I will make no effort to join them, except to say that it strikes me that the deep part of Wittgenstein is the attack on the epistemological picture of the mind which culminates in the publicness constraint on language discussed in the last section. If he also put a further social externalist constraint, that, I am arguing, lacks the depth and the motivation of the publicness constraint.

39  See McDowell (1984b) for a most forceful and detailed statement of this criticism. See also Blackburn (1984) for the same scathing criticism of Kripke's social view even though in the end Blackburn, unlike McDowell, opts for an individualist perspective. In fairness to Kripke, it must be pointed out that he fully anticipates their criticism and raises it explicitly himself; but it is less clear that his skeptical solution's appeal to the community can get out of being subject to the criticism.

40  By "altogether" I mean both the official Platonism which lies in the metaphysical abstractions but also what I am below calling the *ersatz* Platonism which lies in the drive to an objectivity and normativity in lexical matters; and I am saying that it is the latter, which finding the former unpalatable, will look elsewhere for surrogates: in inner convictions, in neurophysiological states, in social practice, in scientific essences, etc.

41  When I say "behavioural," I have in mind intentional behavior. See the next few paragraphs for more on this.

42  The word "naturalism," like the word "disposition" itself, of course, can be used in a way that need not involve any commitment to a reduction of content to non-intentional and purely causal terms. See Strawson (1985) for an explicit defense of such a use. Strawson is by no means alone in this and in fact attributes the use to Wittgenstein himself. It is possible, invoking Davidson's (1970) distinction between questions of

ontology and explanation, to distinguish between naturalism in ontology and naturalism in questions of explanation. One may think human behavior is characterizable and explainable only in non-naturalistic terms and yet not make any concessions to an unscientific non-naturalist ontology of a mental substance. However, in all uses of the term "naturalism" in this book I will, following the dominant current use, mean the stronger commitment to a reduction of intentionality to the non-intentional.

43 See Bilgrami (1987) for a discussion of this point with regard to Fodor's more naturalistic view.

44 I am laboring this point which distinguishes me from the dispositionalist because my view has been the target of much misguided criticism and comment when I have presented it to audiences, who should have been guiding their criticism and comments to the dispositionalist. See n. 62 below and the discussion in the text to which it is attached for ultimate proof of the distinction between my position and the naturalist dispositionalist position.

45 If McDowell and Blackburn are correct about Kripke substituting social dispositions for individual ones, then wrongly rather than rightly.

46 I deliberately emphasize the conjunction. As my constraint (C) makes clear *both* my externalism and anti-foundatinalist holism are part of non-reductionist or anti-naturalist idea. Holism about the mental is not in general and by itself an anti-naturalist idea. By itself, it is perfectly compatible with a reductionist position which has no place for the intentional idiom. Functionalisms of certain varieties are holistic positions which are reductionist in precisely this sense. These functionalism characterize functional role in non-semantic, non-external, inner and purely causal terms. So externalism is necessary to bring in a semantic and intentional element to thwart the reduction of these functionalisms. On the other hand, externalism is by itself not enough to thwart a naturalist reduction of meaning either. Jerry Fodor's denotational, information-theoretic semantics mentioned in chapter 2 is an externalist view whose main point is a naturalist reduction. Thus the holism of my constraint (C) is necessary to thwart Fodor's naturalistic and reductionist exeternalism, which is why Fodor eventually rejects holism. The anti-naturalist force of my constraint lies, therefore, in a conjunction of things. It lies in its *anti-foundationalist holism* but also in that it is an anti-foundationalist constraint on *externalism*. This combination of externalism and anti-foundational holism ensures that the intentional or semantic element is part of the characterization of the states involved.

47 McDowell attributes the view to Wittgenstein but that is a hermeneutical controversy that it would be foolish (for me anyway) to enter.

48 Kripke does not himself make the confusion of thinking that irreducibility in the sense of non-naturalism amounts, in itself, to an irreducibility in the sense of groundless norms. That confusion will occur only in the minds of those who think that any view, such as mine for instance, which opposes the sense of norms demanded by Kripke, must be naturalistic and dispositionalist in the sense we have been discussing above. Kripke does not himself say that the dispositionalist who is his target is restricted to a non-intentional idiom. This is evident from the quotation cited in n. 36 ("Is not the dispositional view an equation of performance and correctness?") He does not anywhere say or even suggest that the performance in the equation is non-intentional.

So his target is not merely the naturalist who functions with only a non-intentional idiom, but any position which has no place for norms in the sense which allows one to say that agents like Bert and Kwert are mistaken in their use of "arthritis." For example, my position would be his target because even though it helps itself to an irreducible intentional idiom, it insists that there is no necessity to seeing those agents as mistaken.

I should add that, as it happens, Kripke also finds the idea of the further irreducibility, i.e. the idea of groundless norms to be very odd (see p. 51), which is why, presumably, he looks for a ground in social practices. It is this aspect of Kripke that McDowell finds mistaken since he thinks Kripke turns to the dispositions of the community and thus gives up on the first sort of irreducibility.

49  See Wright (1989, p. 292) for this criticism and this suggestion of a blunt non-reductionism providing a fact of the matter for Kripke's skeptical question. Wright himself is eventually skeptical that this blunt non-reductionism can be a resting point on the question of the nature of meaning.

50  See Bilgrami (1986) for an appeal to such holism as a means for resisting Dummett's charge that only a reductionist view of meaning along verificationist (or as he calls it "assertibilist") lines can say something informative about meaning. My idea of how to say something more and remain non-reductionist is already implicit in the constraint I have imposed on externalism.

51  Not just orthodox externalism but any externalism is primarily addressing itself to this part of the lexicon. It is addressing itself to the non-logical terms.

52  See also Chomsky (1986, ch. 4) for a rejection of norms in the study of language. I should nevertheless distance my position from his because I know that he has objections to my positive remarks on the regularity-based, externalist-holist nature of concepts. In Bilgrami (1985,1987) I made some very primitive remarks, first, to dissociate normativity in Kripke's sense from the question of meaning and content (suggesting instead that normativity in the sense that is involved in logic were fare more relevant) and, second, to separate the question about the normativity of meaning from the publicness of meaning. In making them I was clearly influenced by the general individualism that both Chomsky's and Davidson's philosophy of language make possible, though I was not aware that Chomsky had written explicitly on Kripke.

53  My use of the word "lexicon" in drawing the distinction with logic might be a little misleading since logical words like "and" and "or" may be said to be part of the lexicon. What I am really distinguishing are the logical terms and the non-logical primitive predicates and singular terms. As stated in n. 51, these non-logical terms are the terms to which any sensible and well-motivated externalism addresses itself.

54  See the discussion of Robinson Crusoe below for more on this.

55  In Bilgrami (1987) I explicitly make the point that this constraint on interpretation that there be overlap in material inferences is not what is driving Kripke and Burge's notion of normativity.

56  It is also probably arguable that the codifications of inductive logic also lack this freedom from context.

57  See Putnam (1962) for a concession that there are such uninteresting cases. There may also be cases of norms governing some concepts which may not quite amount to definitions such as transitivity for the concept of length.

58  I think the philosophers who are most clearly guilty of this are John McDowell and Philip Pettit (1986), esp. p. 13. Here they explicitly invoke Davidson's arguments for the imposition of norms of consistency and coherence in order to defend Burge's social externalism about terms such as "arthritis" and other natural kind terms. If all that I have been saying about the difference between Davidson's interest and the interest in the lexicon is correct, the kind of defence they argue for is simply unavailable.

59  This is a large and disputed claim and I have made it more dogmatically than I would have cared to. It is not something that I can discuss here and I do not make any crucial use of it for my other claims.

60  Let me repeat once again that the sense of regularity is not the one of the naturalistic dispositionalist picture but in the sense which you find in a holistic theory of interpretation for individual agents.

61  See Davidson (1967) for a statement of the need to fulfill these desiderata and Chomsky (1957) for the first statement of such desiderata but with an emphasis on grammaticality rather than meaning or understanding.

62  Notice that the fact that I allow this sense of norms which are based on *intentions* of speakers makes it absolutely clear that my opposition to Kripke's notion of normativity is not a result of some hidden commitment to a naturalist dispositional picture of the mind. The fact that Kripke demands more of normativity (see below) than is offered by this sort of normativity which I am allowing, and which is secondary to speakers' intentions to communicate, makes it absolutely clear that he is just as opposed to non-reductionist, non-naturalist views which fall short of his demand for normativity as he is to reductionist, naturalist views.

63  Of course, often, as when we are being poetic or perverse, we may *deliberately* flout this tacit hypothetical norm. Those, however, are cases essentially different from Bert.

64  Notice that I am not saying that this hypothetical norm is sufficient for meaning. Someone may think I am saying that, since I am denying that the categorical norm I am contrasting it with is necessary. But to say it is sufficient would be false since, I suppose, someone may not ever have the desire to be easily understood and so the antecedent of the conditional would be false – and here one would want to deny that there was meaning even though the conditional remained true. Rather my point simply is that there are no categorical or intrinsic norms of the lexicon, but, given the desire to communicate, one often implicitly thinks one ought to do whatever it is that fulfills and facilitates that desire. If that is a norm, then it is at best a hypothetical norm in precisely the sense that Kant defined and criticized. It is a norm which tells us how best to bring about something extrinsic which we want.

65  This example is not intended as suggesting that the host mishears the Cambridge philosopher nor that he is too polite to acknowledge what she said. Rather, the scene intended is that he hears correctly and interprets the utterance as an expression of gratitude. See Davidson (1986) for examples put to similar use.

66  I assume that Kripke's discussion is meant to cover this more extreme example of Crusoe we are considering.

67  I say "may be" all right deliberately because there is the perfectly serious claim that radical interpretation begins at home; so the fact of there being the same sounds need not get us around the problem of how to interpret him discussed in the next few paragraphs.

68 That is the interesting case here since it brings up the question of mistakenness, i.e. the case where Crusoe's translator belongs to the community in which the word "arthritis" is used in the way we use it (for a disease of the joints only) but Crusoe himself uses 'gavagai' for a wider class of ailments.

69 This may not be quite right. There is a question as to whether the demand that meaning and belief be public actually requires there to be an attributor or not. See below for more on this.

70 Davidson actually thinks more than a second person is needed for thought and meaning. He thinks a triangulation of two persons and the external world is needed. Since I am only concerned here with the need for a second person I have not brought in this further requirement.

71 It is possible, of course, that someone should want to say that Kripke had got Wittgenstein wrong and that Wittgenstein's talk of "custom" and "practice" had in mind just this Davidsonian idea of the social and nothing stronger, that his idea of norm was only this minimal sense of what is required to ground the notion of similarity. (He could point out as evidence of this that the Davidsonian argument from judgments of sameness is almost identical to the anti-private language argument in Wittgenstein.) But this would mean interpreting the significance of Wittegenstein's own remarks about the gap between inner convictions of what seems to be the case and what is the case, not as reflecting a Kripke-like demand for normativity in the use of items in the lexicon; but rather as just this very much more underlying demand for an inter-subjective basis of similarity judgments, a demand so underlying that it might well be made even of the regularity-based, individualistic picture of concepts I am promoting. That would, in turn, mean that Wittgenstein would have repudiated Kripke's view that KWert poses a serious skeptical threat to meaning; and it would also mean that he would have rejected Burge's (1979) view about the Bert case, i.e. rejected a view explicitly presented by Burge at the beginning of that paper as being a Wittgensteinian view. Both these views are only supportable by a conception of normativity relevant to meaning that is over and above the minimal and underlying sense of norm just mentioned.

Actually, though I do think it is possible to say that Wittgenstein probably had in mind to argue for something much closer to Davidson's view than Kripke's, I think my remark in parenthesis earlier in the note is an exaggeration. It is very hard to find Davidson's argument clearly in the Wittgenstein text and it would require a certain amount of interpretative adding and subtracting to make it come out so. That is an interesting subject, but not for now.

72 The case of Burge is a little complicated. A lot depends on whether Burge takes reference or extension in the sense defined by Kripke and Putnam as being primary or whether he takes social externalism as we have been discussing as being primary. The difference is that the latter emphasizes the constitutive force of the community and its experts rather than the scientific essences and objective natures of natural kinds. And that amounts to a real difference because communities and their experts can be wrong about the objective natures and scientific essences of natural kinds. In a recent paper Burge himself seems to have changed his primary emphasis from the social view to the Kripke/Putnam view. See especially n. 13 of Burge (1989) where he criticizes

Loar's (1985a) reading of his view. The significance underlying the shift for the question of theory-change is simply this. If we emphasized the social externalism only we could only provide for theory-disagreements within communities but not between communities. We could not allow that because the anchors provided by social externalism can, *ex hypothesi,* only be intra-communal. So Burge's view, prior to the shift in emphasis, may have only a limited usefulness for this line of motivation. Hence this line of motivation motivates the two other orthodox externalism more obviously than it motivates social externalism.

73  Even Davidson, who with his emphasis on interpretation eschews the metaphysics underlying the causal account and with his rejection of Burge eschews social externalism, nevertheless insists on reference in a way that is motivated by a desire not to give up entirely on the distinction we are discussing. I cannot cite a reference for this motivation in him because it was conveyed to me in conversations. I will discuss Davidson in chapter 4 and show why his view, though it shuns these other views of reference, nevertheless in many ways approximates the idea of wide content.

74  That is, if I insist on holding on to *my* notion of externalist content I must at least add on wide content to it as a further kind of content which allows for our intuitions about there being theory-change. In other words, I must bifurcate content myself, if not into wide and narrow content than into wide content and my externalist content which meets constraint. (C)

75  The distinction has of course, been a subject of much discussion in the philosophy of science, especially since the appearance of Kuhn (1962). Scheffler (1967) is an explicit attempt to save the distinction from collapse by introducing a theory of direct reference for the theoretical terms in scientific theories. Scheffler, of course, does not extend the line of thought to the wider philosophy-of-mind consequences for the nature of intentional content. There is, in fact, hardly any explicit treatment that I know of which does extend it in this way to motivate wide content, thought in Putnam (1975) there are some remarks to that effect, as there are in White (1983). And Fodor (1987) raises the issue in the context of a discussion of holism about intentionality.

Since I cannot here take up the question of meaning change and theory change with any depth or sophistication as it applies to the details of the nature of scientific theories, I will restrict my discussion to the more general issue about wide content. The crudeness of my suggestion below about how my view can account for intuitions about theory-change without an appeal to wide content, though it is introduced with a simple scientific example, obviously would need much refinement in the narrower context of philosophy of science. Since that is not the context of my present discussion, I will not try to refine it below. But I hope the suggestion does bring out the uncompulsoriness of wide content for the intuition that an agent may change his belief or theories rather than his meanings. For a fuller treatment of the consequences of the suggestion for the philosophy of science, see Khalidi (1991).

76  For the reason given in n. 72, the causal rather than the social versions of orthodox externalism are more appropriate for dealing with such cases of theory-change. So, I will only talk about the causal accounts during this discussion.

77  Obviously in the example being discussed where different natural languages are involved, the causal account as we find it in Kripke, will need to include, as a part of

the causal chains it posits, events that involve translations. Fodor's causal account which is given directly for a "language of thought" bypasses the complication, at this level, of their being two natural languages.

78 Such indexical beliefs, as I pointed out in chapter 1, are absolutely essential to my externalism, about concepts and contents, in any case. They are the points at which external items enter thought. It is inevitable, then, that they should play a key role in fixing the common subject matter of changes and disagreements in beliefs. But equally, as I have said in chapter 2, there is no reason to think that these indexicals in these thoughts, despite their ineliminability, are not mediated by descriptions and beliefs. No rigidity is being admitted, not even in descriptions. That is one of the effects of imposing (C). I say more about indexicals in chapter 4.

79 It is true that I have nothing to say against those who claim that they have an intuition that even if there were absolutely no shared beliefs between agents, they are still talking about the same thing. I simply do not share that intuition and in fact find the idea that we are still talking about the same thing highly unintuitive. So, I have not argued that my unified picture of content can accommodate the notion of theory-change, if one is working with what I take to be a highly extreme and unintuitive idea of when there is theory-change. Such claims to intuition are impossible to argue against. One can only listen to the examples that are offered to jog one's intuition and then respond. I have unfailingly found that whenever my intuition has been jogged toward admitting theory-change or toward admitting genuine singular thought, it has always been because I have found some shared beliefs or some descriptions present, even if, in the limiting case (but *only* in the limiting case) they take the form of relatively trivial metalinguistic specifications. I stress again that these metalinguistic specifications are not a routine part of the individuation and specification of concepts. They are dictated by the particular facts of given localities. As I make clear in chapter 2, n. 28, most concepts in most localities do not get metalinguistic specifications. So, my concession that metalinguistic specifications must minimally be allowed in particular extreme cases of intuitions about theory-change is no concession at all to the referential individuation of concepts which I am opposing. It would only be a concession if I also allowed that these specifications are always routinely there in all concept-individuation. That would compromise the work being done by the non-metalinguistically characterized descriptions. I insist that in most localities the work of concept-individuation *is* being done only and entirely by the non-metalinguistically specified descriptions.)

Many of the examples presented tend to involve the presence of two objects and a single term. Here is one. A boy goes to a party and meets two other boys, each called Tom. Much later he tells his parents "Tom was nice" but he has no distinguishing memory of which of the two Toms was nice. In fact, he does not even recall that there were two Toms. The intuition that we are supposed to have is that his term "Tom" refers to one of the boys he met and he is talking about that boy. And only unmediated causal links can account for that since, *ex hypothesi*, there are no distinguishing descriptions or beliefs that he has. I simply lack the intuition that he is talking of one of the boys he met. Let us try to jog one's intuition further by adding a bit of additional information to the example: the parents know that their son would have found one of the Toms nice but not the other, i.e. they know their son well and they know what sort of person he likes and they know which of the two Toms was such a person. Doesn't that add weight toward the intuition that he was talking of one of the Toms? It honestly does not for me, unless one is prepared to say that the son, at least inarticulately, had the distinguishing beliefs that his parents could articulate.

### *Chapter 4   Truth and the Locality of Content*

1   See Davidson (1967) for an initial statement of the relevance of Tarski-style truth-theories to the themes of meaning and intentionality. The relevance is spelt out in much greater detail in Davidson (1973b).
2   The context of McDowell's proposal is to handle Frege's puzzle about identity.
3   This objection was raised against me by Loar in (1985b).
4   I am repeating here, what has come up before in earlier chapters, that those who thing it is enough just to say "'water' refers to *water*" with a thump of the table as they utter "water" on the right-hand side, without making any concession that this summarizes something else much richer, must be seen to have a mysterious and unsatisfactory account of concepts and term-meanings.
5   Fodor has, himself, made this criticism of my locality thesis.
6   Indeed, Fodor's anti-holism can be seen as motivated by the desire to save meaning against holism despite giving up on the analytic-synthetic distinction. For him, it is saved by denying holistic meaning-theories and making concepts purely local and primitive via strict denotation in the causal-informational account he favors. But for me, it is saved by the locality thesis I have been sketching, which grants holistic meaning theories and shuns the idea of primitive concepts and denotational semantics in his sense.
7   I should point out that there may be *other* reasons (such as, for instance, those having to do with the difficulty of saying in advance what goes into *ceteris paribus* clauses) which make psychological generalizations low grade. But they raise a quite different problem from the one we are addressing in this objection to holism. The objection to holism arises for even these low-grade generalizations.
8   Of course, there may be cases when all that is aggregated is carried over to the local level. The cases in which this is likely to happen are when an agent relies almost exclusively on another for some concept of his and does not have many other beliefs of his own. In such a case there is not much else to carry to a locality except the belief that $x$ is whatever Maggie the expert calls "$x$".
9   There may, of course, be quite independent reasons for Fodor's desire to make a naturalistic reduction from the one we are considering here. Since this not a book on the subject of the naturalistic, or any other, reduction of content, I need not take up those reasons here. I only wanted to put aside any reason in favor of naturalism which sees naturalism as the only way to provide an atomistic, anti-holistic, denotational semantics. Such a semantics is not necessary because, if I am right, Fodor's fears about what follows from holism are unfounded.
10   It is an interesting fact that anti-holistic foundationalism is the common element in

both Fodor's and Michael Dummett's (1973) views on meaning. (Dummett calls his anti-holism "molecularism." ) They both, of course, end up with very different positions. Fodor seeks to combat holism by trying to provide a denotational semantics that invokes, via information theoretic means, an atomistic version of naturalistic reduction of content and meaning. Dummett, on the other hand, combats holism by means of the idea of the canonical verification of all sentences in terms of a class of privileged sentences, whose verification is direct and non-problematic, and which forms a proper fragment of the totality of sentences. Thus, anti-holism respectively promotes a version of naturalism and verificationism in these two philosophers. My externalist position embraces holism and rejects both these forms of reduction, at the same time as it rejects truth-conditional theories of meaning, in the standard sense, which understand the meaning-giving truth-conditions to be other than agents' conceptions of the truth. See Bilgrami (1986) for a full discussion of the intimate connections between Dummett's verificationism, his anti-holism and his commitment to the idea that meaning is public.

11 I say "in effect" because various things he says about such truth-theories in McDowell (1976) would contradict the idea that their clauses summarize agents' beliefs. In extensive unpublished comments on the material of this chapter he has explicitly expressed this disagreement.

12 Unlike, for instance, Fodor who thinks that puzzles of this kind can be solved without appeal to beliefs with contents but by appeal to different causal roles (see chapter 2).

13 See Dummett's (1973) discussion of Frege's notion of sense. See also Chomsky (1965).

14 Even the knowledge which allows for the derivation of "truth"-conditions from the beliefs summarized in the base "reference"-clauses of the truth-theory (non-austerely conceived in my way) is surely recognizable by agents in a way that is unthinkable for the highly structural knowledge posited by generative grammarians. There is some marginally greater justification in thinking of this more constructive axiom as being different from the base-clause axioms, different in the sense of being less within the ken of recallability to an agent's awareness upon reflection. But this admission does not amount to a serious problem since the puzzles are solved by the modified *base* clauses of the truth-theory.

15 Actually, McDowell grants that the hallucinating agent has a singular thought in second intention, as it were. He grants that the agent *thinks* that he has a content that he could express by saying "That table is round", but he, in fact, does not have it. I believe, and I believe many others believe, that it is very unintuitive to say that he in fact does not. These others, however, are motivated to think it unintuitive and draw consequences from thinking it unintuitive that I disagree with as much as I disagree with anything in McDowell. These disagreements between me and the others will emerge below.

16 Again, not every single concept but see chapter 1 for that caveat.

17 I have stressed the unique role of demonstratives in accounting for agency. I have not stressed the other aspect Evans (1982) stresses of how demonstrative thought is acquired. In a subtle and powerful but, all the same, unconvincing discussion of this aspect of demonstrative thought, Evans stresses that a proper understanding of this

aspect shows that demonstrative reference is, as he puts it, "identification-free." If he is right that would repudiate my insistence on the mediation by belief and description involved in demonstrative thought, and it would redeem the Russellian view. His argument turns on the idea of the normal functioning of our information-acquiring and information-retrieving mechanisms of perception and memory; the idea is supposed to account for the special features of demonsrative-thought, including I-thoughts, without the need for identifying beliefs.

I do not wish to deny that the normal functioning of our information-acquiring and retrieving mechanisms is a necessary condition for having demonstrative-thought. I have said as much when I insisted that there must, in general, be causal (sensory) relations with the external world in order to have demonstrative-thoughts at all. But I deny that the agent who, for instance, says "That is round" should always have an answer to the question "which object is that object?" The answer could in some cases be as trivial as "The object I am focussing on" but it cannot be so trivial as "The object that my expression 'that' refers to." My insistence on there being such an answer available from the agent is because if there is not, then it leaves things with a mystery as to what thought the agent really thinks he has. Talk of "information-acquiring mechanisms," though true, does not remove this mystery. For more on this notion of mystery, see my discussion of the 'Third Objection' in the section entitled "Some Objections to the Charge of Disunity" in chapter 2. For a convincing description-theoretic treatment of "I", see Rovane (1987).

18 I say "eventually" because obviously the object is not always going to be present, so the demonstrative need not at any given time and place be used in the strict sense of pointing. If the agent has at no time been in the presence of the object, then he must be relying in some way on others who have. In this case the "eventually" is even more emphatic.

19 McDowell (1982) makes this point explicitly, saying that it is supported by our ordinary ways of thinking about and reporting content.

20 They both have said so explicitly in the articles already cited.

21 This is the argument in the section 'The Refutation of Idealism' Kant (1929).

22 I have also discussed this response in Bilgrami (1987).

23 Putting aside the worry just means that one does not have to work with the subscripted ways of representing his concepts – "London" and "*Londres*" will do.

24 See Colin McGinn (1982a, p. 240) for an interpretation of Davidson that sees him as a bifurcationist. But McGinn gets the bifurcation wrong when he says that it is bifurcation into wide and narrow content. It should be stressed again, therefore, that my reason for saying Davidson may in the end encourage bifurcation does not turn in any way on any commitment on his part to a second notion of content that is motivated by *internalism*.

25 I should point out again what I have pointed out throughout Chapter 2 that though I have talked of Burge as one of these other externalists, who is committed to a bifurcation, he does not count himself a bifurcationist. But others, such as Loar, who embrace Burge's view of content, do, plausibly, see Burge as forcing it.

26 I say "extra" brand of holism because it is more than the holism I have committed myself to with constraint (C). It is more than the holism which says that a concept is

the concept it is because it stands in inferential relations with other concepts. It is more than the holism which says that a belief cannot be the belief it is unless there are other beliefs with which it is inferentially related. For more on this extra holism see below.

27 For this example, see Davidson's Dewey Lectures, in particular Dewey Lecture 2, given at the University of Minnesota and as yet unpublished. The point is made in different ways in many other published sources.

28 It should be pointed out in fairness to the social view of externalism that it is not so starkly different from Davidson's position in this respect as the other externalist views he differs from. The social view can claim that truth-conditions are "fixed" only to the extent that the social linguistic practices are stable. But still the fluidity that changes in social linguistic practices would bring is very different from the fluidity proposed by Davidson, which comes from the dialectic interplay between two interdependent components and not from the fact of a diachronic instability in social practice.

29 See my "Meaning as Invariance" (unpublished) for a detailed treatment of such an idea of meaning from within a Davidsonian framework on meaning. This treatment was a large part of my PhD dissertation. And though the idea still strikes me as right, I would now embed it in a different framework.

30 I discuss all three below in the text. There is a fourth aspect of Fregean sense which many also find undesirable – its Platonism – which I will ignore, since it is too obvious that my way of developing Frege's relevance to intentionality cannot possibly be associated with it.

31 The idea of such a cluster view of the sense of proper names was famously proposed by Searle (1958, 1969) and has been the subject of much discussion since then. It was seen not to have overcome the problems that arose for the stricter view, only to have complicated them. Here I am only discussing the charge that both views lead to definitions and to analyticity. There is also the charge that comes from Kripke's attack in (Kripke 1972) on all versions of the description theory of the sense of proper names. I said something about that charge in the discussion of theory-change in the last chapter.

32 Chomsky has long argued that semantics has nothing to do with the study of language or concepts. This has seemed perverse and wrong-headed to almost all philosophers and even many linguists. But that judgment is based on an unsympathetic interpretation of his view. If the position on meaning and content that I have been elaborating over these many chapters has convinced anyone, it should make good sense of Chomsky's allergy to the pursuit of semantics. Chomsky has often said that the study of syntax is where the study of mental representation must take place. A careful and sympathetic reading of Chomsky's claims to this effect should properly understand his use of the label "syntax" here as stemming from an instinctive repudiation of a certain standard idea of semantics, and understand it *broadly* so as to include the idea of agents' conceptions. I do not deny that it is confusing to call it "syntax." Even if a study of meaning gives up on the standard idea of semantics, and instead gives a central place go something like agents' conceptions, it can only lead to misunderstanding to call it "syntax." And I believe that Chomsky has had more than his share of being misunderstood by philosophers. But his deep point remains. The rest is mere amicable dispu-

tation about words. The point sympathetic to Chomsky which is worth emphasizing is that because of the stranglehold that the standard idea of semantics has had, philosophers and linguists have failed to see something important which drove Chomsky to put things the way he does.

33 Loar's point has been made before by many who have taken a truth-conditional view of meaning but Loar himself explicitly connects it with wide content, and in putting the point this way I will follow him. Without mentioning wide content, Hartry Field (1972) makes the same point in response to the question: why do we ever need to introduce the concept of truth? Field's later work makes fully clear that what he has in mind is the concept of truth which goes into the individuation of wide content. See also Lepore and Loewer (1981) and Lycan (1986) for a defence, roughly along Field's lines, of Davidson's way of connecting meaning and truth-conditions.

34 See Putnam (1978, pp. 99-103) for this appeal to success. Also Schiffer (1981). They both appeal to success to show what function the concept of truth has in our conceptual scheme, but, as stated in n. 33, I am making the explicit connection with the concept of wide content.

## *Chapter 5   The Case for Externalism*

1　The main problem, as pointed out in the earlier discussion, was to account for error.

2　Here again, as throughout the book, I am ignoring the motivation for internalism which claims that it is a necessary condition for psychology to be a strict science, that externalism will not allow for a genuinely naturalistic psychology. My interest is only in whether content as it performs in commonsense psychological explanation (that-clause content) demands internalism or externalism. A number of philosophers–Searle, Loar and a host of others–do think that it demands internalism, and it is they whom I am addressing.

3　Though Searle voices the concerns and intuitions of a number of philosophers on important details, there are not many philosophers who take the position that we have no need for any externalist notion of content. At any rate the position does not have the sort of powerful and concerted community voice that makes the bifurcationist position such an orthodoxy in our times.

4　The only notion of internalist content which would, perhaps, not be the target of these arguments is a notion of narrow content which is defined parasitically on wide content. That notion, though, would only doubtfully fulfill the motivations with which narrow content is usually posited. See my brief discussion of such a notion (Bilgrami 1986).

5　The word "satisfies" is used by Searle to mark the relation that some states of affairs, events, objects ... have to a belief, which would make the belief true; or have to a desire, which would fulfill the desire, and so on. His notion of satisfaction is thus a generalization of the notion of truth-conditions; a generalization made in order to individuate the content of beliefs and intentional states other than beliefs as well; such as, for instance, desire.

6　See Bilgrami (1989b) for a more thorough critique of Searle's internalism and his view of intentionality, generally.

7 Kant himself did not raise this particular question since he did not ever raise the question of judgment in communication, but only judgment in experience. For an interesting discussion of the limitation of Kant's interests and its possible broadening in the philosophy of language and mind, see Rovane (1986).

8 See also Bilgrami (1985, 1987) for this argument for externalism.

9 I discuss this reduction in my "Comments on McDowell's Functionalism and Anomalous Monism" (unpublished) presented at a symposium with McDowell on "The Philosophy of Donald Davidson" held at Rutgers University, (May 1984).

10 I shall take it for now that the issue of skepticism about other minds *is* the issue about publicness. A little later I will discuss a view, due to Nagel, which tries to force the two issues apart, but for the purposes of the present discussion of McDowell, nothing misleading or unfair is being perpetrated by making this equation, which is implied by his own answer.

11 See McDowell (1981, 1987). The view was already to be found in his earlier paper which we considered in chapter, 4 (McDowell 1976).

12 Stroud earlier suggests that Kant saw clearly that direct realism should not involve the impossibility of error such as in hallucinations. It is possible that the specific appeal to space as a form of sensibility does not produce a form of direct realism about outer objects that entails difficulties for accounting for error. If so that would depend on details in Kant that cannot be investigated here. In any case, Stroud does not say how Kant avoids the problem. Even if he avoids it, the point I am arguing remains: his direct realism, via transcendental idealism, is not necessary if he has an independent and general argument to show that inner experience, in general, is dependent on outer experience, in general.

13 Famously, Strawson (1966). Both the cited sections from Kant are, of course, in Kant (1929).

14 As an aside, I should say that I believe that Wittgenstein, who did so much to raise the question about publicness, himself often took this simple stance and relied heavily on the second of our unsatisfactory alternative answers to the publicness question. He did not deny externalism but he nowhere explicitly demanded that meanings be constituted externally in the way I have. His emphasis, like McDowell's, was on the direct perception of meanings which encourages the simple stance. This was especially so in those passages where he asked the reader not to indulge in philosophy but to "look and see," The "look and see" idea is part of the directness of our observation of meaning – and the external world – so that skeptical questions about these things cannot even arise. When he stresses this aspect, the social aspect that Kripke stresses in his skeptical solution becomes more problematic. We could reconcile these two aspects by saying that the social aspect makes possible the direct perceptual aspect in the sense that we can directly perceive the meanings of other in our linguistic community but not in other linguistic communities. But that would be to change Kripke's subject to a phenomenological one which he did not intend it to be.

15 My claim here is not the Davidsonian claim that Nagel discusses i.e. any language, thus a language of super-knowers, is translatable by any other language user, thus translatable by us. This seems to imply that it is translatable by us now. I am not claiming that as the discussion above should have made obvious. That claim is,

*possibly*, susceptible to the objection that some have raised against it, viz. that a spectrum of increasingly unshared beliefs between an initial agent and others at the further end of the spectrum – though at each interval there would be mostly shared belief between immediately adjacement agents – may lead to an agent at the other extreme who has hardly any overlap of belief with the initial agent, and is therefore, by Davidsonian standards, uninterpretable by him. No claim I have made above is susceptible to any such argument.

16  See Peacocke (1988) for an excellent and satisfying discussion of a notion of a post-verificationist principle of intelligibility in empirical matters.

17  Burge does not use my words "internalism" and "externalism" but instead "perceptual individualism" and "perceptual non-individualism." Since I have argued that externalism and individualism are perfectly compatible, I have substituted my words for his. The substitution in no way misrepresents his position in the paper under discussion, because the paper makes no appeal, in its argument, to the social externalism that contrasts with both individualistic externalism and internalism. The paper's argument can be carried on, and assessed for its plausibility, even if Burge is wrong in his other papers where he argues that content is socially constituted in a way that I have been resisting in earlier chapters.

18  I am compressing a lot in the exposition. As a result, I have left out many refinements and motivations since I do not want this primarily to be a discussion of Burge's (1985) paper but rather, as I go on to say below, a way of contrasting the more and less ambitious things one can try to say against internalism in its epistemological context. One of the things I have left out is the precise role of the second premise, and another is the reason for his fastening on such small objective entities as cracks and shadows. The reader interested in the issue for their own sake and independent of my dialectic is advised to look at Burge's text for those details.

19  I say "miracles" generally rather than talk of evil demons because strictly speaking evil demon explanations of content should count as externalist. But, it should be understood that, given the externalism that Burge and I and everyone else who is an externalist wants to establish, these explanations must count as capitulation to internalism, as Descartes's use of them makes clear.

20  Descartes himself claims innateness for mathematics and therefore the concept of extension; and, as for the vast lexicon of concepts regarding material objects we are concerned with, his view, in the Meditations, is that since he has as much reality as material substance, he has the concept of material substance. This provides all the ingredients for his appeal to innate ideas to justify them: these concepts are presumably constructs out of three things: what is given in sense experience, the idea of material substance and the innate concept of extension. It is a curious mix of phenomenalism, nativism and the wholly obscure notion of the possession of degrees of reality and its implications.

21  See Burge's discussion in the early pages of his paper (1985) for a brief but excellent analytical and historical treatment of formulations of internalism, and of the difficulties of formulating a single characterization that is both precise and historically accurate.

22  In this passage he does not mention the social accounts but only the causal-theoretic. He later criticizes the social accounts as well for leaving out the introspective or phenomenological element (see Loar 1987, p. 97).

23 I should add that I have given no argument against reduction of intentionality in this book. I am only saying here that while my constraint is in place, reduction is being denied. I have said little to justify it against the reductionist.

24 I should point out that Loar, himself, in both these papers I have cited, wished eventually to give a strict naturalistic account of content and show the phenomenological properties of content he presents as eventually illusory; but that is irrelevant to the present discussion. I wish no such eventual illusory status for the irreducible representational content presented in my account. I use the word 'strict' naturalist account because I take my own irreducibilist account to be naturalistic in the more casual sense that merely requires things to be in the realm of the causal order but not necessarily non-intentional.

25 Searle strongly hints at this position in various places, especially in his "What is Wrong with the Philosophy of Mind" (Unpublished manuscript, 1991).

26 I am not here able to compare my objection to the significance of this question to thoughts, with a somewhat more complicated and different response I would have to the significance of this question to other mental states, such as pain.

27 See the beginning of the chapter for a discussion of the two assumptions, and the promise of the connection between them in one of the criticisms brought against them.

28 By "no more," I mean no more to the necessary conditions for realism only in the context of the question about the interest-relativity of third-person attributions. It should be obvious that, more generally speaking, this is only one necessary, and not a sufficient, condition for realism about intentional states. Other necessary conditions would be a certain holistic complexity, and also a self-reflexivity regarding intentional states on the part of the agent. This is why, of course, talk of the vending machine as having such states is instrumental. A further necessary condition might be that there are certain limitations on the extent of indeterminacy that the attributions are subject to. Imposing the right constraints goes a long way towards reducing indeterminacy. Of course, it will not eliminate it altogether. But see the ensuing discussion on the indeterminacy that remains.

29 I should make clear that I am leaving out of this discussion, Quine's idea of indeterminacy as involving something over and above undertermination in theory of meaning; an idea that seems to me, as it did to many others before me, to make its case by adopting an unargued-for physicalism. That further notion of indeterminacy is not relevant to my dicussion.

30 Also there is some doubt that the actual example of interpretative indeterminacy in belief-attribution, which he offers in the paper, is one that Davidson will even consider as genuinely a case of indeterminacy in the sense that Davidson discusses it, a sense which requires no controversy about empirical equivalence. This requires a level of (non-trivial) description of the predictions of behavior and of pattern of assent and dissent, in which the predictions are the same on both theories. Dennett nowhere offers such an example in his paper. So there is a real question as to whether, in attacking Davidson's temperature analogy, he is keeping faith with the specific indeterminacy problem that that analogy was supposed to speak to in Davidson.

31 See the discussion of the relation, in Davidson's theory, between the belief component and the meaning or reference component in chapter 4.

32 I had, in my dissertation 'Meaning and Invariance' (University of Chicago, 1983), spelt out in some detail what this more complicated invariance would look like. But now, as I said in chapter 4, I think that the whole idea of a theory of interpretation having two such components (meaning, belief) is wrong.

## Epilogue

1 Thomas Nagel, too, might be counted as committed to a version of Cartesian internalism. I am being careful to say Cartesian internalism because in neither of these philosophers is the internalism of the mental one can trace to Descartes accompanied by the Cartesian view that the mind is a separate substance. There is no accompanying commitment to Descartes's dualism.

2 Specially when narrow content is seen as specifiable independently of wide or externalist content generally.

3 This has sometimes been said to me by those who have themselves defined externalism explicitly in their writing as nothing more and nothing other than a doctrine about content which denies that content is constituted independently of our relations with the external world.

## Appendix

1 For something short of this see my "Self-knowledge and Resentment" forthcoming in *Philosophical Topics*.

2 He first raised the problem in Wright (1984) but has subsequently been more explicit about it (Wright 1989a,b,c).

3 I am careful to say "some form or other" for various reasons but most particularly because I would not, myself, want intentionality to be seen as judgment-dependent in any significant way resembling the model of judgment-dependence that Wright pursues for color, earlier in the same paper (See Wright 1989c, s. III).

4 Readers will recognize that this is a starting point for Strawson's non-metaphysical account of freedom and accountability. This is not surprising since I want to tie the question of self-knowledge with the question of moral responsibility. Thus my strategy for self-knowledge is akin to his strategy for free will. Frustrated with the efforts at giving a metaphysical justification of our free will, he turns to the reactive attitudes. Frustrated with the efforts to give an epistemological justification of our self-knowledge, I turn to them too. I do, however, think that there is more to be said by way of justifying our reactive attitudes than he does or I do in stating the first step in my argument.

5 See n. 3 above for a partial hint of what I mean by this.

6 For the idea that propositional attitudes themselves should be seen as commitments on the part of agents and, therefore, caught up with intellectual responsibility and self-knowledge see Levi (1980). The idea is, in many ways, an attractive one but it is not clear to me that it is compulsory to see propositional attitudes along those lines.

This is another of the issues that needs to be discussed in greater detail. See my forthcoming paper, cited in n. 1, for a more detailed discussion of it.

7   By "never fully" I intend to gesture to the failure in Wright – unarmed with something like my proposal – to provide a real argument against alternative explanations of the presumption of self-knowledge which allow us to deny the constitutive thesis.

# Bibliography

Armstrong, D. M. 1968: *A Materialist Theory of Mind* (London: Routledge and Kegan Paul).

Bilgrami, A. 1983a: Meaning as Invariance. Unpublished dissertation submitted to the University of Chicago.

Bilgrami, A. 1983b: Review of Christopher Peacocke's *Holistic Explanation. Journal of Philosophy* 80.

Bilgrami, A. 1984: Comments on John McDowell's "Functionalism and Anomolous Monism." Paper presented at a Symposium with John McDowell on "The Philosophy of Donald Davidson., Rutgers University, May 1984.

Bilgrami, A. 1985: Comments on Loar. In *Contents of Thought,* eds R H Grimm and D. D. Merrill (Tucson, Arizona: University of Arizona Press).

Bilgrami, A 1986: Meaning, Holism and Use. In *Truth and Interpretation, Perspectives on the Philosophy of Donald Davidson,* ed. E. LePore (Oxford: Basil Blackwell).

Bilgrami, A. 1987: An Externalist Account of Psychological Content. *Philosophical Topics* 15.

Bilgrami, A. 1989a: Comments on James Higginbotham's "Knowledge of Reference." Paper presented at a Symposium with James Higginbotham on "Representation and Realism", Columbia University, December 1989.

Bilgrami, A. 1989b: Realism without Internalism. *Journal of Philosophy* 86.

Bilgrami, A. 1991a: Objects of Thought. In *Consciousness,* ed. Enrique Villanenva (Rowman and Littlefield).

Bilgrami, A. 1991b: The Unity and Autonomy of Content. Unpublished MS.

Bilgrami, A. (1992): Self-Knowledge and Resentment. *Philosophical Topics* (Special Issue on the Philosophy of Hilary Putnam). In the press.

Blackburn, S. 1984: The individual Strikes Back. *Synthese 58.*

Block, N. 1987a: Advertisement for a Semantics for Psychology. In *Midwest Studies in Philosophy* 10: *Studies in the Philosophy of Mind,* eds P. French, T. Uehting, H. Wettstein (Minneapolis: University of Minnesota Press).

Block, N. 1981: Psychologism and Behaviourism. Philosophical Review 90.

Block, N. 1987b: Functional Role and Truth Conditions. *The Aristotelian Society* 61.

Burge, T. 1979: Individualism and the Mental. In *Midwest Studies in Philosophy* 6: Studies in Metaphysics, eds P. French, T. Uehling, H. Wettstein (Minneapolis: University of Minnesota Press).

Burge, T. 1982: Two Thought Experiments Reviewed. *Notre Dame Journal of Formal Logic* 23.

Burge, T. 1985: Cartesian Error and the Objectivity of Perception. In *Contents of Thought,* ed. R. H. Grimm and D. D. Merrill (Tucson: The Univeristy of Arizona Press).

Burge, T. 1986a: Individualism and Psychology. *Philosophical Review* 95.

Burge, T. 1986b: Intellectual Norms and Foundations of Mind. *Journal of Philosophy* 83.

Burge, T, 1988: Individualism and Self-Knowledge. *Journal of Philosophy* 85.

Burge, T. 1989: Wherein is Language Social? In *Reflections on Chomsky*, ed. A. George (Oxford: Basil Blackwell).

Chomsky, N. 1957: *Syntactic Structures* (Mouton: The Hague).

Chomsky, N. 1965: *Aspects of the Theory of Syntax* (Cambridge, Mass.: MIT Press).

Chomsky, N. 1986: *Knowledge of Language: Its Nature, Origin and Use* (New York: Praeger).

Chomsky, N. 1989: Mental Constructions and Social Reality. *Proceedings of the Conference on Knowledge and Language,* Groningen, May 1989.

Churchland, P. M. 1981: Eliminative Materialism and Propositional Attitudes. *Journal of Philosophy* 78.

Churchhland, P. M. 1987: Epistemology in the Age of Neuroscience. *Journal of Philosophy* 84.

Davidson, D. 1967: Truth and Meaning. *Inquiries into Truth and Interpretation* (Oxford: Clarendon Press).

Davidson, D. 1973a: Belief and the Basis of Meaning. *Inquiries into Truth and Interpretation* (Oxford: Clarendon Press).

Davidson, D. 1973b: Radical Interpretation. *Inquiries into Truth and Interpretation* (Oxford: Clarendon Press).

Davidson, D. 1974: Dewey lectures delivered at the University of Minnesota.

Dawidson, D. 1977: Reality without Reference. *Dialectica* 31.

Davidson, D. 1982: Rational Animals. *Dialectica* 36.

Davidson, D. 1984a: Theories of Meaning and Learnable Languages. *Inquiries into Truth and Interpretation* (Oxford: Clarendon Press).

Davidson, D. 1984b: On the Very Idea of a Conceptual Scheme. *Inquiries into Truth and Interpretation* (Oxford: Clarendon Press).

Davidson, D. 1986: A. Coherence Theory of Truth and Knowledge. In *Truth and Interpretation,* ed. E. Lepore (Oxford: Basil Blackwell).

Davidson, D. 1987: Knowing One's Own Mind. *Proceedings and Addresses of the American Philosophical Association* 60.

Davidson, D. 1991: What is before the Mind. In *Consciousness* ed. E. Villanueva (Oxford: Basil Blackwell).

Dennett, D. 1982: Beyond Belief. In *Objects of Thought*, ed. A. Woodfield (Oxford: Oxford University Press).

Dennett, D. 1987: Evolution, Error and Intentionality. In his *Intentional Stance* (Cambridge, Mass.: MIT Press).

Dennett, D. 1990: Real Patterns. *Journal of Philosophy* 87.

Descartes, R. 1911edn: Meditations on First Philosophy. *The Philosophical Works of Descartes*, Vol. I, ed. E. S. Haldane and G. R. T. Ross (Cambridge: Cambridge University Press).

Devitt, M. 1981: *Designation* (New York: Columbia University Press).

Dretske, F. 1981: *Knowledge and the Flow of Information* (Cambridge, Mass: MIT Press).

Dummett, M. 1973: *Frege: Philosophy of Language* (London: Duckworth).

Dummett, M. 1976: What is a Theory of Meaning? II. In *Truth and Meaning*, eds G. Evans and J. McDowell (Oxford: Oxford University Press).

Dummett, M. 1978: The Social Character of Meaning. In his *Truth and other Enigmas* (Cambridge, Mass.: Harvard University Press).

Evans, G. 1980: Comment on Fodor. *The Behavioral and the Brain Sciences* 3.

Evans, G. 1982: *Varieties of Reference* (Oxford: Oxford University press).

Field, H. 1972: Tarski's Theory of Truth. *Journal of Philosophy* 69.

Field, H. 1975: Conventionalism and Instrumentalism in Semantics. *Nous* 9.

Fodor, J. 1975: *The Language of Thought* (New York: Thomas Y. Cromwell).

Fodor, J. 1980: Methodological Solipsism Considered as a Research Strategy in the Cognitive Sciences. *The Behavioral and Brain Sciences* 3.

Fodor, J. 1987: *Psychosemantics* (Cambridge, Mass: MIT Press).

Fodor, J. 1989: Is Content What 'That' -Clauses Pick Out?

Grandy, R. 1973: Reference, Meaning and Belief. *Journal of Philosophy* 70.

Grice, H. P. 1957: Meaning. *Philosophical Review* 66.

Hampshire, S. 1965: *Freedom of the Individual* (Princeton, NJ: Princeton University Press).

Harman, G. 1982: Conceptual Role Semantics. *Notre Dame Journal of Formal Logic* 23.

Hempel, C. G. 1962: Deductive-Nomological vs. Statistical Explanation. In *Minnesota Studies in the Philosophy of Science*, vol. I, eds H. Feigl and G. Maxwell (Minneapolis: University of Minnesota Press).,

Higginbotham, J. 1989: Knowledge of Reference. In *Reflections on Chomsky*, ed. A. George (Oxford: Basil Blackwell).

Kant, I. 1929: *Critique of Pure Reason*. trans. by N. K. Smith (London: Macmillan).

Kaplan, D. 1979: Demonstratives. In *Propositions and Attitudes*, eds N. Salmon and S. Soames (Oxford: Oxford University Press).

Khalidi, M. 1991: *Meaning Change and Theory Change*. Unpublished dissertation submitted to Columbia University.

Kripke, S. 1972: Naming and Necessity. In *Semantics for Natural Language*, eds D. Davidson and G. Harman (Boston: Reidl).

Kripke, S. 1979: A Puzzle about Belief. In *Meaning and Use*, ed. A. Margalit (Dordrecht: Reidel).

Kripke, S. 1982: *Wittgenstein. On Rules and Private Language* (Oxford: Basil Blackwell).

Kuhn, T. 1962: *The Structure of Scientific Revolutions* (Chicago: University of Chicago Press).

Lepore, E. and Loewer, B. 1981: Traslational Semantics. *Synthese* 55.

Levi, I. 1980: *The Enterprise of Knowledge* (Cambridge, Mass.: MIT Press).

Lewis, D. 1972: Psychophysical and Theoretical Identifications. *Australasian Journal of Philosophy* 50.

Lewis, D. 1973: Radical Interpretation. *Synthese* 47.

Lewis, D. 1979: Attitudes De Dicto and De Se. *Philosophical Review* 88.

Loar, B. 1981: *Mind and Meaning* Cambridge: Cambridge University Press).

Loar, B. 1985a: Social Content and Psychological Content. In *Contents of Thought*, eds H.Grimm and D. D. Merrill (Tucson: The University of Arizona Press).

Loar, B. 1985b: A New Kind of Content: Reply to Bilgrami. In *Contents of Thought*, eds H. Grimm and D. D. Merrill (Tucson: The University of Arizona Press).

Loar, B. 1987: Subjective Intentionality. *Philosophical Topics* 15.

Lycan, W. 1986: Semantics and Methodological Solipsism. In *Truth and Interpretation*, ed. E. Lepore (Oxford: Basil Blackwell).

McDowell, J. 1976: On the Sense and Reference of a Proper Name. In *Reference, Truth and Reality*, ed. M. Platts (London: Routledge and Kegan Paul)

McDowell, J. 1981: Antirealism and the Epistemology of Understanding. In Meaning and Understanding, eds H. Parret and J. Bouveresse (Berlin and New York: Water de Gruyter).

McDowell, J. 1982: Double Vision. *Times Literary Supplement* 4317.

Mcdowell, J. 1984a: De Re Senses. *Philosophical Quarterly* 34.

McDowell, J. 1984b: Wittgenstein on Following a Rule. *Synthese* 58.

McDowell, J. 1985: Functionalism and Anomalous Monism. In *Actions and Events*, eds. E. Lepore and J. McLaughlin (Oxford: Basil Blackwell).

McDowell, J. 1986: Singular Thought and the Extent of Inner Space. In *Subject, Thought, and Context*, eds J. McDowell and P. Pettit (Oxford: Oxford University Press).

McDowell, J. 1987: In Defence of Modesty. In *Michael Dummett: Contributions to Philosophy*, ed. B. Taylor (Dordrecht: Martinus Nijhoff).

McDowell, J. And Pettit, P. 1986: Introduction. In *Subject, Though and Context*, eds J. McDowell and P. Pettit Oxford: (Oxford University Press).

McGinn, C. 1982a: The Structure of Content. In *Thought and Object*, ed. A. Woodfield (Oxford: Clarendon Press).

McGinn, C. 1982b: Realism and Content Ascription. *Synthese* 56.

Nagel, T. 1974: What Is It Like to Be a Bat? *Philosophical Review* 83.

Nagel, T. 1979: Subjective and Objective. In his *Mortal Questions* (New York: Oxford University Press).

Nagel, T. 1986: *The View from Nowhere* (New York: Oxford University Press).

Peacocke, C. 1988: The Limits of Intelligibility. *Philosophical Review* 96.

Perry, J. 1979: Thc Problem of the Essential Indexical. *Nous* 13.

Putnam, H. 1962: The Analytic and the Synthetic. In *Scientific Explanation, Space, and Time. Minnesota Studies in the Philosophy of Science* 3, eds II. Feigl and G. Maxwell (Minneapolis: University of Minnesota Press).

Putnam, H. 1974: Some Issues in the Theory of Grammar. In *On Noam Chomsky: Critical Essays*, ed. G. Harman (New York: Doubleday).

Putnam, H. 1975: The Meaning of "Meaning." In *Language, Mind and Knowledge: Minnesota Studis in the Philosophy of Science*, 7, ed. K. Gunderson (Minneapolis: University of Minnesota Press).

Putnam, H. 1978: *Meaning and the Moral Sciences* (London: Routledge and Kegan Paul).

Quine, W. 1960: *Word and Object* (Cambridge, Mass.: MIT Press).

Ramsey, F. P. 1929: Theories. In *Foundations*, ed. D. H. Mellor (London: Routledge and Kegan Raul).

Russell, B. 1951: Mr Strawson on Referring. *Mind* 60.

Rorty, R. 1979: Philosophy and the Mirror of Nature (Princeton, NJ: Princeton University Press).

Rorty, R. 1986: Pragmatism, Davidson and Truth. In *Truth and Interpretation*, ed. E. Lepore (Oxford: Besil Blackwell).

Rovane, C. 1986: The Metaphysics of Interpretation. In *Truth and Interpretation*, ed. E. Lepore (Oxford: Basil Blackwell).

Rovane, C. 1987: The Epistemology of First Person Reference. *Journal of Philosophy* 84.

Salmon, N. 1986: *Frege's Puzzle* (Cambridge, Mass.: MIT Prewss).

Scheffler, I. 1967: *Science and Subjectivity* (Indianapolis: Bobbs Merrill).

Schiffer, S. 1989: Content and Explanation. Unpublished MS.

Searle, J. 1958: Proper Names. *Mind* 67.

Searle, J. 1969: *Speech Acts* (Cambridge: Cambridge University Press).

Searle, J. 1983: *Intentionality* (Cambridge: Cambridge University Press).

Searle, J. 1987: Indeterminacy and the First Person. *Journal of Philosophy* 84.

Sellars, W. 1963: Some Reflections on Language Games. In his *Science, Perception, and Reality* (London: Routledge and Kegan Paul).

Stalnaker, R. 1989: On What's in the Head. In *Philosophical Perspectives* 3, ed. J. E. Tomberlin (California: Ridgeview Press).

Stampe, D. W. 1977: Toward a Causal Theory of Linguistic Representation. In *Midwest Studies in Philosophy*. 2: *Studies in the Philosophy of Language* eds. P. A. French, T. E. Euhling and H. Wettstein (Minneapolis: University of Minnesita Press).

Stich, S.P. 1983: *From Folk Psychology to Cognitive Science* (Cambridge, Mass: MIT Press).

Strawson, P. F. 1950: On Referring. *Mind* 59.

Strawson, P. F. 1962: Freedom and Resentment. *Proceedings of the British Academy*, reprinted in *Freedom and Resentment and Other Essays* (London: Methuen, 1974).

Strawson, P. F. 1966: *The Bounds of Sense* (London: Methuen).

Strawson, P. F. 1985: *Skepticism and Naturalism* (Columbia University Press).

Stroud, B. 1984: *The Significance of Philosophical Skepticism* (Oxford: Oxford University Press).

Taylor, C. 1975: *Hegel* (Cambridge: Cambridge University Press).

Wallace, J. 1977: Only in the Context of a Sentence do Words Have Any Meaning. In *Midwest Studies in Philosophy* 2: *Studies in the Philosophy of Language*, eds P. A. French and T. E. Uehling and H. Wettstein (Minneapolis: University of Minnesita Press).

White, S. 1982: Partial Character and the Language of Thought. *Pacific Philosophical Quaterly* 63.

While, S. 1986: Curse of the Qualia. *Synthese* 60.

White, S. 1989: Transcendentalism and its Discontents. *Philosophical Topics* 17.

White, S. 1991: Narrow Content and Narrow Interpretation. In his *Unity of the Self* (Cambridge, Mass.: MIT Press).

Wittgenstein, L. 1953: *Philosophical Investigations* (Oxford: Basil Blackwell).

Wright, D. 1984: Kripke's Account of the Argument against Private Language. *Journal of Philosophy* 81.

Wright, C. 1989a: Wittgenstein's Later Philosophy of Mind: Sensation, Privacy and Intention. *Journal of Philosophy* 86.

Wright, C. 1989b: Wittgenstein's Rule-following Considerations and the Central Project of Theoretical Linguistics. In *Reflections on Chomsky*, ed. A. George (Oxford: Basil Blackwell).

Wright, C. 1989c: Wittgenstein on Meaning. *Mind* 98.

# Name Index

# Subject Index